D1739803

Reintegrating Armed Groups
After Conflict

This book looks at the political reintegration of armed groups after civil wars and the challenges of transforming 'rebel', 'insurgent' or other non-state armed groups into viable political entities.

Drawing on eight case studies, the definition of 'armed groups' here ranges from militias, paramilitary forces, police units of various kinds to intelligence outfits. Likewise, the definition of 'political integration' or 're-integration' has not been restricted to the formation of political parties, but is understood broadly as active participation in politics, policy-making or public debate through parties, newspapers, social organisations, think tanks, NGOs or public service.

The book seeks to locate or contextualise individual cases within their distinctive social, cultural and historical settings. As such it differs from much of the donor-driven literature that has tended to abstract the challenge of disarmament, demobilisation and reintegration (DDR) from their political and historical context, focusing instead on technical or bureaucratic issues raised by the DDR process. Among the issues covered by the volume as a whole, three stand out: first, the role of political settlements in creating legitimate opportunities for erstwhile leaders of armed factions; second, the ability of reintegration programmes to create genuine socio-economic opportunities that can absorb former fighters as functional members of their communities; and third, the processes involved in transforming an entire rebel movement into a viable political party, movement or, more generally, allowing it to participate in political life.

This book will be of great interest to students of security and development, peace and conflict studies, and IR in general, as well as practitioners and policymakers.

Mats Berdal is Professor of Security and Development in the Department of War Studies at King's College London. From 2000 to 2003 he was Director of Studies at the International Institute for Strategic Studies (IISS) in London. Mats Berdal is a Visiting Professor at the National Defence and Command College, Oslo. **David H. Ucko** is Programme Coordinator and Research Fellow for the Conflict, Security and Development Research Group, King's College London, and a Transatlantic Fellow at the RAND Corporation, Washington, DC.

Routledge studies in intervention and statebuilding
Series Editor: David Chandler

Contents

Figures

Tables

Contributors

Mats Berdal is Professor of Security and Development in the Department of War Studies at King's College London. He is formerly Director of Studies at the International Institute for Strategic Studies (IISS).

Anna Borzello is a journalist who between 1994–2001 was based in Uganda, working first at the independent *Monitor* newspaper and then as the BBC Uganda correspondent.

Antonio Giustozzi is Research Fellow at the Crisis States Research Centre, where he runs a project on state building in Afghanistan.

Alexandra Guáqueta holds a DPhil in International Relations from Oxford and is currently Public Affairs Advisor at Cerrejon in Colombia.

S. Neil MacFarlane is Lester B. Pearson Professor of International Relations and Head of the Department of Politics and International Relations at the University of Oxford.

Zoë Marriage is a Senior Lecturer at SOAS, where she teaches on the MSc Political Economy of Violence, Conflict and Development.

Kieran Mitton is currently an Economic and Social Research Council (ESRC)-funded PhD candidate based at the Department of War Studies, King's College London.

Bereni Oruitemeka was during the production of this book a consultant research assistant for the Africa Programme at Chatham House.

Stina Torjesen is a Senior Research Fellow at the Norwegian Institute of International Affairs.

David H. Ucko is Programme Coordinator and Research Fellow for the Conflict, Security and Development Research Group, King's College London, and Transatlantic Fellow at the RAND Corporation, Washington, DC.

Alex Vines is Director of Regional and Security Studies and Head of the Africa Programme at Chatham House.

Acknowledgements

This book grew out a research project sponsored and supported by the Norwegian Ministry of Foreign Affairs. The editors wish to thank Ambassador Johan Vibe and his colleagues in the Section for Peace and Reconciliation for their generous support and encouragement over the past three years. We would also like to thank David Keen for his typically helpful advice during the early stages of the project and Sabiiti Mutengesa for his constructive contributions. Earlier versions of some of the case studies covered in this volume were first published in the *Journal for Conflict, Security and Development*.

Mats Berdal and David H. Ucko
London

Abbreviations

ACC	Anti-Corruption Commission
ADF	Allied Democratic Front
ADFL	Alliance of Democratic Forces for the Liberation of Congo
AD M-19	Alianza Democrática M-19
ADRP	Angola Demobilisation and Reintegration Programme
AFRC	Armed Forces Revolutionary Council
ALiR	Army for the Liberation of Rwanda
AMF	Afghan Military Forces
ANA	Afghan National Army
ANAPO	Alianza Nacional Popular
ANBP	Afghanistan New Beginning Programme
APC	All Party Congress
AQI	al-Qaeda in Iraq
ARLPI	Acholi Religious Leaders' Peace Initiative
AUC	Autodefensas Unidas de Colombia
CAR	Central African Republic
CDF	Civil Defence Forces
CGG	Campaign for Good Governance
CIPE	Interministerial Commission for the Electoral Process
CIS	Commonwealth of Independent States
CISPKF	CIS Peace Keeping Force
CNDP	National Congress for the Defence of the People
CNE	National Electoral Commission
CNR	Commission on National Reconciliation
CONADER	National Commission for Demobilisation and Reinsertion
CPA	Coalition Provisional Authority
CRS	Corriente de Renovación Socialista
CSOPNU	Civil Society Organisations for Peace in Northern Uganda
DAS	Departamento Administrativo de Seguridad
DDR	disarmament, demobilisation and reintegration
DDRRR	disarmament, demobilisation, repatriation, reinstallation or reintegration
DfID	Department for International Development

DIAG	Disarmament of Illegal Armed Groups
DoD	Department of Defense
DRC	Democratic Republic of Congo
ECOMOG	Economic Community of West Africa States Monitoring Group
ELN	Ejército de Liberación Nacional
EPL	Ejército Popular de Liberación
ex-FAR	ex-Rwandan Armed Forces
FAA	Armed Forces of Angola
FAC	Congolese Armed Forces
FARC	Fuerzas Armadas Revolucionarias de Colombia
FARDC	Armed Forces of DRC
FDD	Forces for the Defence of Democracy
FDLR	Democratic Forces for the Liberation of Congo
FNLA	National Front for the Liberation of Angola
FOB	forward operating bases
GAO	Government Accountability Office
IAF	Iraqi Accord Front
ICC	International Criminal Court
ICG	International Crisis Group
ICTJ	International Center for Transnational Justice
IDA	International Development Association
IDP	internally displace person
IGC	Iraqi Governing Council
IIG	Interim Iraqi Government
IISS	International Institute for Strategic Studies
IMF	International Monetary Fund
IMU	Islamic Movement of Uzbekistan
IRC	International Rescue Committee
IRIN	Integrated Regional Information Networks
IRSEM	Institute for the Socio-Professional Reintegration of Ex-Combatants
ISCI	Islamic Supreme Council of Iraq
JICA	Japan International Cooperation Agency
JMC	Joint Military Commission
JSS	Joint Security Stations
KDP	Kurdistan Democratic Party
LDU	Local Defence Unit
LRA	Lord's Resistance Army
M-19	Movimiento 19 de Abril
MAPP-OEA	Mission to Support the Peace Process of the Organisation of American States
MAQL	Movimiento Armado Quintín Lame
MB	Ministry of State Security
MDRP	Multi-Country Demobilization and Reintegration Programme
MLC	Movement for the Liberation of Congo
MoD	Ministry of Defence

MoI	Ministry of the Interior
MONUA	United Nation's Observer Mission in Angola
MONUC	United Nations Mission in the Democratic Republic of Congo
MPLA	Movement for the Popular Liberation of Angola
MRD	Motorised Rifle Division
MVD	Ministry of the Interior
NEC	National Electoral Commission
NPRC	National Provisional Ruling Council
NRA	National Resistance Army
NRC	National Reconciliation Committee
NRM	National Resistance Movement
NSD	National Security Directorate
OAS	Organisation of American States
OAU	Organisation of African Unity
OCHA	United Nations Office for the Coordination of Humanitarian Affairs
ORHA	Office of Reconstruction and Humanitarian Assistance
OSCE	Organisation for Security and Cooperation in Europe
PD	Polo Democrático
PDA	Democratic Party of Angola
PGDR	Programme for Demobilisation and Reintegration
PMDC	People's Movement for Democratic Change
PRDP	Peace, Recovery and Development Plan
PRIDE	Post-conflict Reintegration Initiative for Development and Empowerment
PRT	Partido Revolucionario de los Trabajadores
PSOE	Spanish Socialists Worker's Party
RCD	Rally for Congolese Democracy
RFCT	Ready First Combat Team
RPA	Rwandan Patriot Army
RUF	Revolutionary United Front
RUFP	Revolutionary United Front Party
RVC	Regional Verification Committee
SADC	Southern African Development Community
SCIRI	Supreme Council for the Islamic Revolution in Iraq
SIDDR	Stockholm Initiative on Disarmament, Demobilisation and Reintegration
SLA	Sierra Leone Army
SLPP	Sierra Leone People's Party
SoI	Sons of Iraq
SPLA	Sudan Peoples Liberation Army
SSR	security-sector reform
SSR	Soviet Socialist Republic
TAL	Transitional Administrative Law
TNA	Transitional National Assembly
TR	transition and reintegration

TRC	Truth and Reconciliation Commission
TRIC	Transition and Reintegration Implementation Committee
UIA	United Iraqi Alliance
UNAMA	United Nations Assistance Mission in Afghanistan
UNAMSIL	United Nations Mission in Sierra Leone
UNAVEM	United Nations Angola Verification Mission
UNDP	United Nations Development Programme
UNHCR	United Nations High Commissioner for Refugees
UNICEF	United Nations Children's Fund
UNITA	Union for the Total Independence of Angola
UNMA	United Nations Mission in Angola
UNMOT	United Nations Mission of Observers in Tajikistan
UNSC	United Nations Security Council
UPDA	Ugandan People's Democratic Army
UPDF	Uganda Peoples' Defence Forces
USAID	US Agency for International Development
UTO	United Tajik Opposition

Introduction

The political reintegration of armed groups after war

Mats Berdal and David H. Ucko

The story of Angola and the DDR literature

In the autumn of 1992, Angola was plunged back into a murderous civil war, shattering the hopes generated by the Bicesse Peace Accords signed in May 1991 and the brief respite it had provided from nearly three decades of violent conflict. The immediate trigger to war was the decision by the leader of the Union for the Total Independence of Angola (UNITA), Jonas Savimbi, to reject the outcome of the first nation-wide democratic elections ever to be held in the country. These had taken place in September 1992 as stipulated in the peace agreement reached the previous year; an agreement that also envisaged what proved to be a wholly unsuccessful attempt to demobilise government and UNITA troops and to create a unified armed forces. By the time the 'peace process' appeared to be back on track in late 1994, an estimated 200,000 people had perished and many more had been displaced. Under the so-called Lusaka Protocols signed in November 1994, the government and UNITA renewed earlier pledges to disarm and demobilise, though this time the DDR process would be under the auspices of a large-scale UN peacekeeping operation, UN Angola Verification Mission III (UNAVEM III). Even so, within four years the Lusaka Protocols had gone the same way as the Bicesse Accords and Angola was once again in the thrall of bloody civil war. The war finally came to an end with the death on the battlefield of Jonas Savimbi in early 2002 and the military defeat of UNITA. By the time the nation-wide elections were held again in 2008 – the first since the disastrous elections of 1992 – the country, as Alex Vines and Bereni Oruitemeka note in this volume, had gone 'from being one of the most protracted conflicts in Africa, [to] one of the most successful economies in sub-Saharan Africa'.[1]

There are several reasons for treating the story of Angola's tortuous and blood-stained road to peace after the Cold War as an entry point into the subject of this book.

The most obvious is that the repeated failures to bring Angola's civil war to an end in the 1990s was instrumental in focusing the attention of international organisations, NGOs and policy analysts on the overriding importance of meeting the challenges posed by the continued presence of military personnel, arms and organisational structures *within* a war-torn society following the formal end of hostilities.[2]

A measure of success in the disarmament, demobilisation and reintegration (DDR) of combatants came to be recognised – and still is – as perhaps the single most important precondition for post-war stability and, by extension, for more ambitious attempts to facilitate 'a society's transition from conflict to normalcy and development'.[3] DDR is now a central component of nearly all large-scale peace operations, whether under UN auspices or that of regional organisations. Involvement in some aspect of the 'DDR process' has become an important, in many cases a mainstream, activity for development agencies in leading donor countries, within the UN Development Programme (UNDP) and even to the Bretton Woods institutions. In Iraq and Afghanistan – cases both covered in this book – the DDR context is plainly very different from that of UN operations, yet the fundamental issue that DDR is meant to address is the same: ensuring that armed groups that have prospered during the active phase of hostilities do not return to the battlefield or find other ways of undermining local and international efforts to build lasting peace, and to do so by finding ways of integrating ex-combatants into the social, economic and political life of post-war society.

The heightened interest in the subject and the recognition of its importance have generated a diverse and substantial body of 'DDR literature', the beginnings of which can also be traced to the early efforts to assess the sources of failure in Angola.[4] Much of that literature has been prescriptive and policy-oriented in character, focusing on those engaged in the delivery of DDR programmes and concerned with the identification of specific and transferable lessons from the experiences of now nearly 40 DDR processes since the mid-1990s.[5] Perhaps inevitably, this literature – especially that generated by NGOs, government and UN agencies and exemplified by the 'UN Integrated DDR Standards'[6] – has tended to concentrate on the 'mechanics' of DDR activities: how best to plan, organise, coordinate and fund what are often formidable logistical and technical challenges. In this literature, discussion of the relationship of DDR to *political context* and *processes* tends to be of a perfunctory and often merely question-begging kind, as in 'success in DDR depends on political will'. This is not, of course, to suggest that questions relating to the organisation of DDR are unimportant or that lessons in this area cannot be learned from the range and variety of DDR experiences we now possess. In Mozambique, where the UN in 1993–94 was charged with shepherding another war-torn society from civil war to peace, a conscious effort was made to learn precisely these lessons from Angola and the relative success of the ONUMOZ mission was attributable no doubt in part to these issues having been addressed.

Concern with the organisation, management and implementation of DDR activities has continued to preoccupy donors and international organisations and is especially evident in numerous reports designed to identify lessons and synthesise best practices.[7] One notable example of this is the Stockholm Initiative on Disarmament, Demobilisation and Reintegration (SIDDR) whose explicit aim was 'to propose ways and means that can contribute to an improved framework in which DDR processes can be planned and implemented'.[8] Another is the UN's own work on so-called 'Integrated DDR Standards': a set of 'policies, guidelines and procedures for UN-supported DDR programmes in a peacekeeping context'.[9] While the SIDRR recognises the dangers of divorcing DDR programmes from their political context, its detailed recommendations focus on the mechanics of DDR and the report makes a valuable contribution in this respect. In particular, it draws attention, as have similar reports since the surge in complex peace operations after 2003, to the special requirements of social and economic reintegration of combatants after conflict; a reflection not only of earlier neglect but, more importantly, of the realisation that this phase of activities represents a more complex and multifaceted challenge than demobilisation.[10] Likewise, the UN's work on Integrated DDR Standards represents, in many ways, an impressive effort to distil lessons about how best to design and implement DDR programmes.

Aims and underlying themes

The present volume is less concerned with the 'supply side' challenges raised by the design and implementation of multi-donor and multi-agency DDR programmes than it is with the politics of DDR and the nature of the armed groups at the receiving end of DDR treatment. In part, and as indicated above, this is because the mechanics of DDR have already been expertly and extensively covered elsewhere. More fundamentally, however, the project from which this book emerged was also conceived in response to certain deficiencies and perceived areas of neglect evident both in the aforementioned body of DDR literature and the *actual* practices of donor countries and the UN. In this respect, the cases covered here draw attention to and help rectify three sets of deficiencies, all of which are closely connected.

First, the effort to draw lessons of a policy-oriented kind from a range of different cases, especially when focused on technical and administrative challenges, is almost bound to underplay *qualitative* differences in the historical, cultural and political context that necessarily exist among different DDR processes. These differences include enormous variations among armed groups in terms of their organisational and leadership structure; ideological and political coherence; internal dynamics and sociological make-up; potency and self-sufficiency as a fighting force; levels and quality of external support; and in the degree to which, in the case of 'rebel' groups, the cause they espouse enjoys a measure of societal recognition and legitimacy.

One of the aims of this volume is precisely to bring out the diversity in the character of armed groups that have, with very uneven levels of success, been subject to DDR treatment. Thus, the Lord's Resistance Army (LRA) resembles, in important respects, a millennial movement and whatever popular support it initially enjoyed among the Acholi people of Northern Uganda has been largely forfeited by its use of terror tactics. The Revolutionary United Front (RUF) in Sierra Leone, Kieran Mitton observes, represented 'a largely illiterate, politically and socially dislocated body of brutalised youths, who despite possessing a myriad of legitimate grievances, were ill equipped to return (or to be introduced) to civil society and channel these grievances through peaceful political discourse'.[11] By contrast, the Kurdish *Peshmerga* and Shia *Badr Brigades* in Iraq, though never really disarmed or demobilised, are highly organised, well-trained and capable military formations.[12] In Tajikistan, the warring factions were loosely 'structured fighting groups' based on 'kinship, community, or workplace ties', led by commanders and sub-commanders that served as 'community leaders, police officers, and army servicemen' before the war.[13] To highlight such differences does not mean that any and all efforts to draw lessons from across different cases are, necessarily, exercises in futility. It does, however, point to the dangers of adopting what Zoë Marriage, in looking at demobilisation efforts in the Democratic Republic of Congo (DRC), identifies as an essentially 'static approach' to DDR challenges;[14] of thinking in terms of readily transferable templates and of divorcing the discussion of ideal 'technical' solutions from realities on the ground. All of the cases covered in this volume powerfully underscore these dangers.

Second, in the short to medium term, efforts to disarm, demobilise and reintegrate combatants invariably present external actors and sponsors of DDR with *policy choices* and *dilemmas*, which, though they vary in their acuteness, are insufficiently recognised in the aforementioned DDR literature. It is, for example, impossible to disagree with the 'recommendation' contained in the final report of the SIDDR that programmes should be 'designed to make a contribution to security and stabilisation in the immediate post conflict environment *and* lay the foundation for future sustainable long-term development'.[15] The difficulty is not merely that these two aims frequently conflict with one another but also that when they do, the policy choices favouring 'security and stabilisation in the immediate post-conflict environment' often run counter to what Stina Torjesen and Neil MacFarlane have aptly described as the 'liberal democratic script'.[16] 'It might be the case,' they argue in their study of Tajikistan after the civil war in the 1990s, that this DDR process, 'worked precisely because it did *not* follow a liberal democratic script.'[17] This was a process that set aside any attempt at disarmament, overlooked transitional justice issues and offered instead comprehensive amnesties, positions in government and even economic assets to former fighters and commanders. This route to short-term stability, as Torjesen and MacFarlane are careful to acknowledge, may well have come at a heavy long-term price, even though it nonetheless did create 'a number of important goods for Tajikistan in the immediate years after the war'.[18] As such, the case brings out what is often a very real dilemma: 'Is there a breaking point when an "over-facilitation" of former combatants' interests will jeopardise the overall economic wellbeing of a country and perpetuate cycles of underdevelopment, grievance and insecurity?' It is a dilemma that is likely to be particularly acute where the capacity for armed groups to engage in 'spoiling behaviour' and return to war is high.

The tension that often exists between what are legitimate demands for justice after conflict on the one hand, and the requirements of political stability in immediate post-conflict environment has given rise to similarly complex and morally uncomfortable dilemmas elsewhere. As Anna Borzello illustrates in her chapter on Uganda, seeking to reintegrate the former fighters of the LRA poses difficult questions regarding the role of justice versus reconciliation: What are the prospects of reintegrating an armed group that abducts and press-gangs children and adolescents and that is also responsible for massive human-rights abuses? How best to repair the damage of two decades of violent conflict when many rebel fighters – but, notably, not all – are themselves victims? As Borzello notes, the notion of bringing senior LRA commanders into the political fold 'stretches the whole notion of forgiveness to its very limits'.[19]

The dilemma recurs in Colombia, where the prospects of successful engagements with the paramilitary groups of the Autodefensas Unidas de Colombia (AUC) have been similarly undermined by its involvement in human-rights abuses and, in this case, drugs trafficking for self-enrichment. As Alexandra Guáqueta explains, the group's behaviour in wartime has elicited strong and entirely understandable criticism, both internationally and domestically, against its reintroduction to political life and transformation into a legitimate political entity. At the same time, the decision not to provide the AUC with political space risks perpetuating their illegal activity, intimidation and informal control of politics. Here too, in other words, tension exists between the need to balance reconciliation and stability on the one hand with legitimate demands for justice on the other.

In all these instances, the case studies throw light not only on the short- and possible long-term consequences of the policy choices taken and the actions supported by external actors, but also, crucially, on the contextual reasons for why these were taken. It would be tempting to conclude that the policy choices always present themselves in a 'right or wrong' variety and indeed, in retrospect, cases examined here do point to the potential long-term costs of decisions taken or not taken. Too often, however, context and circumstances mean that choices are between 'bad and very bad' options, which require difficult judgments to be made about the balance of risks involved in each case.

Third, while getting the mechanics of DDR right is undoubtedly vital, it is far from the only lesson to be drawn from DDR operations after the Cold War. And this brings us back to the case of Angola, which suggests that it may not even be the most important lesson. After all, the resources given to UNAVEM III, when it deployed in 1995 to assist with the implementation of the Lusaka Protocols, were considerable compared to its predecessor – a ten-fold increase in personnel strength alone – precisely in order to avoid a repeat of the events in 1991–92. And although this time around the UN was also able to draw on the positive lessons of the UN operation in Mozambique, war nonetheless returned with undiminished ferocity in 1998. It was only with the death of Savimbi and UNITA's effective military defeat that Angola's long history of war came to an end. Since then, demobilisation and disarmament in the country has been 'dogged with logistical problems', disarmament has been patchy and reintegration has proved especially difficult.[20] Even so, as Vines and Oruitemeka conclude in this volume, the DDR process can nonetheless be 'judged as largely successful' because 'returning to war is no longer an option' for UNITA, which has after its defeat 'made a successful transition from armed guerrilla movement to opposition party'.[21] It is from the developments over the past five years that the critical lesson offered by the Angola case emerges most clearly: DDR programmes, however well designed and resourced, can never carry 'peace processes' on their own but must, if they are to be successful, form part of wider political process. One obvious implication to flow from this is that greater attention needs to given, as this volume explicitly seeks to do, to the requirements for the effective *political reintegration* of armed forces after the formal end of hostilities.

The meaning of political reintegration

This immediately raises, however, the question of how political reintegration should be understood. The findings here point to a more permissive approach than that conventionally adopted. Specifically, limiting the meaning of political reintegration to the formal creation of political parties for the purpose of partaking in democratic political processes may be overly restrictive.[22] One reason for this is simply that in post-war settings, as the present volume certainly bears out, the prospect of meaningful and properly functioning party politics is at any rate often very remote. Indeed, in some cases the very attempt to create parties with all that this entails – funding, organisation, peaceful competition for posts – may itself become an all-consuming challenge in delicately poised war-to-peace transitions. In the case of Sierra Leone, attempts to transform the RUF into a functioning political party were seriously undermined by the group's lack of a cohesive political agenda, the illiteracy and political unfamiliarity of its membership and the strong bifurcation of its power-hungry leaders and politically disengaged rank-and-file. According to Kieran Mitton, 'the unsuitability of the RUF for political transformation remained a major obstacle' and, in many ways 'the dismantling of the group, rather than its political consolidation, would [have been] of greater benefit to the peacebuilding project'.[23]

An alternative understanding of reintegration, one here explicitly adopted by Guáqueta, involves focusing on a wider range of spaces for active and legitimate political participation at the local and national levels after violent conflict. In practice, she suggests further, this may involve members of armed groups actively participating in 'policy-making and public debate through think tanks, NGOs, journalism and jobs in the public sector'.[24] For a number of smaller Colombian guerrilla groups in the early 1990s, involvement by demobilised guerrillas in these areas provided a non-violent outlet for airing political grievances and, crucially, also helped to 'strengthen liberal political ideas and human-rights norms'.[25] Likewise, in Sierra Leone, several former RUF combatants 'found that they were able to pursue their concerns through established political parties and the wider institutions of Sierra Leonean civil society without recourse to their RUF identity'.[26] In both instances, the *political reintegration* of soldiers was relatively successful though none of the rebel groups survived as political parties.

There is another reason to de-emphasise the creation of political parties as the *chief* criterion for successful reintegration, while still recognising it as a long-term objective. As this book's chapters on Iraq, Afghanistan and the DRC illustrate, efforts to form political parties out of armed groups all-too-often mistake their successful transformation for political reconciliation per se. As David Ucko demonstrates, the hurried search for 'local' Iraqi groups to be transformed into political parties and turned into a new Iraqi government resulted in the co-option and elevation of various sectarian and militia-wielding elements, none of which enjoyed much legitimacy or support among ordinary Iraqis. Their further entrenchment through two elections, commonly perceived as a positive marker of post-conflict state-building, only consolidated these groups' power and has contributed to a seemingly irredeemable corruption of Iraqi governmental affairs, threatening, even, the progress seen in that country since early 2007. The transformation of irregular armed groups into political parties here resulted in a 'false process of political reintegration', which was less about 'bringing armed forces under legal and civil control' and more a means for militia leaders 'to insert their supporters in the emerging security structures as a power base, and to exclude those of potential rivals'.[27]

A similar subversion of 'state-building' is found in Afghanistan. As Antonio Giustozzi notes in this volume, the lack of time, patience and international commitment to Afghanistan served to turn the noble purposes and ambitions of the national reintegration process into a mere 'façade', behind which

> non-state armed groups of various types [were] allowed to continue to exist and sometimes prosper, as long as they were willing to pay at least lip service to the bureaucratic process and abstained from actively working against the government in charge.[28]

For many years, this arrangement provided Western donors with the image of limited success and Afghan warlords and other armed groups with an opportunity to thrive and operate much as before, albeit now within the government and its local security forces. While this largely unconditional co-option did guarantee a measure of security in the short term, such gains were often transient and furthermore came 'at the expense of considerable medium- and long-term loss of support for the foreign intervention by the population at large'.[29]

Zoë Marriage's study of the DRC reveals a similar lesson. Here too, the provision of political power to former rebel commanders, and the nominal transformation of their armed groups into political entities, was conducted in the hope of forestalling further violence and marking a first step towards peace. However, as the case study makes clear, the result of this form of reintegration has been a political pillage – akin to the pillages that took place across Congo in the 1990s – by which some parties made immediate gains, all while shaping the conditions for longer-term losses and creating new and destabilising systems of power. As Marriage notes, 'the pillage in this context is political in nature – the short-term gains and confidence tricks sustain the process, but risk establishing political institutions that are, in the long term, destructive and abusive'.[30] Again, this case study points towards the need for a broader conception of political reintegration, one that moves beyond the mere formalisation of political parties, and is informed by the strong continuities that can persist during the passage from war to peace.

Politics and local context: no universal strategies

Since the early 1990s, attempts to disarm, demobilise and reintegrate soldiers after years, sometimes decades, of armed conflict have been undertaken in a huge variety of 'post-conflict' settings. Today, DDR is the main business of nearly all of the UN's ongoing large-scale peacekeeping operations. The troubled effort by outsiders and national authorities to bring stability to Iraq and Afghanistan is closely linked to the 'DDR challenge' in both countries, even though the precise nature of the challenge may, at times, have been poorly understood. The case studies covered in this volume highlight the many contextual factors that shape these different undertakings: the alignment of regional interests and influences bearing on a DDR process supposedly taking place within a country; the political economy of war and peace distinctive to each conflict zone and cutting across formal borders; the unique characteristics of armed groups and their leadership; the evolving global and normative environment in which DDR is conceived and carried out. All of these impact on the political complexity of DDR and underscore the overriding lesson to emerge from the book: there are real 'limitations and perhaps dangers, of applying universal DDR strategies in highly specific local conditions'.[31] This simple, seemingly straightforward conclusion should not detract from its fundamental importance.

Notes

1 Vines and Oruitemeka, 'Beyond Bullets and Ballots': the reintegration of UNITA in Angola'.
2 Berdal, *Disarmament and Demobilisation*.
3 Report of the Secretary-General, par. 3.
4 See World Bank, *Demobilisation and Reintegration of Military Personnel in Africa*.
5 Ministry of Foreign Affairs, Sweden, *Stockholm Initiative on DDR*, 9.
6 See United Nations, *UN Integrated DDR Standards*.
7 Ball and van de Goor, 'DDR – Mapping Issues, Dilemmas and Guiding Principles'.
8 *Stockholm Initiative on DDR*, 1.
9 United Nations, *UN Integrated DDR Standards*.
10 One example of this is the challenge posed by the reintegration of child soldiers, a subject that has received increased, if belated, attention in recent years.
11 Mitton, 'Engaging with Disengagement: The Political Reintegration of Sierra Leone's Revolutionary United Front'.
12 Discussed more fully in Ucko, 'Militias, Tribes and Insurgents: The Challenge of Political Reintegration in Iraq'.
13 Torjesen and MacFarlane, 'Reintegration before disarmament'.
14 Marriage, 'Flip-Flop Rebel, Dollar Soldier: Demobilisation in the Democratic Republic of Congo'.
15 *Stockholm Initiative on DDR*, 31 (our emphasis).
16 Torjesen and MacFarlane, 'Reintegration before disarmament'.
17 Torjesen and MacFarlane, 'Reintegration before disarmament'.
18 Torjesen and MacFarlane, 'Reintegration before disarmament'.

19 Borzello, 'The Challenge of DDR in Northern Uganda: The Lord's Resistance Army'.
20 Vines and Oruitemeka, 'Beyond Bullets and Ballots'.
21 Vines and Oruitemeka, 'Beyond Bullets and Ballots'.
22 This is the explicit focus adopted in de Zeeuw, *From Soldiers to Politicians.*
23 Mitton, 'Engaging with Disengagement'.
24 Guáqueta, 'The Way Back In: Reintegrating Illegal Armed Groups in Colombia Then and Now'.
25 Guáqueta, 'The Way Back In'.
26 Mitton, 'Engaging with Disengagement'.
27 Ucko, 'Militias, Tribes and Insurgents'.
28 Giustozzi, 'Bureaucratic Façade and Political Realities of Disarmament and Demobilisation in Afghanistan'.
29 Marriage, 'Flip-Flop Rebel, Dollar Soldier'.
30 Marriage, 'Flip-Flop Rebel, Dollar Soldier'.
31 Torjesen and MacFarlane, 'Reintegration before disarmament'.

References

Ball, Nicole and van de Goor, Luc, 2006. 'DDR – Mapping Issues, Dilemmas and Guiding Principles', *Conflict Research Unit*. Netherlands Institute for International Relations, The Hague.

Berdal, Mats, 1996. *Disarmament and Demobilisation After Civil Wars*, Adelphi Paper 303. Oxford University Press, Oxford.

De Zeeuw, Jeroen (ed.), 2008. *From Soldiers to Politicians: Transforming Rebel Movements After Civil War*, Lynne Rienner, Boulder, CO.

Ministry of Foreign Affairs, Sweden, 2006. *Stockholm Initiative on Disarmament, Demobilisation and Reintegration* (Final Report). The Swedish Government Offices, Stockholm.

Report of the Secretary-General, 2000. 'The Role of UN Peacekeeping in Disarmament, Demobilisation and Reintegration', S/2000/101, 11 February.

United Nations, 2006. *UN Integrated DDR Standards*, UN, New York.

World Bank, 1993. *Demobilisation and Reintegration of Military Personnel in Africa: The Evidence from Seven Country Studies*, Report No. IDP-130, Africa Regional Series, Discussion Paper, Washington DC, October.

1 The way back in

Reintegrating illegal armed groups in Colombia then and now

Alexandra Guáqueta

Introduction

Colombia has been a democracy for most of the 20th century, has no ethnic or religious divides and it is ranked as a mid-level developing economy. Nevertheless, internal violence in the form of armed conflict has been a critical feature over the past decades. Seven left-wing guerrilla organisations emerged between the 1960s and the 1980s, along with a series of right-wing illegal forces, the so-called 'paramilitary'. Through their armed struggle against the state, Marxist guerrillas aimed at redressing grievances related to inequality, social exclusion and the concentration of political power in the hands of a few, and proposed installing a socialist regime. Paramilitary forces, on the other hand – who grouped loosely as Autodefensas Unidas de Colombia (AUC) in 1997 – have sought to repel guerrilla influence and, as we now know, frequently served as natural allies of the state security forces in the battlefield.

Five out of the seven guerrilla groups, the Movimiento 19 de Abril (M-19), the Movimiento Armado Quintín Lame (MAQL), the Ejército Popular de Liberación (EPL), the Partido Revolucionario de los Trabajadores (PRT) and the Corriente de Renovación Socialista (CRS) – totalling approximately 5,000 combatants – demobilised after peace negotiations in 1989–94 and temporarily became a 'relevant political force'.[1] While it is true that none of the original political movements they created ultimately survived democratic political competition, it is possible to argue that these guerrillas underwent a relatively successful *political reintegration*. Ever since their demobilisation, many have participated in policy-making and public debate through think tanks, NGOs, journalism and jobs in the public sector, and their sustained political engagement has contributed to strengthen liberal political ideas and human-rights norms in Colombia.[2] Moreover, several former guerrilla leaders are currently key figures of the Polo Democrático (PD), a left-wing party with important public appeal created in 2003. Whether as groups or individually, guerrillas found space for legitimate political participation at the local and national levels and they did so despite the continuation of war waged by the remaining armed groups, the Fuerzas Armadas Revolucionarias de Colombia (FARC), the Ejército de Liberación Nacional (ELN) and the paramilitary.[3]

Almost two decades later, Colombia is once again attempting to reintegrate ex-combatants: 31,671 from AUC who demobilised between November 2003 and August 2006 as the result of negotiations between the Álvaro Uribe government and the commanders of the various blocs; and approximately 15,800 'individually demobilised combatants' – members of FARC, ELN and AUC who have since 2002 deserted their group. This time, however, the task of transforming illegal armed groups into legitimate political entities or finding other means for combatants to participate in policy-making is much harder than before. The AUC's reintegration has not only elicited criticism from around the globe due to the group's previous human-rights abuses. Domestically, the participation of former combatants in politics has become anathema and individually demobilised guerrillas have experienced social rejection, such as the demand by Bogotá citizens in 2005 that reintegration hostels be relocated 'far away'.[4] Before, bringing guerrillas in was not only convenient from a security standpoint; it was seen almost as a moral obligation because of their grievances and even as connoting a positive contribution to social order given their ideals. In contrast, while the demobilisation and reintegration both of the right-wing paramilitary and of left-wing rebels may still be convenient, it is undoubtedly less palatable to Colombian society and the international community. Surely FARC and ELN, the two guerrilla groups that chose not to participate in the early 1990s peace processes and remain active, will encounter higher entry barriers when they do demobilise, as their popularity among Colombians and the international community has eroded.[5]

Why are things so different today? By examining and comparing the processes of political reintegration of M-19 and the paramilitary, this chapter will argue that there are at least four critical factors that either allow or bar former combatants from becoming legitimate players with a capacity for political interlocution: the international and domestic political and normative contexts; the nature and behaviour of the illegal armed group (how much power they command, to what extent groups use war for personal profit and whether they commit egregious crimes); the terms of the peace negotiations; and the practical dimensions of exercising political interlocution. The analysis does not focus on the menu of incentives that drove these illegal armed groups to demobilise but rather on the barriers of entry. These factors relate to issues of acceptance and permanence. Acceptance into the sphere of legitimate politics stems from the congruence of rules, both explicit and implicit, that allow entry (the normative, legal and political contexts) and the combatants' identity and behaviour. As to permanence, the capacity to perform as a political party, an NGO or as a public official is often conditioned by more practical aspects of the transformation process, such as political and organisational skills and the availability of funding.

The question of political reintegration is as important to sustainable peace as the technical aspects of DDR. Power sharing, in particular within a democratic framework, is a means of reducing the potential for renewed violence, as it may harness illegal armed groups' motivations and capacity to resort to violence. Current academic and political debates on conflict resolution and peace building, though, have tended to downplay or elude this fundamental issue. Apart from the institutionalisation of DDR in international organisations as a technical and administrative process to find jobs for combatants and to transform the state security sector, this may be explained by the 'economic turn' in the analysis of armed conflict. By highlighting the economic dimensions of civil wars, the new conceptual lens has portrayed fighters as greedy individuals who do not have a legitimate political cause and, therefore, can or should not be politically reintegrated.[6] In addition, greater access to information regarding the conduct of illegal armed groups on the ground (which has exposed the cruelty of many); the reduced salience of prior 'good causes', such as rebellions against dictatorships, due to democratisation and the globalisation of liberal political ideas; a deeper internalisation of human-rights norms and other anti-crime regimes; and the War on Terror that followed the events of 11 September 2001 have shaped the debate and contributed to the shunning of political reintegration as an issue. Combatants no longer hold the same idyllic aura of former 'well-intended rebels'; note that the term 'guerrilla' is hardly used anymore and many armed organisations are now labelled 'terrorists.' As a result, the reintegration of rebels, criminals and terrorists today faces different political and legal challenges. For instance, opponents of AUC's demobilisation and reintegration have alluded to the group's close connections to the drug trade, its mafia-style behaviour, its relatively high degree of influence over economic and political transactions in certain Colombian localities, and its appalling human-rights record as reasons why it should be barred from politics. However, even though greed can be an important variable in conflicts and moral imperatives call for strict punishments for perpetrators of human-rights abuses, the practical issue of what to do with former combatants who wield influence over entire communities – and how to stop them from re-arming – remains.

The chapter is organised as follows: the first and second sections examine M-19's and AUC's experiences, respectively; and the concluding remarks reflect on the above-mentioned critical dimensions affecting acceptance and permanence.

The good old days: the reintegration of M-19

M-19 emerged in 1974 in response to a reported case of fraud in the 1970 presidential elections, which favoured the Conservative Party's candidate, Misael Pastrana. The group was formed by urban middle-class progressive activists, intellectuals, communist youths, disgruntled members from Alianza Nacional Popular (ANAPO) – the party that had lost the elections – and former FARC and ELN members, and defined itself as a nationalist, democratic, revolutionary movement. The guerrilla group demobilised 791 combatants in 1989–90 during peace negotiations with the Virgilio Barco government (1986–90) and became a political party, Alianza Democrática M-19 (AD M-19), joined later by EPL and PRT members. It had important victories at the local and national levels and obtained the second largest representation in the National Constituent Assembly that redrafted Colombia's constitution in 1991, a process that consolidated key democratic reforms and introduced modern liberal ideas on human rights. However, AD M-19's popularity then declined and the party disappeared after the 1998 elections. How did M-19 become a legitimate political party and why did it decline in later years?

It should be noted that AD M-19's decline as a party did not end the group's political reintegration process, which proceeded apace but took other forms. Many of its leading members, like Antonio Navarro Wolf and Gustavo Petro, remained active in politics and have become cornerstones of the PD. Today, the PD has become the first social democrat/leftist party with national appeal in the history of Colombia, a remarkable development considering the country's 150-year-old bipartisan tradition that had privileged both the Liberals and Conservatives. For the sake of brevity, the section will focus on the AD M-19 party and not the developments thereafter. It is suggested, though, that many of the same elements that allowed AD M-19 to exist can also explain the political survival of many of its leaders up until today.

A politically favourable window of opportunity

M-19's peace agreement and demobilisation occurred in tandem with substantial political reforms, carried out through a one-off National Constituent Assembly, which updated Colombia's 1886 constitution. Both events were perceived as key in overcoming the deep national crisis caused by weaknesses in Colombia's democratic institutions. It was a unique moment of great optimism and hope in which M-19's entrance into the political arena – as well as that of other guerrilla groups that demobilised right after M-19 – symbolised Colombia's passage to an improved political stage based on democratic values.[7]

The moment also provided respite from the anguishing sense of crisis and chaos that had emerged because of increased violence and crime in Colombia in the mid-1980s. The illegal drug industry flourished, traffickers amassed great wealth and power and launched a war against the state to prevent anti-drug laws that could land them in jail and, in particular, to avoid extradition to the United States. The war led by Pablo Escobar and the Medellín cartel featured the assassination of government officials, politicians, journalists and judges, for which the cartels had trained squadrons of mercenaries, the *sicarios*. Drug barons also resorted to targeted and indiscriminate bomb attacks in Bogotá, Medellín and Cali. 'Narco-terrorism' combined with the systematic bribery of authorities and the contamination of legal politics, extravagant spending and money laundering (which distorted the economy) and the use of violence to settle vendettas.[8]

Drug-trafficking and drug-related violence intertwined with conflict. In the 1960s and 1970s, guerrilla groups had remained small, survived on petty theft and extortion, recruited in less populated rural areas and acted as authority figures in localities with little state presence. Confrontation with the armed forces was infrequent and usually occurred far from Bogotá. Besides, unlike other Cold War conflicts, neither side was supported by the United States or the Soviet Union. Nevertheless, in the early 1980s, illegal armed groups, especially FARC, began to swell.[9] To fund its military expansion, FARC taxed the production of cocaine and the farming of coca bushes that was by then gaining ground in Colombia.

Estimates in 1985 claimed that FARC earned $99 million in a single year through such practices.[10]

Boosted by the illegal drug industry, but also by other sources of funding (ELN, for example, relied more on extortion and kidnapping), the guerrillas gained power and in turn served as a trigger to the rise of AUC. In the 1980s, right-wing paramilitary groups emerged as independent counterinsurgency forces in different parts of the country, supported by cattle ranchers, emerald traders, agricultural entrepreneurs and large landowners frustrated at the lack of state protection.[11] In time, some of the old leadership of these paramilitary groups was replaced by drug traffickers and their allies. Other paramilitary groups, like the *Muerte a Secuestradores* ('Death to Kidnappers'), were from the start directly tied to drug traffickers and aimed to protect their business and ill-gotten properties from extortion. It was then that the struggle took the form of a 'dirty war' against guerrillas and the left in general, waged by *sicarios* and the paramilitary, at times in collusion with public security forces.[12] Conflict and crime combined to claim some 20,000 deaths per year;[13] and, driven by the drug-based economy of war, Colombia went from a few hectares of coca bushes in the early 1980s to approximately 40,000 hectares in 1990.[14]

Colombia's problems overwhelmed state institutions and the political system, which had remained weak and outdated. Slow and partial reforms and fringe improvements (like anti-corruption purges in state security forces) were deemed insufficient. Therefore, many in Colombia began calling for 'structural' changes to solve what was seen as the root causes of conflict and crime, such as the lack of security guarantees and legal opportunities for the left, the concentration of power in Bogotá and in the hands of the elites, the absence of the state in many parts of the territory, administrative weaknesses of the public sector and poverty, inequality and underdevelopment.[15]

Against this turbulent landscape, the peace talks with M-19, officially announced in 1989, and the settlement of March 1990 came as a much-needed respite. Most political forces received the breakthrough positively, as a step to save Colombia from 'chaos'.[16] The optimism was also connected to the political reform underway, which was in part a product of the peace process, as M-19 had requested as a condition for its demobilisation that the government commit to a deep constitutional reform through a national assembly.[17] The mood was reflected in the *Séptima Papeleta* student mobilisation in the first months of 1990, which summoned constituents to vote in favour of an assembly and managed an impressive 86 per cent turnout.[18] The feeling among many was that Colombia was being catapulted into a new age and shedding some of its backwardness.

This political context and the related perception of the conflict as a legitimate expression of social grievances helped the reintegration of M-19 in several ways. First, it garnered public support for the peace accord and the reintegration of guerrillas into the legal political system. A transformed M-19, with relevant political participation, embodied Colombia's change. Second, by demobilising through a widely accepted peace process and through political discussions with the government, M-19 was able to frame itself as a 'political actor' in the public sphere.[19] Third, the state of institutional flux caused by the reforms provided bureaucratic and legal flexibility, which eased M-19's transition. The group quickly registered as a party with no checks on whether it complied with the rules, and was granted the *circunscripción especial*, two guaranteed seats in Congress. Fourth, the Assembly also served as a unique forum to construct a new political identity and as a window for public relations.

M-19 trustworthiness and the terms of the agreement

The terms of the peace negotiations also helped generate a favourable reception for M-19. On the one hand and unlike President Betancur (1982–86), who was criticised for being too lenient with FARC, Barco advanced a 'Peace Initiative' that combined carrots and sticks and was, thus, able to gain the support of the armed forces and main political sectors. The legitimacy of the peace negotiations bestowed legitimacy on the outcome: the birth of AD M-19. On the other hand, the way M-19 managed the negotiations portrayed them as 'serious' and 'trustworthy', as genuinely committed to peace and democracy and as worthy of becoming a legal political force.[20] When the rebel group held initial conversations with Barco's team in 1988, it had already decided to demobilise whatever the outcome of the deal so long as basic guarantees were met: a legal pardon and the physical protection of M-19 members.[21] Accordingly, M-19 made important concessions, especially taking into account that the group had not been defeated: it committed itself to a unilateral ceasefire and agreed to demobilise even though the government's political-reform bill was facing setbacks in Congress (the Barco government chose to withdraw the bill in late 1989 because corrupt legislators had introduced amendments that favoured drug traffickers).

Norms and the M-19 conduct at war

Legally and socially pardoning M-19 members and thus morally accepting them rather than treating them as pariahs was relatively uncontroversial, which also contributed to their subsequent legitimacy as political actors. Between 2 and 3 per cent of M-19 members were imprisoned for acts other than 'political crimes' (typically homicides committed out of combat),[22] but most combatants, leadership and rank-and-file received full pardons for their 'political crimes', including the hostage-taking of the Dominican Republic Embassy and the Palace of Justice and kidnapping, defined back then as a political crime connected to rebellion. There was a sense that forgiveness was fair given the flaws of the state and the undeniable existence of some of the 'objective' causes behind rebellion, such as poverty and inequality. Besides, the normative and legal contexts were conducive to forgiveness. At that time, the national human-rights regime was still underdeveloped: there was little public awareness regarding human rights, the issue was not a priority in the state bureaucracy and investigative capacities were weak.[23] For instance, neither the Ombudsman Office (Defensoría) nor the Fiscalía and its Human Rights Unit existed at the time. It was afterwards, during the intensification of armed conflict beginning in the mid-1990s, that tolerance towards violence decreased and legal dispositions hardened. In fact, former guerrillas played an active role disseminating human-rights norms in their work through NGOs and think tanks, a case in point being the work of former EPL combatants. Something similar occurred with regard to drug trafficking. Colombia had always endorsed the drug-prohibition regime, but there was a certain degree of social leniency vis-à-vis trafficking. It was only after the narco-terrorist wave of 1989–92 and the subsequent degradation of war, fuelled by the increasing participation of illegal armed groups in the illegal drug industry, that anti-drug laws were stiffened and the public began to view drug trafficking as an evil.

However, if Colombia afforded the guerrillas relatively lax standards or low barriers of entry, it is also true that M-19's identity played in its favour. M-19 departed from the more militaristic, Colombian Marxist insurgency groups, such as FARC, that hoped to install a communist or socialist regime. The M-19 leadership perceived orthodox communists waiting for an urban proletariat critical mass to form, or rebels seeking an authoritarian regime à la Fidel Castro in Cuba or a peasant uprising as in China, as disconnected from Colombia's realities.[24] What the country needed, they argued, was not communism but political and economic reforms that would open up the elite-controlled bipartisan system and effectively channel the interests of 'the masses', not just the oligarchy. In that respect, M-19 was far less radical than the other guerrillas and even legal parties to the left and expected to become a broad-based political force that could compete in democratic elections. These ideas and expectations shaped M-19's conduct during the war with regards to the use of violence. 'Shooting is not the way to take over power. Power is not obtained that way here. The thing is that this democracy is so closed, so bipartisan … that bullets are needed to get some attention', said one member.[25] Rather than engage in military combat with state security forces, launch indiscriminate attacks on civilians or gain territorial control through coercion, M-19 often opted for symbolic actions and selected political targets for its attacks. Of course, operations could go astray, as happened with the Palace of Justice takeover of 1985, when more than 100 people died including magistrates, public security officials, dozens of civilians and even M-19 members. However, in this case, much of the blame was placed on the armed forces and the police, who apparently disobeyed orders and used overwhelming force to avoid bargaining with M-19.[26]

Much like other illegal armed groups, M-19 stole from banks, food trucks and armoured vehicles.[27] Moreover, it has been claimed that M-19 was the first rebel group to experiment with drug trafficking and arms-for-drugs deals and that it introduced kidnapping as a way to raise funds, not only to exert political pressure.[28] However, M-19's involvement in such activities was not systematic.[29] In fact, during the 1980s, there was much debate among M-19 leaders on these specific issues. Leaders feared a revolutionary expansion would push the group deeper into drug trafficking and increased kidnapping and thereby tarnish the group's image (as has effectively happened with FARC today).[30] Then, in 1989, when narco-terrorism intensified and as the group was demobilising and preparing to enter legality, the organisation publicly condemned drug trafficking and spoke of its 'harmful effects' such as 'corruption' and 'violence'.[31] In general, M-19, as well as all the other guerrillas, managed to escape the degradation of war that occurred following their demobilisation.[32]

An enabling international atmosphere and the absence of foreign players

The international context also had an enabling effect on M-19's reintegration. The end of the Cold War brought a favourable climate for the resolution of ideologically driven conflicts in the Third World, while the concomitant triumph of liberal political ideas spurred the 'third wave' of democratisation in Eastern Europe and the South. As a result, former outcasts could be rehabilitated, especially if their grievances had related to authoritarianism and so long as they embraced Western democracy. This was also the time of relatively generous amnesties, offered to both rebels and dictators and justified in the name of democracy. Amnesties were possible, at least for a while, as the human-rights regime and other laws defining and punishing criminal behaviour had not yet become particularly robust or globalised. For instance, transnational NGO advocacy of human rights had not focused on Colombia and the few existing investigations and pronouncements by organisations like Amnesty International or Human Rights Watch dealt solely with the flaws of the government, at times implicitly siding with the guerrillas. Given this context and the features of the Colombian conflict, the international community generally welcomed the early 1990s' peace negotiations and political reforms.

International support, however, did not translate into mediation, assistance or any type of pressure to shape the terms of the settlement or collaborate with the disarmament, demobilisation and reintegration (DDR) of former fighters. Often, international actors have played leading roles in ending armed conflicts and in the peace-building process thereafter.[33] However, neither foreign states nor international institutions like the UN and the Organisation of American States (OAS) influenced the Colombian peace negotiations of the early 1990s. The US gave its approval but refrained from interfering – an unusual course of action given its record of intervention in Latin America, its 'backyard'. The laissez-faire approach stemmed from the particular friendship between the two states since the 1920s and the consequent 'prudent distance' maintained by the US with regard to Colombia's armed conflict and domestic politics, which had provided Bogotá a free hand to solve the guerrilla problem according to its own preferences.[34] In the end, the external presence in Colombia during the peace process was limited to a handful of representatives from the Socialist International, the Spanish Socialists Worker's Party (PSOE), the World Council of Indigenous Peoples and the Dutch NGO Pax Christi, who served as witnesses during protocol events and played a marginal role in verifying disarmament and in economic reintegration programmes.[35]

In retrospect, and when compared to the recent paramilitary demobilisation and the attempts to lure FARC and ELN into a peace settlement, it seems that the limited foreign presence reduced the political complexity of the peace negotiations and avoided vetoes to the reintegration of former combatants.

M-19 at the ballots

The transition from an illegal armed group to a political party required not just domestic and international political acceptance, but also the resolution of certain practical issues, beginning with the entry into electoral competition. Since M-19 had all along envisaged becoming a party, it explicitly addressed the point during the negotiations and secured its entry in the 1990 election. The amnesty removed possible legal obstacles in running for public office and the so-called *circunscripción especial*, the formula invented to provide former guerrillas with a concrete political landing strip, offered M-19 two guaranteed seats in Congress for the 1990–94 term.[36] The *circunscripción especial* was both a symbolic concession, part of the give-and-take of peace and democracy, and a technical advantage justified on the grounds that M-19 had no previous electoral experience and was, therefore, not in a condition to compete against the traditional parties.[37] In addition, M-19 was allowed to keep its financial assets, which it used for early proselytism,[38] and government subsidies for maintenance further helped its members finance their time in politics. Total expenditure in DDR programmes for M-19, PRT, EPL, MAQL, CRS and deserters (approximately 2,500) during 1990–2002 was estimated at $108.59 million.[39]

M-19 was officially reincarnated as AD M-19 just days after the settlement and it achieved outstanding electoral results during its first years of existence. The charismatic M-19 leader, Carlos Pizarro, obtained third place for the mayorship of Bogotá and gained much sympathy as a presidential candidate – however, he was assassinated in April by the Medellín drug mafia. Antonio Navarro took his place and obtained 12.5 per cent of the votes for the presidency, an important third position vis-à-vis the Liberal and Conservative parties that no other force had occupied since 1970. This result prompted the winning party to offer AD M-19 a permanent position in the cabinet, the Ministry of Health. In December 1990, when the National Constituent Assembly was voted in, AD M-19 obtained 19 of 70 seats, the second largest representation, and managed to set up a tripartite presidency shared with the Liberal Party and a dissident faction of the Conservative Party, the Movimiento de Salvación Nacional. At the Assembly, AD M-19 led important developments such as the inclusion of ample human-rights guarantees in the new charter. In 1991, it won 22 seats in the new Congress instated after the constitutional reform and, in 1992, it obtained promising results at the provincial and municipal levels. However, AD M-19's appeal began to wane in 1994, when the party obtained only one vote for the lower chamber, no votes for the Senate and just 3.7 per cent of the presidential ballot. Then, in 1998, AD M-19 was massively defeated.[40] In addition to the context and to Colombia's political cultural traits (clientelism and its relatively conservative tradition), a number of other important factors influenced the rise and decline of AD M-19 (see Table 1.1).

Table 1.1 AD M-19 in local and national elections

1990 (regular local and national elections)
2/161 Representatives
2 Mayors
5 Municipal council members
12.5% of the votes for the presidency, third place

December 1990 (election of the National Constituent Assembly)
The second largest representation, 19 of 70 seats

1991 (special Congress and Governorship elections after the reform)
9/102 Senators
13/165 Representatives
T5 Governors, elected in coalitions with other parties

1992 (first local elections after the reform)
17 Provincial Assembly members
1 Mayor
260 Municipal council members
10 *Ediles* (town-neighbourhood representatives)

1994 (local and first national elections after the reform)
1/165 Representative
3.79% of the votes for the Presidency in the first round, third place
7 Provincial Assembly members
5 Mayors, elected in coalitions with other parties
129 Municipal council members
40 *Ediles* (town-neighbourhood representatives)

Source: Ministerio del Interior, *Huellas de paz.*

One of them was strategy. M-19 believed that communism had little appeal among Colombians, an idea that had shaped their initial identity as a rebel group. It was also aware that its past as an illegal organisation could play out negatively unless voters were assured of its transformation into a democratic actor.[41] Accordingly, to send the right signals and come across as a 'safe option' to a broader audience, AD M-19 resorted to an inclusive discourse that referred to 'democracy', 'peace', 'national reconciliation' and 'consensus'.[42] Going beyond rhetoric, they invited public figures from other political tendencies to join their lists, such as Carlos Ossa Escobar from the Liberal Party and retired anti-Communist military general, José Joaquín Matallana, and indistinctively struck alliances with other parties for local elections. Initially, this seemed to have yielded the desired outcome. Later, however, M-19 was criticised for being 'more of the same' rather than a real alternative.[43] In retrospect, M-19 leaders argue that their discourse and proposals became too vague.[44]

Another issue was AD M-19's relations with its constituents. M-19 was a small rebel group but an efficient communicator and, therefore, was able to make the most of its public appearances and the media during the peace talks and the National Constituent Assembly sessions, which were given ample coverage in television and the radio. This served as a positive publicity campaign. However, M-19 was unable to build a more structured relationship with its constituents to guarantee their loyalty at the ballots over the long term. The government had agreed to social investment in key areas of interest to the former guerrilla groups, a form of 'peace-dividends' that could be capitalised on by AD M-19 for electoral purposes.[45] However, once demobilised and without a vertical structure in place, it was hard to keep contact with the base; the activities and routines attached to rebellion goals were no longer in place and communication among members became less frequent. Moreover, as time passed, middle- and lower-rank combatants grew increasingly preoccupied with day-to-day life, their interest in politics fading. As for new 'enthusiastic sympathisers', those discontent with both the Liberal and Conservative parties and expecting some kind of structural change, the party 'never figured out how to make them part of AD M-19 … we thought about registration cards, but never did much', admitted Vera Grabe, who was elected to Congress in 1990.[46]

'We simply did not know how politics was actually done', she added. Specific political skills were needed. M-19 was not a peasant organisation; its leadership and middle tiers were educated, accustomed to political debating and familiar with urban life, which clearly facilitated the group's entrance into the Colombian political arena. Nevertheless, AD M-19 was still a 'beginner' at politics and did not know how to manage a party, the inner workings of the Legislature or bargaining with the Executive. AD M-19 also suffered collective action problems that caused internal power struggles. All this led Otty Patiño, former M-19, to conclude that the transition from war to peace should be seen as a relatively long process and that new political parties must be given minimum safeguards in terms of electoral advantages for several terms to ensure their survival in difficult moments.[47]

Still, with all the difficulties encountered by AD M-19, it is remarkable that the former guerrillas who joined the party did not return to conflict.[48] They effectively became peaceful, law-abiding citizens, and many of the leadership and middle tiers became recognised public figures or members of NGOs, universities and think tanks advancing democracy and human-rights norms. More significantly, former M-19 leaders have become instrumental in the consolidation of the PD party. In 2006, the PD was joined by a small leftist party, Alternativa Democrática, and together they obtained 11 out of 102 seats in the Senate and nine out of 166 seats in the lower chamber in the Congressional elections that year, while the presidential candidate Carlos Gaviria came in third.[49] In the 2007 elections for local authorities, the PD obtained once again the mayoralty of Bogotá, the second most important position after the presidency; 19 other mayoralties across the country; the governorship of Nariño; 22 members in provincial assemblies and 378 in municipality town councils. Despite the high approval rates of Uribe, the PD could pose as an actual competitor in the coming 2010 presidential elections.

Efforts to reintegrate the paramilitary: a different game in a different time

The scattered independent paramilitary groups of 20 to 100 combatants that emerged in the 1980s formally turned in 1997 into AUC, a loose, pragmatic alliance of blocs. AUC's two main purposes were to coordinate a rapid expansion plan throughout Colombia and to gain political status rather than be treated like ordinary criminals. The former would give them leverage and the second would facilitate some sort of negotiation with the government that included pardons for their abuses and guarantees of no extradition to the US under drug-trafficking charges. Because the notion of a peace process had usually applied to the state and rebel forces, and technically speaking the paramilitary were not fighting the state, the paramilitary had not been part of Colombia's ongoing peace talks since the 1970s. Besides, 'self-defence organisations', as they called themselves, had even been legal in certain periods.

Not long after Álvaro Uribe's inauguration as president in August 2002, AUC signalled to the government its willingness to 'demobilise'.[50] The 'exploratory talks' began in December 2002 and the first Santa Fe de Ralito agreement, a short and vague document, was signed in July 2003 by 22 of 26 AUC blocs (all except for the Bloque Central Bolívar, the Bloque Élmer Cárdenas and the so called 'Eastern Alliance'). In November and December 2003, the Cacique Nutibara demobilised in Medellín, but a crisis in the negotiations followed and demobilisations stopped. Talks eventually were renewed, more blocs joined and in May 2004, another agreement was finalised, this time with greater details about the DDR process and stricter conditions for the paramilitary. The committed paramilitary blocs withdrew from the conflict in a staggered calendar from November 2004 to April 2006 and entered an 18-month reintegration programme, which was later lengthened depending on the needs of each individual, until he or she was 'ready'. In all, about 31,671 combatants claimed to have demobilised collectively.[51] Some of the terms of the agreement and the key features of the transitional justice regime that was set up to treat crime wars and human-rights abuses were written in the 72 article-long 2005 Justice and Peace Law and in related decrees and court rulings.[52] These were the object of heated public debate, discussions in Congress and court ruling from August 2003, when the first draft of an 'alternative justice' law was circulated in Congress, up until 2007, when critical implementation decrees were being issued.

Whereas the transformation of guerrillas into political parties had been a desirable and unquestioned development in the early 1990s, the political future of the paramilitary following demobilisation was uncertain, further divided Colombian society and faced fiery opposition in international policy-making circles. Some believed paramilitary combatants had won legitimate support in their respective territories by mending the troubles caused by decades of state neglect and guerrilla abuse and, therefore, were worthy of political acknowledgement and acceptance by society. Others were critical but concluded that the paramilitaries were a de facto political force by virtue of their power and thus impossible to isolate. But the political mainstream thought otherwise and insisted on disarticulating paramilitary structures, meaning not just disarming the groups but making sure that their political and economic influence over local and national authorities would come to an end. Whether for moral reasons or convenience, most politicians, business leaders and citizens felt the need to dissociate publicly from paramilitary 'contamination' or hush about existing contacts. In the 2006 presidential elections and in the 2007 local elections political parties, including Uribe's new Partido de la Unión, ended up purging suspected paramilitary supporters and demobilised paramilitaries from their lists. The connections between paramilitary and politics became anathema and, in 2007, the 'para-politics' scandal broke out, landing more than 35 congress members, governors and mayors in jail for illegal actions connected to the paramilitary.[53] What was the controversy about? Why were former paramilitary combatants denied political reintegration? Why were they treated differently from the guerrillas that demobilised in the early 1990s?

The paramilitary: part criminal, part political

AUC was not a 'common' rebel organisation. The deep concerns and often-outright rejection of paramilitary participation in politics after their demobilisation relates to three specific features of their identity and conduct: an appalling human-rights record, trafficking drugs for self-enrichment and abusing politics and public institutions to get their way.

Like other combatants, the paramilitary committed grave crimes. However, they also displaced thousands of people from their homes, engaged in mass killings and used brutal methods. Cinep, a Colombian think tank, registered 14,476 victims of homicide, torture and forced disappearances and 64 massacres between 1988 to 2003.[54] In Mapiripán in 1997, approximately 70 alleged FARC collaborators were tortured and killed, their body parts thrown into the Guaviare River; in 2000 in Carmen de Bolivar, paramilitaries of the Autodefensas Campesinas de Córdoba y Urabá tortured, beheaded and raped more than 40 peasants; and in 2001, the Farallones Block killed 46 indigenous persons of the Naya with machetes and chainsaws. Their extreme cruelty was later confirmed in 2007, when demobilised combatants revealed how they trained on assassination techniques, including cutting people's bodies into pieces while still alive.[55] Many of their victims were civilians, including women and children. Besides, the fact that the paramilitaries often received collaboration from public security forces, in the form of information, equipment or military support during operations, further eroded their reputation and, of course, that of the state. These connections between the paramilitary and the state, though not institutionalised or supported by high-level authorities, reminded audiences of the stereotypical behaviour of Latin America's right-wing dictatorships, reinforcing the idea that they were not on the side of the weak, to defend them, but on the side of the strong to sustain their privileges.

Second, the paramilitary were heavily entrenched in drug-trafficking rings, which became a great obstacle to peace and DDR processes and specifically to political reintegration. Allowing a drug trafficker to benefit from transitional justice and to become a legitimate political interlocutor in a democratic society was unacceptable to local and foreign audiences. The first paramilitary groups, such as the ones commanded by landowners like Ramón Isaza from the

Magdalena Medio, were mostly self-financed and supported by rural businesses seeking protection from FARC and ELN. But drug-traffickers-turned-landowners began setting up their own armies and partnering with paramilitary leaders, who subsequently grew dependent on drug money as conflict expanded. Soon economic motivations became as important as any security incentive. For instance, the Castaño brothers and 'Don Berna' were among those who filled the vacuum in domestic and international smuggling left by the dismantling of the Medellín cartel in 1993 as well as the fall of the old Cali cartel in 1995.[56] Finally, during the last stages of the paramilitary expansion, a new wave of drug traffickers joined up using as an entry door the paramilitary 'franchise' system, whereby the Castaño brothers and Mancuso sold the 'paramilitary brand', along with training and contacts, to ambitious criminals willing to conquer new territories and eventually benefit from a political negotiation. This was how 'The Mellizos', 'Gordo Lindo', 'Macaco', 'Johny Cano' and 'El Tuso' became part of the paramilitary structure.[57] In May 2008, following increasing evidence that key paramilitary commanders had cheated the peace process, 14 of them were extradited to the US on drug-trafficking charges.[58]

Paramilitary forces were also involved in many other illicit businesses like gasoline theft and contraband, arms trading, and the buying and selling of land forcefully appropriated or abandoned by displaced persons.[59] They laundered and invested money in legal activities, from jeweller's shops in Margarita Island, to stocks in Panama, to gold mines, pharmacies, transport companies, armoured vehicles, car dealers and agri-business.[60] They also participated extensively in extortion and in 'paid security protection' to raise funds, control local populations and compromise key business-leaders or politicians by virtue of their illegal payment. One important case that reached the media during paramilitary confessions in 2007 was the payments made by the American multinational Chiquita Brands to paramilitary in the Urabá region.[61] Particularly commanders and middle-rank combatants made sure to profit personally from war and crime. Their wealth was such that the Central Bolívar bloc alone announced at one point that it would allocate $53 million – in the form of properties, cattle and cash – as reparations.[62] Their affluence and individual profiteering clearly differentiated paramilitary from the Colombian guerrillas to have demobilised previously and justified higher barriers of entry, including asset forfeiture to pay for victim reparation programmes, a measure M-19, EPL and the other groups never faced.

The third feature of paramilitary conduct was the manipulation of local politics. While 'armed clientelism' – the practice of using elections and public office as a tactical war instrument – had been used by prior guerrilla movements, the paramilitary forces managed to perfect and extend this practice, thereby gaining control of entire regions and even affecting national politics. The common practice was to intimidate local voters through massacres and selective murders, bribe or strike political alliances with politicians if need be, handpick their own candidates and often intimidate opponents to reduce competition for mayor and governorships, and then organise voting districts to maximise the results for Congressional posts. In 2005, paramilitary leader Salvatore Mancuso boasted having 35 per cent of the Congress in paramilitary hands. Later on, in 2007, the true reach of paramilitary involvement in politics was uncovered in the 'para–politics scandal', in which at least 35 mayors and congress members, including Álvaro Araujo, brother of Minister of Foreign Affairs Consuelo Araujo, were imprisoned. Reports claim that at least 11 of 33 provinces in Colombia, including César, Córdoba, Magdalena and Sucre, became true paramilitary bastions.[63] As with their wealth and connections with public security forces, this penetration of politics portrayed the paramilitary as an extremely powerful organisation.

In sum, the paramilitary were a special breed of combatants. Like the other Colombian illegal combatants, they wore military fatigues and engaged in armed fighting. However, they had intricate economic and political networks, part legal and part illegal, that served as solid pillars from which to exercise great power – greater than any other illegal armed group in Colombia's history. This meant that although paramilitary leaders and base too had grievances, even grudges against the traditional urban elite, they certainly did not resemble the idealistic guerrillas seeking to defend society's poor and excluded. They looked more a right-wing, cruel, overgrown *mafiosi* organisation, which had clear implications for their reintegration process.[64] Most forcefully, the possibility of AUC transforming into a legitimate political entity, such as a political party, was eliminated by their own prior conduct, as the paramilitary came to be seen as driven not by politics, but by greed.

The issue deserves further analysis, as it touches upon fundamental aspects of peace-building. One innovation in the theory and practice of managing armed conflicts has been to bring the economic dimensions of conflicts to the fore, thereby downplaying the political and power-sharing components of war. For instance, the Colombian paramilitary, despite their *mafiosi* appearance, were indeed 'political'.[65] This does not mean buying into the paramilitary's own self-serving discourse. Since before their demobilisation, the paramilitary made an effort to portray themselves as a politically motivated organisation. They began using language that alluded to an 'ideological platform' and that referred to the 'natural right' of 'legitimate self-defence', the state's duty to defend its citizens and the right to protect private property.[66] As the debates around the Justice and Peace Law and its related decrees progressed, paramilitary leaders continued to make an effort in that same direction: 'it must be acknowledged that using arms to defend your own life, given the weaknesses of the state ... is as political as using weapons to attack the state', claimed a paramilitary article posted on the AUC website.[67] Of course, there was much at stake in gaining a political status due to legal technicalities; the Colombian law specified that political criminals (as opposed to drug traffickers) can be exempted from extradition. With such political status, they were also seeking to reduce asset forfeiture and their time in prison.

Discourse apart, the paramilitary were political in that they exercised power over important parts of the territory, mediated in disputes among inhabitants, provided security and regulated economic transactions. Carlos Alonso Lucio, a former M-19 but also a 'friend' of the paramilitary pointed out that 'the paramilitary are more a *political phenomenon* as opposed to a *political organisation*'.[68]

This may be different from being a cohesive rebel organisation with a specific political ideology and a defined and comprehensive public agenda on how to run the state for the common good (the guerrilla 'political' identity), but it is nevertheless 'political'. Notwithstanding criminality, paramilitary forces constructed an alternate order in many localities in Colombia, in which they were even recognised as the local authority. In this way, they gained some degree of legitimacy – even if it ran counter to the Colombian mainstream culture and foreign Western standards of legitimacy in a democracy. Such appeal, even with their non-democratic behaviour, was clear during the first round of court hearings. Commander 'Macaco' from the Central Bolívar bloc, for instance, was cheered by more than 600 fans outside the court during his first voluntary deposition; they wanted to 'welcome him with whistles, drums and chants supporting his social work – according to fans – in eight provinces around the country'.[69]

What does this mean for reintegration? Being 'political' in this way is not a blank cheque in terms of justice, but does raise the question of what to do with armed groups like the Colombian paramilitary, who are wealthy, have strong economic interests, have committed crimes against humanity but can still control territory and people, thereby posing risks to the state and to state-building.

In Colombia, since disarmament and demobilisation had not necessarily dismantled their power networks, the risk that irregular and grey-area practices, not to speak of violence, could still be used to determine the outcome of elections was, for many, precisely a reason to keep the paramilitary away from politics. They believed that it was better to keep paramilitaries out of politics altogether so as to avoid this 'shadowy' way of doing politics. Others, such as Senator Rafael Pardo, who had been a leading figure of the Barco and Gaviria administrations during the peace processes of the early 1990s, suggested letting them in so as to exercise explicit control over their political conduct. In practice, this would have meant checking party and personal bank accounts, implementing transparency best practices and inducing self-constraint to keep extremists out (as the Partido de la Unión and *Cambio* Radical had voluntarily done with the purges). The argument of many others was that it did not matter whether the paramilitary were political or not, the main theme had to be their egregious human-rights violations, on which grounds they had to be punished and barred from becoming legal political entities.

Grappling with the mixed identity of the paramilitary was not easy. Neither Colombians nor the Justice and Peace Law really settled the issue. Demobilised combatants were allowed to create civil-society organisations – such as the NGOs Corporación Democracia from the Cacique Nutibara block, the Fundación Iniciativas por la Paz close to commanders Mancuso and Báez, Buscando Caminos Buenos and Semillas de Paz from the Central Bolívar bloc, and Senderos from the Mineros bloc – but they were not allowed to create political parties. The law granted them the 'political treatment' they were asking for, largely the exemption from extradition, so long as they complied with certain rules, but made no reference to their 'political reintegration' (understood as the legal exercise of politics). It acknowledged their economic dimension by stating that they had to repay victims with their own assets and introduced asset forfeiture of goods obtained illicitly, including by drug trafficking, but stopped short from categorising them as drug traffickers, the 'eligibility' criteria for the legal benefits of the Justice and Peace Law defining a true paramilitary as those not originally created solely for trafficking or illicit enrichment purposes.

In the end, paramilitary reintegration has been complicated and success partial, partly because of this mixed identity. AUC no longer exists; the strategic expansion plan that so rapidly extended paramilitary presence across the country stopped; homicide rates dropped and paramilitaries' negative impact over democratic institutions has been undermined through the legal prosecutions that followed the 'para-politics' scandal. Still, 'normality' has not been reached and residues of the paramilitary phenomenon pose grave threats. Immediately after the collective demobilisation, local communities and authorities began reporting the emergence of new illegal organisations, such as the Águila Negras.[70] In 2007, a National Reparation and Reconciliation Commission report said authorities had detected at least 34 new criminal structures with a total of about 3,500 to 5,000 men. There has been much debate on the nature of these organisations and whether they are composed of old and new recruits attached to former high commanders, a new generation of the paramilitary phenomenon only commanded by a different leadership, or just 'criminal bands' taking advantage of the vacuums in security and drug trafficking left by the paramilitary. Moreover, the 2007 local elections showed that, in some municipalities, several paramilitary structures still wielded political power. In some regions, such as Medellín, it is claimed that while violence is constrained, paramilitary combatants continue to operate, albeit with a lower profile, and still act as the local authority. Finally, in 2008, the Colombian government decided that several paramilitary leaders had cheated to such a degree as to deserve one of the punishments they so feared: extradition to the US.

Changed political and normative contexts

The domestic political and normative contexts of paramilitary political reintegration, 15 years after the first wave of guerrilla demobilisation in the early 1990s, were very different and presented high entry barriers. Colombians were less willing to embrace illegal armed groups, whether guerrillas or paramilitary; there was no broad-based transformative episode, like the National Constituent Assembly, to provide political momentum; and the system was endowed with tougher human-rights and anti-drug regimes.

In the mid-1990s, Colombia's conflict witnessed another turn in magnitude and severity.[71] FARC, ELN and AUC grew and expanded their influence across the country. FARC went from having a couple of thousand combatants in the early 1980s to approximately 15–18,000 in 2000; ELN reached its peak, 4–5,000, in 1996; and AUC was estimated at 6,000 in 1999 and at 13,500 in 2003 – although this figure nearly tripled during the 2004–06 demobilisation.[72] Expelling and blocking one another from territories and obtaining new sources of funding to sustain a bigger war became key objectives for guerrillas and paramilitaries. For that, they sought tighter territorial control, resorting to coerced co-option and bribery of local authorities, military combat against opponents, selective murders, massacres and forced displacement of civilians, all with increasingly gruesome methods. All groups stepped up extortion, illegal trading and theft, the paramilitary and FARC delved deeper into coca production and drug trafficking, while FARC and ELN invented mass kidnapping. Meanwhile, the Colombian security forces intensified their response, first under President Pastrana and then more vigorously under President Uribe's Democratic Political Security, by recruiting more troops, improving intelligence-gathering and combat capacity and strengthening coca eradication. Eventually, the conflict began to take its toll, constituting, to some, a true humanitarian crisis: two million people were internally displaced,[73] more than 3,000 kidnappings occurred per year,[74] around 100 small towns were wiped out annually, and even the big cities – previously isolated from the conflict – began witnessing bomb attacks.[75] In addition, Colombia turned into to the world's largest coca producer: in 2000, illegal crops reached an all-time high of 136,200 hectares, 74 per cent of total world cultivation.[76]

In 1997 and 1998, thousands of Colombians took to the streets in unprecedented massive demonstrations against violence.[77] At first, this prompted another round of peace-talks. In 1998, the Andrés Pastrana administration (1998–2002) launched new negotiations with FARC, and invited the international community to support the process politically and economically. It was the first time Colombia had called for international help. The UN and EU responded by increasing economic and humanitarian assistance, while the US helped with Plan Colombia, a large anti-narcotics/anti-terrorist aid package with a strong military component, designed as the hard persuasion element of the overall peace strategy. Pastrana offered FARC a temporary demilitarised zone, but the rebel movement used this locality for further training and regrouping. Domestic and international observers began to question whether FARC had turned into a greed-based criminal organisation. At the same time, the state stepped up the pressure on AUC, which was also increasingly in the limelight because of its involvement in criminal activities.[78]

The collapse of peace talks with FARC and the growing public perception of illegal armed groups as greed-driven tilted the balance back in favour of stick rather than carrot. President Uribe, who proposed tougher security measures, was elected with a 22 per cent margin over his rival in the first round of the 2002 presidential elections. He launched an all-out war against FARC and ELN, and pledged to combat right-wing paramilitary groups.

Meanwhile, the legal and normative contexts with regard to human rights and drug trafficking, two central features of armed conflict in Colombia, had stiffened. In the 1990s, the judicial system was reformed and law-enforcement agencies strengthened. Specific state agencies with the mandate to promote and oversee human rights were created, such as the Defensoría del Pueblo (Ombudsman) along with the figure of *personeros* in municipalities, the Human Rights Unit of the Fiscalía (Attorney General's Office), the Ministry of

Defense's Human Rights Office and the Human Rights Observatory at the Vice-presidency.[79] Moreover, international humanitarian law was formally integrated in 1994 when Colombia signed Protocol II of the Geneva Convention and in 1997, at the government's request, the UN High Commissioner for Human Rights opened a field office in Bogotá. The further institutionalisation of the human-rights regime was stimulated by the 1991 Constitution; Colombia's own process of modernisation; heightened domestic and international attention to conflict dynamics, as reflected in the increased presence of international human-rights NGOs in Colombia, the proliferation of local NGOs and the work of UN agencies.[80] Occasional pressure by the United States through new human-rights certification requirements attached to military aid and 'institution-building' assistance connected to the war against drugs also played a role in entrenching human-rights norms and laws.[81] The human-rights community, composed of Colombian and foreign NGOs, local and national public agencies, UN officials, the Inter-American Human Rights System and foreign donors, shaped the terms of the agreement between the Uribe government and the paramilitary by demanding higher prison sentences for war crimes and effective reparations, restitution and rehabilitation of victims, and served as watchdogs of both para-military and state compliance with the agreements.

A similar development occurred with the drug-prohibition regime. In this case, narco-terrorism, the narco-corruption scandal of 1995 linking several politicians to drug cartels, the intertwining of conflict and drug trafficking and the United States' ever-larger anti-drug aid were key drivers. Colombia signed and updated anti-drug and judicial cooperation treaties with other countries; the Fiscalía created an anti-narcotics unit; Law 190 of 1995, the so-called Anti-Corruption Statute, criminalised money laundering; and other laws passed in 1996–97 strengthened asset forfeiture and increased sentences for drug traffick-ing, money laundering and connected crimes. Aerial and manual eradication and alternative development became permanent features of Colombia's counter-drug policy, boosted later through Plan Colombia. Interdiction was expanded through maritime, riverine and land operations by the military and the police, and radar control systems were enhanced to detect smuggling aircraft. In addi-tion, Colombia reintroduced the extradition of nationals in 1997, allowing the sentencing of Colombians in US courts for crimes (typically pertaining to drug trafficking) committed on US soil.[82]

As the illegal drug industry and conflict became more connected, prohibition laws and counter-narcotic operations reached the illegal armed groups. Counter-narcotics army battalions and massive aerial coca-crop eradication began target-ing guerrillas and paramilitaries and, for the first time, illegal combatants were extradited. From 1991 to April 2006, the US requested 109 combatants in extra-dition for drug-related offences,[83] and the first to be condemned in US courts were three 'narco-terrorist' paramilitaries.[84] In fact, extradition to the US on drug-trafficking charges turned into a key negotiation leverage in the peace process, since paramilitaries feared that punishment the most.[85] It was so, that in March 2008, after accumulating evidence that various paramilitary leaders had cheated the Justice and Peace Law, President Uribe decided to extradite them to the US using the anti-drug regime as a mechanism. Moreover, the Justice and Peace Law introduced some of the same language and rationale in anti-drug laws with regards to asset forfeiture.

The lower tolerance for violence and crime and the moves to combat and prosecute illegal armed groups more forcefully were inevitably accompanied in public discourse by the reconstruction of armed groups as criminals as opposed to 'political others'. Thus, although the paramilitary were eventually able to find a receptive government when it proposed demobilisation, the public was less sympathetic to the idea of political reintegration or of granting them a space as legitimate citizens. Neither was Colombia in the midst of deep national reform and so lacked the flexible political juncture that had helped M-19 and other groups reintegrate through the National Constituent Assembly in 1990.

International constraints

Another difference relates to the presence and pressures of foreign countries and international institutions. Whereas Colombia's old peace negotiations were designed and implemented with no external third eye playing a substantial role, paramilitary peace negotiations and implementation of accords were entirely permeable to international dynamics and the actions of foreign actors. These effectively influenced the negotiations with paramilitaries and the Justice and Peace Law, making them more severe than what the state and the combatants had originally envisaged, and took on to monitoring compliance thereafter for several years. Notwithstanding some differences among states, international organisations and NGOs, the general verdict of the international community was to veto the immediate transformation of paramilitaries into a political force, by issuing public and private warnings, using assistance as leverage and, in the case of the US, threatening to execute extradition.

Despite the close Bush–Uribe alliance, the US supported the paramilitary demobilisation process but not without conditions. The US tendency to expand its missions, the bureaucratic dynamics of a bigger and better war against drugs and Colombia's cry for assistance in the face of conflict escalation did away with the old 'prudent distance' in US–Colombian relations. Then, in 1998, the first 'Plan Colombia' was born, to assist the 'troubled democracy' against guerrilla-related drug cultivation and trafficking. Then, after the 9/11 attacks were articulated into the War on Terror and mainstreamed in foreign policy, the US turned to help Colombia combat 'terrorists', which was, according to the US State Department listings as of 2001, the official label not only for guerrillas but for AUC as well. US military assistance, economic development, judicial strengthening and human-rights-related aid entered Colombia – approximately $5.34 billion were disbursed from 2000 to 2006, more than the total aid given in the previous three decades. Along with it came US political intervention in Colombia's decisions on conflict management.[86] The US had turned into the main standard-setter of paramilitary demobilisation and reintegration.

The general effect of US policy was to echo and promote the hardening of Colombian domestic audiences towards all illegal armed groups, thereby raising the barriers to paramilitary transformation into a legitimate political entity. 'I'm not sure the self-defense groups have a political goal or that they have a political agenda. They have only one program: narco-terrorism', said Ambassador William Wood in 2004 as the Justice and Peace Law was being debated.[87] Wood did at one point acknowledge the paramilitary's 'political dimension' but referred to it as 'vile, violent, brutal and anti-democratic'[88] and harshly condemned Mancuso's and Baez's appearance at an official hearing in the Colombian Congress, which friendly Congress members had arranged for them.[89] It must be noted, though, that the US did not impede talks with either FARC or with AUC, despite the hard rhetoric warning against negotiating with terrorists – but it made sure to express its preferences on the bargain and its outcome. In general, the US wanted the Colombian state to negotiate from a position of strength, the assured enforcement of drug prohibition and compliance with US laws. With regard to the paramilitary, this translated into the US pushing for stiffer terms in the Justice and Peace Law, which contained the agreement between the Uribe government and AUC; requesting the extradition of paramilitary commanders as a stick; helping Colombia strengthen its capacity to punish paramilitaries who defected from the deal; supporting the OAS verification mission; helping Colombia provide employment opportunities to the foot soldiers; while keeping the paramilitary out of politics.[90]

Such intervention did not come only from the state, in a 'billiard ball' fashion, but by the whole gamut of actors shaping policy-making in Washington. Bush critics – Democrats and progressive think tanks and NGOs like the Center for International Policy, the Washington Office on Latin America and especially Human Rights Watch through its Washington DC office – harshly condemned the US policy of lending support to the demobilisation despite its shortcomings, to Plan Colombia, to President Uribe, and to the idea of granting AUC any possibility to participate legally in politics.[91] In 2007, the Democrats, after having won back the congressional majority in 2006, implicitly conditioned their support to the Free Trade Agreement and Plan Colombia on the government's willingness to implement the Justice and Peace Law strictly and punish public security forces, politicians and businesses with links to the paramilitary.[92]

This time around, Europe kept a close watch also, thereby shaping the outcome of the process. Since the mid-1990s, various European countries increased their assistance to Colombia, directly and through NGOs and the UN, focusing on economic development, human rights, democracy and the empowerment of local NGOs and civil society in Colombia. This meant that despite their lower position of influence over Colombia relative to the US (because of history, geography and amounts of aid), they still wielded influence over sectors of the Colombian population that were actively involved in the public debates related to the paramilitary demobilisation process. It was through this channel, especially, that they tried influencing the government.[93] Most condemned AUC and had deep concerns about the demobilisation, which was perceived to support the transition of war criminals and drug traffickers into legality with impunity.[94] Sweden and the Netherlands, who decided to cooperate to increase their own influence, were the only European countries to provide financial support and political backing to the OAS during the very first stages of its verification mission, not without fears of criticism from domestic constituents and other European fellows.[95]

The OAS verification mission, MAPP-OEA, created in 2004, also played a role.[96] Weaknesses apart, the mission's reports on paramilitary re-arming and the participation of demobilised combatants in criminal activities were important not only as a way to verify the implementation of the Justice and Peace Law but also in shaping the various debates about the paramilitary's 'true' identity; they highlighted mostly the criminal dimension. As for the UN and its panoply of agencies in Colombia, they were viscerally against AUC, continuously voiced criticism of the Justice and Peace Law and demanded the 'effective dismantlement' of paramilitary structures. Michael Frühling, UN Human Rights Commissioner in Colombia, explicitly faulted the law for not including temporary political inabilities for those implicated in human-rights violations and explicit provisions barring AUC reintegration into the armed forces.[97]

The Inter American Human Rights Commission, which also pronounced itself on the paramilitary peace process, specifically on the Justice and Peace Law and related decrees, did not address the issue of the ex-combatants' political future either as a formal, legal political party or in the form of NGO activism or journalism, but indirectly contributed to the emphasis on punishment rather than reintegration in the public debate. The Commission's declarations after the enactment of the Justice and Peace Law in July 2005 and after the Constitutional Court's sentence C-370, for instance, insisted repeatedly on Colombia's 'international legal obligations' with regard to human rights. This translated into a duty to prevent and combat impunity, to ensure victims' and society's right to know the truth, to apply strictly the established criteria by which former paramilitary would lose the legal benefits enumerated in the Justice and Peace Law and to consider criteria other than the 'original purpose' of the organisation when deciding whether a paramilitary or a block were effectively 'paramilitary' or drug traffickers in disguise.[98]

In addition to the specific discontents of these third parties, recent international experiences with ending dictatorships and civil wars set new expectations with regard to justice, which generally reduced the scope of indults and amnesties and reinforced the moral obstacles to paramilitary political reintegration.[99] For instance, a prosecutor of the International Criminal Court (ICC), Luis Moreno, produced official statements on AUC demobilisation, which acted as a warning to Colombia should it fail to investigate paramilitary crimes and apply appropriate punishments.[100] The implication of any failings, it was implied, would be the ICC intervention, which would be detrimental to Colombia's image as a democratic country. In 2007 and 2008, Moreno visited Colombia, signalling the ICC's close watch over the implementation of the agreements and thereby helping to maintain formal and informal vetoes to paramilitary participation in politics. The ICC even hinted that if paramilitary extradition to the US proved an obstacle to fulfilling the truth requirements of the Justice and Peace Law, it would consider ruling over the Colombian case.[101] Meanwhile, the Inter-American Human Rights Commission supported the above mentioned statements, citing, among other sources, the UN's basic principles and guidelines on the right to a remedy and reparation for victims of gross violations of international human-rights law and serious violations of international humanitarian law – adopted by the General Assembly in 2006.[102]

Paramilitary identity, perceptions of Uribe and the terms of the agreement

While the Uribe government held talks with AUC and the Justice and Peace Law was being discussed, the debates focused on whether the law, which would determine the terms of the agreement, was going to be tough enough and whether it would disarticulate paramilitary structures: actual dismantlement of paramilitary power implied going beyond disarmament and the withdrawal of paramilitary forces from armed conflict; it meant paramilitaries abstaining from influencing economic and political transactions in their local fiefdoms and removing their allies and protégées from public office. The focus was not on how to transform the paramilitary organisations into legitimate political entities as had been the case with M-19 and their contemporaries. In addition to the nature and conduct of paramilitary groups, the perceived lenient terms of the negotiations between the Uribe government and AUC, as embodied in the Justice and Peace Law, and the evidence of paramilitary cheating during the long, staggered demobilisation in 2003–06 served to justify a ban on paramilitary participation in the 2006 elections and a push for the social, economic and political containment of AUC post-demobilisation.

Whether the final version of the Justice and Peace Law was lax or not is relative. For sure, the law was more strict than the requirements faced by M-19: it introduced reparations for victims and a Reparations National Commission; it contained provisions to forfeit money and properties of AUC members (acknowledging the fact that paramilitaries had used war to make profit); it established that kidnapping was not a political crime and consequently could not be pardoned; and created a special unit in the Fiscalía to investigate crimes further. Nevertheless, domestic and international audiences considered the law excessively lenient, given the nature and conduct of the paramilitary and the changed normative context. Critiques constantly hailed over the law as it was being discussed in Congress and even the final text, which was harder than the initial versions submitted by the Uribe government, was deemed unsatisfactory. The *New York Times* spoke of 'Colombia's Capitulation' to crime,[103] and the law was even rebutted by Uribe followers: Senator Gina Parody, complained that the law was 'sending Colombians the message that crime paid', while Senator Rafael Pardo opted out of the pro-Uribe alliance in Congress.[104] For many, the alternative sentence for those found guilty of crimes against humanity – up to eight years in a special prison plus four years of parole – was too low. Other points of contention regarded the lack of actual mechanisms to implement forfeiture, the absence of requirements regarding confessions, and the fact that reparations mechanisms had no teeth.

In part, these concerns stemmed from distrust of President Uribe and his will to prosecute paramilitary crimes. The President had a reputation of being sympathetic to armed self-defence. Opponents and NGOs claimed that he had personally benefited from paramilitary counterinsurgency in Antioquia and Cordoba, where he, as well as paramilitary commanders, owned land, and that Uribe's brother, Santiago, had participated in the Doce Apóstoles group, linked to the paramilitary.[105] Meanwhile, the ongoing reports of links between state security forces and the paramilitary, the infiltration of paramilitary personnel in key agencies such as the Departamento Administrativo de Seguridad (DAS) – the investigative and intelligence agency, the autocratic bent of the government's security policy and the right-wing tone of official discourse only lent credit to the suspicions.[106] In addition, the paramilitaries failed to prove that they were genuinely committed to peace and democracy and thus ready to become law-abiding citizens. While it is true that combat and mass killings nearly stopped following the demobilisation, the paramilitaries still exercised coerced influence in their old war zones, influenced politics in illegal ways, committed homicides, executed social cleansing, extorted local populations and kept links with drug trafficking.[107]

In the end, the 'peace' bargain with the paramilitary did not contain the same type of political issues that had featured in the M-19 peace agreement, such as the introduction of fundamental changes to democratise the political system, steps to transform the armed group into a political force and favourable conditions in electoral competition. Instead, the terms of the settlement resembled the type of plea bargain criminals would strike with law-enforcement agents to reduce their sentence in exchange for good behaviour or valuable information, except that it was written in a bill for Congressional approval and called a 'peace agreement'. This nature of the agreement was the result of, first, the paramilitary focus on having a settlement whose main point was not reintegration but the protection of combatants from extradition to the US and, second, society's understandings of the nature of paramilitary forces. Even if former combatants not guilty of war crimes could legally run for office and form their own movement or join other parties of their liking, the terms of the negotiation did not envisage transition instruments and paramilitaries were anyway morally banned from participating in politics in 2006.

Power and political participation: scenarios of paramilitary reintegration

In practice, paramilitaries still exert influence over politics, not always in entirely illegal ways, while some combatants have expressed their desire to become politicians following mainstream rules. (Others may want to withdraw from the limelight and enjoy any remaining wealth and some, from the middle tiers and rank-and-file, have already drifted into crime rings and carried on with extortion and drug trafficking.) The point is that several AUC members have local appeal in certain regions in Colombia and they are recognised as authority figures. Paramilitary forces may not be legitimate in the cultural mainstream, but they are in a local sub-culture, even if this legitimacy was first constructed using force and the leverage of their money. It is interesting to compare this situation with the case of M-19 and other guerrillas. Whereas M-19 enjoyed legitimacy in the eyes of Bogotá, enough to enter legality and electoral competition, it never exercised as much power in as many regions as the paramilitary did and presumably still do. In addition, crime and brutality notwithstanding, the paramilitary may ironically be better equipped to survive in politics than M-19 was when it demobilised back in the early 1990s. Unlike the guerrillas, AUC leaders were all along connected to the cities and active in legal politics, even if through illegal means, and were therefore familiar with the daily workings of political machineries: they understand pork-barrel politics, manage well the articulation between local and national politics and know how to mobilise constituents during elections. Above all, they have more access to funding through their legal businesses. In the long run, though, former paramilitaries will have to adopt cultural mainstream rules as enshrined in accepted national laws and international standards if they want to sustain their participation in national public spheres as political actors. The political reintegration of the paramilitary might involve a process of selection and self-selection whereby the more criminal elements are weeded out and 'bad' paramilitaries are differentiated from 'good' ones.

Concluding remarks: the critical dimensions of political reintegration

Whenever a conflict ends, there is always the question of what to do with the rebel leaders and forces, or with the state and its security apparatus, depending on the ending of the conflict and the side vanquished. So far, attention has mainly focused on two themes: DDR and justice through tribunals. In the middle stands the issue of political reintegration. Such reintegration envisages letting the irregular armies share political power through electoral competition or transforming them into law-abiding citizens with social recognition and influence in public opinion and policy-making at the local or national levels. It is assumed, of course, that the challenge stems from the fact that the group has legitimacy or power that cannot be ignored and the potential to spoil peace if marginalised. The 'way back in' to social and political spheres is about being accepted by the relevant audiences and having the capacity to perform as social and political interlocutors. This chapter examined the cases of M-19 and AUC in Colombia and found the following dimensions of reintegration to be critical.

The international context

The political aspects of *big power games* and valid *international normative frameworks* sustained by the state system, international institutions and international society (regimes) serve as reference for political reintegration by setting the boundaries on what is and what is not permitted. Admittedly, there is a Western bias, at least for the analytical exercise in this chapter: Colombia defines itself as Western and cares about what Western states and institutions do. In the case of M-19 and the other guerrillas that demobilised in the early 1990s, the international context allowed Marxist rebels to transform into legitimate social and political actors. Given the nature of the Cold War in many places of the Third World – a cover for right-wing extremists in the case of Latin America – Marxist guerrillas were seen as politically-driven, heroic, revolutionary victims, fighting to redress authoritarianism, the exclusion of the left and the concentration of power and wealth in the hands of traditional elites. It was thus almost a moral imperative to reintegrate rebels even if they had previously resorted to illegal and violent acts.[108]

More than a decade later, as AUC demobilised, the international context looked somewhat different. The wounds of the Cold War were no longer as pronounced and rebel groups in general, from the left to the right, appeared less heroic, particularly as the academic and policy emphasis on the economics of war had uncovered its 'dirty' financial aspects and greed. Moreover, the Western human-rights regime, with all of its shortfalls, became more globalised and robust. This meant that violence was less tolerated and pardons and amnesties harder to concede. Then, for Colombia, because of its own history and cultural identity, the drug-prohibition regime also mattered and affected political reintegration by defining AUC members involved in drug trafficking as criminals that ought to be extradited to the US.

The impact of the international context may be assuaged by the distance of a given state or set of actors from key international players. In the case of Colombia, however, that distance shrunk in the early 2000s as the international community became more involved in Colombian affairs. Eventually, the preferences of specific external players directly involved in the politics of conflict management in Colombia, such as the US, Europe and the UN, affected political reintegration by setting the standards for AUC's demobilisation and political reintegration. The outcome for the paramilitary was a veto on its transformation into a legitimate political entity, at least in the short run. Whether such an approach turns out to be effective in preventing paramilitary forces from rearming or fuelling violence in the future has yet to be seen. Snyder and Vinjamuri argue that sustainable peace may require more political expediency and less justice since it takes into account the actual power configuration among a given set of actors.[109] Barring the paramilitary from the political system may, therefore, have been the moral thing to do given their involvement in grave crimes, brutality and corruption, but it induces paramilitaries to carry on exercising influence over politics and legal economic transactions 'underneath the table' and can delay their absorption by the system and mainstream culture. It also places greater strains on the state, which must inevitably enforce the peace agreement by detecting and punishing paramilitary defection. The extent to which the state is capable (or willing) to enforce peace with AUC is unclear.

Domestic politics

The *domestic political context* matters in similar ways, by defining what is and what is not legitimate. M-19 was an accepted actor in Colombia; the paramilitary less so. However, the Colombian experience, specifically the case of the paramilitary, shows that acceptance is a multifaceted category since there are relevant local audiences whose rules may differ from the national and international, or Western, mainstream.

Another dimension of the domestic political level is whether political reintegration takes place in the context of a broad national reconstruction process, for instance the ending of civil war where all groups are readjusting or redrawing fundamental power agreements while constructing new social contracts with civil society. The fluidity of the political and legal systems at the time of the reintegration of M-19 and the other four guerrilla organisations helped their political reintegration in general and concrete ways: by lending a favourable climate to innovation and allowing quick legal and bureaucratic adjustments for M-19's entrance in electoral competition. In contrast, the paramilitaries encountered a political system that underwent reform and progressively enhanced democratic rule of law. They found rigidity and the expectation that all of the adjustments required for political reintegration were to be made on their part, not on the side of the state or society.

The terms of the peace negotiations

The *terms of the peace negotiations* affect the legitimacy of an illegal armed group after demobilisation. If the negotiations appear to be fair to all parties and external observers, former combatants will more easily be accepted into the political system. The reputation of the state and the government are however key variables in this equation. It was very clear how perceptions of Uribe's alleged bias towards the paramilitary and suspicions over how his re-election to the presidency would benefit from the demobilisation impacted negatively on the domestic and international reception of the Justice and Peace Law and, in turn, on the possibilities of former AUC combatants to partake in politics as accepted actors. In contrast, Barco and Gaviria's 'intentions' and 'motivations' in dealing with M-19 were never questioned: they were seen as seeking the common good along the right democratic path.

Identity and behaviour of illegal armed groups

The *identity and behaviour of illegal armed groups* matter in political reintegration, although the way they are perceived is culturally bound. In Colombia, the involvement of the paramilitary in systematic brutal killings, the use of war and crime for personal profit and their record of manipulation of local politics directly affected the terms of the peace negotiation and their path of reintegration: they were denied entry into mainstream political and social spheres.

M-19's more benign conduct helped them become legitimate political entities.[110]

One key discussion here, however, is the issue of political identity: does the group have a political nature or is it in fact a greed-driven, criminal organisation and, if so, how is political reintegration possible? Can thugs be transformed into law-abiding citizens and eventually into responsible, legitimate political parties? Colombia has yet to find an answer to these questions, based on what happens to the various strands of the paramilitary that loosely joined as AUC. This would appear to be more of a medium- to long-term process. Nevertheless, it seems clear that illegal armed groups with a defined national political agenda will have a greater interest in political participation after demobilisation. In contrast, a greed-based illegal armed group will be interested in reduced sentences and access to war spoils for personal use. Moreover, having a political discourse may not guarantee an illegal armed group's successful transformation into a legitimate entity; surely, many other variables count. However, to participate in politics as a party, a social movement or as an NGO in a democratic system, an armed group and its leadership must have, at least, political views on relevant issues for local communities or national policy-making. Moreover, in order to gain legitimacy and the adherence of an audience, such views must fit within the existing national political market place.

Alternatively, power appears to be an important element, apart from whether or not an illegal group has a clear and sophisticated political agenda in conventional ways. The contrast between M-19 and the paramilitary is clear on this point. M-19 might have been more popular among Colombians, but the paramilitary had (and have) more power (economic and military capacity), which they translated into control over entire populations. This not only gave them enough status to obtain the government's attention when they expressed their willingness to demobilise; it also earned them a certain local acceptance. Of course, even local legitimacy and the capacity to exercise coercion can be eroded if the dominant groups continuously abuse their power.

Lastly, political reintegration has critical practical dimensions. M-19's rise and decline as a political party showed that illegal armed groups that demobilise do not automatically turn into viable political parties with the capacity to act as politicians, local administrators or effective public servants. Very often, illegal armed groups have spent too much time 'in the bush' (like the 40-year-old FARC), suffer from high illiteracy or are simply not familiar with the practicalities of running a party or a NGO. DDR packages are frequently narrowly focused on disarmament, immediate humanitarian attention, psychological treatment, assuring the basic livelihoods of former combatants and training and education to help combatants find stable employment – measures seen as key deterrents to the resumption of violence given the assumption that combatants joined illegal armed groups due to deep socio-economic grievances and a lack of economic opportunities. However, as illustrated most forcefully with the case of M-19, combatants also need guided preparation for political reintegration in the form of education for political practice.

Notes

1 Relevance stems from having 'either coalition or blackmail potential'. The term is Giovanni Sartori's and is used by Shugart to analyse guerrillas' incentives to demobilise *and* specifically participate in democratic elections. See Shugart, 'Guerrillas and Elections,' 121–152.

2 Some of the most important organisations are the Observatorio para la Paz by M-19, the Fundación Sol y Tierra by the indigenous-based MAQL, the Corporación Nuevo Arco Iris led by León Valencia from CRS, and the Fundación Cultura Democrática by EPL. CRS was the last to demobilise in 1994, by which time AD M-19 was already in decline, so they chose not to become politicians seeking the public vote but rather focus on the successful economic reintegration of their members and on grassroots work. Conversation with León Valencia, May, 2006.

3 It must be noted that former guerrillas did face serious security challenges. More than 1,000 of the guerrillas that demobilised were assassinated over the years by the usual peace spoilers in Colombia, paramilitary forces, drug traffickers, members of the public security forces and remaining guerrilla groups. Valencia, 'En el pasado, la generosidad fue nuestra, en el futuro tendrá que ser del Estado', 16.

4 'Informe Especial: Cómo va elproceso de reinserción tres años después?', *El Tiempo. com*, 20 September 2005; 'Las múltiples caras de la desmovilización', *Semana.com*, 13 March 2005; 'El drama de los reinsertados', *Cromos* (4546), 14 April 2005; 'Reinserción, un frente complicado para la paz', *El País* (Cali), 13 March 2005.

5 The way sectors from the left such as union leaders, NGOs and left-wing politicians like the Mayor of Bogotá, Lucho Garzón, one of the leading figures of Polo Democrático, harshly condemned FARC's bomb attack against El Nogal Club in February 2003 and the donations to FARC by the Danish NGO Rebellion in 2004 are cases in point. 'La CUT condena acto terrorista', www.cut.org.co; 'Uno no puede escoger entre terroristas buenos y malos, afirma Luis Eduardo Garzón', *El Tiempo*, 17 February 2003; 'La alianza de 125 organizaciones sociales y afines por una cooperación internacional para la paz rechaza la donación de 8.500 dólares a las FARC', *El Tiempo*, 5 November 2004. Due to FARC's increasing involvement in drug trafficking and crimes against humanity, many in Colombia and abroad have questioned its 'true' motivations and see it as a criminalised insurgency. Perceptions on ELN are more benign because of its reduced contact to drug trafficking, its less militaristic structure, its emphasis on social and political work and the use of a public discourse in favour of civil society and wealth redistribution. ELN has also been less frequently involved in terrorist attacks against civilians as compared to FARC, although kidnapping has been high.

6 See Collier and Hoeffler, 'Greed and Grievance in Civil Wars', and Kaldor, *New and Old War* as well as the subsequent debates in Berdal and Malone, *Greed and Grievance: Economic Agendas in Civil Wars*, Ballentine and Sherman, *The Political Economy of Armed Conflict: Beyond Greed and Grievance* and Berdal, 'Beyond Greed and Grievance – and not too soon . . .'.

7 IEPRI, 'Quién cree en la Constituyente?'; Hernández, *Una agenda con futuro*.

8 For an interesting and reliable description of the period, see Pardo, *De primera mano*. See also the journalistic work Duzán, *Crónicas que matan*.

9 On guerrilla expansion, see Echandía, *El conflicto armado*.

10 US Department of State, Bureau for International Narcotics and Legal Affairs, 1985, 62.

11 Romero, *Paramilitares y autodefensas, 1982–2003*.

12 Bejarano, 'La política de paz durante la administración Barco', 97. Bejarano was one of President Barco's peace negotiators.

13 Aguirre *et al.*, 'Colombia's Hydra'.

14 Estimates of the size of the illegal drug industry vary. Two key sources on cultivation and eradication in Colombia are the yearly US International Narcotics Control Strategy

Report, which uses figures from the Central Intelligence Agency, and the UN Office on Drugs and Crime.

15 Bejarano, 'La política de paz durante la asministración Barco', 90–91.

16 'Pleno respaldo de los gremios económicos al proceso de paz del Gobierno', *El Espectador*, 24 February 1989; 'Hay que salvar a Colombia de la guerra civil', *El Tiempo*, 7 March 1989; 'Conservatismo apoya proceso de paz con el M-19', *El Espectador*, 26 October 1989.

17 Bejarano, 'La política de paz durante la administración Barco,' 83; Gómez, A. *et al.*, *Discusiones sobre la reforma del Estado en Colombia*, 65, ss.

18 Ibid. 78.

19 Patiño, 'Armas versus política,' 66–70. The point is interesting if one examines the case of individually demobilised combatants. From 2002–06, more than 9,000 in Colombia deserted illegal armed groups on their own and joined the Ministry of Interior's DDR programme. By 2006, some had formed organisations to advocate better reintegration projects, but most were otherwise politically invisible: they did not constitute a political entity as such. For instance, one middle-rank former FARC attributed the lack of bargaining leverage vis-à-vis the government and the lack of opportunity to exercise politics to the fact that he had demobilised on his own. Several conversations with former FARC combatant in 2005.

20 'El diálogo: un paso a la convivencia, dice Barco', *El Tiempo*, 13 January 1989; 'Hay voluntad nacional para buscar la paz' *El Heraldo*, 18 April 1989; 'Antes de elecciones todo debe haber concluido', *El Tiempo*, 18 March 1989.

21 This had been M-19's calculation, since key demands regarding open political participation had already been addressed by previous reforms and they perceived that the public's sympathy for revolutionary causes had been decreasing due the excesses by rebels. Interview with former M-19, Vera Grabe, Bogotá, October 2005 and April 2006.

22 Villarraga, *Los derechos humanos y el derecho humanitario*, 57. Interestingly, Villarraga says that 10 per cent of CRS went to prison. The difference is most likely related to the legal changes on kidnapping. Laws were stiffened in 1993 before CRS demobilisation as a response to increases in kidnapping connected to narco-terrorism and guerrilla activity.

23 The point on the investigative capacities by the police and judiciary was brought to my attention by Carlos Eduardo Jaramillo, peace adviser during the Gaviria administration (1990–94). He also mentioned that after the 1990s' peace agreements, one lesson learned by the military, traditionally opposed to the left-wing guerrillas, was to open formal criminal investigations against rebels to guarantee their imprisonment. The simultaneous strengthening of the rule of law and the escalation of armed conflict meant that war would also be fought in court, not just through weapons.

24 López de la Roche, *Izquierda y cultura política.*

25 Ibid., 278.

26 Bejarano, 'La política de paz durante la asministración Barco', 82.

27 Lara, *Siembra vientos y recogeras tempestades*, 305–324.

28 Rubio, 'M-19, secuestro y narcotráfico'.

29 See Corporación Observatorio para la Paz, *Las verdaderas intenciones de los paramilitares*, which also narrates M-19's contacts con Escobar and drugs.

30 Wolf, 'La desmovilización del M-19 diez años después', 66–74; interview with Vera Grabe.

31 Corporación Observatorio para la Paz, *Las verdaderas intenciones de los paramilitares*, 28.

32 In his analysis of FARC, Gutiérrez argues that the larger an organisation, the more its involvement in criminal behaviour – greed (or at least criminal fundraising) – can be a function of scale, Gutiérrez, *Criminal Rebels? A Discussion of War and the Criminality from the Colombian Experience.*

33 Crocker *et al.*, *Turbulent Peace*.
34 Guáqueta, *Change and Continuity in US–Colombian Relations*.
35 Fundación Ideas para la Paz files.
36 The term was shortened due to the installation of the National Constituent Assembly and its reforms. After 1994, the political calendar resumed regularity.
37 Interview with Carlos Eduardo Jaramillo, Bogotá, September 2005.
38 Interview with Vera Grabe.
39 LaHuerta *et al.*, *Diagnóstico del programa de reinserción en Colombia*, 1, 15–19. Exchange rate used: 2,000 pesos = 1 US dollar.
40 Ministerio del Interior, Dirección General para la Reinserción, *Huellas de Paz*, 141.
41 Interview with Vera Grabe.
42 López De la Roche, *Izquierda y cultura política*.
43 Zuluaga, 'De guerrillas a movimientos políticos', 61.
44 Patiño, 'Armas versus política'.
45 Interviews with Carlos Eduardo Jaramillo and Alvaro Villarraga, September 2005.
46 Interview with Vera Grabe, 10 August 2005, Bogotá.
47 Patiño, 'Armas versus política', 62.
48 Due to its decline at the ballots, the AD M-19 experience is often portrayed as a failed case of political reintegration, see Bejarano and Reales, *Políticas después de la Guerra*, 101; Zuluaga, 'De guerrillas a movimientos politicos', 55.
49 www.polodemocratico.net.
50 Unlike M-19, which as a group absolutely decided to withdraw from the conflict, the consensus among the different blocks of AUC was brittle.
51 Splinters of the Bloque Héroes de Tolová, Frente Vichada and Bloque Héroes de los Montes de María, as well as the Bloque Cacique Pipintá, Autodefensas del Pájaro and the Autodefensas Campesinas del Casanare, totalling about 1,000, never demobilised. Neither did several mid-ranking commanders of the main paramilitary structures, as we learned later on. Several were killed following vendettas and turf battles or captured by authorities in connection to criminal activities. It seems that paramilitary commanders left several key mid-level combatants behind on purpose, as 'insurance' in case negotiations failed, for personal protection from former rivals or to take care of the illegal businesses they still ran.
52 The first Sante Fe de Ralito agreement was general and vague, the second one somewhat more precise and the Justice and Peace Law a full-length document. Still, several aspects of the peace process, often very substantial ones, required further clarification. This was done through the following decrees and court rulings: Decree 4760, 30 December 2005; Sentence C-370, 2006; Decree 2898, 29 August 2006; Decree 3391, 29 September 2006; Decree 315, 7 February 2007; Decree 3570, 18 September 2007; and Decree 1364, 25 April 2008.
53 Congressmen Dieb Maloof, Luis Eduardo Vives and Habib Merheg were forced to leave Partido de la U and Jorge Luis Caballero and Jorge Castro left *Cambio* Radical. Claudia López, 'Los héroes que no se han reinsertado', *Semana*, (1202), 29 November 2005; Juan Manuel Santos, radio interview in 'La W', 5 October 2005; Casa de Nariño, Secretaría de Prensa, Palabras del Presidente Uribe en los 114 Años de la Policía Nación', Bogotá, 3 November 2005.
54 Cinep, *Paramilitarismo de Estado en Colombia*. It is worth mentioning that FARC has been involved in violent crimes including indiscriminate bomb attacks and thousands of kidnappings, which makes their situation different from M-19 and other guerrillas. So far, however, FARC is either less concerned with its reputation or unwilling to understand the normative changes Colombia has undergone in the last two decades.
55 'Colombia busca 10.000 muertos', *El Tiempo*, 24 April 2007.
56 Carlos Castaño and Don Berna were part of the 'Pepes' organisation, the acronym stands for 'persecuted by Pablo Escobar'. In revenge for Escobar's harassing tactics

to control the drug market, they launched along with others in the business, a fierce man hunt which eventually led to the imprisonment and then assassination of Escobar by Colombian and American authorities in 1993 after he escaped jail.

57 'El hombre de la Sierra', *El Tiempo*, 25 October 2001, 'Habla Vicente Castaño', *Semana*, (1205), 5 June 2005; 'Los archivos de Don Berna', *Cambio*, (663), 15 August 2005.

58 '"Paras" extraditados seguían delinquiendo e incumplían compromisos de ley de Justicia y Paz: Uribe', *El Tiempo*, 13 May 2008.

59 Corporación Nuevo Arco Iris, 'Los grupos paramilitares en las regiones'.

60 Gómez *et al.*, *Y el poder para ¿qué?*. 'Este es el portafolio paramilitar,' *El Tiempo*, 11 February 2007.

61 Arias *et al.*, 'Relaciones peligrosas'.

62 'Hoy conocimos a Macaco', *Semana.com*, 12 June 2007.

63 Valencia, 'Exicraso'.

64 Colombia's case for instance was a chapter in Huggins, *Vigilantism and the State in Modern Latin America*.

65 Romero argues that political and academic emphasis on the economic dimensions of war has downplayed the 'political' dimensions of the emergence of the paramilitary, specifically Autodefensas Campesinas de Córdoba y Urabá (ACCU). The political dimensions he refers to are the desires of regional elites, which eventually became paramilitaries, to maintain their influence over local politics amidst the threat of a possible demobilisation of left-wing guerrillas resulting from peace processes, which would have entailed the sharing of local power. This localised 'political' dynamic is different from the guerrilla's political identity as a national Marxist movement seeking deep overarching reforms. Romero, *Paramilitares y autodefensas*, especially the 'Introduction'. See also discussions in Barón and Gutiérrez, *Re-stating the State*.

66 'En amplio pronunciamiento: Autodefensas reivindican su carácter político', *El Colombiano*, 3 July 1997; see also the document by AUC and ACCU, Estatuto de Constitución y Régimen Disciplinario written around 1996–97.

67 'Paras dicen que deben recibir estatus politico,' *La Patria.com*, 11 September 2006.

68 'Paramilitarismo, desmovilización y política'. forum hosted by Caracol Radio, *El Tiempo*, Fescol, Revista *Semana* and UNDP, Bogotá (21 September 2005).

69 'Hoy conocimos a "Macaco" '. *Semana.com*, 12 June 2007.

70 Fundación Ideas para la Paz (FIP) and International Alert interviews in Barrancabermeja, in August 2006; 'Las "Águilas negras", grupo conformado por desmovilizados de las autodefensas, ya azotan 5 regiones', *El Tiempo.com*, 31 October 2006.

71 Restrepo *et al.*, The Dynamics of the Colombian Civil Conflict' 396–429; Guáqueta, 'The Colombian Conflict'.

72 Information provided by Dirección de Inteligencia, Ejército Nacional de Colombia. See also Rangel, *Colombia: guerra en el fin de siglo*, 12.

73 Displacement statistics vary according source. See 'Las víctimas: una guerra injusta', in UN Development Programme, *El Conflicto: callejón con salida*; and documents of the Observatorio del Programa Presidencial de Derechos Humanos y Derecho Internacional Humanitario, Vicepresidencia de la República. Typically, the Colombian NGO Codhes claims that official figures are too low; their estimates of annual internally displaced persons already exceeded 100,000 since 1991, www.codhes.org.

74 'Evolución histórica de los secuestros en Colombia', statistics compiled by the Departamento Nacional de Planeación using figures from the National Police and the NGO País Libre, www.dnp.gov.

75 Dirección de Justicia y Seguridad, Departamento Nacional de Planeación, *Cifras de violencia 1996–2002*.

76 Figures are from the US Department of State, Bureau for International Narcotics and Law Enforcement Affairs, *International Narcotics Control Strategy Report 2001*, Washington DC.

77 www.colnodo.apc.org.
78 In part, this can also be attributed to US demands. As mentioned below, US conditionality increased with Plan Colombia.
79 www.derechoshumanos.gov.co.
80 The Confederación Colombiana de Organizaciones No Gubernamentales, created in 1989 under UN auspices, alone gathers 1,000 local NGOs.
81 Human rights reporting by Colombia to the US was first introduced by the 1996 Leahy Amendment. Later (along with increased Plan Colombia military assistance, approved in 2000) came stricter compliance requirements. See US Public Law 106–246. Organisations such as the Washington Office on Latin America, Amnesty International and Human Rights Watch, however, argue that the US should be stricter with Colombia.
82 US Department of State, Bureau for International Narcotics and Law Enforcement Affairs, *International Control Strategy Report*, from 1992 to 2000.
83 Ninety from FARC and 19 from AUC. Information provided by the US Embassy in Bogotá.
84 Acuscación de Estados Unidos a los paramilitares colombianos, Departamento de Estado de EE.UU., Richard Boucher, portavoz, Bogotá, 24 September 2002, bogotá. usembassy.gov/wwws0069.shtml.
85 They feared the US judicial system because the probability of influencing it was lower than in Colombia and for its harsh treatment of drug offenders. This effect may have waned in 2008 after the extradition of 14 top paramilitary leaders to the US. Sentences had not been determined when this chapter was written, but it is possible that paramilitary leaders could have benefited from the US plea bargain system, receiving reduced sentences for drug-related crimes and no punishment for human rights violations in exchange for valuable intelligence related to the drug market such as international contacts, routes and trafficking methods. See Rubini (advisor to the paramilitary), 'Así la veo yo'.
86 For US aid figures, see Serafino, *Colombia: Conditions and US Policy Options*.
87 'La agenda de la AUC es el narcoterrosimo', *Cambio*, June 2004.
88 See speech at the Woodrow Wilson Center, 14 June 2005, available at www.wilsoncenter.org/events/docs/Wood_Transcript_WWC_6–14–05.doc.
89 'Embajador de Estados Unidos califica de "escandalo" discurso de jefes paramilitares en el Congreso', *El Tiempo*, 29 July 2004.
90 'Congreso de E.U. condiciona apoyo económico para respaldas proceso con los paramilitares', *El Tiempo*, 6 July 2005; 'Y el gringo ahí', *Semana.com*, (1240), 5 February 2006.
91 See, for example, Isacson, 'Peace – or "Paramilarization"', and Washington Office on Latin America, 'New Law in Colombia inadequate to prevent future violence, drug trafficking; US should not provide political or financial support', 24 June 2005; Human Rights Watch, 'Human Rights Watch, Colombia: Letter to US Ambassador William Wood on Demobilization Process', Washington, DC, 24 January 2005; Human Rights Watch, 'Demobilization Scheme Ensures Injustice'. Washington DC, 18 January 2005.
92 'Más requisitos de ayuda de E.U. en el 2008,' *El Tiempo*, 20 June 2007.
93 Guáqueta, 'Colombia: seguridad y política exterior'.
94 Declaration by the Presidency on behalf of the EU on the occasion of the formal start of the talks between the Government of Colombia and the AUC paramilitary groups, Brussels, 30 June 2004; Delegación de la Comisión Europea para Colombia, Declaración del Consejo de Ministros de la Unión Europea sobre Colombia, Luxemburg, 3 October 2005.
95 Sweden took the lead only after intense debates in the Swedish Ministry of Foreign Affairs. Sweden had been a key supporter of the 1999–2002 FARC peace talks and incurred political costs due to its alleged bias in favour of FARC and the failure of the talks. It seems this was at least one factor that weighed in its decision to accompany the paramilitary demobilisation process through the OAS.

96 MAPP-OEA, the OAS verification mission, has been funded by the US, Netherlands, Sweden and the Bahamas.
97 Oficina en Colombia del Alto Comisionado de las Naciones Unidas para los Derechos Humanos, 'Consideraciones sobre la Ley de "Justicia y Paz"'.
98 Interamerican Human Rights Commission (IACHR), Issues Statement Regarding the Adoption of the 'Law of Justice and Peace' in Colombia. Washington, Press Release, No. 26, 2005 and Inter-American Commission on Human Rights Issues Statement on Constitutional Court's Decision Regarding Application of Law of Justice and Peace in the Republic of Colombia, Press Release No. 28, 2006, Washington DC.
99 Snyder and Vinjamuri, 'Trials and Errors', 5–44.
100 'Corte International pide cuentas al país', El Tiempo, 31 March 2005; 'La CPI tiene grabaciones de altercado entre Comisionado de Paz y "paras" en Santa Fe de Ralito', *El Tiempo*, 2 April 2005.
101 'A verificar si Colombia investiga y juzga a criminales vino fiscal de la Corte Penal Internacional', *El Tiempo*, 25 August 2008; 'Corte Penal Internacional actuará si justicia colombiana no lo hace en caso de crímenes masivos', *El Tiempo*, 26 August 2008.
102 A/RES/60/147 of 21 March 2006; Theo van Boven, 'Draft Principles and Guidelines on the Right to a Remedy and Reparation', presented at the Workshop on International Human Rights Standards-Setting Process, Geneva, 13–14 February, 2005.
103 'Colombia's Capitulation', *New York Times*, 4 July 2005.
104 'La nueva ley de Colombia otorga concesiones a Paramilitares,' *New York Times*, 29 June 2005; Rafael Pardo in *El Tiempo*, 10 April 2005.
105 'Petro acusa a hermano de Uribe de tener vínculos con paramilitares', *RCN Radio*, downloaded on 8 May 2006 from www.rcn.com.co/noticia.php3?nt=9616; Contreras, 'A Harsh Light On Associate 82'.
106 'El DAS y los paras', *Semana*, (1226) 31 October–7 November 2005.
107 See OAS, 'Sexto Informe Trimestral del Secretario General'; 'Los archivos de Don Berna', *Cambio* 633, 15–22 August 2005.
108 In El Salvador and Guatemala, the FMLN and the UNRG were the 'benign' forces that triggered desirable democratic reforms. Western international donors, even the United States after having supported cruel dictatorships, did not refrain from assisting the Central American peace processes and in particular the former guerrillas. It is interesting to note that in contrast, the US-funded, Nicaraguan right-wing Contras (counter-revolutionary) never enjoyed such appeal and support.
109 Snyder and Vinjamuri, 'Trials and Errors'.
110 The experience of Sendero Luminoso in Peru is an example of how extreme human-rights violations may undermine the popularity of an insurgency despite the validity of their political and social claims. Sendero encountered strong rejection among peasants who eventually supported strong counterinsurgency policies.

References

Aguirre, K., Muggah, R., Restrepo, J.A. and Spagat, M., 2006. 'Colombia's Hydra: The many faces of gun violence', in *Small Arms Survey 2006: Unfinished Business*. Oxford University Press/Geneva Graduate Institute for International Studies, Oxford.

Arias, G., Guáqueta, A. and Mantilla, G., 2007. 'Relaciones peligrosas: los dilemas de los empresarios en el conflicto', *Siguiendo el conflicto: hechos y análisis* 49, April.

Ballentine, K. and Sherman, J. (eds), 2003. *The Political Economy of Armed Conflict: Beyond Greed and Grievance*. Lynne Rienner Publishers, Boulder, CO.

Barón, M. and Gutiérrez, F., 2004. *Re-stating the State: Paramilitary Territorial Control and Political Order in Colombia (1978–2004)*. Crisis States Programme Working Paper 66. DESTIN (London School of Economics), London.

Bejarano, A.M. and Reales, C.E., 1998. *Políticas después de la guerra: la reincorporación de grupos guerrilleros en América Latina y su impacto en la consolidación de una oposición democrática viable*, Estudios Ocasionales. Cijus, National Endowment for Democracy and Universidad de los Andes, Bogotá.

Bejarano, Jesús Antonio, 1994. 'La política de paz durante la administración Barco', in Deas, M. and Ossa, C. (eds), *El Gobierno de Barco. Política, economía y desarrollo social en Colombia, 1986–1990*. Fedesarrollo, Fondo Cultural Cafetero, Bogotá.

Berdal, Mats, 2005. 'Beyond Greed and Grievance – and not too soon…', *Review of International Studies* 31:3.

Berdal, M. and Malone, D. (eds), 2000. *Greed and Grievance: Economic Agendas in Civil Wars*. Lynne Rienner Publishers, Boulder, CO.

Cinep, 2004. *Paramilitarismo de Estado en Colombia: 1988–2003*. Cinep, Bogotá.

Collier, P. and Hoeffler, A., 2001. *Greed and Grievance in Civil Wars*. World Bank, Washington DC.

Contreras, Joseph, 2006. 'A Harsh Light On Associate 82. A declassified Pentagon report claims Uribe once worked for Pablo Escobar', *Newsweek International Edition*.

——, 2005. 'Los grupos paramilitares en las regiones'. *Arcanos* 8:11.

Corporación Observatorio para la Paz, 2002. *Las verdaderas intenciones de los paramilitares*. Intermedio Editores, Bogotá.

Crocker, Chester, Hampson, F.O. and Aall, P. (eds), 1996. *Turbulent Peace: The Challenges of Managing International Conflict*. United States Institute for Peace, Washington DC.

Dirección de Justicia y Seguridad, Departamento Nacional de Planeación, 2002. *Cifras de violencia 1996–2002*. 0(1). Bogotá.

Duzán, María Jimena, 1992. *Crónicas que matan*. Tercer Mundo Editores, Bogotá.

Echandía, Camilo, 1999. *El conflicto armado y las manifestaciones de violencia en las regiones de Colombia*. Presidencia de la República de Colombia, Oficina del Alto Comisionado para la Paz, Observatorio de Violencia, Bogotá.

Gómez, A., Ignacio, A., Sandoval, B., María, A., Wills, O., Trujillo, Laura, Catalina, A. and Botero, F., 2001. *Discusiones sobre la reforma del Estado en Colombia: la fragmentación del Estado y el funcionamiento del Congreso*, Estudios Ocasionales. Cijus-Universidad de los Andes and Colciencias, Bogotá.

Gómez, I., Hernández, S. and Soto, M.E., 2007. *Y el poder para ¿qué?* Intermedio Editores, Bogotá.

Guáqueta, Alexandra, 2002. *Change and Continuity in US–Colombian Relations and the War Against Drugs*, DPhil thesis. Somerville College, University of Oxford, Oxford.

——, 2003. 'The Colombian Conflict: Political and Economic Dimensions', in Ballentine, K. and Sherman, J. (eds). *The Political Economy of Armed Conflict*. Lynne Rienner Publishers, Boulder, CO.

——, 2005. 'Colombia: seguridad y política exterior', in Ardila, M., Cardona, D. and Ramírez, S. (eds), *Colombia y su política exterior en el siglo XXI Fescol*. Cerec, Bogotá.

Gutiérrez, Francisco, 2003. *Criminal Rebels? A Discussion of War and the Criminality from the Colombian Experience*. Crisis States Programme Working Paper 27. DESTIN (London School of Economics), London.

Hernández, Manuel, 1994. *Una agenda con future: Testimonios del cuatrenio Gaviria*. Presidencia de la República, Tercer Mundo Editores, Bogotá.

Huggins, M.K. (ed.), 1991. *Vigilantism and the State in Modern Latin America. Essays on Extralegal Violence*. Praeger, New York.

IEPRI, 1990. 'Quién cree en la Constituyente?', *Análisis Político*, 10 (May–August).

Isacson, Adam, 2005. 'Peace – or "Paramilarization"', International Policy Report, Center for International Policy, Washington DC.

Kaldor, Mary, 1999. *New and Old Wars: Organised Violence in a Global Era.* Polity, Cambridge.

LaHuerta, Y., Pinto, M.E. and Vergara, A., 2002. *Diagnóstico del programa de reinserción en Colombia: mecanismos para incentivar la desmovilización voluntaria individual.* Departamento Nacional de Planeación, Bogotá.

Lara, Patricia, 1986. *Siembra vientos y recogeras tempestades: la historia del M-19, sus protagonistas y sus destinos.* Planeta editores, Bogotá.

López de la Roche, Fabio, 1994. *Izquierda y cultura política: ¿oposición alternativa?* Cinep, Bogotá.

Ministerio del Interior, 2000. *Huellas de paz: los desmovilizados y su participación en los escenarios de elección popular.* Imprenta Nacional, Bogotá.

Oficina en Colombia del Alto Comisionado de las Naciones Unidas para los Derechos Humanos, 2005. 'Consideraciones sobre la Ley de 'Justicia y Paz', Bogotá, 27 June.

Organisation of American States (OAS), 2006. 'Sexto Informe Trimestral del Secretario General al Consejo Permanente sobre la Misión de Apoyo al Proceso de Paz en Colombia – MAPP/OEA', 1 March.

Pardo, Rafael, 1996. *De primera mano: Colombia 1986–1994: entre conflictos y esperanzas.* Cerec-Norma, Bogotá.

Patiño, Otty, 2000. 'Armas versus política', in Ministerio del Interior, Instituto Luis Carlos Galán (eds), *De las armas a la democracia*, vol. I. Ministerio del Interior. Instituto Luis Carlos Galán, Bogotá.

Rangel, Alfredo, 1998. *Colombia: guerra en el fin de siglo.* Tercer Mundo Editores, Bogotá.

Restrepo, J.A., Spagat, M. and Vargas, J.F., 2004. 'The Dynamics of the Colombian Civil Conflict: A New Dataset'. *Homo Oeconomicus* 21:2.

Romero, Mauricio, 2003. *Paramilitares y autodefensas, 1982–2003.* IEPRI–Planeta, Bogotá.

Rubini, Juan, 2008. 'Así la veo yo. El Proceso de Paz con las Autodefensas está más vivo que nunca', 13 August, www.lapazencolombia.blogspot.com.

Rubio, Mauricio, 2004. 'M-19, secuestro y narcotráfico', draft paper posted on Semana. com, October.

Serafino, Nina, 2001. *Colombia: Conditions and US Policy Options.* Congressional Research Service, Washington DC.

Shugart, Mathew Soberg, 1992. 'Guerrillas and Elections: An Institutionalist Perspective on the Costs of Conflict and Competition', *International Studies Quarterly* 36.

Snyder, J. and Vinjamuri, L., 2003. 'Trials and Errors, Principle and Pragmatism in Strategies of International Justice', *International Security* 28:3 (Winter).

UN Development Programme, 2004. *El Conflicto: callejón con salida: Índice Nacional de Desarrollo Humano, 2003.* UNDP, Bogotá.

US Department of State, Bureau for International Narcotics and Legal Affairs. *International Narcotic Control Strategy Report* (1985, 1992, onwards). Government Printing Office, Washington DC.

Valencia, León, 2005. 'En el pasado, la generosidad fue nuestra, en el futuro tendrá que ser del estado', in Valencia, L., Hernández, F. and Sanguino, A. (eds), *El regreso de los rebeldes. De la firma de las armas a los pactos, la crítica y la esperanza.* Corporación Nuevo Arco Iris and Cerec, Bogotá.

——, 2005. 'Exicraso', *Arcanos* 8:11.

Villarraga, Álvaro, 2000. 'Los Derechos Humanos y el Derecho Humanitario en los Procesos de Paz, 1990–2000'. Ministerio del Interior, Dirección General de Reinserción, Gente Nueva Editorial, Bogotá.

Washington Office on Latin America, 2005. 'New Law in Colombia inadequate to prevent future violence, drug trafficking; US should not provide political or financial support', Washington Office on Latin America, Washington DC.

Wolf, Antonio Navarro, 2001. 'La desmovilización del M-19 diez años después', in Cepeda, F. (ed.), *Haciendo paz: reflexiones y perspectivas del proceso de paz en Colombia.* US Embassy–Fundación Ideas para la Paz, Bogotá.

Zuluaga, Jaime, 1999. 'De guerrillas a movimientos políticos. La experiencia colombiana: el caso del M-19', in Peñaranda, R. and Guerrero, J. (eds), *De las armas a la política.* Tercer Mundo Editores–IEPRI, Bogotá.

2 Reintegration before disarmament

The case of post-conflict reintegration in Tajikistan[1]

Stina Torjesen and S. Neil MacFarlane

Introduction

Tajikistan is interesting in the context of disarmament, demobilisation and reintegration (DDR) for a number of reasons. First, Tajikistan is a success story: over a decade after the formal end to fighting Tajikistan now enjoys remarkable levels of peace and stability. Second, DDR programmes in Tajikistan were accompanied by a comprehensive peace settlement, which called for tough compromises from the two main parties to the conflict. Third, there was an emphasis on reintegration over demobilisation and disarmament. Whole units of anti-government forces were included into state military and police structures, while opposition leaders were given 30 per cent of the top government posts. Given the full-scale integration of opposition units into the government forces, demobilisation was in some ways partial. There were degrees of disarmament of fighters but large weapons stocks remained with commanders and little pressure was levied on medium- and top-level leaders to surrender their weapons. Last, a striking feature of Tajikistan's peace settlement is the set of measures taken by the reconciled parties that helped deter the emergence of spoilers.

This chapter argues that reintegration was prioritised over demobilisation and disarmament in Tajikistan's peace process. The decision of the participants and sponsors of the peace agreement to overlook inadequate disarmament rates created comparatively high levels of trust among the former fighters and commanders. The quick provision of incentives, such as comprehensive amnesties and the offer of government positions and economic assets, also created stakes in the peace process for a number of actors. Transitional justice was largely overlooked. A central claim of this chapter is that the DDR process in Tajikistan, and its eventual success, run counter to the conventional wisdom on what components should form part of DDR and how the process is best implemented. Robert Muggah notes that 'a post-conflict reconstruction orthodoxy' has emerged, which stipulates particular types and sequencing of peacebuilding efforts and DDR activities.[2] The case of Tajikistan runs counter both to the emphasis on 'positive peace' and political liberalisation in conventional approaches to peacebuilding as well as to the stress on demobilisation and disarmament.[3]

The chapter also seeks to draw attention to the Soviet and post-Soviet experience of Tajikistan. This context is central to explaining important features of Tajikistan's civil war (1992–97) and its aftermath. The Soviet legacy is a key to understanding the type of armed commanders that emerged in the conflict as well as the strategies with which President Emomali Rakhmonov and the Commission on National Reconciliation (CNR) sought to thwart spoiler tendencies. Primarily this pertains to the large-scale post-Soviet privatisation process initiated after 1997, which created a number of economic goods to be divided up among the parties to the peace process. Post-Soviet Tajikistan also inherited a complex, albeit malfunctioning, law enforcement system. The Tajik branches of the Soviet secret police (KGB) and police (Ministry of the Interior – MVD) played central roles (mostly on the side of the government) during the war years, and were pivotal in the gradual restoration of order after 1997. In addition, the entrenched Soviet norm in the population and law enforcement of zero tolerance for the illegal civilian possession of guns helped stabilisation efforts and facilitated the campaign to reduce gun ownership and violence. In this way, the chapter demonstrates the usefulness of two different perspectives on the stabilisation process, which are often overlooked: a political economy approach and a constructivist approach that stresses the perseverance of Soviet norms.

Finally, the chapter also seeks to highlight the important synergies between the activities of outside powers and the emergence of potential and actual spoilers after 1997.

This chapter will first explore some of the central features of Tajikistan's civil war, the peace settlement in 1997 and the regional context. It then provides a detailed account of the DDR process and assesses the incentives that it created for the warring parties. The chapter later looks at three cases of spoiler behaviour to assess why, despite provision of incentives, some spoilers nevertheless emerged. The chapter concludes by highlighting the consolidation of both peace and President Rakhmonov's power since 2001, but also raises some questions regarding the viability of Tajikistan's long-term political and economic development.

The chapter builds on work conducted by the authors for the United Nations Development Programme (UNDP) Tajikistan and the Small Arms Survey for the report 'Tajikistan's road to stability: Reduction in small arms proliferation and remaining challenges'.[4] Research for this report included over four months of fieldwork in Tajikistan in 2004 and involved cooperation with over 24 researchers from the country itself. The joint efforts with researchers from Tajikistan included the facilitation of 76 focus groups across the country and sustained attempts (only partially successful) at securing access to relevant bodies of official data. Official sources were supplemented by a press review (1997–2004) focusing on weapons-related information. The authors travelled extensively in Tajikistan and conducted over 160 interviews with government officials and health-sector personnel, representatives of NGOs, journalists, diplomats, and personnel of intergovernmental organisations.[5]

The civil war

Tajikistan is a former Soviet Socialist Republic (SSR) that became independent in 1991. It is a poor and mountainous country bordering Afghanistan, China, Kyrgyzstan and Uzbekistan. Its 7.1 million citizens are largely Tajik (Persian) speaking, though the country also has a sizeable Uzbek-speaking minority (15 per cent).[6] Tajikistan's key exports are cotton and aluminium. It is also a transit-country for significant quantities of drugs flowing from Afghanistan to Russia.

The collapse of Soviet control over the Tajik SSR triggered intense debate on the future political direction of the country, the composition of the leadership, and control over economic resources.[7] As demonstrations flared in Dushanbe from 1991 onwards, two separate alliances emerged; one stressed democratic reforms and Islamic renewal, the other emphasised political continuity and secularism. Both alliances drew support from different areas of Tajikistan, and this gave the conflict a regional, as well as a political and ideological character. Elite tensions merged with grass-roots friction stemming from poverty, shortages, and long-simmering conflicts in communities in Khatlon, which had received large groups of migrants from mountainous areas (the Rasht and Tavildara Valleys). These peasant groups had been ordered to resettle in the cotton-producing areas in the 1950s and 1960s.[8]

Growing tension on the elite and grass-roots levels soon provoked competitive armament followed by open conflict. The war involved massive violence and destruction of property, particularly in Khatlon province, as well as a protracted insurgency in the Rasht Valley. In its first years, the conflict was fought largely by regionally based militias. Some (Kulyabi and ethnic Uzbeks from Khatlon) supported the government led by Emomali Rakhmonov, which had emerged after the overthrow of a coalition Government of National Reconciliation in late 1991. Others (from the regions in and around the Rasht Valley and from resettled communities in Khatlon) supported the Islamic and democratic opposition groups. These latter groups were consolidated into the United Tajik Opposition (UTO) in 1993 at a meeting in Taloqan, Afghanistan.

The conflict occasioned intervention (mainly through the use of air power and arms transfers) by Uzbekistan in support of the government. The opposition benefited from the support of Tajik-dominated factions in northern Afghanistan, and from financial underpinning originating in the Middle East, much of which was used to purchase weapons in Afghanistan. Acting at the behest of neighbouring Central Asian states, which were concerned by the threat of political Islam, and the Russian Federation, which had a strategic interest in the control of the Tajik frontier with Afghanistan, the Commonwealth of Independent States (CIS) inserted the CIS Peace Keeping Force (CISPKF) in 1992 in an effort to stabilise the situation, pending a settlement of the conflict. From 1994, the UN Mission of Observers in Tajikistan (UNMOT) observed this force, monitored developments in the country and facilitated dialogue between the warring parties.

The war – and associated atrocities committed against civilians (notably in Khatlon and Rasht) – generated a massive flow of refugees, principally into Afghanistan: 600,000 people fled and, in exile, provided a mass base of support for the opposition's military campaign. An estimated 50,000 people died in the war, the largest death toll of any conflict in the former Soviet Union.[9]

Key features of the peace settlement and DDR strategies

On 27 June 1997, President Emomali Rakhmonov and the opposition leader Said Abdullo Nuri signed the 'General Agreement on the Establishment of Peace and National Accord'. The agreement created the 26-member Commission on National Reconciliation (CNR). It comprised equal numbers of opposition and government representatives and was given the task of implementing the agreement and related protocols. Sub-commissions, also with equal numbers of representatives from the two sides, were formed on political, military, refugee and legal affairs. Their tasks included overseeing the implementation of distinct aspects of the peace agreement, such as the upholding of the ceasefire, demobilisation and refugee repatriation.

The General Agreement included four protocols that gave detailed provisions on political, military, refugee and amnesty issues. The executive branch of the government (ministries, departments, local government and law enforcement) was to incorporate UTO representatives on the basis of a 30 per cent quota.[10] The government declared its responsibility to reintegrate and assist returning refugees. The UN, the Organisation for Security and Cooperation in Europe (OSCE) and the UN High Commissioner for Refugees (UNHCR) were requested to help ensure the safety of refugees and the government pledged not to open criminal proceedings against refugees based on their participation in the conflict. The protocol provided a set of amnesty measures for the fighters and the National Reconciliation Committee (NRC) subsequently initiated additional amnesty provisions, including the issuing of a list of names of over 5,000 UTO fighters and civilian representatives who were to be guaranteed amnesty for crimes related to the war and committed in the 1992–97 period.

The military protocol laid out a comprehensive four-stage strategy for disarmament, demobilisation and reintegration.[11] The UTO fighters were to gather at ten assembly points in Tajikistan and Afghanistan. The main assembly points in Tajikistan were in Kofarnihon, Khorogh, Vanj, Garm, Komsomolobod, Tojikobod and Lenin districts. Fighters from the mountain areas and the groups in Afghanistan gathered at these points in the autumn of 1997 and spring of 1998. Here they registered, received medical checks and were disarmed. Based on the registration lists, most UTO forces were, still as whole and distinct UTO units, formally incorporated into the regular armed forces of Tajikistan. A Joint Review Board assessed whether individual fighters were fit for further military service and made recommendations for appointments to command positions. Some opposition formations formed new units, such as the MVD forces in Khorogh and Garm, while others entered as separate smaller parts into existing command structures in the army (Ministry of Defence), the police (Ministry of the Interior) and the border guard forces (State Committee of the Protection of Borders). A total of 6,842 combatants were registered by the NRC sub-commission on military affairs. Of these, 6,061 were approved for further service, although many fighters subsequently left or were forced to leave the service.[12] The strategy of preserving original structures reduced the potential for tension among former adversaries and produced some level of trust in the peace process as well as a sense of security on the part of mid- and top-level UTO commanders.

The fighting groups submitted some of their weapons upon registration at the assembly points, though there are indications that guns also remained in the hands of the opposition.[13] The UN records from the initial registration, where the bulk of arms handovers were to occur, testified to the low levels of disarmament. Many of the 60 former fighters that were interviewed in semi-structured interviews as part of our research also stressed that they had handed their weapons directly to their immediate commander. The commanders in turn seem to have surrendered only a small share of the weapons to the disarmament teams.[14]

The weapons that were handed over and registered were later officially transferred, with full documentation, into the government units that the opposition fighters had joined. Some of these weapons remained in the gunroom of the particular unit or were transferred to the central stockpiles of the relevant ministry or government committee in Dushanbe.[15] Officers originally affiliated with government forces in many cases obtained de facto control over the integrated opposition weapons.

Regional dimensions

There were distinct regional and international facets to the conflict that affected the course of the civil war, the peace settlement and subsequent spoiler behaviour.

In Uzbekistan, anti-government, Islam-inspired movements had threatened the political leadership after 1991.[16] The Uzbek leadership responded with a severe crackdown on religious movements. This prompted some groups to flee to Tajikistan and Afghanistan and to form ties with the UTO. Uzbekistan, therefore, came to perceive the Islamic opposition in Tajikistan as a threat to its own national security, particularly as the UTO propagated Islamic political ideals and provided logistical and operational support to Uzbek opposition groups. Uzbekistan gave considerable military and political assistance to bolster the coalition behind the secular Tajik government and support the fight against the UTO. Uzbekistan encouraged the government to take an uncompromising stance towards the Islamic opposition – preferring the military defeat of the UTO to political compromise. The peace agreement defied Uzbek preferences, as it provided for a broad-based compromise between the warring parties and legitimised and installed, for the first time in post-Soviet Central Asia, an opposition Islamic group within a governing coalition. As a consequence, Uzbekistan withdrew its support from Tajikistan, imposed economic sanctions and attempted, as illustrated below, to undermine the peace settlement by encouraging spoiler behaviour.

The situation in Afghanistan affected Tajikistan in a number of important ways. Northern Afghanistan provided a relative safe haven for the opposition civilians and fighters that fled Tajikistan in 1992–93. Opposition fighters regrouped in Afghanistan and formed the UTO. They also delineated clearer command structures and set up training camps. Representatives of the former opposition forces claim that the Northern Alliance military leader Ahmad Shah Massoud gave vital strategic advice and assistance during the initial formation of the UTO.[17] Income from the export of drugs (from Afghanistan through Tajikistan) and financial support from transnational religious organisations enabled the UTO to procure weapons in Afghanistan. There are signs that, as the Taliban grew in strength, it also established links with some military groups within the opposition camps and that these ties, as will be seen below, persisted after 1997 and may have encouraged spoiler behaviour.

Russia was heavily involved in events in Tajikistan during and after the civil war. The Soviet Union's 201st Motorised Rifle Division (MRD) and the border-guard troops stationed in Tajikistan in 1991 were later officially transformed into units with the Russian Federation's armed forces. The border-guard units were on a number of occasions attacked by UTO groups though the 201st MRD did not officially take part in the fighting. In 1993, the 201st MRD took on a peace-keeping role in Tajikistan. A number of commanders and fighters from both sides have however testified that weapons from the 201st MRD stockpiles often reached civilians and fighters alike, and that segments of the 201st MRD also gave active military backup to the pro-government Popular Front in 1992–93.[18]

Russia also played an important role diplomatically. It coordinated the CIS peacekeeping initiative with the UN efforts. It supported and encouraged the UN-facilitated dialogue 1994–97 and formed part of the mediation team along-side Iran and other states in the region. This formed part of a broader strategic rapprochement between Russia and Iran in this period.

The appointment of Evgeny Primakov as Russian Foreign Minister in 1996 coincided with significant Taliban advances and the subsequent fall of Kabul. This was perceived by leaders in the region, in Iran, Russia and the CIS as a dramatic worsening of the security situation, since it raised the spectre of Taliban-affiliated Islamic radicalism spreading from Afghanistan into areas with high concentrations of Muslims within the CIS. Primakov is thought to have played a central role in forging the compromise that allowed for the controversial and large-scale inclusion of the Islamic opposition into the Tajik government as part of a deal to end violent conflict. He may also have convinced Iranian representatives, as well as Ahmad Shah Massoud (who at this time was dependent upon Russian supplies to the Northern Alliance), to encourage elements within the Tajik opposition and the government to seek a peaceful settlement.

Iran played a central diplomatic role throughout the conflict, but little is known of its ties with the opposition, aside from the fact that many UTO political leaders were mainly based in Teheran during the Civil War years.

The role of commanders

The two warring factions consisted of loosely structured fighting groups headed by commanders and sub-commanders. Local community leaders, police officers, and former army servicemen became leaders of formations based on kinship, community, or workplace ties. Some of the leaders who emerged on the two opposing sides had previously operated in the Tajik shadow economy, had criminal records, or had been part of the distinct milieu associated with combat sports in Dushanbe and Kofarnihon.[19] Some analysts have estimated that there were approximately 60 key commanders on each side.[20] Government commanders emerged and operated in much the same way as their counterparts in the UTO. The government forces underwent some restructuring in 1993–94 and were nominally transformed into a national army structure. The government commanders continued, nevertheless, to play a dominant role in organising the government response to the UTO. It does not seem as if there were properly delineated and coherent lines of authority and control among the commanders, the army operating much like a collection of militia groupings rather than as a vertically organised military structure.

The decentralisation in command structures complicated the peace negotiations in 1994–97. A UN military observer who chaired the regular meetings in Dushanbe in these years noted that the representatives of each side had little control over large sections of their respective coalitions. The frequent violations of the ceasefire from 1994 further undermined the dialogue, as representatives had difficulties ensuring that pledges would be upheld.

Some of the military commanders had strong links to particular communities and acted as both protectors of the populations and de facto political leaders in their area.[21] At key turning points, the military commanders' push for peace was vital for the eventual completion of negotiations.[22]

Creation of stakes in the peace

Given the independent, yet locally entrenched, position of a large number of commanders, it is surprising that Tajikistan experienced relatively limited spoiler behaviour. How can this be explained? Arguably, both the intended and unintended consequences of the Tajik settlement gave the majority of commanders on both sides a significant stake in the peace process. A central feature here was the large-scale integration of armed groups into the military and law-enforcement structures. Most military commanders of some standing were offered lucrative and high positions in the MVD, Ministry of Defence (MoD), Ministry of Emergency Situations (MChS), Ministry of State Security (MB) or State Committee on Border Protection (KOGG). In addition, they continued in the years immediately following the peace settlement to enjoy direct control over potent fighting forces since the combatants had followed the commanders into the new state structures. Arguably, this preserved trust in the peace process while it also facilitated a commitment to uphold the peace agreement on the part of the commanders.

The reintegration process was coupled with an initial 'hands-off' policy on the part of President Rakhmonov with regard to the commanders' control of former opposition areas, such as the Rasht and Tavildara Valleys and Gorno Badakhshan. Most of the police and law-enforcement structures in these areas were initially composed of opposition fighters and commanders and there was little direct involvement or control from the central government in local affairs.[23]

The peace settlement, however, also entailed a number of other incentives. Most prominently, political and military leaders from both sides acquired flats, whole apartment blocs, shopping centres, factories, cattle-grazing areas as well as cotton fields and cotton-processing facilities. Most of the prominent political and military leaders from 1997 are now holders of major economic assets that were previously state property. The Tajik state had not embarked upon a large-scale privatisation process before fighting broke out in 1992 and there were no major formal initiatives of this kind during the civil war. This particular set-up meant that there was a range of economically attractive state properties whose ownership could be transferred to the actors who had facilitated and allowed for the peace process.

The transfers were made in different ways. Some leaders had properties formally transferred to them by the Committee for State Property and became de jure owners of these assets. For example, Hoji Akbar Turajonzoda, a former religious and political leader in the UTO, was given the post of first vice prime minister. He was also reported to have acquired a cotton-processing plant in Vakhdat, Khatlon Province, the main shopping centre in Vakhdat ('Univermag') and two flats in Dushanbe.[24]

Others acquired property in similar ways after 1997, but chose to register relatives as formal owners. Suhrob Kasimov, a commander on the government side, is believed to control indirectly a shopping centre ('Sadbarg'), as well as holiday resorts in Varsob district. The factory 'Bordjuma' is reportedly officially registered in the name of a close associate of Kasimov.[25]

Some of the properties that commanders and political leaders formally acquired after 1997 were objects they had obtained control over by force during the war. When the former government commander Gaffur Mirzoev was arrested in 2005, the newspaper *Asia Plus* gave an outline of the economic assets he had acquired.[26] The assets included a meat-processing factory, over 30 flats in Dushanbe, and the bank 'Olimp', and the newspaper stressed that Mirzoev had been able to acquire many of these assets during the war or immediately after because he had 'been in command' and, therefore, had been allowed to 'break the law'.[27]

The former military and political leaders were also favourably placed (due to government connections and the continued command of fighters that guaranteed protection) to initiate new and profitable economic activities in the post-war market economy. Mirzoev, for example, successfully established a major casino ('Jomi Jamshed') in Dushanbe, while Turadjonzoda acquired control over the profitable import of wheat from Kazakhstan.

Theses strategies were accompanied by the decision of President Rakhmonov not to prevent corrupt practices and/or the abuse of government positions for personal enrichment. Tajikistan has one of the lowest scores in the Transparency International Corruption Perception Index (ranked 144 out of 155).[28] There has

been no lawsuit against corrupt individuals – the exceptions being former political or military leaders who have challenged Rakhmonov politically. In these
cases, extensive and detailed compromising material has been presented, docu-
menting deep-seated corruption.[29] The promotion of former military and political
leaders into government position has, therefore, given the dominant civil war
actors an easy means of enriching themselves, while also creating a stake in the
survival (if not the proper functioning) of government institutions.

This wilful and uneven neglect of corrupt practices is compounded by the
drug trafficking through Tajikistan. In 2003, Tajikistan's law enforcement
intercepted over five tons of heroin and small-scale drug couriers are regularly
arrested.[30] However, there have not been any police campaign or court trials
against the main organisers of the drugs trade in Tajikistan – except for
allegations of drug-dealing made during seemingly political trials against
Rakhmonov's opponents. During the war, the commanders financed weapons
purchases through drugs trafficking.[31] The dominant figures on both sides of the
civil war were those best positioned to engage in drug trafficking after 1997.
Some of these leaders sought to remain central figures in the drugs business, and
President Rakhmonov has done little to hinder their activities.

Conventional reintegration initiatives and involvement of the international community

Multilateral organisations, primarily the UN, played an important role during
and after the civil war. The role of UNMOT in facilitating dialogue during the
war has already been mentioned. UNMOT also provided important expertise in
the actual design of the peace agreement, the associated protocol and the conduct
of post-war elections. The other central UN agency was UNHCR, which was
one of the first international organisations to start operations in Tajikistan. It
dealt with the return of refugees from Afghanistan, which was initiated in 1994
and continued for the rest of the decade.[32] The vital role of UNHCR in the war
years enabled it to take a lead role in DDR activities. Together with UNDP, it
implemented a range of reconstruction projects, which employed former combatants for short periods of time.[33]

Tajikistan's government also attempted to initiate a vocational-training programme for former combatants. This initiative was executed by the Ministry of
Labour and it received financing from international donors. However, the project
was launched long after the end of hostilities and, despite the funding it received,
it ultimately trained relatively few ex-combatants. Once its funding lapsed, the
project did not become self-sustainable.[34]

Overall, these conventional reintegration programmes seem to have offered
some material benefits, but to a relatively small segment of fighters and local
communities. In comparison with the large-scale integration of combatants and
commanders into state structures and the opportunities they were given for legal
and illegal income-generating activities, these conventional programmes seem
relatively insignificant.

Spoilers and spoiler behaviour

Despite the overall commitment of most commanders to the peace process, some spoilers did nevertheless emerge. Some commanders challenged the settlement in political-military terms, with the main challenge coming from Makhmud Khudoiberdiev. Others turned to organised criminal activity. The government (with the assistance of former opposition forces) expended considerable effort from 1997 to 2000 in suppressing these groups and confiscating their weapons. This process was largely concluded by July 2001 with the suppression of a group led by Rakhmon ('Hitler') Sanginov and Mansur Muaqqalov the outskirts of Dushanbe.

Three reasons stand out for the emergence of spoilers in Tajikistan: the effect of foreign involvement and regional conflicts; the perception of being denied a reasonable share of economic assets and political influence; and the seemingly aimless and criminal nature of some of the groups that had emerged during the chaotic war years. We present three cases that highlight these factors.

Makhmud Khudoiberdiev

Khudoiberdiev was a leading government commander in the civil war. Khudoiberdiev and many of the men under him were ethnic Uzbek with Tajik citizenship. His forces were among the best-organised fighters on the government side. Khudoiberdiev headed a battalion that controlled areas around Kurgan Tube and Tursunzoda in Khatlon province. Estimates of the number of soldiers in the battalion range from 200 to 1,000. Khudoiberdiev disagreed with the political strategies of the CNR and clashed with other former government and opposition forces in August 1997. He and his men then retreated south via Shaartuz and Beshkent into southern Uzbekistan.

Some observers stress that Khudoiberdiev had sought to restore the original Soviet-era division of the Khatlon province into two separate areas, one encompassing the western and cotton-producing region around Kurgan Tube and the other encompassing less fertile lands in the eastern border regions around the city of Kulyab. Khudoiberdiev is thought to have vied for formal administrative control over the western parts of Khatlon.

After leaving Tajikistan, Khudoiberdiev and his men moved through Uzbekistan into Afghanistan in November 1997 to assist General Dostum (also an ethnic Uzbek) in the campaign against the Taliban. Khudoiberdiev returned to Uzbekistan in June 1998 and set up a base close to Djishar, near the Tajik border. The group was reportedly equipped with Uzbek combat gear in October 1998 and later entered the Tajik border area near Shakristan. Khudoiberdiev's forces launched an attack on 3 November 1998 on key sites in Khujand, including the base of the interior forces regiment, the provincial police station (OVD), the Ministry of State Security offices (MB station), and the post and telecommunications office. Government reinforcements were dispatched to Sughd province the following day and Khudoiberdiev's fighters were quickly defeated. The government is reported to have lost 39 men in the fighting, while approximately

50 of Khudoiberdiev's men were killed. Khudoiberdiev's battalion retreated to Uzbekistan through Nau and Chakalovsk regions.

Several interesting features stand out in the Khudoiberdiev case. First is the inability of Khudoiberdiev to mobilise other factions in the Tajik elite. Khudoiberdiev's forces remained isolated and were easily suppressed by government forces with the support of UTO fighters. Second is the link to Uzbekistan: the fact that Khudoiberdiev used Uzbek equipment and entered from Uzbek territory suggests that Uzbekistan's government supported his bid to challenge the emerging political map in Tajikistan. The Khudoiberdiev case also highlights the trend after 1997 to deny ethnic Uzbeks with Tajik citizenship any benefits flowing from the peace settlement. It also draws attention to the disproportionate criminalisation of ethnic-Uzbek former guerrilla groups relative to their ethnic-Tajik counterparts.[35] Third, Khudoiberdiev's decision to launch a military challenge arose due to various disagreements over how Tajikistan's economic resources were to be divided among the parties to the peace process. Keeping the eastern and western parts of Khatlon in one jurisdiction gave the Kulyab political factions (with which President Rakhmonov was affiliated) better prospects for political and economic control over Tajikistan's cotton production.[36]

Mullo Abdullo

The case of Mullo Abdullo draws attention to the complex regional situation in Tajikistan after 1997 and the challenges this volatile context posed for Tajikistan at a time when the country attempted to secure the peace.

The Islamic Movement of Uzbekistan (IMU) lent support to UTO during the civil war. After the peace settlement in 1997, the IMU maintained close relations with segments of the UTO, including the Minister of Emergencies Mirzo Zioyev and Mullo Abdullo's group. After 1997, the IMU enjoyed the (unofficial) protection of Zioyev and it also operated a base in the mountains above the Tavildara valley – the home region of Zioyev – until February 2001.[37] The IMU strengthened its ties to the Taliban in the late 1990s, and it is likely that the Taliban provided organisational and material support for the IMU attacks on Kyrgyzstan and Uzbekistan in 1999 and 2000. The attacks may have been launched from the IMU's base near Tavildara.

Mullo Abdullo and his group were based in Darband, a region neighbouring Tavildara. Mullo Abdullo had since 1997 rejected formal integration into the Ministry of Defence forces, a move portrayed by the government media as relating to Mullo Abdullo's reluctance to give up illegal drug trafficking. Mullo Abdullo's group appears to have been able to operate relatively freely and without government interference in the Darband area until 1999–2000. The attack by the IMU on Kyrgyzstan and Uzbekistan, however, revealed strong links between Mullo Abdullo, the IMU and the Taliban. Mullo Abdullo was also reported to 'share the same religious convictions as the Taliban'.[38] Following the attacks, Kyrgyzstan and Uzbekistan increased the pressure on Tajikistan's political leadership to crack down on all guerrilla groups operating out of, or near, Tavildara.

The immediate pretext for the attack on Mullo Adbullo was the killing in June 2000 of the Garm region administrative head, Saimudin (AKA Sergey) Davlatov, a murder of which Mullo Abdullo had been accused. Government forces attacked the group in June and later in September 2000. The group fled Darband and sought refuge in Tavildara. Though many of his men were killed in the operations, Mullo Abdullo himself is reported to have fled to Afghanistan where he joined the Taliban forces. It was rumoured that he was captured or killed in Taloqan, northern Afghanistan, in February 2002.[39]

Mullo Abdullo, it seems, chose the role of a spoiler because he shared the political aims of both the IMU and the Taliban: continued instability in the greater Central Asian region that could facilitate an eventual takeover by radical groups in countries like Uzbekistan, Afghanistan and Tajikistan. The combat activities of the IMU and the Taliban drew support from Mullo Abdullo, whose activities in turn came to pose a challenge to the peace and stabilisation process in Tajikistan.

Rakmon 'Hitler' Sanginov

The group of Rakhmon 'Hitler' Sanginov appears, in contrast, neither to have had connections to regional powers, nor to have promoted specific political agendas. This force nevertheless presented a significant challenge to Tajikistan's stabilisation process and was one of the most significant and long-lasting spoiler groups.

Sanginov had been part of the UTO and was offered a position in the Ministry of Defence after the war. Sanginov accepted the position but was later dismissed, having refused to adhere to government instructions. He formed a renegade group of ex-combatants together with Mansur Muaqqalov, also a former UTO commander. The group was based in the eastern outskirts of the capital city (in the Lenin district, 12 kilometres outside Dushanbe). Just before the liquidation of the group in June 2001, Tajikistan's Ministry of Interior claimed that the group was responsible for over 400 crimes and a number of murders.[40]

The government operation against the group lasted several days. It had been initiated by Sanginov's group, which had the previous week taken seven law-enforcement officers hostage. Thirty-six group members including Sanginov and Muaqqalov were killed in the operation, while 66 members were arrested and later faced trial.

The consolidation of President Rakhmonov's power

The eradication of Sanginov's group in the summer of 2001 ended the presence in Tajikistan of large armed groups outside the control of central authorities. The US-led *Enduring Freedom* campaign against the Taliban in 2001–02 further stabilised the regional context of Tajikistan. In January 2002, the Ministry of the Interior announced that 80 guerrilla groups had been eliminated in 2001, with 50 suspected militants killed and 200 arrested.[41]

The campaigns against armed groups were accompanied by extensive efforts by law-enforcement agencies to collect weapons from the civilian population (Table 2.1). Efforts along these lines had started during the war and continued after 1997.[42] It bears stressing that Tajikistan was a society unaccustomed to high levels of small-arms and light-weapons proliferation. During Soviet times, gun possession had been limited to police forces, the army and hunters. Acquiring permission to obtain a firearm was a cumbersome procedure and the repercussions of being caught with an unregistered gun were serious. The Soviet Union, including the Tajik SSR, had low murder and gun accident rates.[43] The strong normative pressure, both among the civilian population and law enforcement, that peace should involve a crackdown on illegally owned weapons helped the collection efforts and explains in part why gun violence remains low in Tajikistan (see Figure 2.2).

President Rakhmonov managed to re-establish the state's monopoly of violence through strategies combining co-option and coercion. President Rakhmonov has since reduced political pluralism in the country and concentrated political power and initiative in the office of the president – a violation both of the spirit and letter of the 1997 peace agreement.[44] From 1997 onwards

Table 2.1 Opposition fighters who handed in a weapon upon registration and disarmament (as recorded by UN observers in 1998)

Area	%
Lenin district	48
Kofarnihon	37
Karategin districts	35
GBAO	29
Total integrated UTO fighters in 1988:	6,238
Total number of weapons surrendered in 1998	2,119 (36% of all weapons, assuming one weapon per fighter)

Note
These figures were made available in UNMOT news briefings and are referred to in Burkhard, 'The Problem of Small Arms'. This source reports only the percentages and not the total numbers.

Table 2.2 The fate of former UTO commanders

Present situation of former UTO commanders	Number
Employed by the state	14
Dead or incapacitated	4
Left Tajikistan	1
Abandoned military activity	3
Imprisoned	3
Unknown	1
Total	25

there has been a gradual weakening of the political influence of the former civil-war commanders and the political groups associated with them. Sumie Nakaya has demonstrated how, in recent years, many of the central commanders have lost power relative to oligarchs closely associated with President Rakhmonov.[45]

A survey of the most important UTO commanders found that the majority had gained state employment, abandoned military activity or were dead (Table 2.2). We have published elsewhere a fuller overview of central commanders on both the government and the opposition side.[46]

Conclusions

Tajikistan has achieved remarkable levels of stability, if measured by rates of armed clashes or gun violence. Figures 2.1 and 2.2 indicate a sharp decline in violence from 2000 onwards.

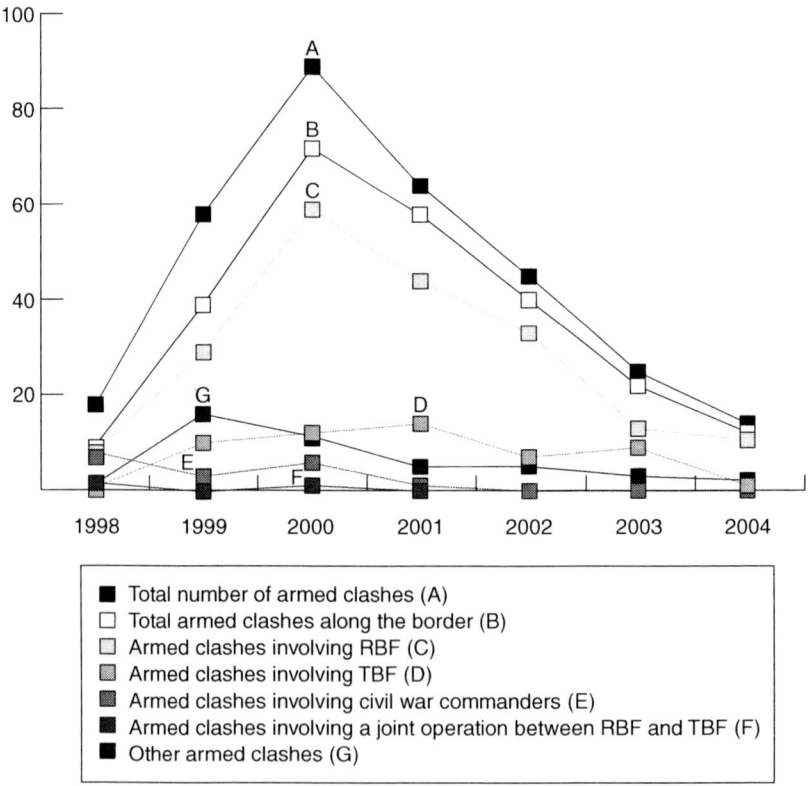

Figure 2.1   Reported armed clashes, 1998 (31 October 2004) (source: Torjesen *et al.*, 'Tajikistan's Road to Stability').

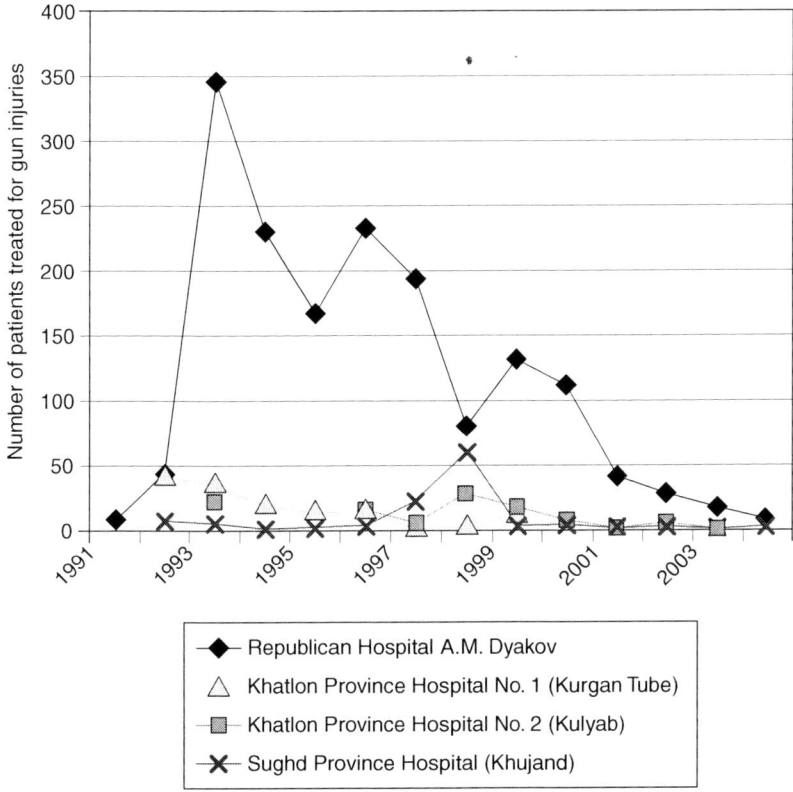

Figure 2.2 Gun injuries 1991–2004   (source: Torjesen *et al.*, 'Tajikistan's Road to Stability').

Arguably a comprehensive strategy vis-à-vis spoilers, combining coercion and co-option, as well as a broad-based and tangible initial reintegration of former combatants into law-enforcement structures, have been key ingredients in the set of policies that have brought high levels of stability to Tajikistan.

A striking feature of the Tajikistan case was the willingness of the central political leadership to accept the reluctance of commanders to hand over their full weapons stockpiles and to tolerate criminal activities, such as large-scale corruption and drugs trafficking. The quick provision of tangible economic benefits and positions for former commanders on both sides was also a key feature of the peace process. These approaches produced both trust and perceptions of safety for many of the former commanders. They also gave strong incentives to maintain and protect the status quo.

In the short and medium term, it is difficult not to regard Tajikistan and the policies of the Rakhmonov administration as successful. The long-term implications of Rakhmonov's strategies, however, are uncertain. Indeed, the Tajikistan case highlights the following questions, which typically arise in the wake of DDR processes: What are the development consequences of an entrenchment of the economic roles of civil war actors? Is there a breaking point when an 'over-facilitation' of former combatants' interests will jeopardise the overall economic wellbeing of a country and perpetuate cycles of underdevelopment, grievance and insecurity? Tajikistan exemplifies these dilemmas. Arguably, the nature of Tajikistan's post-war political settlement has had important implications for post-war developments in governance and the economy. While the commanders themselves have lost some of their power, it seems clear that the system of corruption, patronage networks and shadow business activities has become institutionalised. Over a decade after the signing of the peace agreement, it is becoming increasingly clear that the state's tacit acceptance of a range of criminal activities may jeopardise the very fundament of the state and could distort prospects for economic development.[47] There is a potential for further and large-scale criminalisation of the Tajik state and society because of the multi-billion dollar drug transit through the country. This may seriously affect economic and political development and could, in a worst-case scenario, bring renewed cycles of instability to Tajikistan.

These future dangers aside, the DDR process helped create a number of important goods for Tajikistan in the immediate years after the war. Chief among these is a society that at present has remarkably low levels of violence. This stands in sharp contrast to other countries that have experienced an end to formal fighting but where crime and violence continue – Guatemala forming one of many examples of such a scenario. President Rakhmonov's decision to seek compromise and inclusion and to suspend transitional justice bought time and helped reinstate the conditions needed for a resurrection of the Tajik state. Rakhmonov's subsequent policies of reducing political pluralism, eliminating political opponents (including those formerly associated with the opposition) and concentrating power in the office of the president produced stability. Interestingly, despite the political crackdowns and deviations from democratic principles, Rakhmonov enjoys high levels of popularity and legitimacy.[48] It might be the case that the DDR process in Tajikistan worked precisely because it did not follow a liberal democratic script. Elections were stipulated in the peace agreement and were conducted as part of the post-war process in Tajikistan, but this element was overshadowed by more informal and, in some ways, feudal strategies. President Rakhmonov bought loyalty and trust by creating patronage networks that centred on distribution of material goods and state protection for nominally illegal activities. Former civil war actors from both sides formed the central elements of these patronage networks.

Rakhmonov found a way to move Tajikistan forward after 1997 that matched the local context in Tajikistan. In this sense, Tajikistan is a case that highlights the limitations and perhaps dangers of applying universal DDR strategies in highly specific local conditions.

Notes

1 This chapter draws extensively on research material presented by us (together with Christina Wille) in Torjesen *et al.*, *Tajikistan's Road to Stability*. The report was financed jointly by UNDP Tajikistan and the Small Arms Survey. We are grateful for the Small Arms Survey and UNDP support of this research. We are also thankful for their encouragement to use our findings in this chapter. We also wish to thank the 24 researchers from Tajikistan that were involved in the report, in particular Alexander Sadikov and Bakhityor Naimov. Kamol Atoev produced an in-depth background paper on certain aspects of the DDR process, which has helped us develop the argument presented in this chapter. Finally, we thank Mats Berdal, David Ucko, and John Heathershaw for helpful comments and suggestions.
2 Muggah, 'No Magic Bullet'.
3 Examples of conventional approaches include World Bank, *Breaking the Conflict Trap*. For a comprehensive and critical discussion of peacebuilding and the problematic notions of 'positive' and 'negative' peace in the context of Tajikistan, see Heathershaw, *Peace as Complex Legitimacy* and Heathershaw, 'Peacebuilding as Practice'.
4 Torjesen *et al.*, *Tajikistan's Road to Stability*.
5 Local researchers from the Academy of Sciences research group AFKOR also conducted 60 semi-structured, anonymous interviews with former fighters and other people with particular insights on weapons and disarmament, such as mullahs and mid-ranking personnel in collective farms. Individuals with access to particular target groups were commissioned to seek their opinion on difficult issues. These included conversations with people in positions of power in former opposition areas, privately armed businesspeople and people with access to the weapons black market. Another set of researchers provided insights on the security situation facing ordinary civilians and how small arms and light weapons affect their lives by conducting 76 focus group discussions throughout Tajikistan. Quantifiable information from all focus groups was tabulated, providing a dataset on the opinions of groups across Tajikistan. In total 682 citizens participated.
6 CIA World Fact Book, 'Tajikistan'.
7 At the elite level, the political process in the pre-independence period had undermined the traditional control of the northern Leninabad group within the Tajikistan Communist Party, as well as the hold of the party itself on power when faced with the rise of self-styled democratic and Islamic movements in the *Perestroika* years. For an account of Tajikistan in the late Soviet period and after independence in 1991, see Roy, *The New Central Asia*.
8 Akiner, 'Tajikistan'.
9 RFE/RL, 'Tajikistan: Memories of Civil War Leave Youth Cautious About New Revolution', 11 April 2005.
10 See 'Key points in 1997 General Agreement' in Abdullaev and Barnes (eds), *The Politics of Compromise*.
11 Abdullo, 'Implementation of the 1997 General Agreement'.
12 These figures were made available in UNMOT news briefings and are referred to in Burkhard, 'The Problem of Small Arms'. The latter only reports the percentages and not the total numbers.
13 For example, a former opposition commander who researchers spoke to in the Rasht district centre said that there had been at least 790 registered former fighters in his area. Half of these joined the interior troops battalion, but only 190 guns were handed over, Interview, Garm, 20 August 2004. Staff in the Ministry of Emergency Situations in Khorog similarly noted to researchers that they received 50–60 opposition fighters, but that only nine pieces of weaponry were handed in, Interview, Khorog, 2 August 2004.
14 For more information on the disarmament process, see Section II of Torjesen *et al.*, 'Tajikistan's Road to Stability'.

15 Interview, Garm, 20 August 2004.
16 Horsman, 'Uzbekistan's Involvement in the Tajik Civil War'.
17 Interview, Dushanbe, 26 March 2004.
18 Interview, Kulyab, 5 March 2004.
19 Akiner, 'Tajikistan: Disintegration or Reconciliation?'.
20 Interview, Dushanbe, 24 July 2004.
21 It should be stressed however that there were a number of cases where the human security of civilians was under threat due to the presence of commanders, see Section II of Torjesen *et al.*, 'Tajikistan's Road to Stability'.
22 In September 1996, government forces made contact with UTO commanders in Rasht Valley and signed the 'Garm protocol'. This protocol recognised and acknowledged the central role of the commanders in the peace process. These opposition commanders in turn sent a message to the UTO in Moscow in December 1996, which firmly demanded that efforts to reach a deal continue. See Abdullo, 'Implementation of the 1997 General Agreement'.
23 Since 2001, and the consolidation of President Rakhmonov's power, there is now extensive rotation of the police cadres, and former government fighters or original MVD personnel from other areas are now serving in the former opposition areas.
24 Confidential source material, Dushanbe 2005.
25 Ibid.
26 For more details on the arrest of Mirzoev, see Section II of Torjesen *et al.*, 'Tajikistan's Road to Stability'.
27 *Asia Plus*, 18 August 2005.
28 Transparency International, *Corruption Perceptions Index.*
29 RFE/RL, '"Missing" Tajik Opposition Leader Reportedly Arrested', 26 April 2005. See also RFE/RL, 'Shield or Sieve': Tajikistan Reviews Tactics in the War on Drugs', 2003; RFE/RL, *Central Asia Report.*
30 International Crisis Group (ICG), *Central Asia.*
31 Literaturnaya Gazeta (Moscow). 'Trafficker Outlines Tajikistan's Drug Transit Operations', 12.
32 Interview, Dushanbe, 24 March 2004.
33 Ibid.
34 Interview, Dushanbe, 23 February 2004.
35 In a survey of government-affiliated commanders and criminal proceedings against armed groups, it is evident that a large percentage of the leaders from groups around the area of Tursunzade, a predominantly ethnic-Uzbek area, either received criminal sentences or died during or shortly after the war. This may have reflected the fact that the Uzbeks were not offered significant pay-offs in the peace process, that a number of criminal groupings were formed in Uzbek areas and/or that the Rakhmonov government chose to investigate and prosecute these Uzbek groupings for criminal offences to a greater extent than others. For more insight on the ethnic-Uzbek dimension of the civil war, see 'Comments on Tajikistan' by Barnett Richard Rubin (1996) www.hartford-hwp.com/archives/53/034.html.
36 For further insights on the economic and political significance of cotton production in Tajikistan, see ICG, *The Curse of Cotton.*
37 Russian Army helicopters airlifted IMU fighters from Tajikistan to Afghanistan in February 2001. The group allegedly consisted of 250 people, 'Namangani's Foray Causes Concern among Central Asian Governments', *Times of Central Asia*, 8 February 2001.
38 IWPR, 'Tajikistan Moves against Militants'.
39 Hall, 'Tajikistan'.
40 Asia Plus News Agency, 22 June 2001.
41 Hall, 'Tajikistan'. Hall refers to a piece by AFP on 7 January 2002 that cites 'over 50 armed guerrillas killed and 200 seized in Tajikistan last year'.

42 For more details on the weapons-collection campaigns, see Torjesen *et al.*, 'Tajikistan's Road to Stability'.
43 Interview, Dushanbe, 24 February 2004.
44 For more information on the increasing authoritarian trends of the Rakhmonov administration, see ICG, *Tajikistan's Politics*.
45 Nakaya, 'Politics of Aid'.
46 See Section II of Torjesen *et al.*, 'Tajikistan's Road to Stability'.
47 For a comprehensive discussion of the link between the drug economy and the Civil War in Tajikistan and the way the drug economy is undermining the state, see Cornell, 'The Narcotics Threat in Greater Central Asia'.
48 Shoizmov, 'The Revolt in Kyrgyzstan and Tajikistan's Political Situation'.

References

Abdullaev, Kamoludin and Barnes, Catherine (eds), 2001. *The Politics of Compromise – The Tajikistan Peace Process*, Accord Series. Conciliation Resources, London.

Abdullo, Rashid G., 2001. 'Implementation of the 1997 General Agreement: Successes, Dilemmas and Challenges', in Abdullaev and Barnes (eds), *The Politics of Compromise*.

Akiner, Shirin, 1999. 'Tajikistan: Disintegration or Reconciliation?', Central Asian and Caucasian Prospects Series. RIIA, London.

Burkhard, Conrad, 2000. 'The Problem of Small Arms and Light Weapons in Tajikistan', *Strategic Analysis*, 25:8.

CIA World Fact Book, 2006. *Tajikistan*, US Central Intelligence Agency, Washington DC.

Cornell, Svante, 2007. 'The Narcotics Threat in Greater Central Asia: From Crime-Terror Nexus to State Infiltration', *CEF Quarterly* 4:1.

Hall, Michael, 2002. 'Tajikistan: The Mirage of Stability', *Perspective*, 13:2, November/December.

Heathershaw, John, 2006. *Peace as Complex Legitimacy: Politics, Space and Discourse in Tajikistan's Peacebuilding Process, 2000–2005*, LSE, PhD thesis, London.

——, 2007. 'Peacebuilding as Practice: Discourses from Post-Conflict Tajikistan', *International Peacekeeping* 14:2.

Horsman, Stuart, 1999. 'Uzbekistan's Involvement in the Tajik Civil War 1992–97: Domestic Considerations', *Central Asian Survey* 18:1.

Institute for War and Peace Reporting (IWPR), 'Tajikistan Moves against Militants', *RCA* 19:8, September.

International Crisis Group (ICG), 2002. *Central Asia: The Politics of Police Reform*, Asia Report No. 42, ICG, Osh/Brussels.

——, 2004. *Tajikistan's Politics: Confrontation or Consolidation?*, Asia Briefing, ICG, Brussels/Osh.

——, 2005. *The Curse of Cotton: Central Asia's Destructive Monoculture*, Asia Report No 93, ICG, Brussels/Osh.

Literaturnaya Gazeta (Moscow), 1995. 'Trafficker Outlines Tajikistan's Drug Transit Operations', *Literaturnaya Gazeta (Moscow)* 4:25 January.

Muggah, Robert, 2005. 'No Magic Bullet: A Critical Perspective on Disarmament, Demobilization and Reintegration (DDR) and Weapons Reduction in Post-conflict Contexts', *The Round Table* 94:375.

Nakaya, Sumie, 2008. 'Politics of Aid, Institution-Building, and the Emergence and Consolidation of an Oligarchy in Post-Conflict States', Presentation given at International Studies Association, San Francisco, 26–29 March.

RFE/RL, 2005. *Central Asia Report* 3:29.

Roy, Olivier, 2000. *The New Central Asia: The Creation of Nations*, I.B. Tauris, London.

Shoizmov, Pulat, 2004. 'The Revolt in Kyrgyzstan and Tajikistan's Political Situation', *Central Asia – Caucasus Analyst* 20 April.

Torjesen Stina, Wille, Christina and MacFarlane, Neil S., 2005. *Tajikistan's Road to Stability: Reduction in Small Arms Proliferation and Remaining Challenges*, Occasional Paper 17, Small Arms Survey, Geneva.

Transparency International, 2005. *Corruption Perceptions Index*, www.transparency.org/policy_and_research/surveys_indices/cpi/2005.

World Bank, 2003. *Breaking the Conflict Trap*, World Bank, Washington DC.

3 Bureaucratic façade and political realities of disarmament and demobilisation in Afghanistan

Antonio Giustozzi

Introduction

As in the case of many programmes related to security-sector reform (SSR), there is widespread consensus that the implementation of disarmament and demobilisation in Afghanistan faced multiple contradictions. For example, there was conflict over the ownership of a programme demanded and designed by external actors but which required a high degree of participation by locals. Another contradiction was between the humanitarian concerns of some implementing partners (the welfare of the ex-combatants) and the political interests of those Afghan and international actors who were mainly concerned with maintaining good relations with the military class controlling the Afghan countryside. Finally, the bureaucratic definition of disarmament, demobilisation and reintegration as developed by the implementing agencies did not match the much more complex reality on the ground.

This chapter argues that while the tension between diverging interests was real, the contradictions were eventually resolved. Frustrated middle rank officials of international organisations and diplomatic corps often continued to work on the assumption that SSR was still proceeding as planned. Through a sometimes-harsh confrontation,[1] the political leaderships concerned worked out an unofficial compromise on disarmament and demobilisation. This compromise involved the establishment of a façade process of disarmament, which throughout this chapter will be referred to as DDR and DIAG (Disbandment of Illegal Armed Groups).[2]

Behind this process, non-state armed groups of various types would be allowed to continue to exist and sometimes prosper, as long as they were willing to pay at least lip service to the bureaucratic process and abstained from actively working against the central government. This satisfied international actors, who were not willing to risk destabilising large portions of Afghanistan. It also satisfied international organisations, which were not ready to undertake a major challenge without explicit American support. Finally, it satisfied key Afghan players, all of whom were to various degrees linked to militias in different regions of the country and reliant on them to maintain and expand political influence and leverage.

The chapter first examines the 'bureaucratic' process and its successes and failures. This section is followed by close scrutiny of the political realities both as determined by the anti-Taliban campaign of October–November 2001 and of the actual impact of DDR and DIAG on non-state armed groups.[3]

The bureaucratic process

DDR

Initially laid out in Geneva in spring 2002 as a component of a wider SSR agenda and then specified in Petersberg at the end of that year, the Afghan DDR programme entered the planning phase with President Hamid Karzai's signature of the Decree on Security Sector Reform on 1 December 2002. Two commissions were formed, one to prepare the disarmament component and the other to deal with demobilisation and reintegration. Later, in 2004, Karzai signed another decree to launch the cantonment of heavy weapons belonging to the militias.[4]

The actual implementation of DDR was entrusted to the United Nations Development Programme (UNDP), which created the ad hoc Afghanistan New Beginning Programme (ANBP) in 2003. The latter was meant to work in strict cooperation with the Ministry of Defence (MoD). Figure 3.1 shows how the partners were expected to process the MoD's militias (AMF or Afghan Military Forces). While Afghan partners were playing the main role in disarmament and demobilisation, the reintegration phase would see ANBP collect data about the disarmed combatants and hold sessions with them, explaining the programmes features and aims. Each combatant would then be assigned a caseworker, who would interview him and counsel him concerning different reintegration options, which ranged from joining the new regular army or police, to starting a small business, to entering a profession or to go back to farming. Finally, a food package for the families would be handed over.

At the completion of disarmament and demobilisation, the unit would be declared disbanded and after three weeks, the ex-combatants would start reintegration. The 'template approach' was clearly visible in the design; at the same time this was to some extent necessary, as the programme required strong formal-bureaucratic procedures meant to prevent abuses and manipulation and to address the needs of individual ex-combatants. Standards already used in other contexts were adopted and it drew on know-how and expertise developed by the UN in previous years. There were apparently strict monitoring and evaluation criteria as well.[5] The Regional Verification Committees (RVCs) were attributed a particularly important role in the design, as they represented the only degree of external supervision over the selection process of the ex-combatants. Each of the eight RVCs was composed of one governmental representative, one ANBP representative and 3–5 village elders. Another preventive measure taken to avoid the abuse of demobilisation and reintegration as tools of patronage and self-enrichment was the imposition of an upper ceiling on the number of ex-combatants to be demobilised. Initially, the number was set at 100,000, but it was later cut down to 60,000. There was little Afghan input in its design, except for the fact that the director of the programme, Sultan Aziz, was himself a career

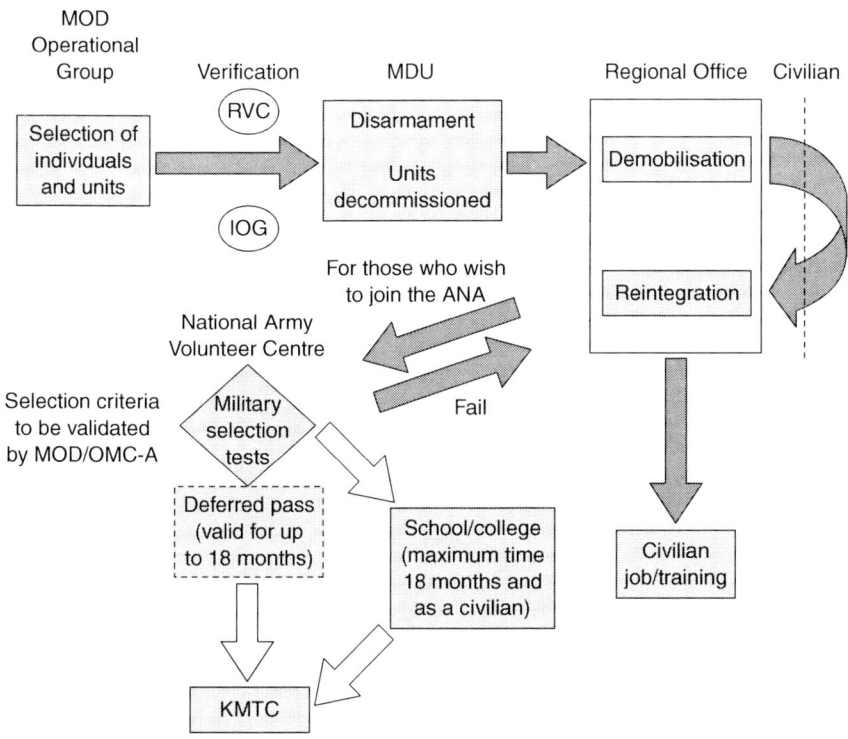

Legend
RVC: regional verification committees; MDU: mobile disarmament units;
OMC-A: Office of Military Cooperation – Afghanistan; IOG: International Observer Group;
KMTC: Kabul Military Training Centre.

Figure 3.1 Role of Afghan and international organisations in DDR process (reproduced from ANBP, *Partnership for Peace: Afghanistan's New Beginnings Program*).

UN official of Afghan origin and with extensive fieldwork experience in Afghanistan. He also had close contacts with some of the formerly warring factions and might well have been instrumental in framing DDR according to their interests.[6]

Even from the standpoint of DDR as a formal bureaucratic process, however, there were flaws. The first one was the delay in starting the programme; it began in October 2003, two years after the end of the conflict and six months later than the original plan had envisaged. Further delays occurred during its implementation, so that it took 21 months rather than the planned 12 to complete disarmament and demobilisation (which was said to have happened in July 2005).[7] The delays had multiple causes, ranging from planning and staffing problems at ANBP to differences between the MoD and ANBP.[8] Among other delaying factors, once the process got underway was the reluctance of some armed groups to hand over their heavy weaponry.[9] This was particularly true of the Panjshir-based militias of Shura-i Nezar (Coordination Council), a faction within Jami'at-i Islami (Islamic Society), the group that had occupied Kabul in November 2001. The removal of heavy weaponry from the valley was repeatedly delayed and when it started, it faced hostility from local authorities and the population. Only a minority of total stockpiles (estimated at 3,000 truckloads) were removed before the completion of DDR, although in subsequent weeks 9–15 truckloads continued to be surrendered each week.[10] Yet another cause of delay was factional infighting in northern Afghanistan, where until mid-2004 the militias of Junbesh-i Milli (National Front) and Jami'at were unable to agree on a schedule for the DDR of their units.[11]

Among the implications of these delays was a deterioration in security, due to the involvement in crime of the often-unpaid militiamen and the 'natural' demobilisation of many ex-combatants, who left their units to tend to the fields or to get other salaried jobs. Apart from the commanders, few militiamen would serve in their units for two years in a row. Many were conscripts or forced recruits, sent by the village elders to serve for just a few months. In the absence of factional conflict, the commanders themselves were not inclined to maintain many men in the ranks. As a result, once DDR actually started in October 2003, relatively few of those still serving were those registered by the MoD in 2002. In fact, ANBP's and UNAMA's (United Nations Assistance Mission in Afghanistan) own records show that demobilisation had already occurred to a considerable extent by 2003–04. From the initial estimate of 94,000 AMF men to be demobilised, a 2004 assessment found that numbers had shrunk to an estimated 45–50,000.[12] In practice, even to meet the revised target of 60,000, AMF units often had to re-mobilise or recruit new militiamen, if only for a few days.[13]

From this bureaucratic perspective, another important flaw was the failure to collect enough weapons, despite ANBP's optimistic claims.[14] By the end of disarmament, according to ANBP figures, over 70,000 weapons had been collected from 63,380 ex-combatants, corresponding to just 56 per cent of the weapons previously registered and suggesting that the militias managed to hand over as little as possible. Moreover, often only scrap weapons were handed over: according to UNAMA sources, 36 per cent of the weapons collected were either unserviceable or cheap (and bad) Pakistani copies.[15] This failure, however, could have been politically motivated by the desire not to alienate militia leaders.

The best indicator of inefficiencies and flaws in the DDR process are found in the reintegration phase, by its nature the most remote from political issues.[16] Typically, the planning of the programme was carried out by one ANBP senior officer and two junior officers, as a desk exercise in Kabul. When it confronted the reality 'on the ground', weaknesses promptly emerged. It proved impossible to assess each ex-combatant's needs and abilities and appropriately counsel them on the selection of reintegration options. During the original ANBP planning and discussions, 'ex-combatants' were rightly identified as 'a fairly heterogeneous group in terms of age, skills and place of origin' and a categorisation into child soldiers, elderly, disabled, literate, commanders, soldiers and urban/rural was considered.[17] This categorisation still failed to identify several relevant groups, such as full-time/part-time soldiers, volunteers/forced recruits, *jihadis*/former soldiers of the communist regime, etc. but, regardless, at the time of implementation, any attempt at taxonomy was abandoned, as the fighters were lumped together as a homogeneous group.

The lack of coordination among the different agencies and organisations involved in the reintegration programme hindered any systematic planning for the activation of local development strategies. Insufficient preparation, logistical capacity and bureaucratic flexibility led to long gaps between the demobilisation and reintegration phases. The absence of technical studies, of market analysis, of feasibility studies and indeed understanding of the complexity of rural livelihoods meant that the advice given by the agencies to the reintegrating ex-combatants was often largely arbitrary. Of those ex-combatants who opted for setting up small businesses, many had to fold up rather rapidly. Trends in the agricultural 'transitional reintegration' were not much different from those for small businesses. Factors of production indispensable to agriculture, such as irrigation systems, rural infrastructure and landed property were not properly addressed. Likewise, an agricultural marketing policy was not defined. Ex-combatants who opted for livestock faced several problems, ranging from confiscation by commanders, the lack of proper training in livestock management, to the extraordinarily cold winter of 2004–05 that caused the death of much of the livestock. Furthermore, because villagers were already frequently competing for natural resources, such as land and water, the lack of proper planning in the distribution of large quantities of livestock concentrated in small areas could well have contributed to generating new conflicts.[18] Vocational training was also implemented in ineffective ways without a preliminary objective labour market assessment, and the quality of the training offered was low. In some cases, for example, a concentration of approximately 15 new tailors per village was being created.

Possibly the most puzzling aspect of reintegration was that it often did not prevent ex-combatants from being re-absorbed by new or old systems of patronage run by warlords and local commanders, which the DDR programme supposedly aimed to break down. In some cases, training courses and projects were organised inside the houses of former commanders, hence backing their position of power and wealth among the ex-combatants and villagers. Elsewhere, small business activities were based on goods provided illegally by their commanders. More generally, the success of ex-combatants depended on their market experience and ability to deal with the patronage-dominated Afghan market. Afghan markets are controlled by mafia-style organisations, which form a sort of oligopoly at every level of the market chain. Thus, new entrants are in competition with existing players for the necessary patronage and 'protection' from government officials and other power holders, as well as for space in the market. It was estimated from different sources that only about 30–40 per cent of ex-combatants' small businesses would have been able to remain in the market. This percentage is mainly composed of those ex-combatants who were already wealthy and well positioned in the market.[19]

The ineffectiveness of the operation was compounded by the lack of coordination mechanisms between the international agencies involved in DDR, such as between the ANBP and the United Nations Children's Fund (UNICEF)[20] or between the Japan International Cooperation Agency's (JICA) DDR programme and the Japanese Embassy's DDR Unit.

DIAG

The problem of the armed groups left out of the DDR process (see 'The civil war and the "ex-combatants"' below) was tentatively addressed by the launch of the follow-up DIAG programme in June 2005, under the aegis of a Disarmament and Reintegration Commission, supported by ANBP and UNAMA. In this case, the process was supposed to be led by the Afghan authorities and in terms of bureaucratic procedures it looked much weaker than the one adopted for DDR (see Figure 3.2), resting as it did on the cooperation of notoriously weak and biased provincial authorities. The D&R Commission was given 'ownership' of the DIAG Strategy and was tasked with providing strategic direction to the executive body of DIAG, known as the DIAG Forum, which in turn provided directives for the Provincial DIAG committees (see Figure 3.3).

Again, there were flaws in the bureaucratic implementation of DIAG. The government approved a Gun Law in June 2005[21] but the Law on Private Security Companies, which was also supposed to be in place before the launch of DIAG, had not been implemented by April 2007. A more important flaw was the toothless character of the programme. The DDR process was not well endowed in this regard, but at least had at its disposal the threat to disband AMF units without demobilisation. This tool was of course irrelevant in the case of DIAG. It was also decided not to consider economic incentives, like handouts or reintegration processes, following the insistence of the main donor (Japan), who did not want to be seen as supporting illegal or criminal groups.[22] As a result, and with the exception of candidates in the parliamentary and provincial elections, the only incentives that could be identified by the DIAG planners were the promise of development spending in areas where DIAG had been successfully implemented, the pressure of public opinion, support of 'social authority', media campaigns and a not very credible threat of intervention by law enforcement agencies.[23]

The impact of a toothless DIAG programme became evident after the parliamentary and provincial elections of September 2005. The threat to disqualify candidates who were involved with illegal armed groups had some impact on the launch of DIAG. Candidates were given until July 2005 to disband and disarm and 124 of them complied at least partially, handing over 4,857 weapons, which accounted for the majority of those collected and verified in June and July. Weapons collection did reasonably well until the end of the year, when its pace slowed considerably (see Figure 3.4). By September 2007, just under 21,000 weapons in working condition had been handed over. Considering ANBP's own conservative estimates of at least 180,000 men active in illegal armed groups, that amount would represent no more than 10 per cent of the presumed total and

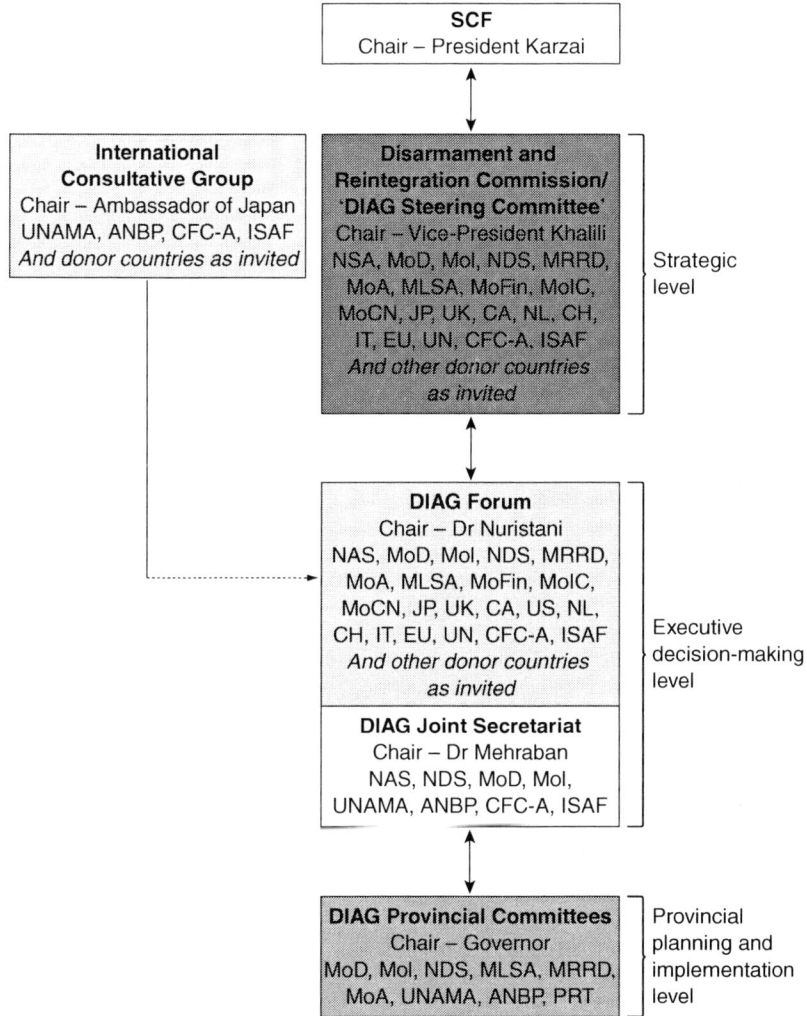

Figure 3.2 DIAG procedures (source: ANBP).

probably even less, as many militiamen would have more than one weapon. At the pace of collection recorded during the first quarter of 2007, it would have taken another 400 months to complete it, assuming no new purchases of guns. Initially scheduled to last from June 2005 until 30 June 2006 and then extended until December 2007, DIAG looked set to continue indefinitely, short of a political decision to terminate it.

Moreover, the piecemeal and unplanned character of the weapons collection process was inevitably bound to limit severely the chances of success. The resulting degree of compliance was very uneven not only between regions and provinces, but

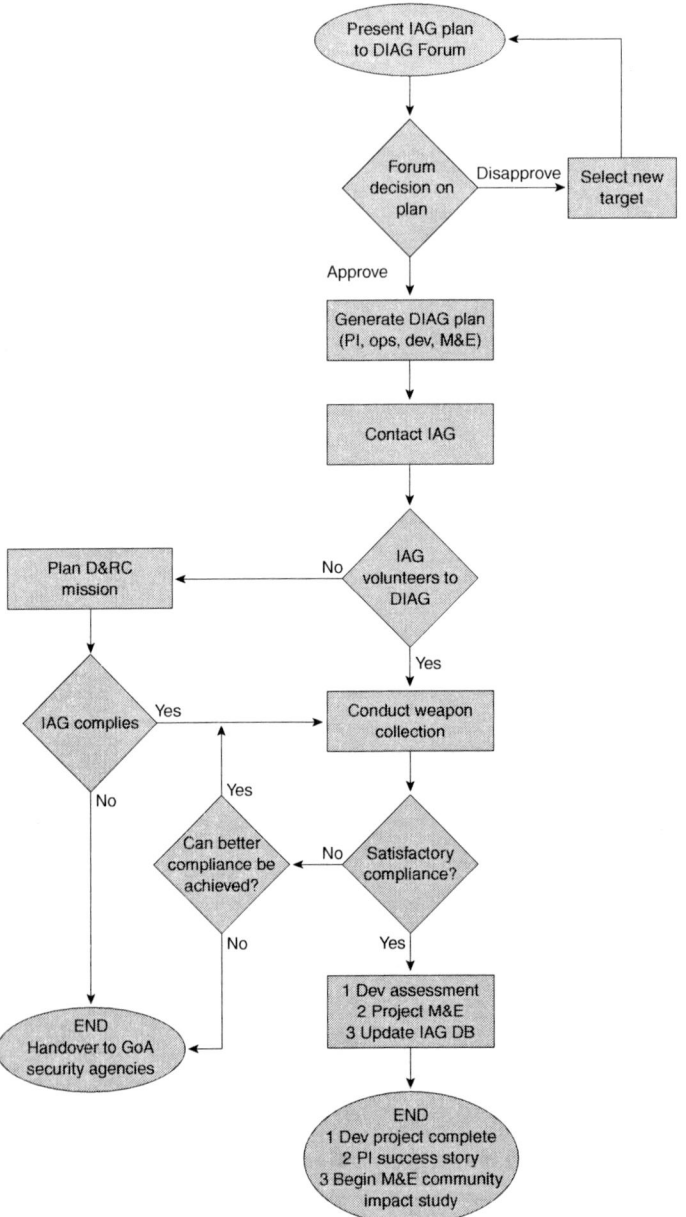

Figure 3.3 DIAG procedure (reproduced from Government of Afghanistan, *Strategy for Disbandment of Illegal Armed Groups in Afghanistan (DIAG)*, Kabul, January 2006; ANBP, *Concept of Operations for Main Phase DIAG*, Kabul, March 2006).

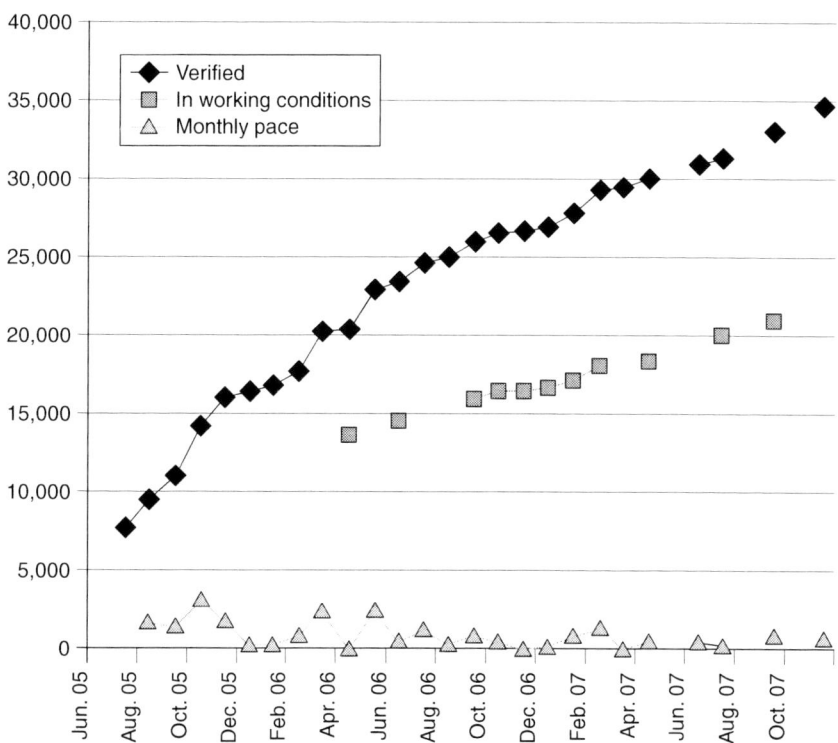

Figure 3.4 Weapons collected under DIAG: total verified by ANBP and weapons in working conditions (source: ANBP).

also within each province. For example, in Takhar province (Table 3.1), of the three districts where the ANBP acknowledged the presence of illegal armed groups, one had returned no weapons, one had returned 42 per cent of the estimated total of illegal weapons and one 13 per cent by October 2006. Similarly, in Kapisa province, the progress of DIAG was very uneven; with Kapisa centre coming in at 52.5 per cent and one of the two Kohistan districts not having handed over a single weapon (see Table 3.2). This means that local military leaders potentially willing to comply might have been restrained by the fear of becoming vulnerable to those neighbours unwilling to disarm.

The slowing pace in 2006 was also due to the resurgence of violence, which was particularly pronounced in southern Afghanistan, but with a tendency to spread to other regions as well. Figure 3.5 shows the uneven compliance between different regions, which again offered an excuse, if not a disincentive, to other armed groups not to disarm. During 2007, the regional imbalance deepened further, with virtually no weapons being handed over in the south and hardly any in the southeast.

Table 3.1 Collection of weapons from illegal armed groups, Takhar province, as of October 2006

	Reported in DIAG database	Handed over	Handed over/ reported (%)	Reported by NSD (2003)
Farkhar	520	214	42	940
Rustaq	1,112	0	0	2,910
Cha'hab	1,050	129	13	710
Yangi Qala				730
Darqad				530
KhuajaBahawodin				500
Kalafgan				420
Dasht-i Qala				1,140
Khwaja Ghar				820
Bangi				1,020
Baharak				920
Namakab				420
Warsaj				760
Eshkamish				920
Hazar-e Sumuch				350
Chal				510
Teluqan				550
Takhar total	2,682	343	13	14,150

Table 3.2 Kapisa province, compliance to DIAG by district, as of October 2006

	(%)
Kapisa centre	52.5
Kohband	21.2
Kohistan 1	0
Kohistan 2	12.5
Nijrab	12.7
Tagab	0
Alasai	0

Source: ANBP, NSD.

The political realities

For all the internal flaws of the DDR process, the argument of this chapter is that it did not matter much, as by the time they were implemented, DDR and DIAG were only meant to be façades embellishing a controversial political compromise, which gained the acquiescence of local military leaders by leaving their ability to maintain control over the villages untouched. In order to understand how this compromise came about, we have first to consider the politico-military situation, that arose at the end of 2001.

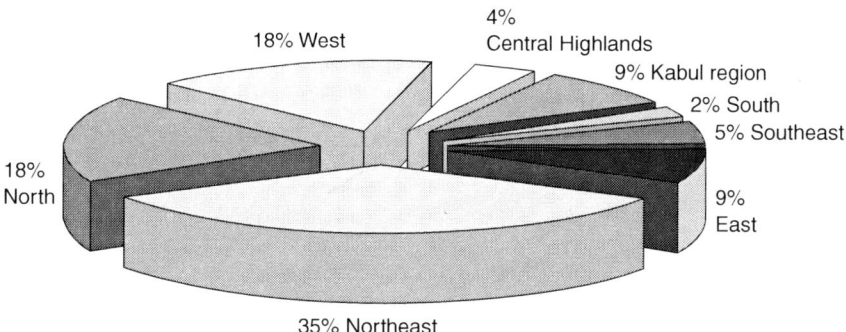

Figure 3.5 Contribution of the different regions to the DIAG programme in terms of weapons handed over, as of October 2006 (source: ANBP).

The civil war and the 'ex-combatants'

The last phase (at least until the Bonn Conference) of Afghanistan's civil wars pitted an ensemble of anti-Taliban militias against a hard-core of Afghan Taliban, supported by numerous foreign volunteers and local militias recruited from among the ranks of the fighters of the previous civil wars. The anti-Taliban front was divided between the United Front, dominated by Jami'at-i Islami but composed of several other groups as well, and several strongmen's militias hastily activated in southern and south-eastern Afghanistan to support the American offensive against the regime. The actual involvement of these disparate groups in the war varied widely. Jami'at's militias had been fighting against the Taliban since the mid-1990s, although their ranks dramatically expanded in the run up to the final offensive thanks to American patronage. The new recruits, mostly former part-time fighters or entirely new recruits attracted by higher pay and the prospect of being on the winning side, saw little fighting during their short service, if for no reason other than the fact that not much fighting took place along most of the frontline. Other groups within the United Front could claim to have at least been fighting the Taliban for a long time, even if most of them had scarcely been active between 1998 and 2001, when northern and central Afghanistan were under Taliban occupation. The only seriously intense fighting of the final campaign took place in a few areas of northern Afghanistan, such as Mazar-i Sharif, and in selected locations around Kabul. The southern strongmen's militias, by contrast, had no real record of fighting the Taliban.[24]

Aside from the political implications of this disparity, it also had important implications for the demobilisation and reintegration plans. Among those who eventually made it to DDR, the genuine ex-combatants, i.e. those who actually took part in fighting for at least a few months, probably did not exceed 15,000. Even among the genuine ex-combatants, few were uprooted individuals lacking a place to return to, as most of them had been fighting not too far from home. Of course, a much larger number of former combatants existed in the country, running into the hundreds of thousands, but they were not considered worthy of incorporating into the DDR process as they either did not figure in the ranks of the armed formations active at the end of 2001 or had been fighting on the wrong side. Thousands of former Taliban fighters were also excluded from the process. Even of those who had mobilised on the anti-Taliban side, only a minority were included in the AMF (see the next section: 'Shadow ownership').

The group which captured Kabul in 2001, Jami'at-i Islami, was clearly in a privileged position to exercise serious influence in the shaping of the demobilisation process (and the political process of reconstruction more generally). By the end of 2001, Jami'at had captured the MoD and its leadership had proceeded to staff it with its own loyalists. A few more armed groups were able to influence the process at the regional level, such as Junbesh-i Milli in the north and Hizb-i Wahdat (Unity Party) in the central highlands. Even in the southern regions Jami'at did not have total power and while trying to place as many close allies as possible everywhere, its leadership had to concede four out of eight military regions to competing groups (south, south-east, east and central highlands), while accepting to share uneasily a fifth region (the north) with Junbesh. Even within the three remaining regions (west, northeast and central), the leadership of Jami'at held far from complete control, not least because it was itself fragmenting among rival personalities, each developing its own network. As a result, the key personalities in control of the MoD, who were coming from the various Jami'at factions, always had to negotiate and bargain with local and regional military leaders. Sometimes the MoD would be able to use the stick of fund-denial to force compliance with orders, but since it was paying only subsistence handouts and, even then, not very regularly, their leverage was limited. In fact, its main power turned out to be its ability to offer militia leaders official appointments as officers, thereby legitimising their role and their possession of weapons. They were also able to bargain over the rank of the appointment, which would determine the status and the influence of the appointee. Jami'at's interest in maintaining and expanding relations with local military leaders derived from its ambition to be the leading force within the coalition government and control as much territory as possible throughout Afghanistan. However, elements from within Karzai's circle, and the President himself, were soon competing with the leadership of various Jami'at factions in courting local military leaders. Neither of these developments boded well for disarmament and demobilisation.[25]

Shadow ownership

It has been claimed that the Afghan DDR process, together with the more general SSR, lacked Afghan ownership.[26] If we focus our attention on the bureaucratic process described above, this is certainly true. However, beneath a superficial layer of bureaucratic norms and procedures, intense negotiations developed from the very beginning, through which key Afghan actors were able to reclaim big chunks of ownership or even seize control over much of the process. In the words of an international observer, 'the decision on who to disarm was the business of local commanders'.[27] The outcome was DDR and DIAG processes that represented an informal compromise between the demands of the 'international community' and the desires of key Afghan allies.

Due to the opposition of the militia leaders, the Bonn agreement (2001) did not include any explicit reference to disarmament and demobilisation, but merely stated that the militias would be brought under the authority of the MoD as a national army and reorganised 'according to the requirements'.[28] During the following months Deputy Defence Minister Baryalai, who was in charge of disarmament and demobilisation but was at the same time closely identified with the interests of a particular faction within Jami'at (*Shura-i Nezar*), proposed a plan that in fact ran counter to disarmament and demobilisation. It envisaged the reorganisation of the militias into a newly trained National Army, with the militia commanders being appointed as officers. The plan sponsored by the UNAMA, the US embassy and others was very different and involved only limited recruitment from the militias into the Afghan National Army (ANA; no more than 10–20 per cent of the size of ANA).[29] The two surveys of militiamen carried out, under the orders of the MoD, by UNAMA and the MoD itself, produced completely different figures, 94,000 and 250,000, respectively. It is widely believed that MoD figures were the result of inflated reports by AMF officers, who were hoping to pocket the food allowances of tens of thousands of ghost soldiers.[30] Presumably, in order to put pressure on its international partners or maybe trying to impose a fait accompli, the MoD actually started its own weapon collection plan in the summer of 2002, which resulted in the stockpiling of the weapons under guarded storage. As international donors were only ready to support the UNAMA/US plan, the MoD plan was abandoned after much foot-dragging by the MoD.

On the surface, this might appear to be an outright victory for the UN and the foreign diplomats. Nonetheless, presumably in exchange for agreeing to the terms sponsored by its international partners, the Jami'ats within the MoD, and by extension the militia leaders, maintained control over key aspects of the DDR process. This consisted chiefly of the ability to select the units to be demobilised/disbanded and, within those, the names of the ex-combatants to be reintegrated. ANBP's planning was entirely based on 'numbers' received from the MoD and local military leaders.[31] The MoD and other key Afghan players made such good use of the manoeuvring room left in their hands, manipulating the process, that the actual DDR programme ended up having only minimal impact on Afghan ground realities.

A first major violation of the spirit of disarmament and demobilisation, as presented to the public, was that a substantial number of militiamen (several tens of thousands) managed to evade demobilisation by being incorporated into the police force, under the control of the Ministry of the Interior (MoI), which was exempted from demobilisation. There is no sign that international organisations or diplomatic corps objected to this exemption. The reform of the police force was initially limited to the slow training of a new generation of police officers from scratch and to short courses (two to eight weeks) for existing policemen, designed to teach them the most basic aspects of policing. Only from 2005–06 would the MoI come under serious pressure to replace key individuals in Kabul and in the provinces. The relevance of the exemption of the police goes beyond the mere number of people evading demobilisation, as the factionalisation of the police force would later come to represent a major disincentive for other non-state armed groups to disarm, by creating a climate of insecurity and distrust.[32] The key question is whether this exemption was overlooked due to incompetence or whether it was functional to a more general political deal.

While there is insufficient information available to answer the question directly, this 'distraction' was not an isolated case. A second example of how political factions within the MoD were able to manipulate DDR was the exclusion of former Taliban fighters, who mostly returned to their villages or crossed into Pakistan on their own initiative. Since the Jami'ats seem to have mainly conceived the DDR process as an opportunity to distribute benefits to followers and allies, they could see no role for the former Taliban fighters in it. Unknown numbers of them would later join the Neo-Taliban insurgency.[33]

Possibly the greatest manipulation of the DDR process was the partial and selective inclusion of armed groups on the MoD payroll. In fact, most of the armed groups existing in late 2001 were not incorporated in the MoD (or in the MoI): the highest estimate of AMF's strength approached 100,000, with tens of thousands more in the police, while UN sources would later conservatively estimate the strength of illegal militias at around 180,000. Those excluded from official appointments were typically local military leaders who were on bad terms with the Jami'at leadership. At the same time quite a few, particularly in remote areas, actually abstained from seeking appointments, contenting themselves with smuggling and other illegal activities and showing little concern for being legitimised by a very distant central state. There was also a strong tendency among local military leaders to maintain parallel structures outside the MoD, integrating only part of their men in the MoD-sponsored units.[34] From 2004, these parallel structures helped the disbanded AMF units to evade demobilisation by reconstituting underground. This reality was implicitly acknowledged by the authorities themselves: Presidential decree 50, which declared non-state armed groups illegal, included among them the 'remnants of the AMF'.[35]

Although the AMF included some representation of the different factions of the anti-Taliban alliance, the regional imbalance was obvious (see Figure 3.6). The attitude of the MoD seems to confirm that Jami'at viewed the AMF as a political tool to expand its influence. With over 40 divisions and a large number of independent brigades, regiments and battalions in existence at the end of 2002, there was indeed much room for patronage. The rank of the commanding officer was not necessarily related to the actual size of his unit, being rather a measure of his political connections. For this reason, some brigades could well be bigger than certain divisions. The initial attribution of military units in early 2002 already showed a factional bias. The large majority of military units anywhere were commanded by those politically close to the Minister of Defence, Marshal Fahim. The main exceptions were the 8th Army Corps, which was dominated by Junbesh-i

Figure 3.6 Distribution of AMF units, 2002 (source: Interviews with UN officials, diplomats and Afghan notables).

Milli, and the 2nd Army Corps, dominated by Gul Agha Sherzai and his allies.[36] The 4th Army Corps, dominated by Ismail Khan,[37] was in a rather ambiguous position as Khan belonged to the same political faction as Fahim but was very jealous of his autonomy. The few additional exceptions were a single division of the 7th Army Corps, which was also under the control of Junbesh, and some commanders who were appointed due to external pressure, such as Atiqullah Ludin, commander of the 3rd Army Corps, allegedly imposed by the US. Interestingly, for a long time Ludin was unable to take up his position effectively in Gardez, due to the hostility of supposedly subordinate officers close to Marshal Fahim, and remained based in his home province of Logar, well outside the military region under his control. Where appointing commanders affiliated with his own faction (Shura-i Nezar) or party (Jami'at-i Islami)[38] caused too much of an uproar, such as in the provinces demographically dominated by Pashtuns, the MoD would normally opt for Pashtun commanders belonging to factions close to Jami'at, often Professor Sayyaf's Ittehad-i Islami (Islamic Union). After that, the MoD continued to make good political use of its ability to create new units, such as 24th Division in Faryab, which effectively appeared in 2003 and was expedient in weakening Junbesh in one of its strongholds.[39]

The MoD also tried to allow as many loyalists as possible into the new National Army, by manipulating the 10–20 per cent quota of recruits allowed to come from the ranks of the militias having undergone DDR (see Table 3.3). The region of Kabul, the core of Shurai Nezar's militias, represented almost nine-tenths of all former militiamen opting for the ANA – double its share of total DDR-ed militiamen. In practice, however, the incorporation of DDR-ed militiamen in the new army could only be implemented minimally, partly due to the screening imposed by international trainers on ANA recruitment.[40]

The initial role of the MoD in determining the names of combatants to be demobilised proved insufficient for the patronage requirements of the militia leaders, not least due to the delay in implementing DDR. Many had left the ranks by the time of actual demobilisation. However, the MoD and its local affiliates maintained the ability to manipulate the lists of combatants introduced to DDR, as reported by different sources,[41] in part due to the weak supervision of ANBP and its unwillingness to confront the MoD over irregularities.[42] A variety of issues related to phoney combatants was reported.[43] It is not surprising that the elderly members of the Regional Verification Committees found the power of the local commanders intimidating. It could prevent them from playing their role in the identification of the combatants and they often seem to have ignored instances of malpractice.[44] The interests of the local military leaders were initially protected also by allowing them to pocket part of the cash hand-outs to 'ex-combatants', though the hand-outs were stopped in most of Afghanistan after the first few months.[45]

As illustrated in 'The bureaucratic process', the DIAG process had sufficient inbuilt flaws not to constitute a serious threat to the influence of local military leaders. In principle, provincial governors were supposed to coordinate with the security agencies to identify the illegal armed groups and put pressure on them to comply with DIAG. The Commission was in charge of establishing whether armed groups had effectively been disbanded. With the collaboration of UNAMA and

Table 3.3 Regional distribution of DDR-ed militiamen and of those among them opting for joining ANA

Regions	Distribution of DDR-ed ex-combatants in %	% of all DDR-ed ex-combatants opting for ANA
Kabul	44.4	88.4
Kunduz	11.3	1.2
Mazar-i-Sharif	11.3	4.1
Gardez, Kandahar, Jalabad, Bamyan, Heart	33.0	6.3
Total	100.0	100.0

Source: ANBP.

ANBP, the Afghan security agencies were expected to build as complete as possible a database of Illegal Armed Groups. Unsurprisingly, such cooperation was always far from wholehearted, as demonstrated quite clearly in Takhar province (Table 3.1). Although National Security Directorate (NSD) estimates might have been imprecise and changes might have occurred between 2003 (when these figures were obtained) and 2005, when the DIAG database was launched, it is extremely unlikely that armed groups in most districts of Takhar would have disappeared without trace. Moreover, figures for the three districts covered by the DIAG database are not so dissimilar; in the case of Cha'hab, NSD figures were actually lower than DIAG estimates. The initial contribution to the DIAG database was done by UNAMA, whose information was integrated by ANBP with information gathered during DDR. It appears that UNAMA very diplomatically decided to list as illegal only selected armed groups, known to have a particularly bad record in terms of harassing the population or of being involved in criminal activities.[46] It is also obvious that NSD was not very proactive in integrating UNAMA's and ANBP's figures with more complete data in its possession.

The management of DIAG openly admits that initial estimates were far from complete and it kept updating the database as more information became available, although, as seen, by October 2006 the picture still diverged significantly from the situation on the ground. From the initial 850 groups with 65,000 men, which figured in the database as of early 2005, numbers had risen to 2,753 groups with 180,000 members by January 2006.[47]

The fact that by April 2006, according to ANBP, 944 leaders of illegal armed groups (roughly a third of the registered total) had been confirmed by the DIAG process as having disbanded their groups, while at the same time handing over just 13,500 functioning weapons (just 7.5 per cent of the minimum estimate), suggests that most of those leaders got away with handing over just a fraction of their weapons. In addition, the inclination of leaders of illegal armed groups to comply genuinely with DIAG does not seem to have improved over time. During the first 11 months of DIAG, 66.5 per cent of the weapons handed over were in working condition. During the following year, only 49 per cent of the weapons handed over were serviceable.[48] Some cases of only partial compliance were all too obvious. Matiullah, the most important and best known militia commander of Uruzgan, 'complied' with DIAG in January 2007 by handing over 264 weapons and then continued to run his militia and play a key role in the fight against the Taliban.[49]

Conclusion: compromise in the shadows

Although the international community imposed ownership over the formal DDR–DIAG processes, the wider disarmament and demobilisation effort was largely owned by Afghan players. It is also difficult to believe that the modest impact of the DDR–DIAG processes, as outlined in this chapter, was an accident and the mere result of less-than-competent ANBP management. Had that been the case, a more direct intervention by the main international player (the US) would likely have taken place in the early stages of implementation. While there is an emerging consensus on the fact that the DDR process might have been weakened by American 'disengagement' or lack of interest,[50] opinions differ with regard to motives. Sometimes this is put down to the desire to avoid dealing with an 'incompetent' ANBP, sometimes to political considerations.[51] In the view of this author, the lame DDR process was only in modest part the result of weaknesses on the side of the implementing agencies. Largely, it was the result of a political decision to limit its impact.

In some cases, the Americans had a direct interest in preventing effective demobilisation. In 2005 throughout southern and southeastern Afghanistan, US forces did not have reliable and effective Afghan partners within the state security agencies and did what they could to maintain bits and pieces of AMF and illegal militias. The case of Matinuddin, a close American ally in Uruzgan, has already been mentioned above. Another example is that of AMF's 25th Division in Khost, which continued to operate even after having been formally disbanded. Eventually the unit disappeared, but its commander, General Khialbaz, even as late as mid-2007, was still leading a militia fighting alongside US troops.[52] Even where American interest was not direct, which was most often the case, the attitude of American officials can only be explained as a concern not to challenge the status quo in rural areas, which translated into an inclination to compromise with local military leaders. Reaching such compromise was neither easy nor painless; it was in fact the result of tough negotiations. International organisations and Western diplomats, after some difficult internal bargaining, appear to have reached a consensus on the demand for at least a façade DDR (to save face) and, at least, a partial purge of militia leaders from official positions, not only in the MoD but also in the administration and the MoI. The Afghans grudgingly accepted the disbandment of official militias, as long as they were allowed to continue to exist in the shadows, but demanded that substantial numbers of militia leaders remain or be incorporated in official positions within the MoD, MoI and other ministries. The international counterparts were only willing to accept a modest number of such appointments. Defence Minister Fahim's reluctance to sacrifice some of his local allies cost him American support and his position in the cabinet, but this did not translate into a more confrontational attitude towards local military leaders as a whole. Post-Fahim reform efforts were not aimed at the militias, but focused on Kabul's headquarters and on the quality of appointments to top field positions. What the international side had been demanding was 'presentable' top layers at the MoD and MoI, not the outright elimination of the militias.[53]

The lack of bite in the DDR process, whether deliberate or not, allowed the MoD and allied local military leaders to impose shadowy renegotiations and eventually get away with the preservation of much militia influence in the countryside. Frustrated Japanese experts, never too keen on confronting the militia commanders, at one point even vented the idea of moving straight towards reintegration without implementing the disarmament phase.[54] The point they missed, however, was that the façade of a formal bureaucratic process of disarmament did matter and was not just a residue of an early attempt to impose a more substantial DDR process. Considerations of international politics dictated that the controversial political deal with the militia commanders be covered by a façade of respectability. Significantly, once the DDR process appeared to be faltering in 2004 due to mutual vetoes from different factions, the administration of George W. Bush started showing some interest and intervened diplomatically to re-establish some impetus.[55] Looking at the hyped way in which the DDR–DIAG effort was marketed to the Afghan public, it would appear that the façade was also meant to attract support for international intervention among the sections of the population not involved with any of the militia social blocs. Some observers also argued that the façade was meant to deliver the image of an uncontroversial Afghan success story to increase the likelihood of President Bush being re-elected in 2004.[56] Finally, the bureaucratic façade was likely meant to legitimise the attempted establishment of a pro-American regime in Kabul, contributing to its presentation to the world as something nobler than a merely 'strategic' move.

Was the compromise ultimately successful? In the short term, it achieved stability and legitimisation but at the expense of considerable medium- and long-term loss of support for the foreign intervention by the population at large. The negative impact was amplified by the great hype that initially surrounded the process, raising great expectations among the Afghan population. The complex web of local military commanders covering the Afghan countryside proved difficult to control, particularly once their political patrons in Kabul and in the regions began to be marginalised. Rearmament of DDR-ed militias was already reported in 2005 and such reports grew more frequent in 2006–07.[57] Sometimes the ex-combatants were recruited back, sometimes their relatives or, in any case, younger men took their place. Abuses against the villagers and non-state taxation continued and according to some NGOs, such as the Norwegian Refugee Council and the AIHRC, the number of cases even increased.[58] As criticism of ANBP mounted during 2003–04, its main remaining selling-point was that it at least sought to de-legitimise the militias by abolishing their legal status.[59] While this is true, the fact that this achievement did not form part of a wider strategy to reduce the influence of local military leaders soon emptied it of any meaning. With their success in the parliamentary elections of 2007, when at least 90 out of the 249 elected were militia commanders or their close associates, the militia leaders were once again legitimised and able to cast their influence wider than ever.[60]

Notes

1 ANBP officials often recognised being under pressure from the Afghan side, pressure that mostly took the shape of relentless sabotage and endless negotiations (personal communication with ANBP officials, Kunduz, March 2003, Mazar-i Sharif, June 2004 and Kabul April 2007. See also Rossi and Giustozzi, *Disarmament, Demobilisation and Reintegration of Ex-Combatants (DDR) in Afghanistan*, 18. At one point in 2006–2007 Afghan officials even repeatedly failed to attend the meetings of the DIAG process (personal communication with UN official, Kabul, March 2007).

2 DDR is the standard initialisation adopted for UN-sponsored Disarmament, Demobilisation and Reintegration processes. DIAG (Disarmament of Illegal Armed Groups) is an acronym adopted specifically for post-DDR in Afghanistan.

3 For a more specific study of the political reintegration of armed factions in post-2001 Afghanistan, see Giustozzi, 'Afghanistan: Political Parties or Militia Fronts?'.

4 President of the Republic, 'On the structural reduction of the Ministry of Defense and Heavy Weapons Cantonment throughout the whole country'.

5 See UN DDR Resource Centre, 'Monitoring and Evaluation: Balanced Scorecard for DDR in Afghanistan', at www.unddr.org/tool_docs/Balanced_Scorecard_for_DDR_in_Afghanistan.pdf, for an example of ANBP's 'scorecard'. See also ANBP, 'Partnership for peace'.

6 See ICG, *Disarmament and Reintegration in Afghanistan*, 6.

7 The Ministry of Foreign Affairs of Japan, 'Chair's Summary'.

8 Thruelsen, *From Soldier to Civilian*, 19–20.

9 The cantonment of heavy weaponry was run as a parallel programme to DDR proper and had to be completely preliminarily for AMF units to proceed to demobilisation.

10 ANBP and UN sources, Kabul, 2004–05; Anita Powell, 'Mujahedeen of Afghan valley slow to warm to disarmament', *Stars and Stripes* (Mideast edition), 27 February 2006. See also UN DDR Resource Centre, 'County Programme: Afghanistan', at www.unddr.org/countryprogrammes.php?c = 121.

11 Personal communication with UN and ANBP officials, Mazar-i Sharif, June and August 2004.

12 Personal communication with UN military liaison officer, Kunduz, April 2004. See also Tarzi, 'Afghanistan: Disarming The Militias'.

13 Personal observation, Kunduz, October 2003.

14 Both the website (www.undpanbp.org/) and the issues of the ANBP bulletin reported statistics, supported by evidence, regarding the number of weapons collected.

15 Personal communication with Eckart Schiewek, November 2005.

16 The following section is based on Rossi and Giustozzi, *Disarmament, Demobilisation and Reintegration*.

17 ANBP, 'Reintegration framework'. Unpublished internal paper, Kabul, November 2004.

18 See Dennys, *Disarmament, Demobilization and Rearmament?*, 4.

19 This section is based on Rossi and Giustozzi, *Disarmament, Demobilisation and Reintegration*.

20 UNICEF ran a parallel programme of demobilisation of child soldiers.

21 Presidential decree 20, 24 June 2005.

22 Dennys, *Disarmament, Demobilization and Rearmament?*, 9.

23 See Thruelsen, *From Soldier to Civilian*.

24 See, for example, Chayes, *The punishment of Virtue*, 25–27, 61. See also Berntsen, *Jawbreaker* passim.

25 Interviews and personal communications with UN officials, MoD officers and AMF commanders, 2003–05.

26 See Sky, 'Afghanistan Case Study: The Lead Nation Approach'.

27 Cited in Rossi and Giustozzi, *Disarmament, Demobilisation and Reintegration*, 4.

28 See the Bonn Agreement, V. Final Provisions, which can be found at www.afghangovernment.com/AfghanAgreementBonn.htm.

29 For more details, see Rubin, *Identifying Options and Entry Points*, 4–5.

30 Thruelsen, *From Soldier to Civilian*, 22.

31 Rossi and Giustozzi, *Disarmament, Demobilisation and Reintegration*, 10.

32 On Afghanistan's police, see Amnesty International, *Afghanistan: Police Reconstruction Essential for the Protection of Human Rights*; Inspectors General, US Department of State and US Defense. *Interagency Assessment*; Serchuk, *Cop Out*; Wilder, *Cops or Robbers?*; ICG, *Reforming Afghanistan's Police*.

33 See Giustozzi, *Koran, Kalashnikov and Laptop.*
34 Personal communication with UN and NSD officials, Kunduz and Takhar, February 2004.
35 Presidential decree 50, Kabul, 14 July 2004.
36 Gul Agha Shirzai, a strongman from the Barakzai tribe, was the main player in Kandahar province in 2002–04.
37 Ismail Khan, one of the key figures in the anti-Taliban alliance, controlled through his private militias most of western Afghanistan after 2001. Linked to Jami'at-i Islami, however, he was keen on maintaining his own autonomy.
38 The 'Islamic Society' is one of the Islamist parties which fought in the jihad first (1978–92) and in the civil wars later (1992–2001). It has a predominantly Tajik membership.
39 Personal communication with UN official, Kabul, September 2004.
40 See Giustozzi, 'Auxiliary Force or National Army?'.
41 See Rossi and Giustozzi, *Disarmament, Demobilisation and Reintegration*, 5.
42 Personal communication with former ANBP official, Kabul, April 2007.
43 Rossi and Giustozzi, *Disarmament, Demobilisation and Reintegration*, 5.
44 Ibid., 4; personal communication with former ANBP officials, Kabul, April 2007.
45 Interviews with UN and ANBP officials, Kunduz, 2003–04. Owing to this, cash handouts were suspended by ANBP.
46 Personal observation, Kunduz, 2003–04 and Mazar-i Sharif, 2004; personal communication with UN officials, Kabul, May and October 2005.
47 ANBP sources, 2005–06. The data still includes information from just 12 provinces out of 34.
48 ANBP sources, 2005–06.
49 *ANBP Newsletter*, January 2007, p. 1; personal communication with UN official, March 2007.
50 See among others Rubin, *Identifying Options*, 7–8.
51 See Rossi and Giustozzi, *Disarmament, Demobilisation and Reintegration*, 5.
52 Personal communication with former ANBP official, Kabul, April 2007.
53 This section is based on personal communications with UN officials and diplomats, 2003–07.
54 See Rossi and Giustozzi, *Disarmament, Demobilisation and Reintegration*, 5.
55 Sedra, 'Afghanistan: Democracy Before Peace?'.
56 See, for example, Roughneen, 'Unhappy prospects for Afghan security'.
57 Dennys, *Disarmament, Demobilization and Rearmament?*, 7; personal communication with UN officials, Kunduz, May 2006; personal communication with police officer, Teluqan, May 2006.
58 Rossi and Giustozzi, *Disarmament, Demobilisation and Reintegration*, 18–19. See also Dennys, *Disarmament, Demobilization and Rearmament?*, 7–8.
59 Interview with ANBP official, Mazar-i Sharif, June 2004.
60 Carlotta Gall, 'Islamists and Mujahedeen Secure Victory in Afghan Vote', *New York Times*, 23 October 2005; interviews with diplomats and UN officials, Kabul, October 2005.

References

Amnesty International, 2003. *Afghanistan: Police Reconstruction Essential for the Protection of Human Rights*, Amnesty International, London.
ANBP Partnership for peace: Afghanistan's New Beginnings Program, 2003–2006. Kabul.
——, 2004. 'Reintegration Framework', unpublished internal paper, Kabul.
Berntsen, Gary, 2005. *Jawbreaker*, Three Rivers Press, New York.

Chayes, Sarah, 2006. *The Punishment of Virtue*, Penguin Press, New York.

Dennys, C., 2005. *Disarmament, Demobilization and Rearmament? The Effect of Disarmament in Afghanistan*, Afghan NGO Network, Japan.

Giustozzi, A., 2007. 'Afghanistan: Political Parties or Militia Fronts?', in de Zeeuw, J. (ed.), *Transforming Rebel Movements After Civil Wars*, Lynne Rienner, Boulder, CO.

——, 2007. *Koran, Kalashnikov and Laptop: The Neo-Taliban Insurgency in Afghanistan*, C. Hurst & Co, London.

——, 2007. 'Auxiliary Force or National Army? Afghanistan's "ANA" and the Counter-Insurgency Effort, 2002–2006', *Small Wars and Insurgencies* 18:1.

Inspectors General, US Department of State and US Defence, 2006. *Interagency Assessment of Afghanistan Police Training and Readiness*, Washington DC.

International Crisis Group (ICG), 2003. *Disarmament and Reintegration in Afghanistan*, Asia Report No. 65, ICG, Kabul/Brussels.

——, 2007. *Reforming Afghanistan's Police*. Asia Report No. 138, ICG, Kabul/Brussels.

Ministry of Foreign Affairs of Japan, 2003. 'Chair's Summary: The Tokyo Conference on Consolidation of Peace (DDR) in Afghanistan – Change of Order "from Guns to Plows"', 22 February, at www.mofa.go.jp/region/middle_e/afghanistan/pv0302/ddr_sum.html.

President of the Republic of Afghanistan (decree dated 27 April 2004), 'On the structural reduction of the Ministry of Defense and Heavy Weapons Cantonment throughout the whole country'.

Rossi, S. and Giustozzi, A., 2006. 'Disarmament, Demobilisation and Reintegration of Ex-Combatants (DDR) in Afghanistan: Constraints and Limited Capabilities', Working Papers series 2, no. 2, Crisis States Research Centre (LSE), London.

Roughneen, Simon, n.d. 'Unhappy prospects for Afghan security', The Oxford Council on Good Governance, Security Briefing no. 4.

Rubin, Barnett R., 2003. *Identifying Options and Entry Points for Disarmament, Demobilization, and Reintegration in Afghanistan*, Center on International Cooperation, New York University, New York.

Sedra, Mark, 2004. 'Afghanistan: Democracy Before Peace?', *Foreign Policy in Focus – Special Report*.

Serchuk, Vance, 2006. 'Cop Out: Why Afghanistan has no Police'. *American Enterprise Institute for Public Policy Research*.

Sky, Emma, 2007. 'Afghanistan Case Study: The Lead Nation Approach', in Nathan, L. (ed.), *No Ownership, No Commitment: A Guide to Local Ownership of Security Sector Reform*, University of Birmingham, Birmingham.

Tarzi, Amin, 2005. 'Afghanistan: Disarming the Militias – Which Militias and Which Arms?', *RL/RFE* 20 April.

Thruelsen, Peter Dahl, 2006. *From Soldier to Civilian: Disarmament Demobilisation Reintegration in Afghanistan*, Danish Institute for International Studies, Copenhagen.

Wilder, A., 2007. *Cops or Robbers?*, Afghan Research and Evaluation Unit, Kabul.

4 Militias, tribes and insurgents

The challenge of political reintegration in Iraq

David H. Ucko

Introduction

The conflict in Iraq, ongoing since the US-led invasion in 2003, presents a uniquely inauspicious context for the political reintegration of irregular armed groups. With the overthrow of Saddam Hussein, the reintegration of Iraqi militias and other armed forces was to occur in an environment where new state structures were only just emerging. Militia and insurgency groups were thus asked to lay down their arms for the sake of a political system whose sustainability and dispensation of power were far from certain and with no guarantee that security be maintained subsequent to their dissolution. The situation distinguishes itself further by the fact that none of the targeted armed groups had won or been defeated in the war leading up to regime change. Rather than as victors and losers, the groups were defined and treated according to their supposed proximity to Saddam Hussein prior to the war. Sufficiently complex, this effort at reintegration was also to proceed alongside a hugely ambitious exercise in state building, conducted by a reluctant 'nation-builder' short on plans and personnel, in a region marked by tension and in which the intervening state suffered a lack of legitimacy. Yet in this context of few positives, the process of political reintegration was perhaps most fatally undermined by the dearth of attention paid, by both the Coalition Provisional Authority (CPA) in Iraq and the Bush administration in Washington, to this critical component of state building.

The purpose of this article is to demonstrate the significance of the low prioritisation of political reintegration in Iraq's subsequent unravelling. The story is familiar: in the years following the US invasion, Iraq experienced a descent into civil war characterised by insurgent violence, militia rule, crime and insecurity. US authorities and forces were badly prepared to counter this downwards spiral and in some ways contributed to it. The Iraqi government and security forces were similarly unable, or even unwilling, to address the growing anarchy, all of which reinforced the scope for vigilante violence and tit-for-tat retaliations among rival militias. By 2006, the situation had reached a nadir, marked by insurgent attacks, roaming Shia death squads targeting Sunni civilian populations and a government infiltrated by sectarian agents.

While these developments have received substantial attention elsewhere, the concern here is the degree to which these challenges grew out of the initial failure to formulate and implement an effective reintegration strategy – one able to transform 'insurgent' and other non-state armed groups into viable political entities; from potential 'spoilers' to groups and key individuals that are prepared to eschew armed struggle and participate in peaceful political intercourse. Within the context of Iraq, such a strategy would have targeted the former armed forces of the Saddam Hussein regime, the insurgency to have arisen soon after its dismantling, and the Shia and Kurdish militias that returned to Iraq following the invasion or that formed shortly thereafter. The focus is thus on the crystallisation of a new Iraqi government and the efforts taken to include or exclude the leaders of Iraq's many irregular armed groups in this deeply political process.

The article concludes with an examination of the United States' so-called 'surge' strategy, implemented in early 2007, and the ensuing improvement in the Iraqi security situation. Though the factors contributing to the lull in violence had little to do with reintegration, it did bring groups and individuals formerly seen as irreconcilable into accommodative arrangements and local ceasefires, resulting in greater stability and leading the way, possibly, towards permanent reintegration. Examining this volte-face sheds light on how reintegration can occur in the most inauspicious of circumstances and in the absence of the formal type of DDR strategy anticipated through much of the literature. Nothing here should suggest that the security gains achieved through the surge are irreversible, uncontested or tantamount to strategic victory for the US. As will be seen, it is also far from certain whether the lack of a comprehensive government-owned reintegration strategy will not, in time, be felt.

Getting off on the wrong foot

Many of the problems associated with militias, insurgents and civil war in Iraq stem from the initial US failure to implement a workable reintegration plan following the overthrow of Saddam Hussein in April 2003. Compounding the lack of a viable strategy, the invading force knew very little about Iraqi society and its actors; it was, therefore, unable to devise effective policy on the fly. Instead, CPA's reintegration policy was an amalgam of unquestioned assumptions regarding the Iraqi state, hunches as to whom could be trusted, and retributive urges targeting all those associated with the former regime. This combination of incompetence and ignorance coloured the CPA's initial approach to Saddam's security forces, the mounting insurgency and to the Shia and Kurdish militias eager to stake a claim in the newly liberated Iraq.

The desire to reform and to punish Saddam Hussein's armed forces led to CPA Order 2, issued on 23 May 2003, which dissolved most of Iraq's official security-related institutions.[1] Perceived as embodiments of Saddam's totalitarian regime, these forces were to be removed and replaced with the yet-to-be-established security structures of the yet-to-be-formed successor regime. The architects of CPA Order 2 have since argued that the edict simply recognised a fait accompli, as the Iraqi forces had self-demobilised during the US invasion.[2] Even so, only a desire for retribution or a lack of planning (or both) can explain the subsequent failure to pay the sacked soldiers, many of whom felt spurned and turned against the occupation.[3] These soldiers were not reintegrated as much as deliberately alienated. With easy access to weapons, in a country awash with munitions, they mounted a potent threat to the US presence in Iraq and to its partners within the emerging government.[4]

The CPA's adversarial approach towards the former security structures of the Ba'athist regime also coloured its response to the low-level violence that emerged soon after the invasion. Even when the threat of insurgency was recognised, there was no talk of placating those opposing the US efforts in Iraq. In general, the CPA

> insisted that all of the problems of the country were caused by the insurgency – rather than that all of the problems of the country were helping to fuel the insurgency – and that ... the insurgency was really about al-Qa'ida operatives and former regime "dead-enders".[5]

While this characterisation was in some cases accurate, blind devotion to Saddam Hussein was rarely the driving force behind the violence; many of those who took up arms felt offended by the occupation and had only a loose affiliation with the Ba'athist party (which had after all dominated most walks of life). Regardless, the CPA's characterisation of the adversary served to obscure the insurgency's nationalist dimension and encouraged strategies of coercion rather than co-option.[6] In many areas, the principal response to the insecurity was to 'kill-capture' insurgents, the flaws of which have been widely discussed. In short, the US lacked the necessary intelligence to locate its enemy; the troop numbers to hold cities and towns; the legitimacy to gain popular support; and the familiarity with counterinsurgency to appreciate the centrality of its 'non-military' components: the delivery of basic services, provision of security and establishment of legitimate governing and administrative structures. The strategy contributed to an escalated insurgency, which in turn generated a climate of insecurity and fear.

This context helps explain the second tenet of the CPA's initial reintegration strategy (or lack thereof) – that concerning Iraq's militias. These paramilitary organisations had long opposed the rule of Saddam Hussein and were operating from various sanctuaries – often Iran in the case of the Shia militias or in Iraq's protected northern territory in the case of the Kurdish Peshmerga. With Saddam's overthrow, the obvious question was how to deal with these forces: the Shia militias were returning to Iraq and the Peshmerga had itself contributed to the US war effort in Iraq's north.

The initial US intention had been to 'DDR sub-state militias' – to disarm, demobilise and reintegrate their members into society – and the Pentagon's Office of Reconstruction and Humanitarian Assistance (ORHA) was pledged a $70-million contract to this end.[7] ORHA hastily put together a plan to establish

DDR offices in the north, centre and south; to inform former fighters of the benefits available to them through the DDR process; and to provide them, upon registration, with a place in the new security services, a pension or vocational training.[8] Whatever its flaws and potential, the plan was never executed: when ORHA was replaced by the CPA on 21 April 2003, and retired general Jay Garner was succeeded by Ambassador L. Paul Bremer, the whole notion of DDR, for the Iraqi armed forces as for the militia, was abandoned.[9] In part, this was because senior officials at the US Department of Defence did not want to spend funds on the defeated forces of Saddam Hussein.[10] Yet in torpedoing the DDR effort for the former security forces, the Shia and Kurdish militia were also left in place.

The CPA did not perceive this outcome as particularly problematic. After all, these groups were opposed to Saddam Hussein; there was a sense that they deserved some sort of reward or recognition.[11] The militia also did not appear to resist the US presence in Iraq. The Kurdish parties were content to let the Peshmerga maintain security in Iraq's northern provinces, where they had operated before the war, and pledged to join the Iraqi security forces once they were created.[12] The Supreme Council for the Islamic Revolution in Iraq (SCIRI) also assumed a seemingly positive stance towards the occupation. On 31 May 2003, it announced that its 10,000-strong militia, the Badr Corps, had relinquished its heavy weapons – a symbolic, if nonetheless spurious claim.[13] In September, SCIRI changed the name of the Badr Corps to the 'Badr Organisation'; to SCIRI leader Abdul-Aziz al-Hakim, the move signalled the force's transformation 'into a civil organisation' that would 'play a role in the restoration of security and the reconstruction and building of a new Iraq'.[14] This was, thus, a further gesture showing just to what extent SCIRI did *not* present a threat to the US state-building effort. Moreover, in terms of its operations, the Shia militia appeared predominantly engaged in security duties, such as the guarding of mosques and other holy places – tasks that the American leadership in any case preferred to delegate, particularly given the shortfall in US troops.[15]

Indeed, between the escalating violence, the lack of US troops and the preoccupation with other issues – the search for Saddam Hussein, or his alleged weapons of mass destruction – the reintegration of seemingly cooperative militias did not present itself as a priority. Given the widespread instability,

> Walter Slocombe, the CPA's director for national security from May to November 2003 ... was sympathetic to the political parties who said their militias were an 'insurance policy' pending a political solution that would ensure their security against other groups.[16]

The Shia and Kurdish militias were thus not reintegrated; they were allowed to thrive because of the security vacuum created through the US occupation. The Peshmerga continued to dominate in the north and, in the south, the Badr Organisation remained essentially intact, all while infiltrating the local security units that would later be subsumed within the national police.

The appearance of a common cause between the Shia militias and the US forces was largely illusory, or at least transient. All while collaborating with the CPA, SCIRI leaders denounced the United States as 'colonialists' for having invaded Iraq; in April, they also shunned a major CPA-organised conference at which Iraq's leaders were to discuss the country's political future.[17] More seriously, Shia militias were quickly assuming control of the south of the country, filling the political space left by the collapse of the central regime; and where Coalition forces were at their thinnest.[18] While their action seldom resulted in armed confrontations with the occupying forces, the militias did insist on total freedom of action. Thus, the one attempt to rein in these sub-state forces – a UK effort to disarm forcibly the town of Majar al-Kabir in June 2003 – resulted in the deaths of six Royal Military Police and was the last such action in the southeast for some time.[19] In the following months, the CPA 'decided that dealing with the militias was not a high priority [and], instead, Coalition military units made tactical arrangements with militias on an ad hoc basis'.[20]

This understanding further encouraged the various Shia militias to assume local control of security and of other functions of state. Not only did this threaten the state-building enterprise in Iraq; it also begged the question of who, exactly, was in charge. The problem was compounded by the fact that the Shia militias themselves competed for power, through sermons in the mosques as well as violence in the streets.[21] In April 2003, the moderate and influential Shia cleric, Abdul Majid Khoei, who was working with US forces, was hacked to death by a Shia mob in Najaf. The same movement surrounded the home of Iraq's most senior cleric, Ayatollah Ali Sistani – another influential and moderate Shia leader – and ordered him to leave town (before being persuaded to disperse by tribal elders in the city). In August 2003, the suspected sponsor of both incidents, Moqtada al-Sadr, founded a new Shia militia, the Mahdi Army, which established itself as a powerful anti-American force and as a counterpoint to the other militias left in place post-invasion, principally the Badr Organisation. In Spencer Ackerman's words, 'as Sadr saw SCIRI grow stronger – with US acquiescence – he felt the need to respond in kind'.[22] In the following year, Sadr established his own law in large parts of the country and geared up for future violence.[23]

A strategy emerges

The CPA did eventually recognise the potential challenge posed by the militias. In November 2003, Walter Slocombe was replaced by David Gompert, who received instruction from Bremer to eliminate the sub-state paramilitaries; their power, it was felt, was threatening the viability of the Iraqi state.[24] The policy shift led to the development of the Transition and Reintegration Strategy, issued on 21 May 2004. As Thomas Mowle explains, the new strategy was in many ways sound: it recognised that the security and social functions served by the militias would have to be supplanted before these forces would stand down. It also acknowledged that, for historical reasons, the militia leaders were distrustful of the central government and that the Coalition, therefore, would face difficulties persuading them to disarm, particularly as the nature and composition of the new government remained uncertain. In recognition of these obstacles, the strategy paper noted that the 'transition and reintegration' (TR) process would need to be long term, lasting years.[25]

On 1 June 2004, following months of negotiations, David Gompert signed reintegration memoranda with nine Iraq militias, representing a combined total of 102,000 fighters.[26] The list of participating groups included the Kurdish parties, SCIRI, Iraqi Hezbollah and the Da'wa Party but excluded the Mahdi Army, which was disqualified as it was created *after* the US invasion.[27] Even so, the participating militias agreed to designate themselves as 'residual elements' and committed themselves to a timetable for their own dissolution through the three tracks presented in the Transition and Reintegration Strategy: reintegration into the security forces; a pension commensurate to that of an Iraqi soldier; or vocational training for civilian employment.[28]

With the memoranda signed, the CPA issued Order 91 on 7 June, which provided the legal basis for the reintegration process.[29] The order set out the conditions imposed on the 'residual elements': until their final dissolution, they were to cease all recruitment and armament; restrict themselves to security operations (which also required the prior approval of the Ministry of the Interior (MoI) and the US military command) and inform the government as to their composition and arsenals. To oversee this process, Order 91 created the Transition and Reintegration Implementation Committee (TRIC), to be chaired by the MoI. Failure to comply with Order 91 would result in a change of status from 'residual element' to 'illegal armed force or militia', at which time the transgressing force would void its temporary right to exist and face punitive measures, the nature of which would be determined by TRIC through discussions with Iraqi and Coalition authorities.[30]

From the policy vacuum of 2003, a plan had emerged. Even so, action taken to reintegrate the militias remained minimal, reflecting a continued disinterest in this component of state building. A RAND report notes that the TR effort 'was unfunded and all but unstaffed as late as the start of 2004' and that by the spring, when the new strategy emerged, 'the CPA TR office was one person strong'.[31] The CPA also assumed that the TR process would not require substantial funding – around $14.3 million – and that it would instead lean on existing programmes and budgets.[32] This assumption proved optimistic: the supporting programmes were rarely fully developed and they lacked the resources to finance the reintegration of some 102,000 fighters. The TR plan had stipulated continued Coalition support and funding for reintegration, but nothing ever materialised on this front.[33] Instead, some reports claimed that 'millions of dollars earmarked for militia demobilisation and reintegration were actually used to address unplanned-for security threats'.[34]

The TR programme was further undermined by its lack of realism. Neither the Iraqi government nor the US military were able to provide the reintegrating militias a security guarantee. Given the Sunni-dominated insurgency and the ongoing power-struggle between Shia militias, the leaders of these forces saw no reason to disarm or to stand down.[35] Misgivings towards the reintegration process were heightened following Moqtada al-Sadr's uprising in April 2004, through which he seized control over Najaf, Kufa and other strategically located cities.[36] In this climate, the vocational training programmes did not seem particularly relevant. Sensing danger, the 'residual elements' also refused to provide the government with information on their composition and armaments – a requirement of Order 91 but not, significantly, of the TR memoranda signed the week earlier.[37]

This context made the short timelines for reintegration particularly unfortunate – and unrealistic. Whereas the Transition and Reintegration Strategy had recommended a five-year schedule for reintegration, to be completed by 2009, the memoranda advanced this deadline to the end of 2005. In addition, when Ayad Allawi, then the prime minister of Iraq, announced Order 91, he declared that 90,000 militia members would be processed by January 2005.[38] As Mowle notes, 'the five-year approach recommended by the strategy had now shrunk to, effectively, seven months'.[39] The narrowing timelines were testament to the desperation of the CPA and the Iraqi government somehow to control the militias, quickly, or to a serious underestimation of what reintegration would require. Either way, Order 91 set unrealistic targets whose eventual transgression served to compromise the integrity of the entire process.

The reintegration process was also undercut by a lack of trust and goodwill. While US authorities viewed reintegration as bringing armed forces under legal and civil control, the militia leadership saw it as an opportunity to insert their supporters in the emerging security structures as a power base, and to exclude those of potential rivals. Hazim al-Shaalan, the interim Defence Minister and an ally of the secular Achmed Chalabi, was for example opposed to the inclusion of 'Islamists' in the security services, which barred the majority of militia fighters from reintegration. Meanwhile, those who sought reintegration demanded ranks beyond what was offered, while those opting for a pension found it difficult to prove their eligibility to sceptical government officials.[40] A final lack of support for the TR strategy, through despondency or disinterest, meant that it floundered. In the months following its formulation, 'job training programs run by Allawi's Labour Ministry were cancelled over personal feuds and pension programs and other aspects of the program of DDR ... were bounced around from one command to another'.[41] With time, the ministries of defence and of labour and social affairs gradually eliminated the first and third tracks: reintegration into the security forces and the provision of vocational training.[42]

Left to their own devices, the 'residual elements' proceeded to breach the many conditions of their reintegration plans. Despite the strong language in Order 91 of 'disciplinary measures and penalties', no significant action was taken to punish the transgressors; nor had Order 91 set out who was to mete out these measures.[43] The militias were thus allowed to operate as before and for the same reasons as before: the US preoccupation with the Sunni-driven insurgency, the lack of troops to provide security and the fear of upsetting the Shia militias and thereby open up a second front alongside the ongoing campaign against insurgents and criminal actors.[44]

Reintegration by default

With Order 91 failing, the political reintegration of militias and of their leaders occurred by default – without any conditions, strategy or monitoring mechanism. This process of transforming militia groups into political entities had already begun with the establishment of the Iraqi Governing Council (IGC) on 13 July 2003, but it was powerfully entrenched through the handover of sovereignty to the Interim Iraqi Government in May 2004 and the Iraqi elections of 2005. The unchecked process of political reintegration embarked upon in 2003 would in the end determine the political balance of power in post-war Iraq and initiate a vicious and seemingly irreversible circle of violence.

Soon after the initial invasion, the CPA appointed a body of Iraqi authorities to the IGC, which was to advise the CPA and lend an Iraqi face to the occupation. The US wanted the IGC to be established quickly and for its membership to reflect Iraq's ethnic composition – as a body founded by the US, this was to be its claim to legitimacy.[45] Problematically, the US was in too much of a hurry to allow and encourage truly representative leaders to emerge from the clean slate that was Iraqi civil society in 2003.[46] Instead, CPA officials distributed political power to 'twenty-five Iraqi leaders well-known *to them*' and who appeared to represent the ethnic constituents of Iraq – that is, the leaders of the political wings of the country's various militias.[47] Appointed to the Council in this fashion were Abdul-Aziz al-Hakim of SCIRI; Abdel-Karim Mahoud al-Mohammedawi of the Hezbollah party in Iraq; Ibrahim al-Jaafari and Ezzidin Salim of Da'wa; and Massoud Barzani and Jalal Talabani, chief commanders of the Peshmerga force. With the possible exception of the last two, these individuals did not enjoy much public support, even among their supposed constituents; their promotion was instead based on their opposition to Saddam Hussein, their unmistakable ethnic identity and the power they held through their control of militias. The influence of these appointed leaders on Council affairs was nonetheless to be significant: four of them served as IGC presidents, a rotating position, and they competed against Council members who were either similarly unknown to the Iraqi population or perceived as illegitimate outsiders.[48]

The placement of militia leaders on the IGC, coupled with the United States' reliance on these Council members to give the appearance of an orderly transition to Iraqi rule, severely limited US options for dealing with non-complying militias. The result can be seen as *a false process of political reintegration*: as Larry Diamond has put it,

> the menace of radical, Iranian-backed armed militias … was mounting rapidly … even as the leaders of their sponsoring political parties were sitting in Baghdad on the Iraqi Governing Council, signing democratic declarations and evincing to their American interlocutors sweet moderation and restraint.[49]

The set-up offered a poor foundation to the Transition and Reintegration Strategy and militated against the notion of an Iraqi government loyal to the state.

This unconditional co-option of militia leaders could plausibly have been reversed with the dissolution of the IGC and the handover of sovereignty to a new Iraqi government. Instead, at an extraordinary meeting on 15 November 2003, the Bush administration elected to transfer authority over Iraq to the members of the IGC, who were to form the nucleus of the new Interim Iraqi Government (IIG). With US presidential elections looming and with violence in Iraq unabated, the ease of transferring sovereignty to the established Iraqi leadership of the ICG seemed all too appealing – at least in Washington. Yet because of the continuity of the transition, 'all the problems that dogged the IGC, its lack of legitimacy, its inability to forge meaningful links with the population and criticisms of it being appointed and not elected' resurfaced.[50]

Nor did this imperfect arrangement guarantee security; much like Order 91, the political incorporation of militia leaders did not apply to Iraq's Sunni tribes and armed groups.[51] The difference was of course that these elements were actively opposing the US effort in Iraq, which raised problems for their reintegration. First, there was the emotive issue of dealing with those responsible for US military casualties. When on 3 August 2004 Deputy Prime Minister Barham Salih announced an amnesty plan to co-opt Sunni insurgents, its scope was immediately curbed by American officials, who insisted that it exclude those responsible for killing US servicemen. The issue of amnesty always presents moral dilemmas. In this instance, the Sunnis perceived their armed activity as resistance against occupation and their exclusion from the amnesty, for having targeted what from a guerrilla-warfare perspective were nonetheless legitimate military targets, was therefore strongly contested. Indeed, both Shi'ite and Sunni leaders vigorously opposed the amnesty deal, arguing that 'those who resist the American occupation are patriots and have no need for official pardon' – a position that clashed with the US desire not to 'reward' its adversaries or allow them, possibly, to launch future attacks.[52] In the end, this and other similar efforts at reintegration came to naught.

It should also be recalled that the US military for a long time saw Sunni insurgents as seeking nothing less than the return of Saddam Hussein – hence their characterisation of the insurgents as 'dead-enders', 'foreign-regime loyalists', 'Ba'athists', etc. 'The logic of this argument', says Toby Dodge, was that 'the violence is highly unrepresentative of Iraqi population opinion … and politically limited to those fanatical enough or unintelligent enough not to realise that the old regime is dead and buried'.[53] The reality was more complex: as Vice President Tariq al-Hashimi explained at the Council of Foreign Relations in 2006, sections within what the US termed 'the insurgency' could be cast as 'resistance', groups opposed to the US presence in Iraq but willing, according to al-Hashimi, 'to contribute and to participate in the political process as long as we offer to them … a workable [and] significant project to accommodate them'.[54] This distinction was not then apparent to the US military, which tended to misconceive the Sunni insurgents as inherently irreconcilable and as impervious to all but armed force.[55] Nor did the US military fully accept that indiscriminate security operations and the mass detention of Sunni Iraqis would fan rather than quash the insurgency.[56]

Through this rushed accommodation of Shia militia leaders – and the refusal to co-opt, while still failing to coerce, the Sunni resistance – the United States sowed the seeds of many of Iraq's later problems. This was also a mess from which extrication would be difficult. Once in government, the militia leaders gained control over specific ministries, which quickly 'turned into party fiefdoms directly breaking governmental coherence'.[57] Henceforth, the arrangements of the Iraqi government were spun to serve the interests of particular leaders and groups rather than, necessarily, those of Iraq. The Transitional Administrative Law (TAL) – Iraq's interim constitution – was produced as a compromise between Shi'ite and Kurdish interests but gave little room to Sunni preferences.[58] Similarly, the emergence of new security structures, including the Army, was heavily politicised and took on a sectarian character, further highlighting the Sunnis' disenfranchisement.[59] The de-Ba'athification Council, overseeing the dismantling of the former regime, allowed Shi'ite Ba'athists to repent and reintegrate but remained firm against their Sunni former colleagues, who were thereby barred from senior government positions.[60] All this time, the Sunni witnessed their weapons being forcibly seized, while the Shia and Kurdish militias were allowed to operate freely.

Elections: entrenching the problem

If the Shia militia leaders were treated all too kindly, the Sunni leaders were indiscriminately excluded – a distribution of power and privilege that soon became self-perpetuating. This vicious circle was only entrenched by the two elections held in Iraq in January and December 2005. The January election was designed to create a Transitional National Assembly (TNA), which would be charged with drafting a new Iraqi constitution. The election passed off without major problems, but it was undermined by the legacy of failed reintegration. Entrenched as the likely political elite, the IIG's Kurdish and Shi'ite militia leaders did comparatively well; in contrast, the Sunni leadership – excluded so far from government and the target, instead, of an aggressive counterinsurgency campaign – decided that political participation was not in their best interest.[61] Their boycott of the elections further strengthened the Shi'ite and Kurdish parties' hold on government; these groups now dominated the TNA and controlled the appointment of senior government officials – while the Sunnis remained excluded and with little to gain through party politics.[62]

By this point, even the recalcitrant Moqtada al-Sadr had found a place in government. Following clashes earlier in 2004, the Coalition reached a deal with Sadr on 9 October, whereby militia members were paid to turn in their weapons and Sadr was offered to join the government.[63] As with the previous round of disarmament and political reintegration, there was no expectation or demand that all arms be handed over or that the Mahdi Army disband or shift its allegiance to the central government. The cost of reducing violence between US forces and the Mahdi Army was thus the unconditional accommodation of al-Sadr within the Iraqi government, where his officials sat side-by-side with those of other militia-wielding parties. Again, the contradiction was palpable: Sadr 'consistently denounced the occupation and displayed sympathy for the armed opposition while simultaneously participating in the political process the US set up and which the armed groups combat'.[64]

Their sectarian rule legitimised through elections, the dominant parties used their position in government to consolidate their power. The new constitution, written by the victors of the January election and completed in October 2005, was widely seen by Sunnis as a 'sectarian text' – one that 'prescribed a form of federalism that would facilitate the dissolution of the state ... [and] that would leave the Sunni Arab community landlocked and without oil'.[65] The constitution also seemed to condone the continued existence of militias: while it prohibited the 'formation of military militia outside the framework of the armed forces', it also reserved the right of 'regional governments' to establish 'the internal security forces for the region such as police, security forces and guards'.[66] It was no surprise that while Shi'ite and Kurdish voters supported the new constitution in the 15 October referendum, the Sunni community overwhelmingly voted against it (while also narrowly failing to defeat it).[67]

The ministries of the new government were also divided up between the dominant parties and transformed into sectarian powerbases. Sadr loyalists gained control of the ministries of health and of transportation, which were purged of their Sunni employees and taken over by sworn Sadrists.[68] In later months, two officials associated with al-Sadr – Hakim al-Zamili, then the deputy health minister, and Brig.-Gen. Hamid Hamza Alwan Abbas al-Shamari, a commander of the ministry's security force – allegedly turned Baghdad's hospitals into 'death zones for Sunnis seeking treatment there'.[69] The two 'were accused of organizing and supporting the murder of Sunni doctors; the use of ambulances to transfer weapons for Shi'ite militia members; and the torture and kidnapping of Sunni patients'.[70]

SCIRI, meanwhile, appointed Bayan Jabr Solagh, a former Badr commander, to the post of Interior Minister. He proceeded to sack hundreds of Sunni officials working in the Ministry, claiming that they were criminals.[71] Henceforth, MoI recruits required a *tazkiya*, or letter of reference, from a SCIRI office or mosque.[72] Jabr also announced that militias would increasingly be incorporated into the Interior Ministry's security structures.[73] This was something President and Peshmerga leader Jalal Talabani could readily agree on. At a meeting on 8 June 2005, he underlined that the 'heroes of Badr' – along with the Peshmerga – were valued by the Iraqi state: 'You and the Peshmerga are wanted and are important to fulfilling this sacred task, to establishing a democratic, federal, and independent Iraq'.[74] The US administration had assumed that political power would provide militia leaders the guarantees necessary to disband their forces.[75] Instead, the militias simply transitioned into the security structures to further the sectarian interests of their masters, but in the legitimising uniforms of the national forces.[76]

This form of reintegration had two broad effects on Iraqi politics and security. First, the reality of a government ruled by militia leaders and run according to sectarian interests prompted many Sunnis to align themselves with the insurgency and with emerging extremist groups, such as al-Qaeda in Iraq (AQI), for protection or for revenge. 'Knowing they could not win democratically, and fearing the consequences of living as a minority, civil war seemed like the best hope.'[77] Frustration and suspicion of the emerging political system led to a rise in attacks directed against the occupying forces and the political institutions that they had put in place. Given the sectarian nature of Iraqi politics, the violence also assumed a distinctly ethnic dimension, particularly following the bombing of the Shia al-Askariyya mosque in Samarra on 22 February 2006.[78]

Second, when the Sunnis did engage in politics, they too mobilised under a strictly sectarian flag, contributing further to the fractured nature of Iraqi politics. Thus, even though a Sunni coalition, the Iraqi Accord Front (IAF), did in the end participate in the December 2005 legislative elections, 'each alliance focused its energy on cementing support among its own base, while doggedly obstructing intrusions by other alliances into its home area'.[79] By the time Nouri al-Maliki, the new prime minister, came to dole out ministerial positions and political authority, he still faced a series of sectarian coalitions, each of which vied to fill ministries with its own lackeys.[80]

No basis for progress

In part, this unfortunate outcome of democratisation stemmed from the constitutional set-up of the Iraqi government, which does not afford the prime minister much bargaining power. Constitutionally, the prime minister is at best a primus inter pares requiring the buy-in of ministers to implement policy. These ministers are, however, loyal to the parties that they represent and which appointed them.[81] Furthermore, Maliki also had to answer to the United States' preferences, which did not always overlap with those of the Iraqi body politic, such as it was. All of this explains why the Iraqi PM was on the whole unable to counteract the false political reintegration of militia leaders or to address the bar on reintegration imposed on the Sunni community since 2003.

In May 2006, for example, Maliki managed to dislodge Bayan Jabr from the MoI and replace him with the independent Jawad al-Bolani. However, as Toby Dodge explains, 'the weakness of the prime minister's position meant that Jabr could not simply be sacked from the cabinet, but was instead moved sideways to become minister of finance' – a position which he has allegedly used to obstruct reconstruction projects in Baghdad's Sunni areas.[82] Lacking a strong backer, al-Bolani by the same logic has struggled to reform the MoI or to dismantle the death squads created during Jabr's reign. Indeed, throughout 2006, the MoI was increasingly penetrated by Sadr's Mahdi Army, which transitioned into the security forces in large numbers.[83]

In June 2006, Maliki announced a 24-point strategy for a National Reconciliation and Dialogue Project, which was to include an amnesty for insurgents and a review of de-Ba'athification regulations. Clearly, this was an attempt to smother the escalating violence and provide a clean break to those who had taken up arms. The amnesty was initially going to apply to those responsible for attacks on US forces; only those guilty for 'the shedding of innocent Iraqis' blood' would be excluded.[84] However, following pressure from the US and from SCIRI, the final version of the bill barred anyone involved in the killing of American or of Iraqi security forces. As Maliki put it, 'The fighter who did not kill anyone will be included in the amnesty, but the fighter who killed someone will not be.'[85] This revision blurred the distinction made in a previous draft between 'national resistance' and 'terrorism' and limited the prospects of successful engagement with the Sunni insurgents.[86] Indeed, the reconciliation plan resurrected the problems faced by the 2004 amnesty: semantically, the definition of 'participation' in the act of killing led to confusion as to eligibility and, more importantly, the Sunnis again felt that their 'nationalist struggle against occupation' was dismissed as terrorism and criminality. The Sunni speaker of the Parliament, Mahmoud al-Mashhadani, reflected a wider Sunni concern when he declared that, 'If we punish a person who killed an American soldier, who is an occupier, we should punish the American soldiers who killed an Iraqi who fought against the occupation.'[87]

As problematically, the reconciliation plan was silent on the topic of militias, offering little more than hopeful injunctions as to their eventual disbandment.[88] The reasons for this were simple. First, Maliki was dependent on the United Iraqi Alliance (UIA) Coalition, which represented SCIRI, Da'wa as well as al-Sadr and had gained 46.5 per cent of the ballot in the legislative elections. 'Efforts to go after these groups risked defection ... with devastating impact on the capacity to govern.'[89] Second, these parties still did not have a compelling reason to disband their militias: the government security forces were either weak or had been infiltrated. Even Pentagon reports candidly predicted that the militias were 'likely to remain active in areas where Iraqi institutions and forces are not yet adequate to meet the social and public safety needs of the local population'.[90] At the same time, their continued existence and operations further dissuaded the Sunnis from accepting the amnesty.[91]

De-Ba'athification, the second tranche of Maliki's reconciliation plan, confronted a similar lack of support and floundered. On 22 July 2006, Maliki established the National Council for the Reconciliation and National Dialogue Plan – a group of 30 leaders drawn from a cross-section of Iraqi society and charged with implementing Maliki's reconciliation plan, such as it was. On 26 August, tribal leaders were convened in Baghdad; statements were made condemning sectarian violence and in support of the government's reconciliation plan.[92] However, there was little substance behind the rhetoric. In the first place, the plan itself was vague, expressing a general desire for progress but proposing no clear means of achieving it. Second, the provisions for de-Ba'athification had initially, and on the UIA's insistence, been removed from the plan; they were only restored following strong US pressure – an indication, perhaps, of a lack of 'local ownership'.[93] Third, the National Council for Reconciliation gained no momentum and its meetings, in June as in December 2006, were marked by suspicion, infighting and notable absences.[94] As Anthony Cordesman noted, 'the initiative did not appear to carry the weight required to end the political deadlock perpetuated by sectarian and ethnic differences'.[95]

The elevation of sectarians within government and their entrenchment within that position through a series of elections had contributed to a seemingly irredeemable corruption of Iraqi governmental affairs. Incoherent at best, at cross-purposes more often, its ministries and parties represented no basis for national policy, for compromise or for reconciliation. Nor was there a Leviathan – a strongman or authority – to repair the damage inflicted through the pragmatic accommodation of these elements. Even the introduction of a Sunni coalition had failed to broaden the scope of Iraqi politics, and in fact contributed to its further fragmentation along ethnic lines. This highly imperfect government was expected somehow to find it within itself to carry through on critical reforms to address the motivation for continued violence. Meanwhile, the US military, perceiving itself as an 'antibody' in Iraqi society and frustrated with the lack of progress, increasingly transferred the responsibility for containing the threat of violence to its Iraqi counterparts – and this in spite of their inadequacies and infiltration by sectarian elements.[96] A veritable recipe for disaster, this set-up led to both political stalemate in Baghdad and a dramatic rise in casualties nationwide.[97] The prospects of salvaging some sort of stability were quickly fading.

Reintegration by other means[98]

From this nadir in 2006, violence in Iraq diminished throughout 2007 and 2008.[99] Starting in late 2006, Sunni tribes and former insurgents increasingly partnered with various US brigades to combat the threat of Sunni extremist – or *takfiri* – groups such as AQI. Simultaneously, some US brigades abandoned the isolated 'forward operating bases' (FOB) for 'Joint Security Stations' (JSS) – small forts constructed across Baghdad and nearby cities to enable the persistent provision of population security. This shift became official strategy with the launch of Operation Fardh al-Qanoon in February 2007, which also saw the deployment of five additional brigades to Iraq. In 2007, this surge in troops and the new US strategy compelled Moqtada al-Sadr to curb his armed activity.

The lull in violence occurred in the absence of a DDR plan. Nor were the conditions on the ground amenable to such a programme: security was lacking, there was no political agreement and no scope for reconciliation.[100] Nonetheless, the security gains grew out of and enabled *informal processes of reintegration*, relying on a series of pacts made between the US military and the more moderate elements of its erstwhile enemies. These pacts were predicated on a shared desire for greater stability on the local level and a mutual dedication to work towards that goal. Through such cooperation, former 'irreconcilables' soon assumed greater responsibility for keeping the peace and enabling reconstruction; in some places, the security gains even brought Sunni and Shia tribal leaders into local peace agreements. The process can be viewed as 'reintegration by other means'.

The schism between moderates and extremists was first felt among the Sunni tribes of Anbar Province, which in 2006 turned against the radical Islamist elements active in the area. Cooperation had hitherto been possible because of the tribes' and extremists' shared Sunni identity and opposition to the Shia government. With time, however, AQI rendered itself deeply unpopular – by disrupting or taking over informal business networks, seeking to marry its members into the higher tribal echelons or by using violence to coerce the tribes into submission.[101] By late 2006, the extremists' efforts to embed themselves had resulted in a backlash.

The US military actively assisted in this decoupling. Doing so would, however, require a complete reconceptualisation of the Sunnis, of their motivation to fight, and of the US military's own role in Iraq. In short, US brigades moved from a narrow focus on rooting out the insurgency to a broader effort to end the cycle of violence, primarily by engaging with its adversaries' initial motivation to take up arms. This helped locate groups and individuals within the insurgency with whom cooperation would be possible. By co-opting this middle-ground and working with it against more extreme elements, the US military not only helped achieve common goals but also improved its own image, all the while contributing to the marginalisation of the hardliners.

As an illustration, when the 1st Brigade, 1st Armored Division, the 'Ready First Combat Team' (RFCT), deployed to Anbar in 2006, then a hornet's nest of insurgent activity, it first conducted a review of its population.[102] The study revealed that in this predominantly Sunni province, the local population did not willingly side with the extremists as previously assumed. Instead, AQI was escalating its intimidation and was generally disliked, yet the tribes were unable to counter this threat for fear of retaliation. Meanwhile, American assurances of an imminent troop withdrawal, intended to placate the Sunni tribes, had in fact heightened their fears of AQI intimidation and of an Iranian power-grab (conducted either directly or through the Iraqi government, widely seen as a 'Persian' stooge). Col Sean MacFarland, RFCT commander, therefore changed the message and the mission: the US troops would not leave, but would stand by the sheiks and help their forces defend the population against AQI retribution and any form of Iranian interference.

A similar partnership was emerging in northwest Baghdad. With a mission statement 'to defeat al-Qaeda and affiliated movements', the 1st Infantry Division's 'Dagger Brigade' also initiated its tour in November 2006 by studying the local population.[103] It emerged that, in this ethnically mixed area, the Sunni population sided with AQI as an imperfect security guarantee against the incursions of Shia death squads conducting ethnic cleansing. As Col J.B. Burton, commander of Dagger Brigade put it,

> We understood their story-line: 'You know that the Government of Iraq is sectarian; you know that the Iraqi Security Forces are sectarian-motivated and members of Jaysh al-Mahdi, and you know that the Coalition Forces are leaving. So as a Sunni in northwest Baghdad, your best hope is to allow al-Qaeda to come in and fight Jaysh al-Mahdi for you.'[104]

This understanding of the Sunni perspective offered an opportunity to 'turn' the moderate fighters in that area: if the US troops could help these Sunnis curb Shia violence, it could drive a wedge between these 'honourable resistance members' and AQI, expand security in the area and build bridges with former 'spoilers'.[105]

The pacts were to be sealed with action rather than words. Even before the shift from FOBs became official US strategy, Colonels Burton and MacFarland, and others, deployed to the most volatile sections of their areas of operations to help provide security. The Dagger Brigade established combat outposts on the fault lines separating the Sunni community from Shia incursions. With the first outpost built, the unit 'saw an increased partnership on the part of the local nationals', which led to the collocation of volunteer Sunni units and US soldiers – one that soon included Shia security-force personnel.[106] In Ramadi, outposts were constructed where AQI violence was at its highest, where US troops would team up with the sheiks' forces to combat the terrorist threat. In subsequent months, tribal fighters joined the security forces en masse and worked with the US military to protect and secure the hospital and other civil institutions against AQI control.[107]

The deployment of US troops in the city rather than in isolated bases became a central tenet of the US military's strategy in February 2007, leading to closer interaction with local communities, who were better protected and more willing to work with the Coalition. Emulating the above approach, several US units teamed up with Sunni moderates against extremist elements.[108] As various collaborative opportunities emerged, more 'Sons of Iraq' – the collective term for the tribal elements, insurgents and civilians to have turned against the extremist groups – were put on the payroll.[109] The recruits were screened and registered using biometric technology and then organised for patrols of their neighbourhoods and towns, where they would help maintain security and produce an overall reduction in bloodshed.[110]

A similar form of bottom-up reintegration was practised by Task Force 134, the US military unit responsible for detainee operations and a microcosm, in some ways, of the overall change in the US approach. Formerly responsible for various prisoner-abuse scandals and criticised for its inadequate detention policies, Task Force 134 had initially contributed to rather than countered the insurgency.[111] Under the command of General Douglas Stone, the unit changed its strategy: from May 2007, the aim was to engage with the prisoners' 'story-line': their motivation for violence, both within the prison and upon their release.[112] To this end, Gen. Stone offered each inmate an 'initial assessment' to identify the prisoner's political orientation, religious beliefs and social concerns. Assessments revealed that many detainees were 'illiterate, disillusioned and angry' and that some became 'security threats to Iraq because they felt they had no other way to make a living or were influenced by radicals'.[113]

Reacting to this information, Task Force 134 launched educational courses in September 2007 for approximately 7,000 detainees, many of whom were uneducated or of school age.[114] Gen. Stone also organised vocational training for lower-risk inmates, who were allowed outside the camp to earn money.[115]

Islamist extremists, meanwhile, were put through religious courses organised by moderate clerics, involving discussions of Islam and the Koran. Psychologists were also made available to deal with traumatised inmates. Finally, the detention facilities held 140 reviews daily to assess inmates' threat level. Those granted release were placed in front of an Iraqi judge to discuss their future and sign a binding pledge to renounce violence. While Gen. Stone says he did not envisage turning 'radicals' into 'choir boys', as of March 2008, his unit had experienced only two returns per 1,000 prisoners released.[116] This ratio of 0.2 per cent contrasts with the 6–8 per cent return rate of January 2007 and illustrated the rehabilitation, reintegration even, of former insurgents and disgruntled young men into society.[117] Within the prisons, moderates had even launched a backlash against the extremist elements that had previously used the facilities as insurgency training grounds.[118]

The new approach, on the ground and in the prisons, relied on the willingness of US commanders to overlook insurgents' past involvement in attacks if they, in return, were willing to forgo violence and participate constructively in Iraqi society. While the RFCT refused to meet with insurgent leaders and promised to punish anyone with Coalition blood on their hands, its leadership did encourage the sheiks to act as interlocutors between the two sides and condoned the mobilisation of insurgents against AQI and their recruitment into the Iraqi security forces (so long as they passed the screening process).[119] The new approach stemmed from a greater understanding of the insurgent's perspective: a lack of options, resentment against occupiers – all understandable and rectifiable causes. The characterisation of the Sunni fighters as 'honourable resistance members' by Col Burton was unprecedented but typical of this understanding, as was Gen. Stone's distinction between 'moderate insurgents' and 'extremists'.[120] Such nuance was rare prior to 2006; it was also foundational to the pacts made with the Sunni community that year and thereafter.[121] At no point did this attitude denote a free-for-all: the point was to separate those who could be co-opted from those who could not; to transform the hardliners into moderates through a variety of means, including military force; and to consolidate successful co-option through localised peace agreements and progressive reintegration.

If the above translated into an 'approach' towards reintegration, similar methods were used to bring Moqtada al-Sadr into the fold. The US military first gained leverage with Sadr by increasing its force levels and positioning itself in the streets of Baghdad.[122] For the first time, the US military also obtained the government's authorisation to enter Shia areas of Baghdad that had previously been off-limits. Some commentators argued that Maliki had realised that he did not need to kowtow to Sadr to keep his government intact – Sadr had withdrawn his party's ministers from the cabinet in November 2006, yet the government did not collapse.[123] It is as likely, however, that Sadr himself agreed to more intrusive US operations as a means of streamlining his militia, which had lost coherence and discipline during the previous year of violence.

During 2006, Mahdi Army elements operated with no real direction from Sadr and engaged in armed activity for personal self-enrichment: renegade units turned on each other for war spoils, targeted civilians – even in Shia areas, and attacked anyone opposing its activities.[124] The movement, which had captured the grievances of working-class Shias, was losing its legitimacy and jeopardising Moqtada's hopes for greater influence – relative, primarily, to the Islamic Supreme Council of Iraq (ISCI, the new name for SCIRI following a May 2007 name-change). Sadr, therefore, 'sought to use the surge as a further opportunity for cleansing his movement, ridding it of notorious troublemakers and giving their names to the government or Coalition forces'.[125] Following a fire fight between the Mahdi Army and the Badr Organisation in Karbala in August 2007, Sadr even imposed a six-month ceasefire, which 'lifted the impunity that many groups – criminal gangs operating in the Mahdi Army's name and Sadrist units gone astray – had enjoyed'.[126] Despite numerous assaults on Mahdi Army units, Sadr renewed the ceasefire in February 2008 and again, indefinitely, in August 2008. In the meantime, he also established the 'Golden Battalion', which was to hunt down rogue Mahdi elements, now referred to as 'special groups'.[127]

Again, by tapping into the motivations of its erstwhile enemies, the US military found common causes that could be used to promote a form of reintegration. It capitalised on the split in the Mahdi Army by supporting the moderates and targeting extremists, much as it had done in Anbar and Baghdad. Accordingly, the US military supported Sadr's Golden Battalion, and reportedly paid some of Sadr's forces to 'help keep the peace' – a reversal on previous policy.[128] Gen. David Petraeus, meanwhile, held secret meetings with senior Sadr officials to discuss security cooperation.[129] The goodwill thus engendered was used to goad Sadr towards peaceful political participation: henceforth, US officials were careful to distinguish between the 'special groups', on whom ceasefire violations would be blamed, and Sadr himself, who was no longer cast as an extremist cleric but as a moderate and important political figure, seeking to rein in his militia. In Gen. Petraeus' own words, 'this is a movement that was built on the principles of the martyr Sadr, Moqtada's father, and it was all about serving the people, not extorting money from them, carrying out criminal actions against them'.[130] Most ambitiously, Petraeus 'started using the honorific "seyed" when referring to Sadr' – used to address descendents of the Prophet Mohammed – and 'asked US officers to do the same'.[131]

Pacts – but no compact

The pacts described above brought about undeniable security gains. However, the viability of disparate security pacts as a form of national reintegration remains uncertain. 'National ownership' over the DDR process is commonly touted as a prerequisite for success. In this instance, it was doubtful whether the Iraqi government – the composition and fragmentation of which lies at the root of the conflict – would react constructively to the changing security situation in Iraq. The local reintegration of Sunni tribes and former insurgents has clearly not displaced the Shia-dominated governmental structures that the Sunnis have so long resisted. Similarly, there was little beyond hope to suggest that Sadr's decision to sell out some unruly elements of his militia would translate into a renunciation of violent means altogether or a peaceful conclusion to his rivalry with other Shia militias. Indeed, would the parties in government be willing to accommodate the new political entities and to share political power? In the absence of a constructive government response to the changing political land-scape, the pacts made with the US military are likely to unravel, along with the security gains that they embody.

The government has taken steps to further the bottom-up reintegration process, primarily by affording Sunnis a greater place in society and government. In October 2007, the Iraqi parliament passed a Unified Retirement Law, granting pensions to former Iraqi soldiers. On 12 January 2008, it passed the Accountability and Justice Law, a de-Ba'athification bill that would provide employment and pen-sions for former lower-ranking Ba'athist officials. On 13 February, it passed an amnesty bill that would see the release of approximately 5,000 suspected former Sunni insurgents from Iraqi prisons.[132] However, these success-stories belie the deep mistrust that still marks Iraqi politics. In August 2007, the IAF walked out of Maliki's government in protest against its failure to deal with Shia militias.[133] In addition, while subsequent legislation might have allayed Sunni concerns, they also prompted further feuding. The Sunni community assailed the Accountability and Justice Law for extending de-Ba'athification to the judiciary and for failing to disband the Higher National De-Ba'athification Commission, the body responsible for de-Ba'athification and that many Sunnis deeply oppose.[134] As serious was the opposition of Vice President Tariq Hashimi to the law's original provision to oust present Sunni members of government to accommodate those heretofore excluded.[135] This last objection points to the emerging rivalry between Sunnis in power and those empowered from the bottom-up, with the former viewing the latter as 'potential organized competitors for support among Sunni Arab Iraqis'.[136] Given these old and new rivalries, legislation passed remains contested, casting doubt as to its implementation.

The Sunni volunteer fighters' struggle to find a place within the government's security services represents a second factor staunching bottom-up reintegration. While fighters with civilian skills can return to a more traditional profession, many Sons of Iraq (SoI) are untrained, uneducated or simply unwilling to abandon the prestige of protecting their community. Moreover, several SoI had formed part of the former security forces, dismissed by the Americans in 2003, and they are eager to reclaim their profession. In theory, only 20 per cent of the volunteers are to be integrated within the security forces, with the rest provided civilian employment opportunities. However, even the process of approving the selected SoI for national service has faced delays and rarely led to integration.[137] By early 2008, several volunteers were threatening to or actually deserted.[138]

The delays stem from bureaucratic impedimenta and government resistance. The Shia and Kurdish parties in power want to maintain their grip on the security structure, currently based around their own militia. The government has also expressed concern that the incorporation of volunteer fighters would bring AQI or insurgent elements into the security forces. These fears should have been allayed by the US registration and screening methods, but have nonetheless continued to retard the reintegration process.[139] Yet the problem is not merely one of Baghdad intransigence: while seeking the legitimacy of national service, some tribal elements have resisted foreswearing the benefits of their isolation, which range from control over local jobs and business opportunities to the significant pay-off provided through the extra-governmental deals made with the US military.[140]

Similar problems surround the political reintegration of Moqtada al-Sadr. Sure enough, the rapprochement resulted in the streamlining of the Mahdi Army and the removal of some elements responsible for significant bloodshed.[141] During the lull in violence, Sadr also took steps towards recasting himself as a national leader, launching a 'reform and reconciliation' project to 'establish a broad coalition of political parties' and sending his envoys to meet with Sunni tribal leaders and politicians.[142] Sadr also recommenced his religious studies, through which he sought to acquire greater credentials as a political leader.[143] Even so, how sincere is this transformation: has the American generals' change in tone really lured Moqtada into civility or were US soldiers used by Moqtada to settle scores within the Mahdi Army? In addition, are US and Sadr's goals at all compatible?

Moqtada's makeover has also intensified his rivalry with the incumbent Shia parties, for whom the threat of a reborn al-Sadr – wielding a more professional and disciplined force and with greater religious authority – represents a threat.[144] In anticipation of a future showdown, the ISCI and Da'wa-dominated government launched major military operations in Basra and in Sadr City in March and April 2008, targeting the Mahdi Army. These ambitious attempts to rid the country of militias were also clearly intended to undermine the comparatively popular Sadr ahead of the provincial elections, then planned for October 2008. To undercut his political aspirations further, the Iraqi government agreed on a draft law that would bar any party from participating in the elections if they also wielded a militia – a telling yet also very ironic decree, given the ruling parties' relation to their own militias.[145] Taking note of this ploy, the IAF allegedly returned to the government in July 2008 in return for guarantees that the SoI parties would also be barred from participating in the forthcoming elections, plausibly through the same draft law.[146]

Continued Shia–Shia violence will further fragment Iraq's identity-driven politics, much as the exclusion of Sunni SoI from government will threaten the country's newfound stability. These, clearly, are the risks of making pacts outside of government. There is a critical difference, in other words, between co-opting various outfits from below and fostering reintegration from the top down. The pacts helped mend rifts and curb violence, but the Iraqi government remains sectarian, even obstructionist. In the words of Gen. Petraeus, 'no one feels that there has been sufficient progress by any means in the area of national reconciliation'.[147] Indeed the US role in this context is complicated, as it seeks to balance its support for the established, yet sectarian government with its support of new political entities such as the SoI, which represent tentative progress, but which the central government seeks to keep weak and isolated.

Conclusion: regime change anew?

In the first year in Iraq, the United States did not pursue any strategy to reintegrate either the defeated security forces of the Saddam Hussein regime or the pre-existing militias that opposed it. Nor did the CPA have a strategy, beyond sheer military power, to bring disgruntled former Ba'athists, nationalists and other Sunni insurgents into the fold. Even the use of military force was ineffective, given the US military's unfamiliarity and ensuing unsuitability for counterinsurgency. In the absence of security, the militias and insurgency groups grew stronger and multiplied. By the time a reintegration strategy emerged, it was irresponsive to political realities and badly implemented.

These political realities were themselves a product of the unconditional and ill-advised incorporation of sectarian elements within the Iraq government. Alongside the narrow, military targeting of the Sunni tribes and wider community, the political elevation of Shia and Kurdish militias helped create a vicious circle marked by ethnic rivalries that soon turned bloody. In retrospect, more time was plainly needed to allow representative Iraqi leaders to emerge, through a bottom-up process rather than as appointed by US officials. Relying on known quantities made the transition to Iraqi rule seem easy, but it critically undermined the long-term goal of state building.

Problematically, holding the line while Iraqi civil society produced representative leaders would have necessitated a longer-term US military occupation and thereby opened up another road to violence. Ironically, it was in the pursuit of greater legitimacy that the US handed power to a sectarian leaders, yet they themselves were neither representative nor legitimate. Iraq thus points to an unavoidable trade-off, inherent to efforts at regime-change, particularly those conducted unilaterally or through a 'coalition of the willing'. Enjoying the most transient of support and legitimacy, the occupier must swiftly locate indigenous authorities to whom power can be transferred, but these national leaders must also be effective and perceived as widely representative and accountable. This conundrum points to the centrality of political reintegration as a component of state building: the process elevates and entrenches the actors by, with or through subsequent action taken. In solving this conundrum, and as forcefully illustrated by the Iraq case study, the need for local knowledge cannot be underestimated. While the starting conditions for regime-change in Iraq were never propitious, some of the grossest of missteps – by the Bush administration, by the CPA – might have been avoided had those responsible for decision-making also taken some time to learn about the society they were so actively trying to reform.

With a vicious cycle set in motion, however, what are the prospects for political reintegration? As seen, progress towards reconciliation in Iraq has been slow. The government set up by the United States in 2003, composed of sectarians and secularists with questionable credentials, has never truly worked for Iraqi national interests, but for their own respective constituencies and power-bases. Correcting this situation has been near impossible because efforts at de-Ba'athification, amnesties and other measures designed to undercut the Sunnis' motivation for violence have had to arise from within structures with a vested interest in perpetuating the problem.

Against this backdrop, the best attempt at reintegration has been the bottom-up cooperative arrangements achieved between US military units and various Sunni groups since 2006. These pacts have compelled formerly alienated and apparently irreconcilable elements to claim an active role in providing security and enabling reconstruction. Similarly, although much more tentative, the partnership achieved in 2007 between the senior US military leadership in Iraq and al-Sadr pointed to a pragmatic yet conditions-based avenue towards reintegration, where commonalities were fully exploited to meet common goals. Yet as these arrangements emerged without much buy-in from the central government, this is still a far cry from proper 'reintegration' – never mind 'reconciliation'. While bringing about unprecedented improvements in security, the long-term consolidation of these achievements would require the government to eschew the particularistic form of decision-making to have marked its policies since the handover of sovereignty in 2004.

Progress on this front has been too slow, but there are grounds for hope. While the long-term effects of Iraq's provincial election in February 2009 are still difficult to predict, these elections – and the national elections planned for later in the year – may provide Sunnis with a chance to elect more representative and legitimate leaders, which might in turn undercut much of their motivation for violence. The Sahawa al Iraq – the Anbar-based council of Sunni tribes to has rejected AQI – has already turned itself into a political party; other Sunni tribes are following suit.[148] In a best-case scenario, the elections 'will consolidate their de facto influence through democratic means, codifying both Sunni rejection of insurgency and lasting status within larger Iraqi society'.[149] Should al-Sadr pursue his transformation into a legitimate politician – and if the US can find a means of working with him – his popular appeal among working-class Iraqis might help challenge the sectarian Shia elements currently in government, who are seen as out-of-touch and as Iranian proxies. If these are the outcomes of the forthcoming elections, the informal reintegration witnessed since 2006 will pay dividends. However, as the elections approach and are held, the central government will most likely seek new ways of marginalising the up-and-coming political leadership that is threatening its hold on power. The US will find itself in the middle of this struggle, an unenviable situation, yet one that will require its continued engagement for the hard-earned progress seen since 2007 not to be squandered.

Notes

1 See CPA Order Number 2, 'Dissolution of Entities', 23 May 2003. In a James Fallows article, Walter Slocombe is quoted as saying: 'We don't pay armies we defeated'. See Fallows, 'Why Iraq Has No Army'. See also, Ackerman, 'Badr to Worse', 13–18.
2 Interview with Walter Slocombe, *Frontline – Public Broadcasting Service*, 17 August 2004. See also L. Paul Bremer III, 'How I Didn't Dismantle Iraq's Army', *New York Times*, 6 September 2007.

3　As Fallows notes, 'Several weeks later the Americans announced that they would resume some army stipends, but by then the damage had been done'. See Fallows, 'Why Iraq Has No Army'.

4　Pollack, 'The Seven Deadly Sins'. The wrong-headedness of this act has been acknowledged by General Garner. See Freedberg, 'Federalism'.

5　Pollack, 'The Seven Deadly Sins'.

6　'Bremer proved unwilling to incorporate the players – Ba'athists and Arab nationalists – who would have been capable of defusing the Sunni-based resistance, and who were, in fact, sending signals that they wanted to talk directly to the Untied States'. See Diamond, *Squandered Victory*, 295.

7　See CPA, *Security Sector Reform: An Example of Structures Designed for Counter-Insurgency and for the Transition*, 29 November 2004 – as cited in Rathmell *et al.*, *Developing Iraq's Security Sector*, 66.

8　It is worth noting that even the creators of the plan described it as hopeful and 'modest'. See Ackerman, 'From Badr to Worse'.

9　Ibid.

10　Fallows, 'Why Iraq Has No Army'.

11　Rathmell *et al.*, *Developing Iraq's Security Sector*, 66.

12　RFE/RL, 'KDP Head Says Peshmerga May Merge with Iraqi Military'.

13　Terrill, *The United States and Iraq's Shi'ite Clergy*, 26.

14　As cited in Terrill, *The United States and Iraq's Shi'ite Clergy*, 26.

15　Ackerman, 'From Badr to Worse'.

16　Mowle, 'Iraq's Militia Problem', 47.

17　John Mintz and Dana Priest, 'Shiite Demands For Control In Iraq Challenge U.S. Plans', *Washington Post*, 16 April 2003.

18　In April 2003, Shi'ite clerics established themselves as local government in Najaf, Karbala and Kut, before moving on to the surrounding villages and towns. As Terrill explains,

> Clerics did this in many cases by assuming control of essential services, including neighborhood security, garbage collection, firefighting, education, and hospital administration. They also appointed administrators and imposed curfews, while offering civic protection, jobs, health care, and financial assistance to the needy. In addition, clerics opened their own newspapers and other media outlets across Iraq.

See Terrill, The United States and Iraq's Shi'ite Clergy, 11.

19　Terrill, *The United States and Iraq's Shi'ite Clergy*, 12. *BBC News*, 'What happened in Majar al-Kabir?', 25 June 2003.

20　Rathmell *et al.*, *Developing Iraq's Security Sector*, 66.

21　International Crisis Group (ICG), *Iraq's Muqtada al Sadr*, 9–10.

22　Ackerman, 'From Badr to Worse'.

23　See Diamond, *Squandered Victory*, 8, 296.

24　Mowle, 'Iraq's Militia Problem', 47.

25　Ibid.

26　Rathmell *et al.*, *Developing Iraq's Security Sector*, 68.

27　The participating groups were: Kurdistan Democratic Party (KDP), Patriotic Union of Kurdistan (PUK), Iraqi Islamic Party, SCIRI, Iraqi National Accord (INA), Iraqi National Congress (INC), Iraqi Hezbollah, Iraqi Communist Party and Da'wa.

28　Mowle, 'Iraq's Militia Problem', 48.

29　See CPA Order Number 91, 'Regulation of Armed Forces and Militias Within Iraq', 6 June 2004.

30　Ibid., 9–10.

31　Rathmell *et al.*, *Developing Iraq's Security Sector*, 68. See also Frontline – Public Broadcasting Service, 'Interview with Matthew Sherman', 4 October 2006.

32　Government Accountability Office (GAO), *Rebuilding Iraq*, 68.

33 In the spring of 2004, a proposal was made to spend $10m over 18 months to create an office of international DDR experts and local Iraqi staff, which could advise the fledgling TRIC. The CPA elected not to fund the effort and the Iraqi Ministry of Finance, for its part, never pursued it. According to a 2005 RAND report, the CPA was at this time 'avoiding new, open-ended financial commitments as the fate for transfer of authority to the IIG drew near'. See Rathmell *et al.*, *Developing Iraq's Security Sector*, 69. See also Frontline – Public Broadcasting Service, 'Interview with Matthew Sherman', 4 October 2006.
34 Schwarz, 'Iraq's Militias', 63.
35 Ackerman, 'From Badr to Worse'.
36 See Diamond, 'The New War for Iraq'.
37 Mowle, 'Iraq's Militia Problem', 48.
38 Ibid.
39 Ibid.
40 Ibid.
41 Allbritton, 'Why Iraq's Police Are a Menace'.
42 Rathmell *et al.*, *Developing Iraq's Security Sector*, 71.
43 See CPA Order Number 91, 9–10.
44 Tom Lasseter, 'U.S. Knew Shiite Militias Were A Threat But Took No Action Largely Because They Were Focused On Sunni Insurgency', *Knight Ridder*, 17 April 2006.
45 The Council membership was to include 13 Shi'ites, five Sunni Arabs, five Kurds, one Assyrian and one ethnic Turk. As Carrie Manning puts it, 'representativeness was defined, then, according to the CPA's mental demographic map of Iraq. So long as someone from each group is represented … the process and the institutions are representative'. See Manning, 'Political Elites', 729.
46 Dodge, 'The Iraq Transition'. See also ICG, *Iraq: Building a New Security Structure*, 8–9. Saddam's elimination of civil society may account for the dearth of suitable political leaders.
47 Pollack, 'The Seven Deadly Sins' (emphasis in original). The IGC selection process is described in Haggard and Long, *On Benchmarks*, 21–22.
48 An October 2003 poll revealed that 69–85 per cent of polled Iraqis had 'not heard enough to voice an opinion on 18 of 25 Governing Council members'. See Office of Research Opinion, 'Iraqi Public'. See also 'Standing of Former Key US Ally in Iraq Falls to New Low', *Washington Post*, 21 May 2004.
49 Diamond, 'The New War'.
50 Dodge, 'The Iraq Transition'.
51 While the IGC did include one Sunni tribal leader, he was not widely respected in his own community. See Pollack, 'The Seven Deadly Sins'.
52 Ian Fisher and Somini Sengupta, 'Iraq To Offer Amnesty, But No Killers Need Apply', *New York Times*, 4 August 2004.
53 Dodge, 'The Iraq Transition'.
54 'A Conversation with Tariq Al-Hashimi, Vice President, Republic of Iraq, and Secretary-General, Iraqi Islamic Party', event held at Council of Foreign Relations, New York, 19 December 2006.
55 Mowle, 'Iraq's Militia Problem', 53.
56 There were a number of important exceptions to this trend, including the experience of the 101st Airborne in Mosul during 2003 and the deployment of the 3rd Armoured Cavalry to Tal Afar. See, respectively, Atkinson, *In the Company of Soldiers*, 294–303 and Ricks, *Fiasco*, 419–424.
57 Dodge, 'Securing America's Interests in Iraq'.
58 'To the Kurds it promises a considerable degree of autonomy; to the Shiite it provides for a parliamentary government'. See Brown, 'Iraq's Constitutional Process', 8. See also Pollack, 'The Seven Deadly Sins'.

59 This process is discussed in detail in ICG, *Iraq: Building A New Security Structure*.
60 ICG, *The Next Iraqi War?*, 10.
61 Katzman, *Iraq: Elections, Government*, 11.
62 Mowle, 'Introduction', 9.
63 Mowle, 'Iraq's Militia Problem', 49.
64 ICG, *Iraq's Muqtada al Sadr*, i.
65 ICG, *The Next Iraqi War?*, 12–13. Partly through US pressure, the Assembly committee drafting the constitution agreed to include Sunni members. However, their opposition to provisions already written into the text was subsequently ignored, as the US – and the Iraqi government – wanted to reach an agreement quickly. See Haggard and Long, *On Benchmarks*, 21–22.
66 See Iraqi Constitution, articles 9(b) and 117(5), 2005.
67 See Dawisha and Diamond, 'Iraq's Year of Voting Dangerously', 95.
68 ICG, *The Next Iraqi War?*, 19.
69 Amit R. Paley and Zaid Sabah, 'Case Is Dropped Against Shiites In Sunni Deaths', *Washington Post*, 4 March 2008.
70 Ibid.
71 *Frontline*, Interview with Bayan Jabr, 21 November 2006.
72 ICG, *Iraq's Muqtada*, 15. A similar method was used by Sadr and by Da'wa with regard to the health and education ministries, respectively.
73 Mowle, 'Iraq's Militia Problem', 50.
74 Edward Wong, 'Iraq's top leaders voice approval of Kurdish, Shiite militias', *San Francisco Chronicle*, 9 June 2005; and 'Iraq's Kurdish president backs Shiite militia'. *USA Today*, 8 June 2005.
75 Tom Lasseter, 'U.S. Knew Shiite Militias Were A Threat But Took No Action Largely Because They Were Focused On Sunni Insurgency', *Knight Ridder*, 17 April 2006.
76 Mowle, 'Introduction', 9.
77 Mowle, 'Iraq's Militia Problem', 49; Mowle, 'Introduction', 9–10.
78 In the aftermath of the al-Askariyya bombing, military sources estimated that Baghdad's homicide rate tripled from 11 to 33 deaths a day, with 365,000 Iraqis being forced from their homes. See International Institute for Strategic Studies (IISS), 'Iraq Under the Surge', 1.
79 Dawisha and Diamond, 'Iraq's Year of Voting Dangerously', 96. See also, Patrick Cockburn, 'Iraq's election result, a divided nation', *The Independent*, 21 December 2005.
80 al-Waeli, 'Iraq: Cultural/Political and Media Observations', 7.
81 Ibid.
82 See Dodge, 'The Causes of US Failure', 97.
83 See ICG, *Iraq's Civil War*, 4–5.
84 Cordesman, *Iraq's Evolving Insurgency*, 74.
85 Joshua Partlow and Bassam Sebti, 'Amnesty To Exclude Killers Of GIs, Iraqis', *Washington Post*, 28 June 2006. See also Solomon Moore, 'Iraq Leader Cites Rebel Interest in Amnesty', *Los Angeles Times*, 28 June 2006.
86 Haggard and Long, *On Benchmarks*, 25.
87 Qassim Abdul-Zahra, 'Iraq's Reconciliation Committee holds its first meeting but differences emerge', *Associated Press*, 22 July 2006.
88 Jamie Tarabay, 'Iraq Reconciliation Plan Is Short On Details', *NPR.org*, 26 June 2006.
89 Haggard and Long, *On Benchmarks*, 26.
90 US Department of Defense (DoD), *Measuring Security and Stability*, 31.
91 'Sunni group endorses national reconciliation plan', *USA Today*, 27 July 2006.
92 DoD, *Measuring Security and Stability*, 8.
93 Haggard and Long, *On Benchmarks*, 24.

94 Sumedha Senanayake, 'Iraq: Reconciliation Conference Fails To Deliver', *Radio Free Europe/Radio Liberty*, 20 December 2006; Qassim Abdul-Zahra, 'Iraq's Reconciliation Committee holds its first meeting but differences emerge', Associated Press, 22 July 2006.
95 Cordesman, Iraq's Evolving Insurgency, 12.
96 Boot, 'Can Petraeus Pull It Off?'
97 Andy Mosher, 'Baghdad Morgue Tallies 1,815 Bodies in July' *Washington Post*, 10 August 2006.
98 This and the remaining sections draw in part on Ucko, 'Upcoming Iraqi Elections'.
99 The Brooking Institute's Iraq Index reports casualties in December of 2005, 2006 and 2007 as 1,348, 2,914 and 550, respectively. See O'Hanlon and Campbell, *Iraq Index Tracking*, 5.
100 A 2007 GAO report cites 'a secure environment, the inclusion of all belligerent parties, an overarching political agreement, sustainable funding, and appropriate reintegration opportunities' as the 'minimum requirements for a successful DDR program in Iraq'. See GAO, *Securing, Stabilizing*, 36.
101 Kilcullen, 'Anatomy of a Tribal Revolt'.
102 Thomas Ricks, 'Situation Called Dire in West Iraq', *Washington Post*, 11 September 2006. See also Smith and MacFarland, 'Anbar Awakens', 47.
103 Interview with Col J.B. Burton, US Army, March 2008.
104 Ibid.
105 Kagan, 'ISW Interview with COL J.B. Burton'.
106 Kagan, 'ISW Interview with COL J.B. Burton'.
107 Smith and MacFarland, 'Anbar Awakens', 44; Long, 'The Anbar Awakening', 80.
108 Notable examples would include, the 1st 'Iron Horse' Brigade Combat Team, commanded by Col Paul E. Funk, and active around the northern and western outskirts of Baghdad; the 'Commando Brigade', commanded by Col Michael Kershaw, south of Baghdad (the 'triangle of death'); the 'Greywolf Brigade', commanded by Col David Sutherland, in Diyala province.
109 By March 2008, nearly 80,000 forces were on the US payroll. See Dehghanpisheh and Thomas, 'Scions of the Surge'.
110 For more details on the workings of the 'Sons of Iraq' units, see Dale, *Operation Iraqi Freedom*, 86–91.
111 Ibid., 91.
112 Gen. Stone's objective was to 'impress upon the [detained] population that there is a mechanism by which their behaviour ... can influence their release and can influence the society'. See Grossman, Elaine M., 'Issues and Ideas – Rehabilitating Iraqi Insurgents'. *Defense and The National Interest*, 1 September 2007. Available from www.d-n-i.net/dni/2007/09/01/issues-and-ideas-rehabilitating-iraqi-insurgents (accessed 7 March 2008).
113 'Bucca Holds First Hasty School Graduation for 60 Detainees', *Multi-National Force-Iraq Press Desk*, 18 December 2007.
114 'Bloggers' Roundtable With Gen. Douglas M. Stone', *Washington Post*, 18 September 2007.
115 As of September 2007, 500 inmates had signed up to this programme at Camp Cropper, with a further 2,000 expected to enrol at Camp Bucca by October. See Grossman, Elaine M., 'Issues and Ideas – Rehabilitating Iraqi Insurgents'. *Defense and The National Interest*, 1 September 2007.
116 'Bloggers' Roundtable With Gen. Stone'; see also 'Department of Defense Bloggers Roundtable with Brigadier General Michael Nevin, 177th Military Police Brigade, Joint Task Force 134', 4 March 2008.
117 'Bloggers' Roundtable With Gen. Stone'.
118 Marie Colvin, 'Tide Turns as Prisoners Turn in Jail Hardmen', *The Times*, 23 September 2007.

119 Correspondence with senior officer of the RFCT, March 2008.
120 Kagan, 'Interview with COL Burton'. 'Bloggers' Roundtable With Gen. Stone'. As Gen. Stone explains, killing Americans is 'a terrible thing … but warriors fight warriors … [and] there's a difference between somebody who is psychologically wedded to al Qaeda's doctrine, and somebody who was unemployed and was forced to go fight us'.
121 Though US officials and Iraqi tribesmen had engaged in dialogue before, the tribes were never compelled to support the US military and sided instead with AQI and other extremist elements. Long, 'The Anbar Awakening', 77.
122 A previous 'surge' – Operation *Together Forward II* of August–October 2006 – had failed because US forces lacked the 'capability to hold areas that have been cleared' and the authority 'to clear neighbourhoods that are home to Shiite militias'. See Baker *et al.*, *The Iraq Study Group*, 15.
123 This is apparently the opinion of David Satterfield, then the Senior Advisor to the Secretary of State and Coordinator for Iraq, as represented in Bennett, 'Underestimating al-Sadr – Again'.
124 The renegade Mahdi Army units would clear neighbourhoods of their Sunni population, take control of their common resources, seize and/or sell on individual property and possessions and engage in kidnapping to extort ransoms. See ICG, *Iraq's Civil War*, 6–10. See also Dehghanpisheh, 'The Great Moqtada Makeover'.
125 ICG, *Iraq's Civil War*, 8.
126 Ibid., i.
127 Nordland, 'A Radical Cleric Gets Religion'.
128 Dehghanpisheh, 'The Great Moqtada Makeover'.
129 See Nordland, 'A Radical Cleric Gets Religion'; Dehghanpisheh, 'The Great Moqtada Makeover'.
130 Gen. David Petraeus, as cited in Deborah Haynes, 'Transcript of The Times interview with David Petraeus', *Times Online*, 21 February 2008.
131 Dehghanpisheh, 'The Great Moqtada Makeover'. See also Amit R. Paley, 'U.S. Deploys a Purpose-Driven Distinction', *Washington Post*, 21 May 2008.
132 The prisoners marked for release were those who had been held 'for more than six months without charge or more than a year without a court appearance'. See Ardolino, 'Inside Iraqi Politics. Part 5'.
133 'Iraq Sunni bloc quits Coalition', *al-Jazeera.net*, 1 August 2007.
134 According to the International Center for Transitional Justice, 'new law is a major victory for the Higher National De-ba'athification Commission and opponents of De-ba'athification reform'. See International Center for Transnational Justice (ICTJ), 'Briefing Paper', 6.
135 Waleed Ibrahim, 'Iraq VP says he won't ratify key Ba'athists law', *Reuters*, 31 January 2008.
136 Dale, *Operation Iraqi Freedom*, 88.
137 Boot, 'We Are Winning. We Haven't Won'.
138 Sudarsan Raghavan and Amit R. Paley, 'Sunni Forces Losing Patience With U.S.', *Washington Post*, 28 February 2008.
139 While Maliki has established an Implementation and Follow up Committee for National Reconciliation (IFCNR), its work has stalled. See Ned Parker, 'The Rise and Fall of a Sons of Iraq Warrior', *Los Angeles Times*, 29 June 2008.
140 Eric Westervelt, 'Iraqi Tribal Leaders Work to Improve Security', *NPR.com*, 12 November 2007. See also Simon, 'The Price of the Surge', 65.
141 'In Baghdad, they retreated to their strongholds; the walls and checkpoints the US erected in late 2007 to surround those neighbourhoods to significantly restrict the movements of their militants'. ICG, *Iraq's Civil War*, 18.
142 Sumedha Senanayake, 'Iraq: Al-Sadr Prepares For The Post-Coalition Era', *RFE/ RL*, 10 May 2007.

143   Soraya Sarhaddi Nelson, 'Iraqi Radical Cleric Al-Sadr Studies for Ayatollah', *NPR. org*, 2 January 2008.
144   ICG, *Iraq's Civil War*, 19.
145   Dean Yates, 'Iraqi cabinet seeks to ban militias from elections', *Reuters*, 13 April 2008.
146   This rumoured deal was reported on in the blog Abu Aardvark and based on reports from the UAE-based paper *al-Khaleej*. See 'Dissolving the Sons of Iraq…?', *Abu Aardvark*, 3 July 2008, abuaardvark.typepad.com/abuaardvark/2008/07/dissolving-the.html.
147   Cameron W. Barr, 'Petraeus: Iraqi Leaders Not Making "Sufficient Progress"', *Washington Post*, 14 March 2008.
148   Correspondence with senior officer, RFCT, March 2008.
149   Ardolino, 'Inside Iraqi Politics'.

References

Ackerman, Spencer, 2005. 'Badr to Worse', *New Republic* 223:4721/4722, 13–18.
Allbritton, Christopher, 2006. 'Why Iraq's Police Are a Menace', *Time Magazine*, 20 March.
Ardolino, Bill, 2008. 'Inside Iraqi Politics: Part 3', *The Long War Journal*, www.longwarjournal.org.
——, 2008. 'Inside Iraqi Politics: Part 5', *The Long War Journal*, www.longwarjournal.org.
Atkinson, Rick, 2004. *In the Company of Soldiers: A Chronicle of Combat*, Henry Holt and Company, New York.
Baker, J.A., III, Lee, H.H., *et al.*, 2006. *The Iraq Study Group Report*, USIP, Washington DC.
Bennett, Brian, 2008. 'Underestimating al-Sadr – Again', *Time Magazine*, 11 February.
Boot, Max, 2007. 'Can Petraeus Pull It Off?', *The Weekly Standard*, 12:31.
——, 2008. 'We Are Winning. We Haven't Won', *Weekly Standard*, 13:20.
Brown, Nathan J., 2005. 'Iraq's Constitutional Process Plunges Ahead', *Policy Outlook: Carnegie Endowment for International Peace*, July, 1–15.
Cordesman, Anthony H., 2006. *Iraq's Evolving Insurgency and the Risk of Civil War: Democracy, Deadlock, and Death Squads: Developments in the Summer of 2006*, Working Draft.
Dale, Catherine Marie, 2008. *Operation Iraqi Freedom: Strategies, Approaches, Results, and Issues for Congress*, RL34387, Congressional Research Service, Washington DC.
Dawisha, A. and Diamond, L., 2006. 'Iraq's Year of Voting Dangerously', *Journal of Democracy* 17:2, 89–103.
Dehghanpisheh, Babak, 2008. 'The Great Moqtada Makeover', *Newsweek*, 19 January.
Dehghanpisheh, Babak and Evan, Thomas, 2008. 'Scions of the Surge', *Newsweek*, 24 March.
Diamond, Larry, 2004. 'The New War for Iraq', *The Hoover Digest* 3, 42–51.
——, 2005. *Squandered Victory: The American Occupation and the Bungled Effort to Bring Democracy to Iraq*, Henry Holt & Company, New York.
Dodge, Toby, 2004. 'The Iraq Transition: Civil War or Civil Society?', Testimony before the Committee on Foreign Relations, US Senate, Washington DC, 20 April.
——, 2007. 'Securing America's Interests in Iraq: The Remaining Options: Political Strategy', Testimony before the Committee on Foreign Relations, US Senate, Washington DC, 25 January.
——, 2007. 'The Causes of U.S. Failure in Iraq', *Survival* 49:1, 85–106.
Fallows, James, 2005. 'Why Iraq Has No Army', *Atlantic Monthly* 296:5, 60–77.

Freedberg, Sydney J. Jr, 2004. 'Federalism Can Avert Civil War in Iraq: An Interview with Jay Garner', *National Journal* 36:7.

Government Accountability Office (GAO), 2004. *Rebuilding Iraq: Resource, Security, Governance, Essential Services, and Oversight Issues*, GAO-04–902R, GAO, Washington DC.

——, 2007. *Securing, Stabilizing, and Rebuilding Iraq*, GAO-07–1195, GAO, Washington DC.

Haggard, S. and Long, J., 2007. *On Benchmarks: Institutions and Violence in Iraq*, Unpublished paper, 1–48.

International Center for Transnational Justice (ICTJ), 2008. 'Briefing Paper: Iraq's New "Accountability and Justice" Law', ICTJ, New York, 22 January.

International Crisis Group (ICG), 2003, *Iraq: Building a New Security Structure*, Middle East Report No. 20, ICG, Baghdad and Brussels.

——, 2006. *The Next Iraqi War? Sectarianism and Civil Conflict*, Middle East Report No. 52, ICG, Amman, Baghdad and Brussels.

——, 2006. *Iraq's Muqtada al Sadr: Spoiler or Stabiliser?*, Middle East Report No. 55, ICG, Amman and Brussels.

——, 2008. *Iraq's Civil War: The Sadrists and the Surge*, Middle East Report No. 72, ICG, Baghdad, Damascus and Brussels.

International Institute for Strategic Studies (IISS), 2007. 'Iraq Under the Surge: Implementing Plan B', *Strategic Comments* 13:2, 1–2.

Kagan, Kimberley, 2007. 'ISW Interview with COL J.B. Burton, Commander of Dagger Brigade, Baghdad, Iraq', *Institute for the Study of War*, 14 November.

Katzman, Kenneth, 2006. *Iraq: Elections, Government, and Constitution*, RS21968, Congressional Research Service, Washington DC.

Kilcullen, David, 2007. 'Anatomy of a Tribal Revolt', posted on *Small Wars Journal*, 29 August.

Long, Austin, 2008. 'The Anbar Awakening', *Survival* 50:2, 67–94.

Manning, Carrie, 2006. 'Political Elites and Democratic State-building Efforts in Bosnia and Iraq', *Democratization* 13:5, 724–738.

Mowle, Thomas, 2006. 'Iraq's Militia Problem', *Survival* 48:3, 41–58.

——, 2007. 'Introduction: The Green Zone in 2004–05', in *Hope is Not a Plan: The War in Iraq From Inside the Green Zone*, ed. T. Mowle. Praeger Security International, Westport, CT.

Nordland, Rod, 2007. 'A Radical Cleric Gets Religion', *Newsweek*, 10 November.

Office of Research Opinion, 2003. 'Iraqi Public Has Wide Ranging Preferences for a Future Political System', *Opinion Analysis*, Department of State, Washington DC.

O'Hanlon, M.E. and Campbell, J.H., 2008. *Iraq Index Tracking Variables of Reconstruction and Security in Post-Saddam Iraq*, Brookings Institution, Washington DC.

Pollack, Kenneth, 2006. 'The Seven Deadly Sins of Failure in Iraq: A Retrospective Analysis of the Reconstruction', *The Middle East Review of International Affairs* 10:4.

Rathmell, A., Oliker, O., Kelly, T.K., *et al.*, 2005. *Developing Iraq's Security Sector: The Coalition Provisional Authority's Experience*, RAND, Santa Monica, CA.

RFE/RL, 2003. 'KDP Head Says Peshmerga May Merge with Iraqi Military', *RFE/RL Iraq Report* 6:21.

Ricks, Thomas E., 2006. *Fiasco: The American Military Adventure in Iraq*, Allen Lane, London.

Schwarz, Anthony J., 2007. 'Iraq's Militias: The True Threat to Coalition Success in Iraq', *Parameters: U.S. Army War College Quarterly* 27:1, 55–71.

Simon, Steven, 2008. 'The Price of the Surge: How U.S. Strategy Is Hastening Iraq's Demise', *Foreign Affairs* 87:3, 57–76.

Smith, Maj. N. and MacFarland, Col. S., 2008. 'Anbar Awakens: The Tipping Point', *Military Review* 88:2, 41–52.

Terrill, W. Andrew, 2004. *The United States and Iraq's Shi'ite Clergy: Partners or Adversaries?*, US Strategic Studies Institute, Carlisle, PA.

Ucko, David, 2008. 'Upcoming Iraqi Elections Must Consolidate Security Gains of "Sons of Iraq"', *World Politics Review*, 20 May.

US Department of Defense (DoD), 2006. *Measuring Security and Stability in Iraq*, Report to Congress, DoD, Washington DC.

al-Waeli, Kadhim H., 2007, 'Iraq: Cultural/Political and Media Observations: Operation Iraqi Freedom 2003, 04, 05, 07', unpublished brief.

5 Flip-flop rebel, dollar soldier

Demobilisation in the Democratic Republic of Congo

Zoë Marriage

Introduction

The Democratic Republic of Congo (DRC) has experienced a series of violent conflicts in the last ten years. Mobutu's rule, which became increasingly violent through the 1990s, was overturned in 1997 by a rebellion led by Laurent Kabila. The following year, a second war broke out in the east of the country, which continued until 2003 when a peace was agreed, although this has remained partial both geographically and categorically. Demobilisation stayed on the political agenda throughout the second war and became a central preoccupation when the peace was signed. The wars in DRC have seen massive recruitment and shifts of alliance, and this chapter explores a particular conundrum that relates to efforts at demobilisation: rebel fighters have been recruited for a few dollars and instability has arisen because soldiers are not paid, yet demobilisation programmes, which bring promises of reintegration grants, have not enticed people to disarm.

The chapter examines three features of the situation in Congo: the informalisation of politics and the economy; the exercise of power through violence; and the multiple crises in which people are living. Against this background, four demobilisation programmes are presented: the regular programme of adult fighters; the programme in Ituri; the demobilisation of children; and the demobilisation of foreign troops. The chapter investigates the implications of the current political situation for demobilisation efforts, and the achievements of the programmes as they stand.

The chapter draws on reports on the demobilisation and peace processes, and on a series of interviews conducted in Kisangani in 2005, which centred on people's perceptions of development and security. Setting the demobilisation within the wider context in Congo, the chapter contributes to a growing body of literature on demobilisation that goes beyond programme evaluation. The work of Norma Kriger, for example, identifies the political winners and losers from the demobilisation of guerrilla forces in Zimbabwe,[1] a theme that is taken up in this chapter. Demobilisation in Afghanistan and Sierra Leone, too, has been analysed with respect to the development trajectory;[2] this has parallels in Congo where forms of insecurity have continued and mutated through the episodes of demobilisation. The experience of Congo provides further evidence of broader political significance of security sector intervention.

Mobilisation and demobilisation in Congo – a conundrum

A Congolese man explained how some people in Kisangani were recruited to the Rally for Congolese Democracy (RCD), the Rwandan-backed insurgency movement that was occupying the town:

> There were some Congolese who were allied to the RCD. It was mainly soldiers, bourgemestres, community leaders, local leaders, and politicians who were allied to the RCD. They went to Rwanda for political-military training – they were sent there for free in the aeroplane. The RCD would give them $10 or $15 to support the rebellion – there are some civil servants who still support the RCD.[3]

International sponsors of demobilisation programmes face contradictory information: individual fighters, brigades or entire armies appear to be volatile and fickle in their support, changing sides for small amounts of money, or with the arrival of a different leadership. Large parts of Mobutu's army joined the advancing forces of Kabila; the following year, the RCD co-opted the security apparatus of strategic towns with apparent ease. Conversely, when demobilisation programmes are rolled out with incentives, income generation, promises of social recovery and reintegration, and at a cost topping $230 million,[4] they meet with significant and sometimes insurmountable obstacles.

Three related factors in Congo are relevant to this conundrum. The first is the informalisation of political and economic life, a phenomenon promoted by Mobutu Sese Seko, President of Zaire (now DRC) from 1965–97, as a means of splintering dissent, and which has continued through the 1990s. It is accompanied by a second factor – the use of violent power, which was meted out in Mobutu's time by the Presidential and Civil Guard, but has been a feature of Congolese life both before and since. The third factor is the multifaceted nature of the crisis that confronts people in Congo: there is a dire economic climate, a host of social and political conflicts, outright wars and international marginalisation and exploitation.

These factors – informalisation, violent power and the multiple crises – combine to create an environment in which demobilisation is extremely complex and problematic to implement. The chapter raises a further issue: the cost of failure for external policy makers and powerful politicians in Congo is low, and there are few incentives to address the weaknesses of the programme. Coupled with this, the power enjoyed by leaders of opposition factions rests on their plausible threat to remobilise, so a political volatility is embedded in a seemingly consensual process.

The conflicts

The conflicts in Congo involve intrastate fighting, transnational violence and interstate wars. Security agendas, too, are pursued at sub-national, national, regional and international levels: each party has an incentive to demobilise the others and impose its own agenda. Rwanda, for example, justified its incursions into Congo as a means of securing its border and disbanding the ex-Rwandan Armed Forces (ex-FAR) and Interahamwe. The arrival of the United Nations Mission in the Democratic Republic of Congo (MONUC), which is involved in demobilisation, coincided with increased international concern about the security threat posed by instability in developing countries. For the fighters, an array of incentives, opportunities and constraints influence decisions to demobilise or mobilise. Demobilisation involves handing over the means of violence – a weapon or a military position – whether by choice (demobilising oneself), or by instruction, incentives or force (being demobilised by others), and submitting to someone else's security agenda.

Informalisation of economy and politics

The present environment for demobilisation is shaped by the informalisation of the economy and political life that occurred during Mobutu's rule. The 1980s and 1990s saw declining terms of trade, the devastation of infrastructure, and the disruptive implementation of structural-adjustment programmes. Mobutu advised: '*debrouillez-vous*' ('fend for yourself') and the break-up of economic and political organisation that followed influenced the ways that wars were fought and the strategies that people employed to survive.

As people attempted to cope in a system that they could not overthrow, con-figurations of tangential support and self-sufficiency emerged that ultimately served to sustain the status quo. During the early 1990s, neglected elements of the army and population systematically pillaged the major towns in Congo. The pillages were apparently acts of protest, but played into the hands of Mobutu by increasing his relative power over the destitute population. One man assessed:

> From 1991 to 1993 it was a culture in the country – it was everywhere, not just here – and it started in Kinshasa. After that there were no more shops or businesses. The population was pillaging too. Since they weren't paid they had to find things to eat. Often they didn't eat it or use it; they just sold it on, but at a silly price, so there was no way of renewing the stock. In the pillage the rich became poor and the poor became rich.[5]

People who participated in the pillages made short-term gains in a process that was, in the longer term, detrimental and out of their control. Other features of the informalised economy include artisanal mining, which became increasingly sig-nificant as infrastructure was destroyed, and the evasion of the state through non-payment of taxes, which discarded any vestigial contract between the population and the leadership.[6] The informalisation of the economy was accompanied by the informalisation of political life. One man summarised the situation: 'Mobutu said, "Eat, dance, drink – do whatever you want, but don't touch my power. If anyone dares to challenge me, I'll kill them." But it was calm.'[7] No effective revolution was mounted and, as Mobutu's power became more tenuous, repression and the elimination of overt opposition forced political life underground.

The shocks came from outside: the termination of US patronage after the end of the Cold War, the arrival of the ex-FAR and Interahamwe following the genocide in Rwanda, and the subsequent invasion of Congo by the Rwandan and Ugandan armies. The scene had been set for massive violence. Mobutu's security machinery had been tuned to protect him and his circle (although it ultimately failed to do so); away from the capital, violence – decentralised and fragmented – allowed for insurgency, counterinsurgency, self-enrichment and self-defence.

Violent power

Seizing and retaining power is associated with direct violence in Congo, and elites have at times deliberately fuelled and exploited insecurity to impose and maintain a particular political order. As leaders arrive and leave with their entourages, armies become rebels and rebels become armies. This affects the formation of political and economic hierarchies, and power is accordingly associated more closely with violence than with bureaucratic political institutions. The colonial regime, the regime of Mobutu and the rebellions of the Alliance of Democratic Forces for the Liberation of Congo (ADFL, led by Laurent Kabila) and the RCD have each demonstrated that force is the means to power.

These regimes have all relied on foreign support, so the culture of violent power has been reinforced internationally. Commenting upon the international responses to events in Congo through the 1990s, Nzongola-Ntalaja observes that, 'changes through democratic means and the rule of law in Africa are not [seen as being] as deserving of unequivocal support as changes through the barrel of a gun'.[8] The intervention by external actors plays a part in defining the legitimacy of violence: in the past ten years, the formal states of Rwanda and Uganda – and the violence they inflict – have been supported or tolerated by their international donors, while Congo is further undermined.

The use of violence to gain political or economic resources has two noteworthy consequences. The first is that differences and inequalities are polarised. Violently concentrating wealth and power into the hands of some has involved the disempowerment and pauperisation of others. This has occurred over successive regimes, through predation and asset stripping as well as by blocking or manipulating trading routes. The second effect is related: the use of violence to determine patterns of distribution is provocative and multiplies existing antagonisms. Inflicting violence potentially fuels hostilities and anger, and the increased militarisation of society and availability of weapons offers the means by which to express violent revenge.

Multiple crises

By the mid-1990s, life in Congo was beset by crisis. The economy had been wrecked, workers were not paid, schools were struggling to function and hospitals were not supplied with medicines or equipment. The situation was rooted in the conflict between the leaders and the population, which was at times violent and, from the colonial era onwards, involved predation and exploitation. Through the 1990s, population movements, attacks and counter-attacks prompted by the Rwandan genocide destabilised the east of the country. The first Congolese war started in December 1996 and brought Laurent Kabila to power in May 1997. The second war started in August 1998, when Kabila's erstwhile backers – Rwanda and Uganda – turned against him and attempted to depose him directly and through their support of armed groups.

The crisis is compounded by the European, US and Asian interests in Congo's resources, wars and security situation. According to Mark Duffield, the development agendas of rich countries have become merged with their security concerns.[9] Congo does not pose a threat to international security and, therefore, has received little foreign aid, given the deprivation and war it has experienced. While Congo has been excluded on a formal level, the growth of transport and communications interactions have created the conditions for informal links to be made through unregulated transnational trade, which brings important benefits, as well as considerable costs to rich nations.

The marginalisation from formal international relations and the partial inclusion in informal international networks place Congo in an ambivalent position globally. The illegal exploitation of mineral resources has been the subject of a UN Panel of Experts and it has been documented by human-rights organisations. The trade in diamonds, coltan and gold, among other resources, responds to international demand but the profits do not reach the Congolese treasury. There is no overarching means of protection against the combination of social, political and economic disaster, the conflict within the leadership, civil and regional fighting and international neglect and abuse.

The situation challenges notions of common security. Whatever has been achieved elsewhere and in Congo has accommodated, promoted or depended on insecurity, isolation and exploitation of some groups. The security claims of Rwanda, particularly relating to the border, have occasioned massive insecurity in Congo; the economic security of foreign mining firms has been bolstered by the weakness in financial systems that would otherwise safeguard Congolese interests. At a personal level, immediate gains from mining often involve medium-term food insecurity and political instability. Various forms of security are competitive, and there is reason to be wary of other people's security agendas.

This begins to unravel one part of the conundrum posed at the beginning of the chapter, regarding the impression that soldiers often, and easily, switch sides between armed groups. David Keen has argued with reference to the Revolutionary United Front in Sierra Leone that the experience of fighters in ostensibly opposing groups can be marked more by similarity than by difference, and therefore, that they can move easily from one 'side' to the other.[10] In Congo, too, soldiers in the army and in other armed groups are unpaid and living a precarious existence. There may only be a small difference between being a foot soldier in one group as opposed to another, and $1 can then facilitate the choice. In investigating why it can be difficult to demobilise fighters, attention needs to turn to the array of conflicts confronting combatants and their decisions as to which ones to fight in order to pursue various – and often incompatible – goals.

The peace

A two-year power-sharing agreement saw the formation of a Transitional Government on 30 June 2003. General elections were planned for 30 June 2005 but were postponed until 30 July 2006 and went to a second round in October. The transition placed a premium on transferring the fighting and the military occupation of the east of the country to a political contest between the major players. The peace is supported by moves towards democratisation, such as the registration of voters and parties, the establishment of the Independent Electoral Commission and the elections. The Inter-Congolese Dialogue has provided a forum for political negotiations, and a new army, the Armed Forces of DRC (FARDC), is under construction at a proposed cost of $546 million.

There was no decisive military victory in Congo, and whatever peace has been established is partial. Following the Peace agreement, militias in North Katanga that were previously allied with the government fought with the army, resulting in the deaths of 5,000 people and the displacement of 1,350,000 between 2003 and 2006.[11] Fighting continues in Ituri district, previously under the administration of the Ugandan army, where the Congolese Lema and Hendu factions clashed over land and differing political and economic agendas. An estimated 50,000 people have been killed in Ituri since 1999, and the fighting has taken on a dynamic beyond the origins of the war.[12] Goma and Bukavu and the surrounding areas remain volatile as parties, including Rwandan groups, vie for access to the mineral resources in the Kivus. The unresolved political conflict between the Rwandan government and the Democratic Forces for the Liberation of Congo (FDLR), many of whose members are wanted on genocide charges, makes for an insecure environment. Human Rights Watch estimate that 400,000 people have been displaced in North Kivus since late 2006 alone.[13]

The political settlement reached in Congo emphasised the need to strengthen the state's institutions, including by restructuring and unifying the Army. As such, it appears to reflect processes of state making associated with the monopolisation of violence.[14] A second feature of the settlement was its conception of justice as being non-retributive: fighters were given political positions, or returned home with an amnesty (with the exception of those suspected of genocide crimes in Rwanda, who were handed to the International Criminal Tribunal in Arusha). Finally, the settlement was notable for including regional players, particularly political figures from the southern African region, which signalled recognition that there were broader interests vested in the conflict and the way that it was managed.

Demobilisation

Peace initiatives began six days after the start of the second war in August 1998, and continued on a monthly basis.[15] These were complicated by the fact that Paul

Kagame, Vice-President and Minister for Defence of Rwanda at the time, initially refused to acknowledge the presence of Rwandan troops in Congo, and
Laurent Kabila, then-President of Congo, refused to meet with the occupying
powers. The question of how to involve the opposition forces in the process was
a major stumbling block to negotiations. The first agreement was reached in
April 1999 in Sirte, Libya. It was brokered by Colonel Muammar Gaddafi, and
was signed by Kabila and President Yoweri Museveni of Uganda; it was also
signed by delegations from Chad and Eritrea, but not by Rwanda nor the RCD.

In July 1999, the Lusaka Ceasefire Agreement was signed by the governments of Angola, Congo, Namibia, Rwanda, Uganda and Zimbabwe. The RCD,
which was experiencing leadership troubles at the time, and the Movement for
the Liberation of Congo (MLC) signed the following month. The strength of the
Lusaka Agreement was that it included the majority of the belligerents but, as a
result, its terminology was weak in defining roles and mechanisms for implementation. The Agreement involved the voluntary withdrawal of foreign forces,
army restructuring, disarmament and UN peacekeeping. The Maimais (Congolese self-defence militias), the Army for the Liberation of Rwanda (ALiR) and
the Forces for the Defence of Democracy (FDD) were not included, and the UN
undertook to disarm these parties separately.

A major weakness of the demobilisation was that it was conceived as being an
unproblematic, technical and short project in which responsibility was not specifically allocated. The Joint Military Commission (JMC) was established to draw up
a demobilisation plan. Article III, clause 22, of the Lusaka Agreement held rather
vaguely, 'There shall be a mechanism for disarming militias and armed groups,
including the genocide forces. In this context, all parties commit themselves to
the process of locating, identifying, disarming and assembling all members of
armed groups in DRC.' This suggests a consensual and uncontentious process.
Disarmament was the subject of Chapter 9, which charged the JMC, with the
assistance of the UN and Organisation of African Unity (OAU), to track, disarm,
canton and document all armed groups, and hand over mass killers and war
criminals to the International Tribunal in Arusha. The disarmament was to take
120 days, and troop withdrawal 180 days – unrealistic timeframes that were subsequently disregarded. Instead, the proposed period of withdrawal saw the training, both by Rwanda and Uganda, of thousands of militia fighters to ensure that
their interests could be pursued post-withdrawal.[16]

There were difficulties, too, with the UN support, which was small and mili-
tarily unconvincing. The Lusaka Agreement led to UN Security Council Resolution 1291, which established MONUC. Despite the elaborate role envisaged for
MONUC, it was initially limited to 90, then 500, military observers. In 2000, the
first troops were deployed, bringing the mission strength to 5,537 (including military observers). Troop ceilings were subsequently raised to 8,700 in 2002, 10,800
in 2003, 16,700 in 2004 and 16,900 in 2005, when the actual strength of MONUC
stood at 16,258.[17] The Lusaka Agreement quietly acknowledged that MONUC's
capacity would be limited, which paved the way for a sustained Rwandan military
presence in Congo to deal with the problems that the UN could not solve.[18]

Prospects for demobilisation were weakened further as security threats persisted. The Lusaka Agreement was a ceasefire, not a peace; it was substantially violated, and its proposals were not implemented. In April 2000, the Kampala disengagement plan was signed, which, like the Lusaka Agreement, excluded the Maimais, FDD and ALiR. In July 2002, a Peace Agreement was signed in Pretoria dealing with the withdrawal of the Rwandan army and the dismantling of ex-FAR and Interahamwe by the Congolese army. On 6 September, Congo and Uganda signed a similar accord – the Luanda Agreement – that pertained to the withdrawal of Ugandan troops from the country.

Some progress was made with the Global and All-Inclusive Agreement on the Transition of the Democratic Republic of Congo. It was signed in Pretoria on 12 December 2002 by the government, the RCD, MLC, RCD-K/ML, RCD-N, Maimais, political opposition and active forces; but in drawing together the leaders, it marginalised many of the rank-and-file. The agreement confirmed Joseph Kabila's position as Head of State during the transition period, and instituted four vice-presidential positions and a government of 36 ministers and 25 deputy ministers.[19] The Pretoria Accords relied on the cessation of hostilities as a precondition for demobilisation. In April 2003, the 'Final Act' was signed in Sun City. An agreement on the cessation of hostilities and a re-launch of the peace process in Ituri was signed in Dar es Salaam in May 2003, and again in May 2004 in Kinshasa.

Demobilisation in Congo has four strands. As is evident from the lack of detail in design and from the consequent shortcomings, all operate on the basis that fighters will demobilise voluntarily and that a few hundred dollars (or in the case of children, a family home) will make demobilisation economically viable. The first strand is the national programme of demobilisation, which is administered by a dedicated governmental body and demobilises adult fighters from the parties' signatory to the Pretoria Accord. The second is the demobilisation of armed groups in Ituri, the district most affected by ongoing fighting. The third is the demobilisation of children, which is carried out by international NGOs, and the fourth process, run by the government and MONUC, relates to the demobilisation and repatriation of foreign troops fighting in Congo.

National Programme of DDR

The National Programme of Disarmament, Demobilisation and Reinsertion is run by CONADER, the National Commission for DDR. CONADER was created in December 2003 with a remit to re-establish security and reform and unite the army.[20] It launched its demobilisation programme in October 2004. CONADER operates in association with the Financial Management Unit, the Structure for Military Integration and the Inter-ministerial Committee for DDR, which comprises the Minister of Defence and the Minister of Social Affairs. The Congolese government provides security and support, and MONUC is responsible for the storage and destruction of weapons.[21]

In April 2004, the World Bank's International Development Association (IDA) agreed to grant $100 million to fund the demobilisation programme. This sum was matched in May 2004 by the Multi-Country Demobilization and Reintegration Programme (MDRP), whose contributing donors are Belgium, Canada, Denmark, the European Commission, France, Germany, Italy, the Netherlands, Norway, Sweden and the UK.[22] Funding has also taken the form of bilateral assistance from Belgium, Canada, Germany, Norway and the UK.[23] The demobilisation is a two-track process: ex-combatants choose between reinsertion into their communities and integration into the new national army, the FARDC. Funds were more forthcoming for demobilisation ($200 million) than for army reform ($14 million),[24] although the Joint Operations Centre and the European Commission sought to harmonise these processes.[25]

All the major armed groups signed up to demobilisation. This includes the Maimais, numbering 20–50,000, RCD-Goma at 45,000, RCD-N at 10,000, RCD-K/ML at 15,000, MLC at 30,000 and the Congolese Armed Forces (FAC) at 100–120,000.[26] Demobilised combatants were to be given an allowance of $125 and regrouped into orientation centres for disarmament, release and registration. Those who chose to join the army were to be moved to *brassage* centres for integration. The common track for demobilisation and integration involved sensitisation, regroupment, identification and orientation. The demobilisation relied on the premise that peace had been established and that there was no necessity for thousands of fighters; it was framed as a technical exercise of reallocating personnel. The combatants were not being realigned with regard to their political inclination, their political systems or their collective means of operating.

There were problems at implementation. In 2005, only six centres were functional (excluding those in Ituri). Some donors intervened bilaterally: Belgium trained a brigade – the first integrated brigade – in Kisangani, and Angola trained a brigade in Kitona.[27] The MDRP reported that 18,800 ex-combatants had been demobilised (including those in Ituri) by the end of June 2005 – the date initially agreed for elections.[28] If the figures on demobilisation in Ituri are in the region of 10,000 (see below), it follows that fewer than 10,000 combatants had been demobilised in the rest of the country at that stage.

Fighting in Northern Katanga eased in May 2006, but the logistics for demobilisation were not in place. Of the three fixed centres in Katanga only one was operational and, even there, there were problems in locating and paying the monthly instalments to demobilised fighters.[29]

Demobilisation and community reinsertion (Ituri)

Rather than abating, war in Ituri intensified after the Lusaka Agreements, and 20,000 or more lives were lost there in the period leading up to the Pretoria Accords.[30] During this time, there were never more than eight MONUC military observers stationed in Bunia.[31] The UNSC mission to Central Africa visited Bunia in June 2003 and, deploring the situation, recommended in favour of the transitional government and for the creation of a unified national army.[32] The demobilisation and community-reinsertion programmes for armed groups in Ituri were launched in September 2004 as a Rapid Response Mechanism. Five centres were opened immediately, followed by two others. Estimates for the number of fighters in Ituri range from 15,000 to 30,000.[33] Demobilisation in Ituri is complicated further by the fact that the Union of Congolese Patriots is not a signatory to the Pretoria Accords.

As with the regular programme, fighters were offered the choice between joining the Army and returning to civilian life. The ex-combatants who chose not to join the FARDC became the responsibility of the UN Development Programme (UNDP), which runs the Community Rehabilitation and Reintegration of Ex-combatants. This project involves a three-day course in preparation for civilian life and provides each former fighter with a $50 allowance and each family with one month's supply of food. The US Agency for International Development (USAID) claims that 12,500 combatants had been disarmed in Ituri by May 2005, while Integrated Regional Information Networks (IRIN) put the figure at 9,000.[34] The policy was in place for reintegration into civilian life, but only a few hundred of those who had disarmed in Ituri by the end of March 2005 were able to reintegrate, and fewer than 200 opted to join the national army.[35] This cast doubt on the viability of both options. Officially, the voluntary disarmament was completed in June 2005 when nearly 16,000 combatants reported to reception centres, but only 780 of these combatants applied for integration into the army. As to the 11,000 who applied for community reintegration, Amnesty International reports that in March 2006, more than 10,000 ex-combatants were still waiting for the projects to start.[36]

Demobilisation of child soldiers

The third process is the demobilisation of child soldiers. There are between 10,000 and 20,000 child soldiers in Congo, recruited to all sides.[37] It is estimated that about half of those fighting in Ituri are children,[38] and MDRP reports that 1,447 children were demobilised in June 2005.[39] A budget of $14.5 million, from the World Bank and UN Children's Fund (UNICEF), was approved for disbursement through four NGOs.[40] The demobilisation of children is linked to the national demobilisation programme, as under-18 combatants who present themselves to CONADER are handed over to the NGOs.

Save the Children supports the reunification of child ex-combatants with their families and reintegration into their communities, while a coalition of the International Rescue Committee (IRC), the International Foundation for Education and Self-help (IFESH) and CARE runs demobilisation projects in Province Orientale, North Katanga and Maniema.[41] The children stay in host families while the NGOs locate their families and arrange for transport home, which is often provided by MONUC. In Kisangani, where the programme is run by the IRC, there is a day-centre with basic recreation facilities and host families are provided with $1-worth of food per day to look after the children. MDRP reported that by June 2005, 11,790 children had left armed groups and 6,643 had been reunified with their families.[42] As with the adult programme, the logistics are designed to facilitate a straightforward return and do not engage with the opportunities or threats faced by the fighters.

Demobilisation of foreign troops

The fourth part of the demobilisation process is the Disarmament, Demobilisation, Repatriation, Reinstallation or Reintegration (DDRRR) programme, which is concerned with the removal from Congo of foreign troops, and is carried out by MONUC and the government. DDRRR was one of the pillars of Lusaka, although it was not implemented. At the time of the Agreement, there were troops in Congo from Angola, Namibia and Zimbabwe (which were allied to Kabila), and from Rwanda and Uganda (which were 'uninvited'). In addition, 15–30,000 Rwandan Hutu troops were fighting alongside the FAC or operating as militias in the Kivus.[43]

The first round of DDRRR was launched after the Global Peace Accord of 17 December 2002, and within days, 1,200 foreign troops had been repatriated. The Pretoria Peace Agreement between Rwanda and Congo laid out a 90-day plan for withdrawing Rwandan troops and dismantling the Interahamwe and ex-FAR. Rwanda withdrew 23,400 troops, but the Congolese government claimed that 20,000 Rwandan Patriot Army (RPA) soldiers remained in Congo and that the RPA was increasingly using the RCD as a cover. Similarly, the Ugandan army (UPDF) pulled out 1,200 troops from Beni and 650 from Gbadolite between late August and 10 September 2002;[44] however, the UN Panel of Experts investigating the exploitation of natural resources in Congo assessed that the UPDF had set up proxies that allowed them to continue extracting after their withdrawal.[45] The demobilisation plan had not addressed dimensions of the conflict beyond the formal agreement to withdraw.

Hostilities continued in the Kivus, and the Congolese government adopted measures to counter the FDLR, including banning its operations in Congo and arresting or expelling some of its more powerful members.[46] By 21 February 2003, UN figures listed 402 Rwandan Hutus as disarming and the FDLR as having not been dismantled.[47] Later that year, the International Crisis Group (ICG) described the demobilisation of foreign troops as a 'failure'.[48] Another round of demobilisation for foreign troops was initiated in October 2004, although the ex-FAR and the Interahamwe did not sign the declaration until 31 March 2005. The government undertook to begin demobilising the FDLR – numbering 8–10,000, and accompanied by twice as many dependents – within six months. FDLR troops were offered $300 to repatriate, but refused to do so as they feared Rwandan justice or reprisals if they returned home.[49]

By December 2004, 11,300 fighters and civilians had returned to Burundi, Rwanda and Uganda, but the programme subsequently floundered. Kabila's announcement, on 29 June 2005, that the army would disarm the FDLR by force was not followed by any orders to do so. The ICG reported that the FDLR and the FARDC were both stationed – apparently amicably – in Mwenga and Rusizi plain.[50] By March 2008, neither the FARDC nor Rwanda had disarmed the FDLR groups along the border,[51] who were estimated to number between 6,000 and 10,000. This was despite a communiqué in November 2007 in which the Congolese government undertook to disarm the militias forcibly and MONUC agreed to provide support. In March 2008, the UN Security Council (UNSC) passed a unanimous resolution that the FDLR and other Rwandan groups in Congo should disarm.[52]

The outcome

Many of the processes promoted in Congo since the accession of Joseph Kabila reflect the contemporary wisdom on demobilisation. Demobilisation took place within a context of Congo being officially reunified and open warfare having ceased in most places. The demobilisation programme was integrated into the broader peace process; in large part, funding has been forthcoming and has supported national institutions such as CONADER, the Independent Electoral Commission and the Inter-Congolese Dialogue. Reversals in the broader peace process, while frequent, have not thrown the demobilisation effort off track completely, and even the postponement of the elections did not result in widespread violence. Despite some amelioration in security countrywide, the demobilisation has been slow.

330,000 – 130,000 = 200,000/t

What went wrong? According to the second draft of the national plan for DDR, there are 330,000 combatants in Congo, of whom 130,000 were to be integrated into the FARDC while the remaining 200,000 were to be demobilised into civilian life. Time was not factored into the equation: the schedules outlined in the peace agreements for troop withdrawals, and for tracking, disarming and cantoning armed groups were so short as to be nonsensical, and there was no acknowledgement that the circumstances could change if the process was delayed. The lack of movement on demobilisation meant that neither the formation of the new national army nor the integration into civilian life of ex-combatants proceeded according to plan. One man in a village in Province Orientale gave his view:

> There was a national programme. It was publicised on the radio, but a lot of people don't have radios, and the language is difficult too – there's no local radio here. So people don't necessarily know about the demobilisation and there's no means of transport, so they can't go to Kisangani. In the east of the country there are some who have demobilised and gone home. But what will they do? The people who had arms – it's hard to return to civilian life when there's nothing to eat. They could take up arms again just to get some food. The Maimais went to Kisangani, but when they went there, there was no work, no money – what are they going to do?[53]

Demobilisation was conceptualised in the Lusaka Agreement and the Pretoria Accords, and consequently in CONADER documentation, as a static problem: there was a caseload of combatants to be demobilised. The language of the agreements themselves, of UNSC reports, and to a lesser degree of CONADER (which accepted the relevance of the political and juridical environment), was of logistical and technical challenges, described in terms of numbers to be demobilised and the allocation of tasks. The approach treated demobilisation as a security issue, and as one that is internal to Congo,[54] rather than acknowledging the multiple dimensions of the choice to disarm and the ongoing tensions, particularly with Rwanda, that make defection and remobilisation attractive.

The poor conceptualisation established an obstructive baseline assessment of the situation. It also restricted any further analysis of the social, economic and political conditions surrounding demobilisation by disregarding the influence of reversals and extraneous factors. Incidents of recruitment and re-recruitment, for example, were omitted from the picture. Nonetheless, recruitment to the FDLR has continued in the Kivus, new groups have emerged in Ituri and Equateur, and Maimai groups in Katanga, who had previously supported Kabila, turned against the government after the peace was signed. Other Maimai groups have returned to arms having been through the demobilisation procedure, as they did not receive what was promised in terms of logistical support, military recognition or security.[55] In particular, the integration of Maimais into the national army has proved problematic as they are from rural areas and many have little formal education.

A second factor omitted in the analysis was the political reorganisation of armed groups, which is sometimes not related to negotiations in Congo, but may have an impact on the political economy of violence. Much of the demobilisation (or demilitarisation) that *did* take place was not part of the official programme: the dissolution of the Union for the Total Independence of Angola (UNITA) following the death of Jonas Savimbi in Angola is a prominent example. Less dramatic, but still of consequence, is the fact that, of the six Ugandan groups that were in Congo when Lusaka was signed, only one was still active in Congo by 2002 – the Allied Democratic Front (ADF). Three had been disbanded, two had left Congo, and one had been subsumed into the ADF.[56] The impact of these realignments was not captured by the demobilisation programme; the provision of material incentives on a person-by-person basis appeals to individual rationality, disregarding the influence of political or psychological incentives or duties. As such, it does not take account of the shifting alliances and misplaces the decision-making process.

A further analytical restriction stemmed from the lack of attention paid to the internal dynamics of armed groups, the dynamics that exist between groups, and the differences in interests or activities. The RCD and MLC are administrative powers with strong political, financial and military backing from Rwanda and Uganda. Their functions, operations and command structures differ greatly from those of the Maimais, who have loose associations and comparatively little external support. Such variations in internal structure and external alliances imply that demobilisation will have different incentives and outcomes for different groups in terms of contingency plans, support networks and opportunity costs; but this variation was not reflected in the demobilisation programming.

These conceptual and analytical shortfalls were accompanied by unwarranted political assumptions about the intentions and capacity of agents directly involved in the fighting and of external actors. The Congolese state has a role in demobilisation, but its actions have been limited: government institutions such as CONADER were established, but laboriously, and the developmental agenda did not facilitate the integration of ex-combatants into civilian life. Roads, schools or hospitals were not built, salaries of civil servants were derisory and often late. The combination of poorly implemented demobilisation projects and limited development provided few reasons to demobilise, and several reasons to be wary of the agenda advanced by the government.

Further miscalculations arose from the assumptions over the role to be played by the FARDC. While FARDC soldiers deployed in many areas, there was an institutional malaise within the Army. There were incidents of desertion (for example, of Rwandophone troops – those who speak Kinyarwanda – on the eastern border in August 2005), and accusations of disparities in pay and conditions. There are also shortages of equipment and salaries, and 'ghost' soldiers on the books.[57] These factors undermine confidence in the Army, altering the decisions facing combatants. The demobilisation plan contained assumptions, too, about the commitment of regional and international players. In fact, there was little backing for the programme: MONUC, even after several increases in troop numbers and the range of personnel, lacked the strength necessary to undertake the tasks allocated to it. Likewise, Rwanda and Uganda's rhetorical commitment to withdraw was not borne out in practice, and only finally occurred after several years of stalling.

The drawbacks identified compromise demobilisation because the efforts made within the official framework did not address or respond to what was happening on the ground or what was in fact possible. This ushers in a further dysfunction, as it reduces the credibility of demobilisation. The choices for individual fighters and armed groups, whether Congolese, Rwandan or Ugandan have remained the same, as was demonstrated by threats made in August 2005 by the RCD general, Laurent Nkunda – heading the National Congress for the Defence of the People (CNDP) – to reinvade eastern Congo. An arrest warrant was issued soon after, but the arrest did not take place and militias allied to Nkunda attacked Rutshuru (North Kivu) in early 2006. Realistic and flexible timeframes for demobilisation supported by adequate logistical and military resources would have allowed very different outcomes and enabled policy makers, politicians and military personnel to respond to unpredictable factors as they arose. In some ways, the observations that demobilisation was poorly conceived, analytically fragile and not backed by a plausible security or development agenda make the situation not easier to understand, but harder: the task is to discover why this form of demobilisation seemed like a good idea, and what can be learnt from the experience.

1 + 4 = 0

While there are inherent shortcomings to the demobilisation in Congo, it is reasonable when analysing policy to identify not only that which is not happening,
but also that which has happened, and to ask: what went right, and for whom?[58]
Demobilisation constitutes one part of a larger political settlement and analysis
of the demobilisation programme accordingly needs to extend to a wider analysis of the peace of which it forms a part.

The peace agreed in Pretoria sought to transform war into a political contest
and saw the inclusion of Abdoulaye Yerodia Ndombasi (government), Azarias
Ruberwa (RCD), Arthur Zahidi Ngoma (political opposition) and Jean Pierre
Bemba (MLC) into the Transitional Government. The inauguration of these four
vice-presidents was lauded internationally, but widely derided in Congo. One
Congolese woman explained the disappointment:

> [Joseph Kabila] promised lots of things, but he's done nothing. We regret
> that. He doesn't pay the civil servants, the teachers or the soldiers, and it's
> not necessary for the people of Congo to have five presidents. I think it's
> because they're all rebels and it's to put an end to the war in the east, but
> they do nothing. We say, '1 + 4 = 0' – they don't do anything.[59]

The accusation of inactivity was supported by the limited progress made in
setting up the disarmament and demobilisation of the foreign forces (particularly
the FDLR) and in establishing the conditions for reintegration. At the same time,
though, there is no evidence that the president or vice-presidents bore any direct
cost for the apparent policy failure; the gulf between the versions of events presented in demobilisation policy and on the ground has allowed the leadership to
claim some success irrespective of the lack of more concrete developments. In
his analysis of warlord politics, William Reno describes a tendency by warlords
to present a façade of formality on the stage of international relations, behind
which more influential politics takes place.[60] When this tendency is coupled with
the observation that the political elites have interests that conflict with those of
the population, it quickly becomes problematic, not only analytically but also
politically, to accept the formal process at face value.

The political elites in Congo made gains from the demobilisation programme
and peace process. Joseph Kabila increased his prestige as a peacemaker within
the southern African region and among international donors. The opposition
movements also gained: they joined the transitional government. The agreement
hinged on its ability to offer incentives to the leadership of opposition factions
and it demonstrated innovation in policy thinking; it is however necessary to
investigate whether it has made other parts of the demobilisation process more
or less likely. None of the politicians in the transitional government was elected
or promoted by popular support, and the economies that they established
violently during the war were not dismantled. Asked if the installation of the
vice-presidents was necessary for peace, a Congolese civil servant assessed:

For the time being it's a reward for those who created trouble in Congo. To satisfy them – it's better. After killing people they lead a better life, but it's time for them to go and leave Congo. Can you believe that someone who has murdered can lead a better life? I saw people buried alive. Someone like Bemba has eaten people and now is a president. We have a country with five presidents – they are eating money![61]

The peace process and demobilisation were palatable for international consumption too. As they took place at the level of formal politics, they did not require broad-based support, and this lack of democratic procedure meant that a notional agreement was relatively easy to achieve. The advantage of including the leadership of opposition-armed groups is that it opens up the possibility of fundamentally changing the dynamics of the conflict. What is instead observable, however, is that the formal political version of events created a reassuring impression of progress, even when there was no change in the structures that were proving destructive. The appeal of the peace and its constituent parts, such as demobilisation, increased the cosiness between international donors and observers and Congolese politicians.

The façade of peace and demobilisation is not merely an agreement of convenience between the political elites of Congo, Rwanda and Uganda and the foreign donors. The shape of the peace – its privileging of certain parties and its oversight of some forms of violence – reflects the prevailing aid agenda in the Great Lakes region in the post-genocide era. Funding to Rwanda and Uganda has enabled these countries to extract resources from Congo, bolstering their domestic development and serving international mineral and timber markets. Aid agendas in Rwanda and Uganda were pursued even when they compromised the security agenda in Congo; the exception came only when the war in Congo endangered other countries in the region. Tensions between Uganda and Rwanda led to repeated clashes between their armies in Kisangani. This antagonism posed a threat to UK-sponsored development in Rwanda and Uganda, and Tony Blair convened talks between Museveni and Kagame in London in November 2001.

While the demobilisation programme and peace process connoted political advantages for the signatory parties and their international funders, it is significant that these advantages did not depend on demobilisation actually taking place in a profound way. Although the negotiations on peace and the developments that followed have started to address some aspects of the war, the mechanisms for implementing the agreements have been described only in vague terms. As a result, no party is responsible for what the programme achieves and, consequently, no party has any incentive to address the weaknesses that arise.

Implications for external actors – untangling the conundrum

This chapter opened with a conundrum: while combatants in Congo appear to be capricious in their support and motivated by small cash rewards, they are not easily persuaded to disarm by expensive demobilisation programmes. It is now possible to untangle this apparent contradiction. First, combatants *appear* fickle – there have been mass desertions in the army, side swapping and collaboration between supposedly opposing groups – but this apparent fickleness may be explained in two ways. In some instances, the incentives to join one group or another are similar, so switching between two Congolese 'sides' does not involve a volte face. Elsewhere, recruitment is forced or changes in the security environment impose a dramatic reordering of priorities and the need to mobilise or defect. Neither of these scenarios implies that combatants can be bought easily by external actors.

Second, to date the demobilisation has not offered much to combatants either financially or in terms of providing security. Its implementation was unreliable – there were numerous delays and logistical problems – and the programme was incapable of responding to dynamic circumstances or competing needs. While demobilisation was ostensibly part of the peace process, peace as it has been delivered did not offer foot-soldiers alternative employment, services or social or economic infrastructure.

A third relevant factor is that the conundrum is based on an apolitical observation. Analysis has illustrated that there are relationships within and between groups, and that the demobilisation programme makes a number of crucial and self-destructive assumptions about the capacities or incentives of key players. Further, the constraints on ordinary combatants have not been fully acknowledged in the demobilisation programming, and questionable assumptions have been made about the nature and outcome of individuals' decisions.

In order to draw out the implications for external actors, it is necessary to investigate the role they have played and the mechanisms by which obstacles to demobilisation are confronted or reinforced by the programme. The preceding two sections have argued that frailties in demobilisation stem both from fundamental limitations in the approach and from the range of incentives that encourage powerful actors to institutionalise these limitations. These two factors need to be taken into account when drawing conclusions.

In assessing the situation, it is also worth considering to what extent the analysis is specific to Congo. The informalisation of political and economic life discussed at the outset of this chapter occurs in many developing countries, although the fervour with which it was pursued by Mobutu was exceptional. With regard to the use of violent power and the multiple crises facing the country, Congo's experience, again, is extreme in both its scale and intensity. The size of the country and the number and diversity of interests represented creates particular logistical and political hazards, and the involvement of regional and international actors exceeds that seen in other conflicts. Therefore, the magnitude of the obstacles is unlikely to be matched in other contexts, but the combination of events and the conclusions arising from their analysis may have applicability elsewhere.

Informalisation of economy and politics

The informalisation of the economy and political life affects what relationships are forged and the arrangements people make for their own security. It is significant in determining the formation of armed groups at sub-national levels, the opportunities for unregulated and transnational traffic in light arms, and the shape and functions of non-formal networks of resource exploitation. By establishing proxies to maintain their mining, trading and communications links, the Rwandan and Ugandan armies were able to profit from the informal political and economic configurations in Congo even as they withdrew from the areas they had been occupying. While the existence of myriad militia groups is a function of reliance on the non-formal sector, the support that they enjoy depends also on the interface between the formal and informal sectors. The Congolese government, in its counterinsurgency operations against the RPA and RCD, supported militias, including the Maimais and the FDLR in the Kivus.

The processes of peace have placed emphasis on strengthening state institutions and monopolising the use of violence, and this could potentially counter the informalised nature of the economy and political life. The process is ineffectual, though, as the links between the state and the population have been corroded by years of abuse; because of this, developments in Congo differ crucially from conventional models of state-building. The government, demobilisation and social development are supported in ways that are not coordinated with, or appreciably linked to, each other and there is no means of forging a contractual relationship between the leadership and the population.

Instead, external support has privileged formal institutions, undermining the accountability of the political elites, as they are answerable to a (not very attentive) set of international donors rather than to any domestic constituency. Rather than fostering a functional state, this increases the gap and conflict between the leadership and the population, reinforcing the need for an informalised economy but without reinforcing the mechanisms by which people are able to cope: salaries are low or not paid and infrastructure is not funded. Formulating demobilisation policy with explicit reference to the informalisation of the economy and political life indicates three possible approaches that could increase the scope and flexibility of donor involvement. These would depend on a nuanced analysis of the political economy of the conflict, tracing in detail what is being achieved and how.

The first approach would be to engage with the informal economy, recognising the political and economic choices that people face and the potential for developments that take place informally and foster security. In the north, this would require a commitment to compromising the interests of powerful groups that benefit from unregulated trade and the opportunities to pursue this through violence. In Congo, it involves working on an understanding of how informal networks of trade and violence operate and the role of history, identity and religion in establishing codes of practice and hierarchies of priorities.

Through such an understanding, support can be withdrawn from informal methods of extraction, investment and trade that lead to violence.

The second approach would be to address seriously the retreat of the elites from responsibility, and not to nurture the façade that has proved to be inert or destructive. This implies closer and less unequal relations between Congo and donors, and a rejection of the superficiality that has characterised negotiations. Fostering accountability to the people and reintegrating violent actors into political life demands a profound understanding of Congolese politics as they are rather than as they seem. The interpretation of politics as resting in decisions taken by faction leaders has proved inadequate in that while they have officially demobilised, demobilisation has been rejected by other combatants and partly because of the way they have seen the leaders treated. Engagement with the politics of demobilisation involves taking strategic decisions on trade-offs and sequencing, rather than assuming that disarmament, demobilisation and reintegration will follow each other and be reinforcing. The re-mobilisation of some fighters, the lack of integration and the shifting of agendas indicate that the process is not linear.

A third approach would be to engage specifically with the interface between the formal and the informal economies. The decentralisation of violence has been shaped by the relationships between the Congolese state, other states in the region and, further afield, mining opportunities and Congolese labour. Poor attention to the links between the formal and informal sectors has resulted in the reluctance of irregular fighters to join the Army. For some, this would be not a formalisation of their position as a fighter but a defection to the other side. For others, there is low confidence in the formal structures, and many Army positions are untenable without recourse to informal means of making money. In practical terms, the task for donors is to maximise the opportunities of people in Congo by decreasing the costs of integration into formal economies.

Violent power

The demobilisation and peace processes in Congo have had some impact on the use of violent power. The incorporation of the opposition into the government has allowed for a cooling of outright hostilities and has delivered some signs of political development. There is a degree of irony, though, as transforming the war into a political contest seems to suggest that fighting is not a legitimate tool, yet, at the same time, this is precisely how most of those in power obtained their position.

Responding to violence can potentially aggravate or diffuse the security situation. In addressing violence, the peace and demobilisation in Congo have issued a combination of rewards, aggression and neglect. Power has been allocated to violent actors, and the success thus achieved in halting their military operations has been undercut by the fact that the privileges granted to them involves no responsibility. This potentially reinforces violence, as these actors may be more likely to use force in the future, particularly if their ambitions are frustrated. In addition, by allocating this form of political power, the peace and demobilisation processes have increased the vulnerability of the population, reduced the incentives for foot soldiers to disarm and potentially fuelled a tendency towards violent self-defence. Therefore, while the apparent intention is reconciliatory, the approach can be inflammatory if aggressors are perceived as being rewarded; this underscores the significance of responding to the needs of non-aggressive parties through the construction of physical and political infrastructure.

A second – and counterproductive – response to violence has involved combinations of neglect and aggression. The neglect originates at the conceptual level, when forms of violence are overlooked. The assumption of the cessation of hostilities is a form of neglect, and it allows for the continuation of the political status quo, as it does not interrogate the distribution or use of violent power. Such oversight has led to catastrophic policy-making and interventions in the past in the Great Lakes region. The refuge and international aid supplied to the ex-FAR and Interahamwe in the camps for displaced people in eastern Congo following the Rwandan genocide stemmed from an uncritical and insufficient political analysis on the part of external actors. On the other hand, more recent international support to Rwanda and Uganda has allowed the build-up of military capacity and has overlooked the role of these countries as aggressors in Congo.

At the level of operations, the neglect inherent to the uneven implementation of the demobilisation combines with forms of aggression to increase the currency of violent power. For example, with regard to the conflict between Rwanda and the FDLR, inconsistency and reneging on all sides has facilitated the continuation of violence in the Kivus. The solutions offered – that Rwanda should engage forcefully with the FDLR or that MONUC receive a mandate to confront them violently – exacerbate the situation. The FDLR have experienced a lot of violence and have not disbanded; the more violence they are subjected to, the greater the salience of their claims to a cause and the greater their ability to recruit.

A further result of this combination of neglect and aggression is the increased vulnerability of some people – particularly those in the east of Congo – as changes in the security environment generate new power imbalances and opportunities to fight. The FDLR are no longer a serious threat to Kigali, and the Rwandan administration is pushed harder to justify its interference.[62] Thus, the strengthening of the Rwandan position leads to a cycle of posturing and provocation between the RPA and the FDLR as aggression towards the FDLR incites further rounds of fighting that justify the continued Rwandan presence. Diffusing this situation can be achieved only if the violence is acknowledged as a meaningful event that shapes relationships between Congo and Rwanda, rather than simply an obstacle to the demobilisation. This moves the analysis away from merely an evaluation of Rwanda's security concerns, often expressed in terms of the number of fighters amassed on the border, and towards an understanding of the political economy that is being pursued in the region by means of violence.

Multiple crises

This chapter has demonstrated that the multifaceted nature of the crisis in which people are living has a bearing on the choices they take regarding demobilisation. If civilian life is not an attractive option for combatants, there is continuing violence and further threats. Entrenching existing hierarchies and uses of violence at local and national levels, by cultivating policy that is blind to the political economy, reinforces the crisis; the demobilisation programme has been based on an assumption that the choices that combatants take can be depoliticised and that there is a linear process of demobilisation.

The peace process and demobilisation programme brought non-state actors into the political arena, rather than imprisoning or eliminating them, and their inclusion could be harnessed to deal simultaneously with different aspects of the multiple crises. Owing to the problems of representation and accountability that have been discussed, this potential has not been fulfilled; in fact, there has not really been an *integration* of ex-combatants. It is more the case that a new layer has been created, and this has generated a stable, politically and economically regressive peace in Kinshasa. The social and economic conditions have proved more conducive to absorbing the top brass than the foot soldiers, but even for the leadership, the possibility of reneging remains should new political developments be perceived as adverse.

Some direction for external actors can be found in the apparent correlation between the numbers of fighters demobilising and the progress (or lack thereof) in the peace process; demobilisation has increased at moments of institutional change.[63] The implication is that, as Mats Berdal has argued, the most significant contribution that can be made to shore up demobilisation is to support a peace process.[64] Following this path in Congo, though, involves not merely implementing the peace process, but critiquing it, to reach an understanding of the interaction of events – the lack of infrastructure, the bias of aid, and the involvement of Rwanda and Uganda. The inability of international funders to assess critically the impact of their assistance in the region has contributed to the insecurity, and has forged alliances with those elements that benefit directly from that insecurity.

The key is the relationship between the government and the people. As has been observed, this relationship has been undermined at a national level by reducing the politicians' accountability to the population, and regionally, by implementing aid agendas that support Rwanda and Uganda but counter efforts towards development and peace in Congo. The implication is that external donors should increase their awareness of their impact on the composition of power, should arrest processes that increase the gap and conflict between the elites and the populations, and should prioritise the establishment of contacts and contracts between the leaders and the population.

Concluding remarks

In the early 1990s, the Zairian population played into the hands of Mobutu and furthered his depredations by pillaging the country's infrastructure and services. There were some winners from the pillage, but for the majority of the population, whatever immediate gains were made were cancelled out by longer-term losses. This chapter has investigated how – in a way that may be analogous – there are tangentially connected incentives and occasions of neglect that result in the dysfunction of the demobilisation programme. The pillage in this context is political in nature – the short-term gains and confidence tricks sustain the process, but risk establishing political institutions that are, in the long term, destructive and abusive.

The regional elites in Congo's wars have incentives to consolidate their power, particularly as the opportunities to profit from direct violence recedes, and international donors have interests in Congo and the development of the Great Lakes region. Support for the demobilisation programme in Congo is varied in the nature and sincerity of its commitment. Some of the signatory parties are interested in being in agreement, but not in demobilising; for donors, the impact of the programme is marginal, whatever the outcome. While demobilisation is just one aspect of the international involvement in Congo, the distance between the decision-making and the responsibility (on the level of international actors) affects what sort of development takes place. This has consequences for the kinds of institutions that are established in Congo and the kinds of relationships that are established between Congo and other countries in the region.

Notes

1 Kriger, *Guerrilla Veterans in Postwar Zimbabwe*.
2 Giustozzi, 'The Demodernisation of an Army'; Fithen and Richards, 'Making War, Crafting Peace'.
3 Interview with bicycle-taxi rider, Kisangani, 8 September 2005.
4 Ball and Hendrickson, *Review of International Financing Arrangements*.
5 Interview with ex-university student, Kisangani, 23 August 2005.
6 MacGaffey, *The Real Economy of Zaire*.
7 Interview with hotel waiter, Kisangani, 20 August 2005.
8 Nzongola-Ntalaja, *The Congo from Leopold to Kabila*, 1.
9 Duffield, *Global Governance and the New Wars*.
10 Keen, *Conflict and Collusion in Sierra Leone*.
11 ICG, Katanga: The Congo's Forgotten Crisis, 1.
12 'Another rebel group gives up arms', Integrated Regional Information Networks (IRIN), 17 March 2008, www.irinnews.org/Report.aspx?ReportId=70449 (accessed 8 April 2008).
13 Human Rights Watch, 'DR Congo. Warring Sides Must Protect Civilians', Human Rights News, 11 September 2007 www.hrw.org/english/docs/2007/12/11/congo17534.htm (accessed 8 April 2008).
14 Tilly, 'War Making and State Making as Organized Crime'.
15 ICG, *The Agreement on a Cease-Fire in the Democratic Republic of Congo*.
16 Ibid. 28.
17 MONUC. www.un.org/Depts/dpko/missions/monuc/background.html (accessed 2 November 2005).
18 ICG, *Disarmament in the Congo*, 13.
19 UNSC, *Thirteenth Report of the Secretary-General*.
20 Government of DRC, 'Programme National de Désarmement, Démobilisation et Réinsertion'.
21 MDRP, 'Country profile: Democratic Republic of Congo'.
22 MDRP, 'Progress Report and Work Plan', 2.
23 Ball and Hendrickson, *Review of International Financing Arrangements*, 42.
24 ICG, *A Congo Action Plan*, 6.
25 MDRP, 'Progress Report and Work Plan', 3.
26 UNSC, *First Assessment of the Armed Groups*; Boshoff, 'Overview of Security Sector Reform'; ICG, *The Congo's Transition is Failing*, 2.

27 ICG, *A Congo Action Plan*, 5.
28 MDRP, 'Progress Report and Work Plan', 4.
29 ICG, *Katanga: Congo's Forgotten Crisis*, 4.
30 UNSC, *Special Report of the Secretary-General*.
31 OCHA, 'DRC: Special Report on Ituri District, Northeastern DRC', 1.
32 UNSC, *Report of the Security Council Mission to Central Africa*.
33 Boshoff, 'Overview of Security Sector Reform'.
34 USAID, 'USAID/OTI DRC Field Report'.
35 'DRC: Reintegrating Ituri's Ex-Militias', IRIN, 8 April 2005.
36 Amnesty International, *DDR and Reform of the Army*, 16–7.
37 OXFAM *et al.*, *No End in Sight*, 4; 'DR Congo Government Begins Demobilising Child Soldiers', Agence France-Presse, 19 December 2001.
38 OCHA, 'DRC: Special Report on Ituri District' 1.
39 MDRP, 'Progress Report and Work Plan'.
40 Ibid., 10.
41 Ibid., 10.
42 Ibid., 4.
43 ICG, *Disarmament in the Congo: Investing in Conflict Prevention*, 2; ICG, *Disarmament in the Congo: Jump-starting DDRRR*, 4.
44 UNSC, *Special Report of the Secretary-General*, 3.
45 UNSC, *Final Report of the Panel of Experts*.
46 ICG, *Rwandan Hutu Rebels in the Congo*.
47 UNSC, *Thirteenth report of the Secretary-General*.
48 ICG, *Rwandan Hutu Rebels in the Congo*, i.
49 ICG, *The Congo: Solving the FDLR Problem Once and For All*.
50 ICG, 'Congo: Deal with the FDLR Threat Now', CrisisWebNews, 14 September 2005.
51 'Kinshasa unable to disarm FDLR rebels', IRIN, 17 March 2008, www.irinnews.org/Report.aspx?ReportId=77320 (accessed 8 April 2008).
52 James Munyaneza, 'Rwanda: FDLR Must Surrender Now, Insists UN Security Council', *The New Times*, 15 March 2008.
53 Interview, farmer, Basua (Province Orientale), 10 August 2005.
54 ICG, *Rwandan Hutu Rebels in the Congo*, i.
55 Interview OCHA representative, Kisangani, 18 August 2005; UN Monitoring of the Humanitarian Situation in DRC, 30/07/05–05/08/05.
56 UNSC, *First assessment of the Armed Groups*, 3.
57 Boshoff, 'Update on the Status of Army Integration in the DRC'.
58 Keen, *Conflict and Collusion*, 166–169.
59 Interview with UDPS campaigner, Kisangani, 30 August 2005.
60 Reno, *Warlord Politics and African States*.
61 Interview with primary school inspector, Kisangani, 25 August 2005.
62 ICG, *The Congo's Transition is Failing*, i.
63 'DRC: Disarmament programme gathers momentum', IRIN, 27 February 2004, www.globalsecurity.org/military/library/news/2004/02/mil-040227-irin03.htm (accessed 10 October 2008).
64 Berdal, *Disarmament and Demobilisation after Civil Wars*.

References

Amnesty International, 2007. *Democratic Republic of Congo. Disarmament, Demobilization and Reintegration (DDR) and the Reform of the Army*. AFR62/001/2007.
Ball, Nicole, and Hendrickson, Dylan, 2005. *Review of International Financing Arrangements for Disarmament, Demobilization and Reintegration*, Phase 1 Report to Working

Group 2 of the Stockholm Initiative on Disarmament, Demobilization and Reintegration (SIDDR), 16 May.

Berdal, Mats, 1996. *Disarmament and Demobilisation after Civil Wars. Arms, Soldiers and the Termination of Conflict*, Adelphi Paper 303, Oxford University Press for International Institute for Strategic Studies, Oxford.

Boshoff, Henri, 2004. 'Overview of Security Sector Reform Processes in the DRC', *African Security Review* 13:4.

——, 2005. 'Update on the Status of Army Integration in the DRC', *Situation Report* Institute for Security Studies, Pretoria, 2 September.

Duffield, Mark, 2001. *Global Governance and the New Wars: The Merging of Development and Security*, Zed Books, London and New York.

Fithen, Caspar and Richards, Paul, 2005. 'Making War, Crafting Peace: Militia Solidarities and Demobilisation in Sierra Leone', in Paul Richards (ed.). *No Peace No War: An Anthropology of Contemporary Armed Conflicts*, James Currey, Oxford.

Giustozzi, Antonio, 2004. 'The Demodernisation of an Army: Northern Afghanistan, 1992–2001', *Small Wars and Insurgencies* 15:1.

Government of the DRC, 2004. Programme National de Désarmement, Démobilisation et Réinsertion – PNDDR (National Programme of Disarmament, Demobilisation and Reintegration) Kinshasa.

International Crisis Group (ICG), (1999) *The Agreement on a Cease-Fire in the Democratic Republic of Congo: An Analysis of the Agreement and Prospects for Peace*, Democratic Republic of Congo Report No. 5, Nairobi/Brussels, ICG, 20 August.

——, 2001. *Disarmament in the Congo: Investing in Conflict Prevention*, Africa Briefing, Nairobi/Washington/Brussels, ICG, 12 June.

——, 2001. *Disarmament in the Congo: Jump-starting DDRRR to Prevent Further War*, Africa Report No. 38, Nairobi/Brussels, ICG, 14 December.

——, 2003. *Rwandan Hutu Rebels in the Congo: A New Approach to Disarmament and Reintegration*, Africa Report No. 63, Nairobi/Brussels, ICG, 23 May.

——, 2005. *A Congo Action Plan*', Africa Briefing No. 34, Nairobi/Brussels, ICG, 19 October.

——, 2005. *The Congo's Transition is Failing: Crisis in the Kivus*, Africa Report No. 91, Nairobi/Brussels, ICG, 30 March.

——, 2005. *Congo: Solving the FDLR Problem Once and For All*, Africa Briefing No. 25, Nairobi/Brussels, ICG, 12 May.

——, 2006. *Katanga: The Congo's Forgotten Crisis*, Africa Report 103, Nairobi/Brussels, ICG, 9 January.

Keen, David, 2005. *Conflict and Collusion in Sierra Leone*, James Currey, Oxford.

Kriger, Norma, 2003. 'Introduction', in Kriger, N. (ed.), *Guerrilla Veterans in Postwar Zimbabwe: Symbolic and Violent Politics, 1980–1987*, CUP, Cambridge.

MacGaffey, Janet, 1991. *The Real Economy of Zaire: The Contribution of Smuggling and Other Unofficial Activities to National Wealth*, James Currey, London.

Multi-Country Demobilization and Reintegration Programme (MDRP), 'Progress Report and Work Plan', Various reports, available at: www.mdrp.org.

——, 2004. 'Country Profile: Democratic Republic of Congo (DRC)', 11 May.

Nzongola-Ntalaja, Georges (2002) *The Congo from Leopold to Kabila. A People's History*, Zed Books, London and New York.

OCHA (United Nations Office for the Coordination of Humanitarian Affairs), 'DRC: Special Report on Ituri District, Northeastern DRC', Integrated Regional Information Networks (IRIN), United Nations.

Oxfam, Save the Children–UK and Christian Aid, 2001. *No End in Sight: The Human Tragedy of the Conflict in the Democratic Republic of Congo*. Oxfam, Save the Children, Christian Aid, August.

Reno, William, 1998. *Warlord Politics and African States*, Lynne Rienner, Boulder, CO.

Tilly, Charles,1985. 'War Making and State Making as Organized Crime', in Evans, P., Reuschemeyer, D. and Skocpol, T. (eds), *Bringing the State Back In*, Cambridge University Press, New York.

United Nations Security Council (UNSC), 2002. *Special Report of the Secretary-General on the United Nations Organization Mission in the Democratic Republic of the Congo*, S/2002/1005, 10 September 2002.

——, 2002. *Final Report of the Panel of Experts on the Illegal Exploitation of Natural Resources and Other Forms of Wealth of the Democratic Republic of the Congo –* S/2002/1146, 16 October.

——, 2003. *Report of the Security Council Mission to Central Africa, 7–16 June 2003*, S/2003/653.

——, 2003. *Thirteenth Report of the Secretary-General on the United Nations Organization Mission in the Democratic Republic of the Congo*, S/2003/211, United Nations.

——, 2005. *First Assessment of the Armed Groups Operating in DR Congo*, S/2002/341, 5 April.

United States Agency for International Development (USAID), 2005. 'USAID/OTI DRC Field Report', May. Available at www.usaid.gov/our_work/cross-cutting_programs/transition_initiatives/country/congo/rpt0505.html (accessed on 17 April 2007).

6 The challenge of DDR in Northern Uganda

The Lord's Resistance Army[1]

Anna Borzello

Introduction

Lord's Resistance Army (LRA) rebels have been fighting in northern Uganda for the past two decades in what has become Africa's longest running conflict. The group, which has little popular support, is notorious for abducting children and targeting civilians. It is led by Joseph Kony, a self-styled prophet, who claims to be fighting to turn the Acholi people back to God. The insecurity is centred in the northern Ugandan districts of Gulu, Kitgum and Pader,[2] sometimes referred to as Acholiland (after the Acholi, who are the predominant ethnic group in the region). However, the rebels have also operated in the north and eastern Ugandan districts of Lira, Apac, Adjumani, Kabaramaido, Katakwi and Soroti, as well as in southern Sudan and, more recently, in northeastern Democratic Republic of Congo (DRC).

The conflict has devastated the region and widened the divide between north and south Uganda. At its height, the conflict caused the displacement of over 1.8 million people, about 90 per cent of the population of Acholi, forcing them to live in squalid, overcrowded camps. Some had been there for a decade. This is against the background of general poverty in a region where 67 per cent of the population live below the poverty line, compared to 38.8 per cent nationwide.[3] The conflict, and the consequent humanitarian crisis, is arguably President Yoweri Museveni's greatest failure since coming to office in 1986.

This is the context in which Uganda's informal disarmament, demobilisation and reintegration (DDR) programme takes place. Rather than being an organised process, set up to help consolidate peace at the end of a conflict, it has been a necessary response to the steady trickle – and sometimes flood – of former rebel abductees, who escape from the LRA, or surrender, or are captured by the Ugandan military. Many are minors; some are girls and women. The process has evolved over the course of the conflict and now includes amnesty for former fighters as well as opportunities for retraining and absorption into the Uganda Peoples' Defence Forces (UPDF), the official military force. The process has also enabled thousands of former fighters to make the transition back into civilian life. However, it has its limits, not least the fact that the former fighters are 'reintegrated' into a situation not just of ongoing conflict but – in the words of the UN Emergency Humanitarian Co-ordinator, Jan Egeland – 'one of the worst humanitarian crises in the world'.[4]

The insecurity dragged on for nearly two decades with no real sign of resolution. However, in the last few years, international attention has finally shifted to the region, and the Sudanese government – who previously backed the rebels – has withdrawn its support to the LRA, denying the group rear bases and a steady supply of weapons. The Ugandan government has also come under pressure to negotiate an end to the conflict. In July 2006, the newly installed Government of South Sudan opened peace talks between the LRA and the Ugandan government in the southern Sudanese town of Juba. This has raised hopes that the war might finally be coming to an end, which in turn has shifted attention onto how best to consolidate peace.

An effective DDR programme could form part of the process of resolving the conflict, and is on the agenda of the Juba talks. Its structure will depend partly on how hostilities terminate and the nature of rebel demands. The logistics of disarming, demobilising and reintegrating the remaining LRA – who will include a core of hardened commanders – will bring challenges. An effective DDR process will also need to include the previously returned LRA, who have essentially been put on hold over the last decade in the camps of the internally displaced.

Ultimately, the only way a DDR programme will succeed is if it is part of a wider peace-building process. 'Reintegration' would mean sending not just all the former fighters, but all the displaced, back to their villages and rehabilitating the region, which has been decimated by conflict. The root causes of the conflict need to be addressed, even though the LRA leadership has largely been unable to articulate them. There also needs to be reconciliation from the clan up to the national level, and beyond, as LRA activity has soured Uganda's relations with both the Sudan and the DRC. Finally, reconciliation raises questions about the role of retributive justice. If there is to be a sustainable peace, should the LRA leadership be punished for their human-rights abuses, or other options of justice be pursued in the hope of ending the conflict, arguably in accordance with 'traditional' Acholi justice? Because of the involvement of the International Criminal Court (ICC), the manner in which this dilemma is resolved may also have wider implications for international arbitration in other conflict zones.

Background to the conflict

There has been fighting in the northern districts of Gulu, Kitgum and Pader since 1986, when the current President, Yoweri Museveni, who comes from western Uganda, seized power following a five-year guerrilla war. Many in the then government military were Acholi. They fled north, and after a few months regrouped as the Ugandan People's Democratic Army (UPDA) – a conventional rebel force that aimed to recapture state power. The group was also motivated by the fear of retaliatory attacks, which were a feature of Uganda's post-independence history. Longstanding divisions and suspicion between the north and south, fostered by

British colonial policies, played into this concern. In addition, many Acholis resented that Museveni had overthrown the brief regime of a fellow Acholi, General Tito Okello Lutwa, in January 1986, having signed a peace accord with him in Nairobi a month earlier.

After a series of engagements with the National Resistance Army (NRA), the new official military, the UPDA negotiated a settlement with the government at the end of 1988 after which most of the rebels laid down their arms, with many electing to join the NRA, renamed the Uganda Peoples Defence Force (UPDF) in 1995. By the completion of the NRA–UPDA settlement, however, a far more unusual force had emerged, which was to have a far-reaching impact. The Holy Spirit Movement (HSM) expressed political discontent in the idiom of Christianity and traditional religion. The group was led by Alice Auma 'Lakwena' ('messenger' in Luo) who said she was seized by the spirit of an elderly Italian soldier. Alice's followers regarded her as a prophet, and she said she was fighting a holy war to purify the Acholi of their sins.

Alice's hymn-singing followers were told that if they smeared Shea butter oil on their chests, they would be protected from bullets.[5] She promised stones would turn into grenades and that snakes were on the side of the insurgents, as long as they followed her 20 Holy Spirit Safety Precautions. She was popular and, initially, successful. Her estimated 10,000-strong force reached within 100 kilometres of Kampala before finally being defeated. Alice fled to Kenya in December 1986, and spent the rest of her life in a refugee camp there. Before her death in January 2006, the Ugandan government made several efforts to bring her home, but these stalled, reportedly because of disagreements over monetary rewards.[6]

In 1987, Alice's father, Severino Lukoya, attempted to take over his daughter's mantle, claiming that God the Father was speaking through him. However, following a brief and somewhat brutal rebellion, Lukoya was arrested. He was later released and now heads the tiny 'New World Meltar, Jerusalem Church', which he is trying to register with the authorities in Gulu town.[7]

This, however, was not the end of the spirit-inspired rebellions, which would mutate under the leadership of Joseph Kony, Alice Lakwena's cousin. Born in Odek village, around 50 kilometres outside Gulu town in 1962, Kony was a traditional healer who had dropped out of primary school and later claimed to be seized by spirits. He says that he went to the bush at the age of 23.[8] In 1987, he joined a unit of UPDA fighters as their 'spiritual advisor' and, in 1988, when most of the UPDA signed the peace accord with the Ugandan government, he was joined, among others, by former UPDA chairman, Brigadier Justine Odong Latek, a professional military officer formerly of the UNLA. Brigadier Latek was reportedly killed in 1989 by the NRA, but not before he and Kony had formed what became, after a series of name changes,[9] the Lord's Resistance Army, with Kony at its head.

The LRA initially enjoyed popular support, partly by feeding off the deep hostility in the region towards the southern-dominated NRM government, led by Museveni. But as this support waned, the group became increasingly brutal – a trend that intensified after the then Minister for Northern Uganda, Betty Bigombe, organised civilians into 'Arrow Brigades', paramilitary units designed for local self-defence against rebel raids. The rebels responded by cutting off the lips, ears and noses of civilians. Joseph Kony later justified this practice in a speech given during the 1993–94 peace talks:

> If you picked up an arrow against us and we ended up cutting off the hand you used, who is to blame? You report us with your mouth, and we cut off your lips. Who is to blame? It is you! The Bible says that if your hand, eye or mouth is at fault, it should be cut off.[10]

These terror tactics were played out on a huge scale after 1994, when – following the collapse of peace talks between the LRA and the Ugandan government – the Sudanese government offered the LRA rear bases, arms, ammunition, medicine and food, in retaliation for Uganda's support for the Sudanese then-rebel group, the Sudan Peoples Liberation Army (SPLA).[11]

The UPDF responded to this upsurge in violence with a heavy-handed counter-insurgency strategy, ordering and in many cases compelling the Acholi into displacement camps, initially known as 'protected villages'. The LRA meanwhile stepped up its campaign of civilian abduction, press-ganging as many as 28,000 people between 1996–2001. About a third of the abductees were children, and they formed the core of the fighting force. Girls and young women were also abducted and forced to become 'rebel wives' and '*ting ting*' (domestic servants) as well as fighters.

In 1999, Uganda and Sudan agreed to normalise diplomatic relations, severed four years earlier. International pressure on the Khartoum government continued to mount and, in 2001, the US declared the LRA a terrorist organisation. Sudan – which was keen to win US favour – officially withdrew support for the rebels in 2002, although collaboration briefly resumed in 2003 when the LRA helped the government troops retake the SPLA-held town of Torit, in Imatong District of the southern Sudanese Equatorial Province.[12]

In 2002, the Ugandan military obtained the Sudanese government's approval to launch Operation 'Iron Fist', a cross-border incursion into south Sudan to pursue the LRA rebels hiding there (the operation was followed by Operation 'Iron Fist Two' in 2004). The engagements sparked off a new round of violence as the rebels flooded back into Uganda, abducting over 10,000 people. The LRA had occasionally in the past targeted the Langi districts of Lira and Apac, but their raids now intensified, and also spread into the eastern districts of Soroti and Katakwi, causing even more displacement and inflaming ethnic tensions, particularly between the Acholi and neighbouring Langi. This was not the first time that the Ugandan military had entered south Sudan – with SPLA support, it had overrun LRA camps in 1995, 1997 and again in 1998 – but it was the first time that it did so with the consent of the Sudanese government.

At the peak of the violence, over 1.8 million people were displaced. Every evening, thousands of children – known as 'night commuters' – streamed into towns for refuge. The renewed fighting also created a flood of returnees. Rebels were dislodged from their bases inside south Sudan and broke up into smaller units. Many seized the moment to escape and take advantage of a government amnesty, while some women and children were released by the LRA in response to the increased military pressure. A number of influential LRA officers surrendered or were captured by the UPDF.

In 2003, the international community finally took note. The UN Emergency Humanitarian Co-ordinator, Jan Egeland, visited northern Uganda and described the situation as 'perhaps the most under-reported story in the world today', as well as one of the worst humanitarian disasters. Foreign NGOs began to arrive in the region in larger numbers and the government of Uganda came under pressure to seek a negotiated end to the conflict. While Museveni – a former guerrilla and, until recently, the Commander in Chief of the Army – has often appeared to prefer a military solution, the vast majority of Acholi support a peaceful settlement, partly because it is their children who die in battle, and partly because they lack faith in the Ugandan military's capacity and commitment to win the war. In the early days of the conflict, it is also possible that some Acholi did not want to see Kony humiliated in an outright military defeat. The rebel leader does not have popular support, but nor does the National Resistance Movement, whose leader, Museveni, has three times – in 1996, 2001 and 2006 – secured only a fraction of the presidential vote in the region.

Rebel and government representatives met at the end of 2004, but the process collapsed in February 2005. Meanwhile, the SPLA and the Sudanese government in Khartoum finally reached a peace deal, further isolating the LRA. Also, in October 2005, the ICC unsealed arrest warrants for war crimes and crimes against humanity against the top five LRA leaders: Joseph Kony, Vincent Otti, Raska Lukwiya, Okot Odhiambo and Dominic Ongwen (Raska Lukwiya was later killed by the UPDF on 12 August 2006).[13] President Museveni had invited the ICC to investigate the conflict in December 2003, presumably in the hope that it would put pressure on the LRA and perhaps garner practical, international support to hunt the rebels down (for example, by making it harder for the Sudan and DRC governments to support/ignore the LRA's presence on their soil). In late 2005, the LRA command relocated to Garamba national park in northeastern DRC and the Ugandan parliament amended the Amnesty Act to allow for the exclusion of the five wanted men.[14] Hopes for a peaceful settlement began to fade.

However, on 14 July 2006, the fledgling southern Sudanese government – in an effort to rid itself of the LRA, secure its territory and raise its international profile – brokered peace talks between a weakened LRA and the Ugandan government.[15] The talks are being mediated by the southern Sudanese deputy Vice President Riak Machar, a former SPLA rebel who in the mid-1990s had reportedly introduced Kony to the Sudanese government.[16] However, Joseph Kony and his deputy, Vincent Otti, declined to attend, citing fear of the ICC, and instead held parallel meetings with the peace team at their bases in the DRC. Kony appointed a 15-person LRA delegation to represent him in Juba – all but two of whom were Acholi from the diaspora.

The level of insecurity in northern Uganda has reduced dramatically since the start of the talks and, on 26 August 2006, government and LRA representatives signed a temporary Cessation of Hostilities. The government of Uganda has promised to amend Uganda's Amnesty Act to include the indicted men if they agree to come out of the bush, even though international legal experts say that the charge of war crimes precludes the possibility of domestic amnesty.[17] It is not clear how this problem will be resolved. At the time of writing, the Juba talks had stalled.[18] Attention has since focused on ways of dealing with ICC involvement in northern Uganda without derailing the peace process. Suggestions include asking the UN Security Council (UNSC) to suspend the arrest warrants on an annual basis (with the provision that the suspension would be lifted if the terms of any peace deal were broken). No solution has yet been found, although any sustainable peace process will need to satisfy international demands for accountability and justice.[19] Nonetheless, despite their slow and faltering progress, the Juba talks have widely been regarded as the best chance for peace in years.

Lord's Resistance Army: ideology, tactics and abduction

Ideology

The LRA blends the intensity of religious ideology with brutal guerrilla tactics. Joseph Kony is at the heart of the movement and has styled himself as a prophet. His aura of mystery has been largely due to his elusiveness: until the 2006 peace process, he had never met with a foreign journalist and avoided virtually all approaches from international organisations interested in facilitating peace. Kony appears to have a genuine hold over his followers. It is rare to meet former rebels who do not believe that he has real spiritual power. Former LRA commanders say Kony's war was prophesied by Alice Lakwena, who predicted that a man would emerge from Sudan to take over her fight. Kony himself says that a young boy will rise up after him and usher in peace.[20]

Thirteen spirits – from America, Sudan, China, Korea, Italy and Uganda – are said to speak through Kony. They are headed by a Sudanese spirit, Juma Oris, and they include one woman, Silly Silindi, who is in charge of operations. Kony says he can see the future: some of his prophecies are specific (predicting that the UPDF will attack at a certain time), while others are more opaque (that he is 'like Moses' and will 'never see the promised land'). Former rebel commanders say that the spirits left Joseph Kony around 1999, and that he now remains with 'wisdom'. It appears that Kony has become more secular in recent years (or has at least chosen to present himself as such): visitors to his base in the DRC say that, unlike meetings during the 1994 peace talks, Kony no longer surrounds himself with elaborate religious rituals and instead attends dressed in military fatigues or smart civilian clothes. In the run-up to the Juba peace talks in July 2006, he described himself as a 'freedom fighter'.[21]

The rebel leader in the past has claimed that, like Alice, he is fighting to cleanse the Acholi of their sins. He also says he wants to create a 'new generation' of Acholi and rule by the Biblical Ten Commandments:

> I would like to declare our political agenda. We are fighting for the Ten Commandments of God. If you look at the Ten Commandments of God are they obeyed? They are violated everywhere. We are fighting because it is God who created us, so we should fight for his rule.[22]

He uses the Bible to justify his brutality and, according to Kony's former personal secretary, Jackson Achama, 'The Acholi are being punished because of their own sins they have committed. Kony is the agent of God because he is bringing about the suffering that will help purify the Acholi'.[23] However, religious justifications and military justifications often run side-by-side: the abduction of children, for example, is explained on the grounds that Jesus 'abducted fishermen',[24] while at the same time Kony's former commanders acknowledge that these children make better fighters because they are nimble, easy to train and quick to forget home.[25]

LRA fighters who return from the bush, including former commanders, rarely justify their fight in political terms, other than to voice opposition to President Museveni.[26] Occasionally, the LRA have released documents suggesting they do have a wider political agenda; for example, in the run-up to the 1996 presidential elections, leaflets bearing the LRA logo were dropped in the region, urging the population to vote for Museveni's rival, Dr Paul Ssemogerere. It is likely that these political views are held by some of the LRA commanders, particularly those who were once in the UPDA, which was a more conventional rebel force. The LRA negotiating team in Juba have issued statements outlining the rebels' political grievances and demands. These include 'basic issues of political persecution and marginalisation, insulting attitudes, land grabbers, cultural diversity, respect for democracy, compensation for all loss including cattle rustling by NRA soldiers ... equal opportunity for all in partisan army'.[27] However, it is not clear whether this team, which mainly consists of Acholi from the diaspora, represents the views of the LRA fighters on the ground or whether it is using the LRA to push their own agenda – previous LRA representatives in the diaspora have had tenuous links with the rebel group.[28] Kony recently told journalists: 'Issues like power-sharing over which people are wasting time is not a big problem. It will come automatically if there is confidence', and observers at the talks have noted that both Kony and his deputy Otti have shown more concern about their safety than with any longer-term political agenda for Uganda.[29] At the same time, it is clear that the rebels exist because of political grievances in northern Uganda, even if the LRA forces on the ground have historically lacked the ability to articulate them.

Tactics and organisation

The LRA is a small group. The Ugandan military estimates that it has probably never numbered more than 5,000, while former LRA commanders put the figure closer to 10,000. Visitors to Kony's DRC base during the 2006 Juba talks estimated that there were about 5,000 rebels, perhaps half of whom were women and children. This is also the number the LRA asked the southern Sudanese government to provide food for when the cessation of hostilities was first signed.[30]

Despite its small size, the LRA has proved remarkably effective. The rebel tactics include moving at night, ambushing the military and targeting civilians both to terrorise them into acquiescence and to secure manpower, food and other provisions. LRA fighters are told that they must fight standing up, 'because Kony says if you bend or squat down while fighting you will be straight away hurt. It is belief that Kony has given us' – and one that makes them formidable in battle.[31] Mysticism and rituals are central to life in the bush (initiation ceremonies, 'blessings' before battles promising immunity from bullets) but harder to carry out when the rebels are on the move. In public at least, Kony now puts less emphasis on the conflict's 'spiritual element'. The LRA are organised into five brigades – Control Altar (the HQ, commanded by Kony), Sinia, Gilva, Stockrie and Trinkle.[32] Each has its own 'chaplain'. These are further sub-divided into battalions, companies and platoons, with the smallest unit being a rebel family (a commander, his wife, their children, escorts and helpers). However, it is not clear how far this structure has survived the fracturing of the group since 2002, nor the more recent relocation to the DRC.

The rebels received weapons from the Sudan government from 1994 until at least 2003. They also have caches hidden in northern Uganda and south Sudan, though it is not known how many of these remain. Former LRA officers say that their pre-2003 weapons supply consisted mostly of small arms and ammunition. The group has also used anti-aircraft weapons, grenade launchers and anti-personnel and land mines.[33] There have been repeated, and unconfirmed, allegations by the Ugandan military that the Sudanese government has continued to supply the LRA through arms drops in Garamba National Park. In 2006, when rebels moved towards assembly points as part of the Cessation of Hostilities agreement, newspapers reported that onlookers were surprised at the number and quality of the weapons carried by the LRA.

Abduction

The LRA relies on abduction for replenishing its ranks, and it has taken over 30,000 people since 1989, including an estimated 20,000 minors.[34] The horrors these kidnapped abductees endure are well documented.[35] This 18-year-old woman, for example, was taken when she was nine years old and held for eight years. The events she recounts occurred when she was ten years old, and are typical:

'Did you see many atrocities yourself?'
'I saw and I was also involved. In killing'.
'Can you tell me about it?'

'I was made to kill four people. I killed two when they were going to Gulu. It's like an initiation. You must kill and pass through the blood. The second time, I was made to kill two. In total, that is four'.

'How were you forced to kill?'

'You are supposed to continue with the journey. But first you must be sprinkled with blood and if you don't have blood on you as you walk along you will be killed. So you have to kill, so you can sprinkle the blood of the person on you'.

'And how did you kill them?'

'We hit them with sticks. There was no way out. The only way was to do it and let my life continue. I always view that spirit of killing. I always see flashbacks of the killing'.[36]

The fresh abductees are marched into the bush, made to murder any recruit trying to escape, are ritually anointed with Shea nut oil and holy water, given two weeks basic military training and then sent into battle. Boys, from ten years and upwards, and men make up the bulk of the fighting force, although females are also fighters. Very young girls are given as servants (*ting ting*) to commanders' wives, but all girls become wives of rebel commanders once they are able to bear children, which they often do soon thereafter. When the LRA still had permanent bases in south Sudan, newly abducted girls were paraded before the officers, who were allowed to pick from them in order of descending seniority. 'Wives' are redistributed to other commanders if their husband dies in battle.

No one knows the total number of LRA abductees. A study carried out by the United Nations Children's Fund (UNICEF) and covering the period 1990–2001, found that 28,902 people had been taken from Gulu, Kitgum, Pader, Apac and Lira; about 10,000 of these were children.[37] By 2001, 16,000 had returned; 5,555 of those who remained missing were children. A further 10,000 children are believed to have been taken in 2002–04, during the 'Iron Fist' operations, but no accurate records were kept during this time due to the insecurity.[38] The LRA have also targeted Sudanese Acholi, who are not counted in abduction statistics. Indeed, until very recently, the impact of the LRA in southern Sudan – despite having bases there since 1994 – was ignored, largely because the civil war in Sudan impeded both access and accurate reporting.[39]

Although there is a popular image of the LRA as an outfit of kidnapped children, it is not known how many children actually remain in rebel hands. Former personal secretary to Joseph Kony, Jackson Achama who surrendered in 2004, claims that LRA usage of children peaked in 1996.[40] Many of these same children have grown to adulthood while in captivity. Achama estimates that there are only 10–15 per cent of children remaining in the bush. The UNICEF data shows that only a third of abductees were children in 1990–2001, but it does not differentiate between abductees held for a day and those held for a year, and adults are often used as 'porters' to carry looted property and then released, while children remain in rebel hands. Reception centre staff say that the profile of returnees has changed over the years and that the average age dropped during the last wave of abductions.[41] A 2005 study of 506 former abductees found that 71 per cent of those taken were 15 or under, of which 16 per cent were less than ten years old. Only 3 per cent were older than 30.[42]

The structure of informal DDR in northern Uganda

This is the unsettled context in which the informal DDR process in northern Uganda takes place, and helps explain both its nature and the challenges facing any future programme. It also explains why up to now the emphasis has been less on producing ex-combatants who will help build peace, and more on mopping up what has at times been a flood of former, often child, abductees, who are more often than not perceived as 'victims', rather than rebels, on their return.[43]

This informal process evolved as follows: before 1994, abductees who ran away or who were captured would go either straight back to their villages/ displacement camps, or pass through the barracks. If they were captured as adults, they might be held on treason charges. If they were children, the military would hold them for a brief time before parading them in Gulu town, where relatives could claim them (although sometimes children were illegally detained on treason charges). Many returnees were granted a presidential pardon, or amnesty. In January 2000, this was formalised into a blanket amnesty and, since then, details of the amnesty have been broadcast over FM radio stations in northern Uganda in an effort to encourage fighters to come out of the bush.[44]

NGOs became involved in handling ex-LRA fighters in 1994, when two agencies – the US-based World Vision, and the indigenous GUSCO (Gulu Save the Children Organisation) – were established in Gulu town to provide trauma counselling for former child combatants. These 'reception' (or 'rehabilitation') centres provide medical checks, basic counselling, and occasionally skills training. Adults were largely left out of the picture. The family of the former abductees were traced, when possible, and they were then sent back home, which often meant an internally displaced person (IDP) camp. Some former abductees moved to town or out of the district over safety concerns in the IDP camps. The role of the NGOs essentially stopped at that point, with minimal follow-up.

Initially, little was done to help the community accept the returnees – the assumption was that these were 'their children' and that they would be welcomed home. In general, the population was, and continues to be, remarkably accepting of the former fighters, not least because this is a war in which victim and perpetrator is often one, and because every extended family has been affected by abduction. Many Acholi explain this attitude by stressing the importance of 'forgiveness' in their culture.

This informal process has evolved over the last decade, although the structure has remained basically the same. The military, for example, has attempted to streamline the way returnees are handled through its Child Protection Unit (despite its name, it caters for all returnees). Over 15,000 Ugandan rebels (not only LRA) have also registered for a formal amnesty.[45] Traditional cleansing rituals have also gained prominence since the late 1990s, largely because of a surge in interest in the use of Acholi rituals, tradition and culture to heal the wounds of conflict.[46] The most common ritual, *Nyono Tong Gweno*, involves returnees stepping on an egg – a ceremony normally used to welcome home those who have been away for a long time. Other, more complicated rituals – for example, to drive out evil spirits (*cen*) – include animal sacrifice. The growth of these ceremonies has developed alongside a more formal articulation of 'forgiveness' into a claim that the Acholi have a distinct form of justice, which is said to be more restorative than retributive – aiming to heal social wounds rather than punish offenders.

After 2002, following a fresh wave of LRA attacks, the number of reception centres in the region increased, with new centres opening in Gulu, Kitgum, Apac, Lira, Soroti and Katakwi. As the military pressure on the LRA increased, many abductees took the opportunity to escape. Some who returned had only been with the rebels a short time, but others were long-term abductees, many of whom were taken as children a decade previously and had become adults while in the bush. NGOs opened more specialised centres to cater for these specific demographics: a centre for adults and another for so-called 'child mothers' – rebel 'wives' who had given birth in the bush. A number of senior LRA commanders were captured or surrendered, including the rebel fourth-in-command, Brigadier Kenneth Banya, and the LRA spokesman, Brigadier Sam Kollo. The UPDF also decided to formalise the reintegration of ex-combatants into the military with a unit, 105 Battalion, composed exclusively of former LRA fighters. Previously the LRA had been absorbed piecemeal into the existing structure of the UPDF.

After 2004, when the number of returnees once again fell, the focus of the informal DDR process shifted to 'effective reintegration', or the ways former fighters cope when they return home. This shift grew in part out of the need of NGOs dealing with returnees to find a new funding category, as there were far fewer abductees returning and needing immediate, emergency attention. More recently, the language of DDR has filtered down into the language of NGOs. It may have originated from the Amnesty Commission, which in 2005 was given $4.2 million to fund resettlement packages from the World Bank's Great Lakes DDR programme. However, perhaps the most important influence has been cautious optimism: when peace talks began in 2006, many hoped that the war might finally end.

The limits of the informal DDR process

Although this informal process of DDR in many ways has served its purpose, and a large number of returnees have been helped to manage the transition period between life in the bush and life in mainstream society, it is far from perfect. Many of the problems marking the process exist because the system has evolved slowly, with inadequate coordination and in response to a changing situation.

Disarmament

Disarmament is, in general, unproblematic. Escaping or captured 'LRA' hand in their guns to the UPDF (or tell the soldiers where they have hidden them). They are asked if they have information about arms caches and mines and in some cases guide the UPDF to these locations. The weapons are then kept by the Uganda military.

Demobilisation

Demobilisation has been more haphazard. A significant number of returnees – one study suggests 25 per cent – are thought to go straight back home without reporting to the authorities.[47] If returnees are not formerly registered as ex-rebels, they are unable to benefit from any reintegration 'packages' handed out by reception centres and, since 2005, the Amnesty Commission. The Amnesty Commission is also only able to provide aid to those ex-combatants who returned after 2000, when the Amnesty Act came into force. Because of inadequate data collection, there is no accurate record of those who have been abducted and those who have returned, which makes tracking returnees difficult.[48]

The process of demobilisation begins with the child-protection units where, some allege, the military has improperly recruited returnees into its own ranks without first giving them the option of returning to civilian life. The majority of returnees then move on to the reception centres, a halfway house between rebel and civilian life, and the subject of a number of studies.[49] Anecdotally, many who pass through the centres say the process has helped them: at the very least the centres provide a way of managing transition, while at the same time reassuring the returnees that they are 'forgiven' for any crimes they might have committed in the bush. Some evidence suggests that those who spend time in the centres are better able to cope with life when they return to their homes.[50]

However, the centres have also suffered from their ad hoc origins. Along with the lack of interagency cooperation, criticisms commonly target the failure to standardise counselling, go-home packages and the length of stay at the centres, as well as the overall approach, which varies widely (some are Christian-based, others secular). It has also been suggested that the Amnesty Act is inadequately understood and that only a fraction of those who are eligible – anyone over 12 years who has been with the rebels for more than four months – registers and receives a certificate.

Reintegration

Displacement

The very notion of 'reintegration' in Uganda is greatly complicated by the massive displacement of populations. What, after all, does 'reintegration' mean to former abductees sent back to live in the squalor of a 'protected camp' and in an environment of ongoing insecurity? In the words of one reception centre manager:

> Life in northern Uganda is a dilemma. We should reunite children with their families so their families can help them. But this same community is again itself undergoing stress and trauma. There is no normal life. Life has broken down.[51]

The camps were created as a counterinsurgency strategy in the Acholi region in 1996 to deny the rebels food and intelligence.[52] They were initially known as 'protected villages', even though they were frequently attacked by the LRA, and are now referred to as IDP camps. The number of displaced persons has risen dramatically since 2002. In 1997, around 500,000 people were displaced. By 2004, this had increased to 1.2 million in Acholi and 1.6 million across the north and east as a whole. The total number of IDPs in northeast Uganda as of February 2006 was 1,699,682 in 251 camps.[53] Some of this displacement was due to spontaneous movement but in most cases the military ordered civilians to leave their villages. In late 2005, the security situation in northern Uganda began to improve and the government started the process of 'decongesting' the camps. The Juba talks hastened this process and in October 2006, Minister of Relief and Disaster Preparedness, Tarsis Kabwegyere, announced that the camps would be disbanded by the end of the year. However, this is not the first time that the government has made such a promise, and people are unlikely to return home in large numbers until they are convinced that the war has reached a conclusive end.

Nonetheless, the situation for the displaced remains appalling. The camps are crowded and there is insufficient provision of water, latrines, medical facilities, schools and food. One survey in 2005 found that an estimated 1,000 people die from war-related deaths each week.[54] Alcoholism is rife and there is virtually no employment, apart from *boda boda* (bicycle taxi) operation, bicycle repair or stallholder (all of which require either capital or training). Around two-thirds of the population in the camps live below the poverty line, a far higher proportion than the national average.[55] As a result, prostitution has soared, as have suicides and depression.[56] People live with the threat of violence from both the LRA and the UPDF, who are regularly accused of human-rights abuses against the very people they were supposed to protect.[57] Elders complain that the young were forgetting Acholi traditions. In the words of the Catholic Archbishop of Gulu, John Baptist Odama, 'The people have left their culture and that is the most painful thing. To lose a culture is to be like someone uprooted, hanging in the air'.[58]

Returnees have to deal with all these problems, as well as the after-effects of trauma, which counsellors say often include nightmares and flashbacks. Many will have lost their family in rebel attacks or still have relatives in the bush. Most fear re-abduction: the LRA, for years, operated a policy of hunting down and killing those who escaped. As the chairman of a group of former fighters in a

Gulu district IDP camp put it, 'We have nothing to do, since we are afraid to go outside and dig. If we are found again we will be captured or killed.'[59]

Stigma and forgiveness

Even though the community in general welcomes the returnees home – there are, for example, few reports of attacks on former fighters – stigmatisation is common. Returnees are often accused of bringing bad luck by carrying '*cen*' – the malevolent and vengeful spirits of those they have killed. Ex-rebel 'wives' are sometimes rejected by their families and left to fend for themselves. The man's family may also reject his rebel wife and children, as this is a culture where a child's identity (and, therefore, claim to clan land) is determined by the paternal line.[60]

Some of these problems are caused by the manner in which the reintegration is carried out. Giving packages or skills training to returnees can cause resentment among civilians in the camp, some of whom complain that the returnees are being rewarded for being rebels. This has led to debate about whether it is better to target former abductees or concentrate on improving the situation of all the displaced, with current thinking favouring the latter approach. Other problems are the result of inadequate planning and coordination. NGOs admit to infrequent and poor follow-up for returnees (because of insufficient funds, insecurity, and lack of documentation). One 2005 study found that only 13 per cent of returnees had received a follow-up visit from reception centre staff.[61]

Cleansing ceremonies – credited with easing the transition back into the community – are also problematic. These ceremonies, like other aspects of Acholi culture, have been altered, weakened and adapted over the years and, despite attempts to revive them, are not universally understood. They are also erratically applied. Some Christian rehabilitation centres shun 'traditional' beliefs, sometimes branding them 'satanic', and prefer to promote prayer ceremonies. The cost of traditional rituals can also be prohibitive, particularly those which involve slaughtering an animal. Studies suggest traditional ceremonies have therapeutic value, but not everyone is able to benefit; one report found that 25 per cent of formerly abducted persons attended prayer ceremonies, 32 per cent took part in communal cleansing ceremonies (introduced in 2002) and 52 per cent were involved in family cleansing ceremonies.[62]

Returnees as 'children' and 'victims'

One factor that may distort the effectiveness of reintegration is the emphasis on children. The phrase 'child mother' for example, refers to abducted girls who were married to rebel commanders and then gave birth. However, they are often youth, who have had their children no earlier than the general population.[63] This focus also affects the manner in which informal DDR programmes have been handled and, potentially, the way in which future formal DDR programmes could be planned. In the 1990s, counsellors at reception centres used to speak of their 'clients' as children, even when they were obviously 16 years or older.[64]

There is equally a tendency to lump all the abductees together as 'trauma victims'. The returnees have been through terrible experiences and many are profoundly disturbed by what they have seen. However, others adapt to bush life and even grow to enjoy it. Counsellors working with returnees say the longer someone has stayed in the bush the more able they are to adapt upon their return, perhaps because they have grown accustomed to the strict discipline of LRA life.

'Child mothers' (who make up only a small proportion of LRA returnees) have suffered a particularly brutal life. Many are appalled and disturbed by what they have been through: forced 'marriage', beatings, exposure to high levels of violence.[65] Nonetheless, some say they would like to stay with their husbands if they were to return from the bush.[66] This 19-year-old woman is one of 21 wives of an ICC-indicted LRA commander:

> He is a good, kind man. He did not torture or beat me. Well ... he only became good to me when I conceived. What he always has at heart is when a lady is pregnant. He has to respect and not beat her. But before I was pregnant, any slight mistake and he would beat me. I feel I will go back to him as a wife, as he is already the father to my children. I will willingly go back with him.[67]

One researcher interviewed formerly abducted girls and concluded that many – particularly those with children, sometimes referred to within the LRA as 'bearers of the new generation' – were accorded respect and status by the rebels, and had also acquired skills, such as nursing, trading, soldiering, translating and accounting, while with the LRA. The author concluded that reintegration programmes were not making the most of the young women's abilities and, by so doing, were chipping away at their strength and resilience. She also noted that some of the skills training ended up stigmatising the former fighters – tailoring, for example, is now considered a 'rebel trade'.[68]

Reintegrating senior LRA commanders

The position of high-ranking LRA officers is slightly different and highlights problems that may arise if peace talks succeed and large numbers of senior LRA rebels return from the bush. A number of them have been captured or have surrendered since 2003. These commanders have great propaganda value for the Ugandan government, who hope that by treating them well, they will lure more senior LRA officers from out of the bush. However, while the populace is generally willing to reconcile in the name of peace, it is harder when the person to be forgiven is not an abductee, but a rebel commander who willingly went to fight, like Brigadier Kenneth Banya, once the fourth most powerful commander in the LRA hierarchy. He now happily moves around Gulu town, despite having taken four abducted adolescent girls as his wives, and has a monthly salary of 600,000 Ugandan shillings, paid by the government.[69] In 2005, two other commanders were staying in the Acholi Inn, the best hotel in Gulu, which is owned by the most influential UPDF officer in the northern region. Major Jackson Achama, Joseph Kony's former personal secretary, with no apparent sense of irony, has even started an NGO – a known way to secure funding – to 'help rehabilitate former child soldiers'.

The situation is tolerated for now, because it is seen as promoting peace, but it stretches the whole notion of forgiveness to its very limits. In the words of one reception centre manager:

> If I look at these top commanders, they were the ones who ordered the abduction of children. These children are going back to the IDP camps. But these top shots are enjoying first class life in Gulu, watching TV … with someone even doing their washing for them![70]

These top LRA commanders are also among the few returnees to have been given work on their return. Brigadier Banya was initially put in charge of Labora Farm – 800 acres of land, 14 kilometres outside Gulu – set up as a project to help returnees feed themselves and funded by the World Bank's Northern Uganda Social Action Fund (NUSAF) and the Ugandan government. Labora has been controversial, not least because it is run by former LRA commanders, some who earned brutal reputations in the bush, and who are now among the few returnees in Gulu not only to have jobs, but also the power to provide employment.

Absorption into the military

Because of the lack of jobs, many returnees – abductees and commanders alike – have opted to join the UPDF. Former fighters have been absorbed into the Ugandan military since the start of the conflict, but in 2002, 105 Battalion was set up to cater specifically for the new arrivals. As of August 2005, the unit, based at Cet Kana, about 30 kilometres from Gulu town, consisted of 912 soldiers. The number has since increased. Soldiers from 105 Battalion are attached to UPDF units in southern Sudan and northern Uganda and they use their knowledge of LRA tactics to track down the rebels and hunt out arms caches. The recruits are allowed to keep their rebel ranks until they are sent for UPDF training, at which time they are reassessed.

The Ugandan military has a long and successful history of incorporating former rebel fighters. The inclusion of ex-LRA did initially cause some concern, not least because of the group's appalling human-rights record. However, UPDF officers say that the LRA make remarkably good soldiers and are extremely disciplined – perhaps because they are used to following orders on pain of death.

The UPDF describes the battalion as a 'great success', but that has not stopped allegations that the military is recruiting minors into the force, wooing them soon after their return and before they have had a chance to pass through a reception centre. The UPDF has also been accused of further stigmatising the former rebels by keeping them in a separate unit. It is hard to assess the truth of these claims, although the times the author visited Cet Kana (albeit in the company of a UPDF escort), the ex-LRA appeared to be adults and did not complain about maltreatment. Several new recruits said that they had been asked if they would like to join the UPDF while they were still in the barracks, but added that they felt free to turn down the offer. Asked why they had joined the UPDF, the following replies were typical:

> I was abducted when I was very young and now this is the only opportunity I can have.
>
> > (24-year-old man, with rebels for ten years)

> There is nothing else I can do apart from being in the army. I wanted to teach but it is difficult for me to start now as I don't have anyone to pay for me. Once you are a soldier, you are a soldier. It doesn't matter which side you are on.
>
> > (29-year-old man, four years in the bush)

> I decided to stay in the army as now I have no parents and no family and I don't have anywhere to go.
>
> > (28-year-old man, ten years in the bush)[71]

Perhaps more controversial is the recruitment of returnees into Local Defence Units, or LDUs.[72] As with the military, returnees join because they have nothing better to do, because it is a life they know and because they sometimes cannot get into the military. Others are reportedly press-ganged, and there have been numerous reports of 'children' joining the force. LDU life is not easy, and the government frequently fails to pay its members their wages, which are in any case meagre. As a result, many abscond.

Planning ahead

Formal DDR programme

The Juba peace process has been the most serious attempt thus far to negotiate an end to the conflict. The talks have also provided the first real opportunity to focus on the mechanics of a formal DDR programme, dealing mainly with those rebels remaining in the bush. The manner in which the conflict ends will determine to some extent the nature of this programme. Also relevant to the content and long-term success of any formal DDR programme will be the final resolution of the problem posed by the ICC's intervention in northern Uganda.

Museveni insists that the purpose of the Juba talks is to provide a 'soft landing' for the rebels, not to discuss power sharing or other political concerns (such as disbanding the UPDF, which was proposed by LRA delegates in their August 2006 DDR position paper at the Juba talks – and immediately rejected by the government).[73] This soft landing would first require convincing the indict-ees that they are safe from prosecution by the ICC. All LRA fighters would then gather in designated areas in South Sudan and hand over their weapons, before being repatriated. They will also be given the opportunity to either return to school or join the UPDF. In addition, the LRA delegation has requested that the children of ex-combatants are provided with education and that funds be made available for skills training and business opportunities. The former fighters' re-entry into the community will be supported by Acholi traditional and religious leaders, who will 'sensitise' the community and oversee reconciliation ceremo-nies. Newspaper reports suggest that Joseph Kony (and other indictees) may prefer to settle and seek asylum in a third country that has not signed the Rome Treaty, while the remainder of his force returns to Uganda.

If the conflict does end, the immediate logistical challenge of carrying out a formal DDR programme that deals only with the rebels remaining in the bush is unlikely to be complicated, given the relatively small numbers involved and the fact that many of them are there against their will. The government has a 20-year history of successfully buying off former fighters and accepting them back into civilian and political life. The community has been dealing with returnees for years and Ugandans, particularly the Acholi, are actively encouraging the rebels to return if it means peace. It is not clear who would pay for a formal DDR process: the Amnesty commission is the government body mandated to receive and reintegrate returning rebels, but lacks funding. Any foreign nationals who have been abducted and held by the LRA will also need to be repatriated and rehabilitated.

In addition (although it is unlikely to be part of any formal DDR programme), the government will need to address the local militias across the north and east, which were raised following the LRA influx in 2002 to help ward off rebel attacks. If this is not adequately tackled, it raises the prospect of guns floating around a region that is already strongly anti-government. In 2005, the govern-ment began to deal with the problem and some former militias have since been absorbed into the police. There are no plans, however, to downsize the UPDF – perhaps because a recent 'ghost soldier' scandal revealed that thousands of soldiers on the payroll were either deceased or demobilised.

Effective long-term DDR

In whatever way the war ends, a DDR programme will only be meaningful if the underlying causes of the conflict are tackled. This does not mean they have to be addressed in direct talks with the LRA. However, the conflict in the north is an expression of very real grievances: feelings of exclusion from national politics, marginalisation and underdevelopment, as well as newer grievances, like dis-placement, which are a consequence of the conflict itself. If these are not tackled, there is little to prevent former fighters from returning to the bush and forming new fighting groups. Uganda is a country where people readily turn to the gun: there have been 22 rebel groups since 1986 alone. As an official of an adult reception centre puts it:

> Everyone working with the formerly abducted fears that they could form the basis of another rebellion … particularly the ones who have joined the army and the LDUs. Many don't have parents. They have nowhere to go, and if they begin rebel activity … they will fight terribly.[74]

Four crucial issues need to be addressed for DDR to have any real meaning: resettlement and rehabilitation; justice and reconciliation; regional politics; and political stability.

Resettlement and rehabilitation

The efforts to dismantle IDP camps will have to be sustained and their former occupants will have to be resettled if the region is to be rebuilt. This will require significant financial resources. The clearing of mines and other unexploded ordnance, left during earlier phases of the conflict, needs to be addressed (although there is little information on the existence of mines or on the extent of the problem). The process will be expensive and require long-term commitment on the part of the Ugandan government and international donors.

Resettlement is already in its initial stages. Camps in the north are being decongested (broken up into smaller satellite camps) while in the eastern districts, 90 per cent of the population had returned home by 2006. Decongestion began in 2005, and in March 2006 – before the Juba peace talks had even been mooted – the government set up a committee to implement what one government minister described as Uganda's own 'Marshall Plan' (a reference to the 1947 proposal put forward by Secretary of State George C. Marshall to reconstruct Europe after the Second World War). The goal is to reduce IDP numbers from '10,000–60,000 persons per camp to 1,000–3,000, to improve service delivery and enable them to get closer to their parishes and villages'.[75] By December 2006, IDPs were increasingly returning to their land during the day to farm, taking advantage of the improved security. However, while decongestion is an improvement on the current situation, it is not the same as returning home. Ultimately, many of the displaced will want to go back to the site of their original villages and will require basic tools and seeds to restart their life. The war-weary population is unlikely to return home until they are convinced that the conflict is really over.[76]

Resettlement is liable to be fraught with difficulties. Land is a touchy subject in the region: for many people, it is all they have left after years of conflict. Hostility towards the NRM is sometimes expressed as a fear that the government wants to grab land.[77] Much of the land in Gulu, Kitgum and Pader is owned customarily or communally (with no written records), which means that ownership disputes are to be expected.[78] The government is likely to be flooded with requests for compensation, particularly from those whose land was occupied by IDPs. At the same time, settlement patterns could very well change. A generation has grown up in congested camps. Young men may not want to become farmers and may choose to migrate to towns, with attendant social consequences.

Rehabilitation will be time-consuming and costly, and much of the money will need to come from donors. There has been no significant development in the region, apart from the main town of Gulu (which has had an inflow of aid, as well as investment from the diaspora). There are also few natural resources to fund development, apart from fertile land for agriculture. The region is so poor that there is not even a real war economy, barring the limited number of people who have benefited from aid agency contracts or, in the past, the military officers who enriched themselves from inflated pay rolls. Any funds will need to be carefully monitored as previous World Bank funds targeted for northern reconstruction have failed to make a significant impact.

Justice and reconciliation

Justice is crucial to long-term peace. It needs to be achieved on two levels: first, by strengthening the police and courts, which have been profoundly weakened by years of military dominance in the region and, second, by laying the past to rest. Trust has been broken and there are individual, clan, ethnic, national and regional conflicts and divisions. In July 2006, for example, civil and religious leaders from south Sudan asked the UPDF to address some of the atrocities that they accused the military of committing, on their soil, during Operation 'Iron Fist'. Increasingly, there has been a push for some kind of truth and reconciliation commission, which will include the government as well as the rebels. This is particularly important, as many northerners feel that the UPDF has not been held to account for its misconduct during the conflict. However, there is still disagreement over whether there should be punishment for those found guilty of war-related crimes. Should amnesty be granted to those responsible or does this create a culture of impunity? Moreover, is there a distinctive Acholi Traditional Justice – restorative rather than punitive – that can satisfy a demand (locally and/or internationally) for accountability? The debate centres on whether peace bought without justice is sustainable. In addition, there may be a need for a wider political conference to discuss feelings of political marginalisation, neglect and underdevelopment in the country's northern districts.

It is worth noting the debate about the possible role of traditional justice mechanisms in the post-conflict north. The ceremony of *Mato Oput* ('tasting the bitter root') is often proposed as a reconciliation ritual, which could satisfy international demands for accountability for the indicted rebel leaders.[79] However, it is not clear if such ceremonies can be adapted to deal with the scale and the type of atrocities committed in the region, or even whether these ceremonies are as robust and viable as sometimes suggested.[80] The rituals are also likely to have little meaning to non-Acholi caught up in the conflict. Furthermore, although the Acholi say they are willing to forgive and reconcile for the sake of peace – and although they have been remarkably tolerant so far – this cannot be taken as a given.[81] Betty Bigombe, who arranged talks with the LRA in 1994 and again in 2005, suggests that attitudes might change after the war has ended:

> Traditional methods of reconciliation exist. The only challenge is that there has never been a problem of this magnitude. I think the people of Acholi are so desperate for peace that they are saying they are ready to forgive. Probably one day when the war is over and you have former LRA, especially those who have committed atrocities in the most brutal manner, walking down the street … I do not know how people will relate to that then.[82]

Finally, the approach to justice and reconciliation taken will have implications for ongoing attempts to pursue justice at the international level. Museveni invited the ICC to investigate the conflict in the north because he hoped that this would put pressure on Sudan (and later the DRC) to hunt down the LRA on their territory. This did not happen, which, he says, is largely why the government agreed to negotiate with the rebels. Whatever decision is reached, this creates potential difficulties. The ICC now risks being seen either as weak (if it backs down) or as an impediment to peace (if it stays firm). Although there have been several solutions proposed to circumvent this problem (suspending the prosecution annually, persuading a country that has not ratified the Rome Treaty, like Sudan, to give asylum to the indictees, proving that traditional reconciliation ceremonies are sufficiently robust to provide adequate accountability), there is no clear solution as of yet.

The regional context

The LRA existed before the Sudan Government gave them backing, but they could never have been as effective without the security of rear bases at which to train abductees, and the steady supply of arms and ammunition. The regional situation has changed dramatically since the Sudanese government and the SPLA signed a peace deal in early 2005. Officially, the LRA no longer receives support from the Sudanese government and the new Southern Sudanese government, which originally promised to hunt the LRA down, has made the dramatic move of instigating peace talks between the rebels and the Ugandan government. If these talks fail, the SPLA has promised to expel the LRA from its territory (although previous military threats against the LRA have failed to deliver). However, it is still possible that elements within the Sudan government could have an interest in funding the LRA, either to destabilise the south or to discredit the Kampala government, which remains the object of deep-seated suspicion and animosity. Until there is stability in southern Sudan, the region could potentially provide succour to Ugandan rebel groups and/or provide a route for arms.

The DRC has also been a haven for various Ugandan rebel groups over the last decade – this is how Museveni justified twice invading the country in the 1990s. The LRA have historically preferred operating among the Ugandan and Sudanese Acholi (or other Luo speakers, like the Langi). However, in late 2005, the LRA entered Garamba National Park, in the northeast of the DRC, far from their normal area of operations. This was previously the hideout for the Ugandan rebel West Nile Bank Front in 1996, some of whose fighters joined the LRA in

1997. It is not clear how long the rebels can stay in this region and still function as an effective rebel group. However, as long as the DRC remains unstable there is nothing to stop a new rebel group from using the park as a base. The LRA reportedly moved to Garamba at the urging of a Ugandan Acholi in the US diaspora, who promised that they would be able to join up with other anti-government forces. Even after the Juba talks started, the Ugandan press suggested that the LRA were actively trying to establish contacts with other Ugandan rebel groups to open up 'a new war front'. Furthermore, an insecure DRC is also a potential supply route for arms.

Political stability

Finally, and crucially, there needs to be a healthy democratic climate. In 2005, Uganda returned to a multi-party political system, following 19 years of operating what Museveni called a 'broad-based' Movement system of government.[83] Unfortunately, the initial gains of opening up the political space were offset when parliament was persuaded to lift the constitutional two-term presidential limit. Museveni stood again and won his 'third term' in the February 2006 general election. However, he gained few votes in the north, which remains resolutely anti-government. Despite economic (and other) successes in the south and west of Uganda, Museveni has failed the north. His challenge in the coming years is to convince the Acholi that he is on their side. He also needs to demonstrate that, despite the lifting of term limits, he is committed to opening up real political space. If the Acholi, and indeed all Ugandans, are left feeling that politics is not an avenue through which they can express their discontent, violence may end up looking like a more attractive option.

Postscript

This piece was written at the start of the Juba peace talks, in 2006. The security situation in northern Uganda has since improved greatly, mainly because the rebels have relocated away from the country's borders. As a result, there has been no abduction in the north and a halt to the trickle of former fighters escaping. The humanitarian situation has improved, although life for many remains grim. Around half of the displaced have gone back to their villages or to 'satellite camps'.[84] In October 2007, the government announced a $606 million Northern Ugandan Peace, Recovery and Development Plan (PRDP),[85] although concerns about its implementation remain.[86]

Despite this positive trend, the future in northern Uganda is still uncertain. In April 2008 – after the LRA and government of Uganda had reached five agreements, including one on DDR[87] – Joseph Kony failed to turn up to sign the final peace agreement. There is now little hope that the negotiations will deliver a settlement. The LRA may not be active in northern Uganda, but they maintain a presence in south Sudan and have bases in DRC and Central African Republic (CAR) – a development that prompted one analyst to remark that Kony had mutated from 'rebel/predator in northern Uganda' into a 'genuine regional warlord'.[88] Uganda, South Sudan and the DRC, as well as the UN Mission in Congo (MONUC), have discussed taking military action against the rebels[89] – who in 2008 abducted between 350 and 500 people from Sudan, DRC and CAR.[90] Joseph Kony, meanwhile, decided not to come out of the bush until the ICC arrest warrants are withdrawn, even though the LRA agreed in Juba that the indictees would be tried in a Ugandan court in the event of a peace deal being signed.[91]

Notes

1 This chapter was originally written in December 2006 and is based on primary research undertaken in Northern Uganda in August/September 2005 and February/March 2006. It has been edited for this volume to include some reference to subsequent studies and reports.
2 Pader was created from Kitgum district in December 2001.
3 Uganda Human Development Report, *Linking Environment to Human Development.*
4 UN Radio Interview, 8 May 2005, www.un.org/av/radio/unandafrica/transcript47.htm.
5 Behrend, *Alice Lakwena and the Holy Spirits.* See also, Allen, *Understanding Alice.*
6 Alice Auma Lakena died in Ifo refugee camp in Kenya on 28 January 2006. Emmy Allio, Arthur Okot and Cyprian Musoke, 'Former Rebel Chief Lakwena is Dead', *The New Vision,* 19 January 2007.
7 Interview with Severino Lukoya, Gulu, August 2006.
8 Translated speech by Joseph Kony to religious and cultural leaders in northern Uganda. Nyakairu and Gyezaho, 'Uganda: Kony Talks'.
9 Lord's Salvation Army; United Democratic Christian Force; the Lord's Army.
10 Quoted in Nyeko and Lucima, 'Profiles of the Parties to the Conflict'
11 The SPLA/M and the Khartoum government signed a peace agreement on 9 January 2005.
12 Marieke Schomerus suggests that it was a different rebel faction fighting alongside the government of Sudan. See Schomerus, *The Lord's Resistance Army in Sudan,* 23.
13 The Ugandan government announced on 30 September 2005 that Dominic Ongwen had been killed in Soroti district, northeastern Uganda in a battle with the military. However, on 13 July 2006, DNA analysis led the ICC to conclude that the body was not his.
14 The amendment gave powers to the Internal Affairs Minister to forward to parliament the names of those to be excluded from amnesty. Frank Nyakairu, 'Uganda: Museveni amnesty to Kony illegal – ICC', *The Monitor,* 7 June 2006.
15 For an overview of the talks, see ICG, *Peace in Northern Uganda.* This report also discusses ways out of the peace/justice dilemma.
16 In 1993, William Nyuon Bany, SPLA chief of staff, fell out with the then SPLA chairman, Dr John Garang. He joined Dr Machar, a former SPLA officer, who had rebelled against Dr Garang in 1991. Because Uganda was supporting the SPLA, Dr Machar and William Nyuon Bany decided to hit back and introduce Kony to Khartoum. Machar later met Kony on behalf of the group. See: Izama and Bisiika, 'Kony/SPLA talk, but why?'.
17 According to Article 86 of the Rome Statute (which established the ICC in 2002), all state parties to the Rome Statute have an obligation to cooperate fully with the court.
18 This chapter was completed in December 2006. Subsequently the Juba talks have broken down and then resumed (on 26 April 2007). For an analysis of the events leading up to the resumption of the talks, see ICG, *Northern Uganda: Seizing the Opportunity for Peace.*
19 In March 2008 the LRA delegation and the Ugandan government agreed that, in the event of a peace deal being signed, ICC indictees would be tried in a Ugandan court,

rather than in the Hague. Other fighters would face traditional justice. The Agreement on Accountability and Reconciliation, Between the Government of Uganda and the LRA/M, www.csopnu.net/?jc=juba.

20 Interviews with former LRA commanders, Gulu, March 2006.

21 Interview, BBC *Newsnight*, 28 June 2006.

22 Interview with Former LRA Major, Jackson Achama, Gulu, September 2005.

23 Interview with Jackson Achama, Gulu, September 2005.

24 Interview with Captain Ray Apire, Former LRA 'chaplain', Gulu, February 2006.

25 Former rebel commanders justify their actions on 'Inside the LRA', Reporter, Anna Borzello. Broadcast on Al-Jazeera, January 2007. www.youtube.com/watch?v=uYURvl8WXFU.

26 This could partly be because senior ex-LRA commanders who have been granted amnesty and, sometimes, cash since leaving the bush, may feel dependent on the goodwill of the Ugandan government and fear they will jeopodise their position if they voice political concerns.

27 LRA delegation opening speech in Juba, 20 July 2006. See: www.radiorhino.org/htm_material/archiv/text/press/monitor/Rria%20060715%20-%20Opening%20speech%20of%20LRA%20delegation%20at%20Juba%20talks.htm.

28 See account by James Obita, the former LRA external spokesman, on his attempts to mediate peace between the LRA and the government. Obita, 'First International Peace Efforts'.

29 'Uganda rebel boss Kony sincere about peace', *Reuters*, 17 November 2006.

30 Later reports suggest the LRA deliberately inflated their number, so as to sell the excess food in the DRC. See, for example, Katy Glassborow, 'LRA Accused of Selling Food Aid, ICC prosecutor says the rebels are using the money they make to rearm', *Institute for War and Peace Reporting*, 25 October 2007.

31 Interview with Joseph Kony's bush doctor, March 2006.

32 Former rebel commanders describe Trinkle as a distinct battalion, but some commentators have suggested that it is an alternative name for Control Altar. Interviews with Senior Commanders, February 2006.

33 For details of LRA weapons see Small Arms Survey, *Fuelling Fear*.

34 Government of Uganda–UNICEF, 'Abductions in Northern and South-Western Uganda'.

35 Amnesty International, *Uganda: Breaking God's Commandments*; Human Rights Watch, 'Abducted and Abused'.

36 Interview, Kitgum Town, March 2006.

37 Government of Uganda–UNICEF, 'Abductions in Northern and South-Western Uganda'.

38 A 2008 study estimated that 72,000 people had been abducted by the LRA since the start of the conflict, of which 38,000 were children. Pham *et al.*, 2007. *Abduction*.

39 See Schomerus, *The Lord's Resistance Army in Sudan*, for a detailed history of the LRA in Sudan, September 2007.

40 Interview, Gulu, September 2005.

41 Veale and Stavrou, *Violence, Reconciliation and Identity*.

42 Liu Institute for Global Issues, *Roco Wat I Acholi*.

43 In a conflict in which so many of the fighters were unwilling, it is hard to know what to call those who return. 'Former rebels/combatants' or 'ex-LRA' suggests agency and hence accountability while 'abductees' ignores that some of the senior commanders went to the bush freely. The commonly used terms today are 'Formerly Abducted Person (FAP)' and 'Returnee'.

44 Kony is said to have warned his troops that they will be killed upon surrendering to the government. However, he clearly knows that this is not the case. When a group of LRA 'wives' and children were released by the rebels in 2002, they were given a note asking that the authorities look after them.

45　The LRA made up the bulk of this number, which included former fighters from five other Ugandan rebel organisations. The project was funded by the World Bank's Multi-Country Demobilization and Reintegration Programme (MDRP).

46　For an in-depth discussion of traditional ceremonies, the role of traditional justice and its limits, see Liu Institute for Global Issues, *Roco Wat I Acholi* and Allen, *Trial Justice*.

47　Liu Institute for Global Issues, *Roco Wat I Acholi*.

48　Allen and Schomerus, *A Hard Homecoming*; Veale and Stavrou, *Violence, Reconciliation and Identity*.

49　Allen and Schomerus, A *Hard Homecoming*.

50　MacMullin, C. and Loughry, M., *An investigation into the psychosocial adjustment of formerly abducted soldiers in Northern Uganda.* Field Report (Enhanced) for International Rescue Committee, March 2002. Cited in Veale and Stavrou, *Violence, Reconciliation and Identity*.

51　Interview with reception centre manager, Gulu, February 2006.

52　The then Presidential Advisor on northern Uganda, Major General Salim Saleh, said at the time that the camps were temporary and would only be in place for six months. Interview with author, 1996.

53　UN OCHA. This figure includes 63 camps in Katakwi District, which has had a long-term displacement problem due to attacks over the last decade from neighbouring Karamajong.

54　Health Ministry, Government of Uganda, and the World Health Organisation, *Health and mortality survey*. The report found that the mortality rate is well above emergency thresholds, and in the districts of Kitgum and Pader, four times higher. The leading causes of death are malaria/fever, Aids and violence.

55　Dolan and Bagenda, *Militarisation and Its Impacts*.

56　A 2008 study found that levels of Post Traumatic Stress Disorder in Northern Uganda are higher than in comparable populations in Afghanistan and Bosnia. Of those surveyed, 54 per cent displayed symptoms of post-traumatic stress disorder (PTSD) and 67 per cent showed signs of depression. See Roberts *et al.*, 'Factors Associated with Post-Traumatic Stress'.

57　Human Rights Watch, 'Uprooted and Forgotten'; CSOPNU, *Nowhere to Hide*; HURIFU, *Between Two Fires*; ARLPI, *Let My People Go*.

58　Interview, Gulu, March 2006.

59　Interview, Gulu District, February 2006.

60　For a detailed account of the problems returnees can face, see Liu Institute for Global Issues, *Alice's Story*.

61　Liu Institute for Global Issues, *Roco Wat I Acholi*.

62　Ibid.

63　Youth in Acholi culture are generally defined as being between 14–30 years of age. Annan and Blattmann, *The State of Youth and Youth Protection*.

64　Discussed in Allen and Schomerus, *A Hard Homecoming*.

65　For further discussion see Liu Institute for Global Issues, *Youth Mothers, Marriage and Reintegration*.

66　A study of 148 young LRA mothers found that, of those who knew their husbands were still alive, 97 per cent were uninterested in reuniting with them. The study also details the difficulties facing women on their return from the bush. See Liu Institute for Global Issues, *Youth Mothers, Marriage and Reintegration*.

67　Interview, Gulu town, February 2006.

68　Lenz, *Armed with Resilience*.

69　Banya was captured in battle by the UPDF in 2004, but maintains that he allowed himself to be captured and insists he was an 'abductee'.

70　Interview, Gulu, February 2006.

71　Interviews at Cet Kana, August 2005 and February 2006.

72　See Human Rights Watch, 'Child Soldier Use, 2003'.

73 Museveni's stand reflects concern about legitimising the LRA, by treating the group as if it represents the political ambitions of the Acholi people.

74 Interview, Kitgum, August 2005.

75 Emmy Allio, 'Master Plan for North Unveiled', *The New Vision*, 31 March 2006.

76 There are also a large number of urban displaced who have been largely ignored in the government's resettlement programme. Refugee Law Project, 'What About Us?'.

77 For an example of land-grabbing allegations, which also named senior Ugandan officials, see Yasiin Mugerwa and Agness Nandutu, 'Saleh names in Acholi land saga', *The Monitor*, 11 December 2006. www.monitor.co.ug/artman/publish/news/Saleh_names_in_Acholi_land_saga_35125.shtml.

78 Adoko and Levine, *Land Matters in Displacement*.

79 For example, if the case against the top LRA leadership was suspended or dropped and Uganda wanted to satisfy the ICC that it had the internal capacity to deal with the indictees.

80 *Mato Oput* involves the perpetrator – through the mediation of elders – admitting guilt, asking for forgiveness and paying compensation to the clan of an individual who has been killed. For further discussion, see ICG, *Peace in Northern Uganda?* and Liu Institute for Global Issues, *Roco Wat I Acholi*.

81 Although, anecdotally, the Acholi overwhelmingly say they are willing to forgive if it will bring peace – and stress that it is part of their culture – some academic research suggests that the underlying feelings may be more complex. Two studies in 2005 reached apparently contradictory conclusions about the Acholi desire for justice: Pham *et al.*, 2005. *Forgotten Voices: A Population-Based Survey* and Hovil and Zachary, 'Whose Justice?'.

82 Interview Betty Bigombe, Kampala, March 2006.

83 President Yoweri Museveni's 'Movement' system of government (1986–2005) was described by its supporters as a broad-based, 'no-party' system of government, as well as an alternate form of democracy, and by its detractors as a thinly veiled version of a one-party state. Under the Movement, political parties were allowed to exist, but their activities were severely restricted, and politicians were not allowed to campaign for office under a party ticket. For further discussion on the democratic limits of the 'Movement' see Human Rights Watch, *Hostile to Democracy*.

84 Internal Displacement Monitoring Centre, *Uganda: Uncertain Future for IDPs*.

85 'The overall goal of the PRDP is to consolidate peace and security and lay foundations for recovery and development'. Government of Uganda, *Peace Recovery and Development Plan*. Amnesty Commission funding for DDR also falls under this programme.

86 Refugees International, 'Northern Uganda'.

87 The agreements reached at the Juba talks included: Cessation of Hostilities Agreement, Comprehensive Solutions Agreement, Permanent Ceasefire Agreement, Agreement on Accountability and Reconciliation and Agreement on Disarmament, Demobilization and Reintegration. Available at www.csopnu.net/?jc=juba.

88 Spiegel and Prendergast, *A New Peace Strategy for Northern Uganda*.

89 'Congo To Attack Ugandan Rebels', *BBC News*, 4 June 2008.

90 'Hundreds Abducted in Central Africa', *Amnesty International*, 22 April 2008.

91 Agreement on Accountability and Reconciliation, Between the Government of Uganda and the LRA/M. The annex allowing that war crimes be tried in a special section of the Uganda High Court was signed on 19 February 2008.

References

Acholi Religious Leaders' Peace Initiative (ARLPI), 2001. *Let My People Go: The Forgotten Plight of the People in the Displaced Camps in Acholi*, ARLPI, Gulu.

Adoko, Judy and Levine, Simon, 2004. *Land Matters in Displacement: The Importance of Land Rights in Acholiland and What Threatens Them*, CSOPNU, Kampala.

Allen, Tim, 1991. 'Understanding Alice: Uganda's Holy Spirit Movement in Context', *Africa* 61:3.

——, 2006. *Trial Justice: The International Criminal Court and the Lord's Resistance Army*, Zed Books, London.

Allen, Tim and Schomerus, Mareike, 2005. *A Hard Homecoming: Lessons Learned from the Reception Center Process on Effective Integration for Former 'Abductees' in Northern Uganda*, Management Systems International, UNICEF and USAID, Washington DC.

Amnesty International, 1997. *Uganda: Breaking God's Commandments: The Destruction of Childhood by the Lord's Resistance Army*, Amnesty International, London.

Annan, Jeannie and Blattmann, Christopher, 2006. *The State of Youth and Youth Protection in Northern Uganda, Findings from the Survey for War Affected Youth*, UNICEF, Kampala.

Behrend, Heike, 2000. *Alice Lakwena and the Holy Spirits: War in Northern Uganda, 1985–7*, James-Currey, Oxford.

Borzello, Anna, 2007. 'Inside the LRA', Broadcast on Al-Jazeera, January, www.youtube.com/watch?v=uYURvl8WXFU.

Civil Society Organisations for Peace in Northern Uganda (CSOPNU), 2004. *Nowhere to Hide: Humanitarian Protection Threats in Northern Uganda*, CSOPNU, Kampala.

Dolan, Chris and Bagenda, Emmanuel, 2004. *Militarisation and Its Impacts: Strategic Conflict Analysis*, Christian Aid, London.

Government of Uganda, 2007. *Peace, Recovery and Development Plan, 2007–2010*, September.

Government of Uganda–UNICEF, 2001. 'Abductions in Northern and South-Western Uganda 1986–2001', *Country Programme 2001–2005*, www.internal-displacement.org/8025708F004CE90B/(httpDocuments)/2F68FFB88812387C802570B7005A54EF/$file/UNICEF+Abducted+Children+Database+(November+2001).pdf.

Health Ministry, Government of Uganda and the World Health Organisation, 2005. *Health and Mortality Survey Among Internally Displaced Persons in Gulu, Kitgum and Pader Districts, Northern Uganda*. www.who.int/hac/crises/uga/sitreps/Ugandamortsurvey.pdf.

Hovil, Lucy and Lomo, Zachary, 2005. 'Whose Justice? Perceptions of Uganda's Amnesty Act 2000: The Potential for Conflict Resolution and Long-Term Reconciliation', Working Paper No. 15, Refugee Law Project, February.

Human Rights Focus (HURIFO), 2002. *Between Two Fires: The Human Rights Situation in Protected Camps in Gulu District*, HURIFO, Gulu.

Human Rights Watch (HRW), 1999. *Hostile to Democracy: The Movement System and Political Repression in Uganda*, HRW, New York, Washington, London, Brussels.

——, 2003. 'Abducted and Abused: Renewed Conflict in Northern Uganda', *Human Rights Watch* 15:12a, July.

——, 2003. 'Child Soldier Use, 2003: A Briefing for the 4th UN Security Council Open Debate on Children and Armed Conflict', Coalition to Stop the Use of Child Soldiers, London.

——, 2005. 'Uprooted and Forgotten: Impunity and Human Rights Abuses in Northern Uganda', *Human Rights Watch* 17:12a, September.

Internal Displacement Monitoring Center, 2008. *Uganda: Uncertain Future for IDPs While Peace Remains Elusive*, Norwegian Refugee Council, Geneva, 24 April.

International Crisis Group (ICG), 2007. *Northern Uganda, Seizing the Opportunity for Peace*, Report No. 124. ICG, Kampala/Nairobi/Brussels.

——, 2006. *Peace in Northern Uganda*, Africa Brief, No. 4. ICG, Nairobi and Brussels.

Izama, Angelo and Bisiika, Asuman, 2006. 'Kony/SPLA talk, but why?', Uganda Office, Konrad-Adenauer-Stiftung, 31 May.

Lenz, Jessica, 2003. 'Armed with Resilience, A Study Addressing the Issues of Reintegration and Resiliency of Formerly Abducted Girl Child Soldiers in Northern Uganda and Their Potential Role as Peace Builders', MSc Dissertation, Oxford Brookes University.

Liu Institute for Global Issues, 2006. *Alice's Story: Cultural and Spiritual Dimensions of Reconciliation in Northern Uganda*, The Justice and Reconciliation Project: Field Notes, 1. Gulu District NGO Forum.

——, 2005. *Roco Wat I Acholi, Restoring Relationships in Acholiland: Traditional Approaches to Justice and Reintegration*, Gulu District NGO Forum/Ker Kwaro Acholi.

——, 2006. *Youth Mothers, Marriage, and Reintegration in Northern Uganda: Considerations for the Juba Peace Talks*, The Justice and Reconciliation Project: Field Notes, 2. Gulu District NGO Forum.

Nyakairu, Frank and Gyezaho, Emmanuel, 2006. 'Uganda: Kony Talks – "We Are Fighting for 10 Commandments"', *The Monitor*, 2 August.

Nyeko, Balam and Okello, Lucima, 2002. 'Profiles of the Parties to the Conflict', in Okello, Lucima (ed.), *Accord Protracted Conflict, Elusive Peace: Initiatives to End the Violence in Northern Uganda*, Conciliation Resources and Kacoke Madit, London.

Obita, James Alfred, 2002. 'First International Peace Efforts 1996–1998', in Okello, Lucrma (ed.), *Accord – Protracted Conflict, Elusive Peace*, Conciliation Resources and Kacoke Madit, London.

Pham, Phuong, Vinck, Patrick and Stover, Eric, 2007. *Abduction: The Lord's Resistance Army and Forced Conscription in Northern Uganda*. University of California, Berkeley Human Rights Center and Tulane University Center for International Development.

Pham, Phuong, Vinck, Patrick, Wierda, Marieke, Stover, Eric and di Giovanni, Adrian, 2005. *Forgotten Voices: A Population-Based Survey on Attitudes about Peace and Justice in Northern Uganda*. International Centre for Transitional Justice (ICTJ) and the Human Rights Centre, University of California, Berkeley.

Refugee Law Project, 2007. 'What About Us? The Exclusion of Urban IDPs from Uganda's IDP Related Policies and Interventions', Briefing paper, Makerere University, Kampala, December.

Refugees International, 2008. 'Northern Uganda: Give Displaced People Real Options', *Bulletin*, July.

Roberts, Bayard, Ocaka, Kaducu Felix Ocaka, Browne John, Oyok, Thomas and Sondorp, Egbert, 2008. 'Factors Associated With Post-Traumatic Stress Disorder and Depression Amongst Internally Displaced Persons in Northern Uganda', *BCM Psychiatry* 8(38), 19 May.

Schomerus, Mareike, 2007. *The Lord's Resistance Army in Sudan*. Small Arms Survey, HSBA Working Paper 8, September.

Small Arms Survey, 2006. *Fuelling Fear, the Lord's Resistance Army and Small Arms*, Oxford.

Spiegel, Julia and Prendergast, John, 2008. 'A New Peace Strategy for Northern Uganda and the LRA', Enough Strategy Paper 19, May 2008.

Uganda Human Development Report, 2005. *Linking Environment to Human Development: A Deliberate Choice*, UNDP, Kampala.

Veale, Angela and Stavrou, Akri, 2003. 'Violence, Reconciliation and Identity: The Reintegration of Lord's Resistance Army Child Abductees in Northern Uganda', Monograph No. 92, South Africa, Institute for Security Studies.

7 Engaging with disengagement

The political reintegration of Sierra Leone's Revolutionary United Front

Kieran Mitton

Introduction

The conflict between the Revolutionary United Front (RUF) and the Sierra Leonean government represents a highly instructive study for reintegration projects, primarily due to the motives underpinning violence and the identity of the main protagonists. Far from being a conventional political insurgency readily lending itself to peaceful political transformation, the RUF possessed within the ranks of its young and brutalised recruits a fundamental rejection of Sierra Leone's political structures. As such, Sierra Leone presented a unique challenge for reintegration efforts, requiring not only the immediate reconciliation of ex-combatants with victims and civil society, but also the long-term political incorporation of a group of youths defined by their very disengagement from and distrust of the political system.

The conflict began in early 1991 when a small group of combatants crossed the Liberian border into eastern Sierra Leone, seeking to topple the one-party regime of Joseph Momoh.[1] Met by a weak and ineffective counterinsurgency effort, a decade of brutal conflict ensued in which two-thirds of Sierra Leone's population were displaced and up to 50,000 were killed. It was not until 2002, following a series of failed negotiated settlements, that peace was officially declared by a new civilian government. The cessation of hostilities owed much to the intervention of British and Guinean troops in 2000, which precipitated the deployment of 17,500 UN peacekeepers, the largest such force at the time. These developments enabled the full operation of a DDR programme, which had suffered repeated interruption since its initial introduction in 1998. A Truth and Reconciliation Commission (TRC) and Special Court were also established, and in December 2005, the United Nations Mission in Sierra Leone (UNAMSIL) withdrew its peacekeepers. In 2007, Sierra Leone conducted national elections, returning the All Party Congress (APC) to power.

The DDR process, which ran in three distinct phases between September 1998 and January 2002, disarmed 72,490 combatants (including 24,352 from the RUF) of which 71,043 were demobilised and 55,000 received reintegration assistance.[2] Despite the relative effectiveness of the demobilisation and disarmament programmes, Sierra Leone remains in a state of abject poverty, with high levels of youth unemployment and limited opportunities, serving to undermine the reintegration of ex-combatants. Former RUF fighters make up a significant portion of those struggling to find work, with many expressing dissatisfaction with the lack of prospects and cynicism with regard to the ruling authorities in Freetown – factors that proved instrumental to the original onset of conflict. Success in politically reintegrating ex-combatants, therefore, should not be judged solely by the absence of renewed violence or the conduct of free and fair elections. Rather, it must also appreciate the extent to which ex-combatants hold faith in the political system, and peace generally, to deliver solutions to problems of social and economic disparity or decline, and the extent to which ex-combatants themselves are shaping this process. In this light, this chapter argues that despite progress in many key areas, former fighters of the RUF have yet to be fully politically reintegrated. The Sierra Leone experience demonstrates that successful political integration does not simply amount to political participation per se, but rather requires specific *forms* of political participation, which reinforce the primacy of peaceful political interaction over and above other means for affecting change.

The RUF: 'not so much a movement as an environment'[3]

To assess the political reintegration of the RUF, it is first necessary to understand that the rebel group was not by nature overtly 'political' in the conventional sense. The RUF differed from many non-state armed groups in that it lacked widespread popular support or a coherent overall political and military strategy.[4] Rather than appeal to the civilian population for logistical support, or to establish a political constituency, the RUF's relation to the people was characterised by brutal atrocities, which often rendered it deeply unpopular, both domestically and internationally.[5]

With much of its rank-and-file membership comprised of child soldiers, many of whom had been forcibly recruited, the RUF represented a largely illiterate, politically and socially dislocated body of brutalised youths, who despite possessing a myriad of legitimate grievances, were ill equipped to return (or to be introduced) to civil society and channel these grievances through peaceful political discourse.

The initial invasion of Sierra Leone, launched across the border from Liberia in March 1991 with Charles Taylor's sponsorship, involved little more than 300 combatants, many of whom had limited connection with Sierra Leone.[6] While the border populations in the south and southeast may at first have been sympathetic to the fighters' grievances against the APC regime, any support was quickly squandered through the RUF's looting and atrocities. As the conflict developed, former Sierra Leone Army (SLA) corporal and RUF leader, Foday Sankoh, continued to claim an ideological basis for the insurgency, framing the rebellion as an attempt to deliver Sierra Leone from decades of mismanagement by a corrupt and self-serving elite.[7] Nevertheless, this rhetoric was consistently undermined by RUF abuses against the civilian populace, often conducted for economic profit. Despite such abuses, the insurgency was able to grow by incorporating a large body of economically and socially marginalised youth, many of whom already existed on the fringes of Sierra Leonean society prior to the conflict, eking out a living in diamond mining and illicit trade. For those resentful of a government operating by an inequitable system of patrimony, the rebellion offered an opportunity both to defy political authority and to gain access to resources from which they had previously been excluded.[8] The RUF sustained itself logistically through the systematic extraction and trade of such resources, particularly alluvial diamonds, which it exchanged for weapons and ammunition. To a considerable degree, therefore, the political economy of war ensured that conflict became, for many, an end in itself.[9]

The motivation of combatants also related to physical security and social empowerment – the capacity to exact revenge on those deemed responsible for peacetime inequalities and the status and camaraderie shared among fellow fighters.[10] In this sense, the RUF was far less a political movement with a definite goal as it was an environment facilitating modes of behaviour perceived as beneficial by combatants. Even so, many rebel fighters enjoined conflict not through some cost–benefit analysis but through direct abduction into RUF ranks. For many such fighters, the effects of brutalisation rather than the lure of loot defined their relationship to violence, yet as such, their motives were also far removed from any overarching political ideology. This is not to suggest that combatants were without genuine political grievance or conviction. Indeed, the disillusionment with ruling elites was itself a factor in determining the RUF's apolitical nature: it did not represent a political alternative but an alternative to politics altogether. Violence was often manifested as a war against authority and as a total rejection of traditional hierarchies, with many combatants expressing a desire to punish Sierra Leonean society or to bring it to ruin. RUF activity displayed a clear determination to postpone political resolution and, accordingly, the language of democratic elections and peace prompted spates of violence clearly intended to deter potential voters and punish those pushing for political reconciliation.

The implications for political integration

The nature of the RUF has rendered its political reintegration far more complex than that of an armed group defined by a readily identifiable political agenda. In seeking through conflict a resolution to problems of economic and social disparity, and in finding in violence a means by which to achieve empowerment or a degree of basic welfare security, many RUF combatants were far less concerned with political concessions or governmental reform. Rather than formalising the RUF's political legitimacy, political reintegration would involve building a trust among combatants in political interaction over and above violence as a means to secure their basic welfare needs and address problems of corruption and economic underdevelopment. However, for those who had more to lose in peace than in conflict, political incorporation represented at best a useful façade for the continuation of abuses, and at worst a direct threat to their status and position.

Included in this group were the commanders and leaders for whom conflict had secured wealth from looting, diamond mining, illicit trade and the availability of cheap labour in the form of loyal fighters. Through their involvement in atrocities, many commanders also feared prosecution and peacetime reprisals, reinforcing their reluctance to renounce violence for reconciliatory discourse. As such, the RUF leadership was in many respects an obstructionist presence at peace negotiations, with commanders across the movement actively deterring rank-and-file combatants from entering DDR programmes, taking on the role of the proverbial 'spoiler'.

If the RUF leadership was uncommitted to political reintegration, the group's rank-and-file were ill equipped for political reintegration. For those who spent many years in the RUF, particularly those abducted at a young age or recruited at the inception of the conflict, the divorce from society was so complete as to require political *induction* rather than *reintegration*. For such fighters, the norms and codes of civil society, the historical context of the conflict and the very notion of political interaction simply lay beyond their sphere of experience. Combatants commonly shared an entrenched fear and hostility towards civilian society, which in combination with a lack of basic education and high levels of illiteracy, served to obstruct their engagement in public debate and formal political participation.

Ending the conflict: 'spoilers' and the spoils of peace

The above complexities are highlighted by the successive attempts to find a peaceful resolution to the Sierra Leone conflict. These attempts also illustrate the general principle that political reintegration efforts are often ineffective if they are not grounded in an understanding of the unique context and nature of the non-state armed group at hand. Initial peace agreements failed to understand the nature of the rebel movement, the motivations of its leadership and the concerns of combatants – they treated the RUF as a conventional political insurgent group and sought to establish political reconciliation with the higher echelons of its leadership. These peace agreements were derailed by a lack of real commitment by RUF leaders, who continued to seek the perpetuation of conflict, preferring the spoils of war to those of peace.

The Abidjan Accord

The Abidjan Accord of November 1996 represented the first major breakthrough in bringing the RUF to the negotiating table and establishing an agreed platform for peace. Following elections – a product of internal pressure from civil society groups, who had the support of the international community – the military regime of the National Provisional Ruling Council (NPRC) was replaced by the civilian government of Ahmad Tejan Kabbah of the Sierra Leone People's Party (SLPP). Kabbah promised amnesty to the RUF on condition that it sought terms of peace, threatening military action should the rebels fail to comply.

Revealingly, it was the latter factor that proved most significant in bringing the RUF to the negotiating table, following as it did a series of military setbacks at the hands of the increasingly effective Civil Defence Forces (CDF), acting in conjunction with private security firm Executive Outcomes. Having failed to prevent elections through the violent intimidation of the electorate and last-minute negotiations with the NPRC, the RUF now saw peace talks as a means of halting the progress of the CDF and expelling Executive Outcomes from the military equation.[11]

The Abidjan Accord provided clear incentives and provisions for the political reintegration of the RUF into the democratic process, including the establishment of an international trust fund to finance the RUF's transformation into a political party. However, reflecting perhaps the RUF's weakened military position, Kabbah's government did not offer the RUF any leadership posts, either in central or local government. Rather than politically incorporating the RUF into the existing regime where it could share power, the government sought to incorporate it into the *democratic system* where it would have to contend for power. Such democratic competition did not favour the RUF, which lacked broad political support as well as allies on the international scene. The Accord therefore failed on two key fronts. First, it offered the RUF leadership no real incentives for peace. While the invitation to form a political party held little appeal for those motivated less by political ideology as by the pursuit of status and economic wealth, the RUF's lack of support made the prospect of a democratic contest all the more unattractive. Furthermore, despite assurances of amnesties, RUF commanders remained convinced that some form of retaliation would occur once they take their place among a hostile civilian population.

Second, the accord failed to appreciate the relationship between the RUF leadership, who on the most part profited from conflict, and its rank-and-file members, who gained less economic advantage and were generally more willing to seek peace should it provide welfare and security.[12] The provision to establish a RUF party mistakenly treated the rebel leadership as politically representative of combatants, risking a consolidation rather than a weakening of their hold over fighters. In this context, the arrest of RUF leader Foday Sankoh in Nigeria in March 1997 did appear to offer a real window of opportunity to prise young rebels away from their jungle enclaves; reports at the time confirmed that many combatants felt confusion and ambiguity over their leadership and were demoralised by diminishing supplies and increasing desertion. Nevertheless, simply decapitating the organisation proved insufficient, as other senior RUF leaders, also with a vested interest in conflict, were quick to fill the vacuum created by Sankoh's arrest. Under Sam Brockerie, who emerged to replace Sanko as RUF leader, illicit trade and diamond-mining operations actually increased.[13] Furthermore, commanders across the RUF actively misled combatants as to the precise details of the Abidjan agreement: rank-and-file RUF were not informed of the crucial offer of immunity from prosecution nor of the benefits promised by the DDR programme.[14] Rather, commanders played on the common belief that the government sought to prosecute RUF combatants for their war crimes.

This misperception was reinforced by the failure of Kabbah's government to rein in the CDF, leading to violent clashes that undermined the trust and security required for DDR and signalled the collapse of the accord.

The Lomé peace agreement

The lack of real commitment to the Abidjan Accord was made clear in May 1997 when disaffected elements of the SLA, calling themselves the Armed Forces Revolutionary Council (AFRC), seized power from the civilian government and immediately invited the RUF, their supposed military opponents, to join them in government.[15] While the AFRC/RUF junta was eventually dislodged from Freetown, its devastating return to the capital in January 1999 convinced many international parties that Kabbah's government should seek a speedy power-sharing deal with the RUF. Accordingly, in July 1999 and under significant international pressure, the Lomé peace agreement was signed. The settlement provided for the RUF's direct incorporation into government; it offered the leadership immunity from prosecution and appointed the newly freed Foday Sankoh as Vice-President and as head of the Commission for Strategic Mineral Resources, National Reconstruction and Development.[16]

While Lomé offered economic and political benefits, such as official control over lucrative resources in Kono, along with a degree of legitimacy, commanders continued to pursue personal gain through conflict and at the very least, in forestalling disarmament and demobilisation. Aware that the RUF would not fare well in national elections, Sankoh sought to maintain his political status as leader of the rebel force. He therefore viewed DDR as a direct threat to his position and bargaining power, a logic shared by commanders across the RUF who had also profited from the looting and illicit trade conducted by their combatants. The RUF cadres themselves widely supported a move towards DDR, reflecting a growing war-weariness and general disillusionment with rebel life.[17] However, the DDR programme lacked provisions to counteract the obstructionism of RUF leaders. Commanders again restricted combatants' knowledge of the agreement's provisions and, in some instances, forcibly re-mobilised those attending demobilisation camps.[18]

Full implementation of the Lomé settlement only occurred once the prospect of a RUF defeat was raised, again reflecting a military rather than political logic at the heart of the group's leadership. Following the abduction of UK soldiers in August 2000 by a faction of the AFRC, known as the West Side Boys, British troops struck a decisive blow against the group, effectively destroying it.[19] The involvement of the UK signalled to many RUF fighters that the conflict could not be won, or perhaps more accurately, that it could not be maintained, and this proved an important factor in their decision to enter the subsequent DDR programme.[20] Of even greater significance in this regard was the role of Guinea, which responded to RUF incursions with a devastating counter-offensive.[21] These developments led to the Abuja Ceasefire Agreement being signed in November 2000 and to the deployment of a 17,500-strong UN force to Sierra Leone in 2001.

With most RUF leaders arrested or routed by the Guinean counter-offensive, their hold over rank-and-file combatants had largely been broken. In the presence of a bolstered UN force, RUF combatants demobilised in large numbers.[22] In contrast to the Lomé negotiations, the RUF's military situation meant that it was in no position to insist on the disarmament of the SLA as a precondition for its own demobilisation, nor could it demand the expulsion of foreign troops operating outside of the UN mandate. Instead, the RUF recommitted to the Lomé agreement in full, enabling President Kabbah to declare the war officially over in 2002. That same year elections were held, with the RUF, as a newly transformed political body, fielding its own candidates.

The difficulties encountered in reaching peace in Sierra Leone demonstrated three requirements for political reintegration relevant to this context. First, any lasting settlement would have to involve more than the satisfaction of a particular grievance against the state. Offering the RUF an opportunity to compete for the vote of an electorate against which it had committed a decade of atrocities was also insufficient for winning its commitment to the peace process. Instead, the incentives that truly held value for combatants were the promise of security (or, conversely, the threat of physical defeat), the offer of amnesty, the provision of employment and basic social and economic welfare – ends previously achieved through violence.[23] Second, the political integration of the RUF also required the dismantling of the rebel leadership, whereby rank-and-file combatants could be prised apart from the negative influence of RUF commanders. By negotiating exclusively with RUF leaders, arranging for the creation of a RUF party and attempting to incorporate the RUF in a power-sharing agreement, previous peace agreements had actually threatened to empower and legitimise the very individuals perpetuating the political disengagement of combatants. In the end, effective military power was required to eliminate the RUF's spoiler leadership, allowing for a genuine attempt at political reintegration and peace. Third, the successful implementation of DDR hinged on the provision of a secure environment once negotiations were initiated. In Sierra Leone's case, the security required for DDR was heavily dependent on external actors, a factor that, as will become clear, has complicated the task of political reintegration in the long term.

The failure of the RUF party

In line with the experiences of other peace processes, it was perhaps inevitable that some attempt would be made to transform the RUF into a viable political entity, as opposed to dismantling the organisation entirely. This move was intended to aid political integration in a number of ways. First, it would act as a visible sign of political acceptance and incorporation, whereby demobilising fighters were assured of their stake in a new and more inclusive political landscape. Second, it could help to incorporate remnants of the RUF leadership, which might prove disruptive to continued efforts at reconciliation and reintegration if not brought into the political fold. Third, and perhaps of greatest importance to long-term peace, the creation of a political RUF party would provide ex-combatants with a conduit for political expression and an alternative to violence as a means of realising personal, social and economic goals. The Lomé agreement therefore included provisions to help the RUF transform into a political party, which were implemented by the government in the run-up to the 2002 elections. In Freetown, Bo and Makeni, offices were purchased to enable the official registration of the Revolutionary United Front Party (RUFP), with Nigeria contributing equipment and training to RUFP representatives in party management.

Despite successfully fielding 203 parliamentary candidates for the 2002 election, the RUFP performed poorly, a consistent outcome throughout the party's short existence. In 2002, it failed to win a single seat, securing just 2.2 per cent of the parliamentary vote and 1.7 per cent for its presidential candidate. In contrast, the ruling SLPP of Ahmad Tejan Kabbah secured a landslide victory with 69.9 per cent of the vote. In July 2007, the RUFP as a political project ended when it opted to merge with the APC, the very target of its original violent invasion. The failure of the RUF to garner the votes of former combatants and to reinvent itself as a political party is the key to understanding more generally why previous attempts to integrate its leadership politically had failed, directly reflecting the nature of the RUF as an organisation, the factors that had fuelled conflict and the needs and priorities of its combatants.

On a purely practical level, the RUF was not equipped to operate as a political entity in the democratic system. Its members, whether at leadership level or at grass roots, had little knowledge of political campaigning or management, with experiences shaped instead by a decade of conflict beyond the bounds of civil society. More than 30 per cent of combatants lacked formal education, with illiteracy in RUF ranks particularly high and political awareness largely determined by the commanders' selective control of information.[24] Indeed, the RUF was defined as a movement by the political disengagement of its young membership. A 2003 survey found that more than half of ex-RUF combatants held no political affiliation prior to the conflict and continued to hold no affiliation post-conflict.[25] With much of the RUF leadership under arrest, its remnants were hardly in a position to appeal to the Sierra Leonean electorate or manage the party effectively.[26] This problem became particularly clear in 2003 when five of the RUF's most senior leaders, Foday Sankoh, Sam Bockarie, Issa Sesay, Morris Kallon and Augustine Gbao, were indicted by the Special Court on 17 counts of war crimes and crimes against humanity. The RUF had neither the personnel to staff a competent party and election campaign, nor a politically sensitised constituency of its own members from which to launch.

The attempt to transform the RUF into a political party not only misunderstood the technical capacity of the movement but, crucially, also its nature and the motives of its young membership. Throughout the conflict, RUF combatants had primarily been concerned with basic needs, personal security and economic advantage as opposed to political ideology.[27] In the context of peace, therefore, the RUF became redundant to many ex-combatants. Yet not only did ex-combatants often lack political motive; many had originally exercised little choice in joining the RUF. Eighty-seven per cent of RUF respondents to a 2003 survey confirmed that they had been abducted into the faction, with only 9 per cent stating that they joined in sympathy with the movement's political aims.[28] With such a high rate of forced conscription, many ex-RUF combatants also viewed themselves as victims of the conflict, and as such did not see the RUF as the natural champion of their concerns in the post-conflict environment.[29]

The RUFP was also unfeasible due to the immediate post-conflict attitude of demobilised combatants. For many former RUF combatants, the end of the conflict marked a new start, with their hopes for an improvement in living conditions strengthened by a significant international presence and the extensive flow of aid. Looking to integrate into Sierra Leone's communities, former RUF fighters had to navigate a delicate reconciliation process, living side-by-side with victims of atrocities and within a population where the rebel group was deeply unpopular. In such circumstances, there was an understandable inclination for ex-combatants to distance themselves from the RUF, with some bypassing the official DDR process altogether to avoid the social stigma of being labelled a former rebel.[30] Ex-combatants wishing to play down their former RUF credentials were particularly unlikely to support the hard-line RUF leaders that were gaining influence in the absence of Foday Sankoh, himself indicted for war crimes.[31] These leaders were not perceived by combatants as representative of their political concerns, but as corrupt, as gaining considerable economic benefits (which contrasted starkly with the situation of the rank-and-file) and – particularly in the run-up to elections in 2002 – as obstructing the demobilisation and reintegration programme.[32] Internal leadership disputes and bitter infighting further served to undermine support, ensuring that ex-RUF fighters sought other avenues for political expression, ultimately condemning the RUFP to electoral failure.

It is arguable that the creation of the RUFP was undertaken for political expediency in the full knowledge that its prospects were severely limited.[33] Some commentators have argued that in contrast to UNAMSIL, the Government of Sierra Leone actively sought to undermine the establishment of the RUFP, obstructing the process in favour of pursuing a total military eradication of the RUF.[34] Nevertheless, even if active governmental support had been clearly provided, the unsuitability of the RUF for political transformation remained a major obstacle to its achievement. The damaging effect of RUF leaders on the political integration of the rank-and-file further showed that the dismantling of the group, rather than its political consolidation, would be of greater benefit to the peacebuilding project.

Political reintegration: beyond the RUF party

The RUF's inability to reinvent itself as a political party did not mean that the political reintegration of its combatants had failed – but rather the opposite. In the immediate post-conflict environment, ex-combatants found that they were able to pursue their concerns through established political parties and the wider institutions of Sierra Leonean civil society without recourse to their RUF identity. That the RUF failed to secure a single seat in the 2002 elections was not only testament to the RUF's unsuitability to political transformation but also a sign that civil society had, to some extent, successfully undertaken the role of voicing and addressing the concerns of ex-combatants. Nevertheless, despite this apparent progress, ex-combatants' interaction with civil society groups and political bodies has not been accompanied by an associated investment of confidence in domestic institutions, but rather stemmed from a trust in the capacity of *outside* actors. The disconnect between the former RUF combatants and the Sierra Leonean government is disconcerting, particularly when one considers that their sense of disengagement has in the past facilitated the outbreak of hostilities.

An institution that played a key role in recognising the link between political, social and economic disengagement and RUF violence was the TRC.[35] Crucially, its 2004 statement on the causes of the conflict acknowledged the part played by previous administrations in rendering Sierra Leone vulnerable to conflict through political abuses and mismanagement.[36] This recognition in itself assisted the RUF's political reintegration, not only by facilitating reconciliation and understanding between victims and perpetrators, but also by signalling that addressing RUF political grievances was deemed integral to the formation of a more equitable Sierra Leonean political landscape. The TRC's final statement was also highly significant to the political reintegration of the RUF and its attempt to move beyond a simple recognition of these legitimate issues and towards the formation of government policy designed to incorporate them in the national project of peacebuilding.

Of pressing concern to the TRC was tackling the 'youth question', which it viewed as central to the disengagement of RUF combatants and as representing a 'national emergency that demands national mobilisation'.[37] The TRC recognised the devastation caused during the conflict by the 'lethal cocktail of youth marginalisation and political manipulation', and noted with alarm that youth continued to 'languish in a twilight zone of unemployment and despair'.[38] The commission's final report, therefore, recommended the legal incorporation of youth in party political representation and the establishment of a National Youth Commission to 'address the youth question as a fundamental priority in post-war reconstruction'.[39] In June 2003, the Sierra Leonean government launched the National Youth Policy, which promised to provide youth 'empowerment in a post-conflict context' and affirmed a cross-governmental commitment to 'mainstreaming youth related activities in the overall process of national reconstruction'.[40] Complemented by the establishment of the Ministry of Youth and Sports, the government of Sierra Leone made every indication to young ex-combatants that, following demobilisation, they would receive special political attention in their own right, allowing them a stake in society denied by pre-conflict administrations.

However, tangible results of this commitment have been somewhat limited.[41] Neither the establishment of a National Youth Commission nor the party political reforms recommended by the TRC have been implemented. To some extent, the Ministry of Youth and Sports took on the role intended for the youth commission, yet it was precisely because the TRC concluded that 'the Ministry of Youth does not have the means to address the youth question' that it had advocated the creation of the commission in the first place.[42] Following its success in the 2007 elections, the APC government chose to merge the Ministry of Youth and Sports with the Ministry of Education, seemingly further reducing the capacity of a ministry already under-funded and acutely lacking in political impetus. While there was some expediency in merging ministries that clearly overlap in their relevance to youth, the APC move was perhaps more reflective of a financial logic, which strikes at the heart of the weakness of government-sponsored political integration efforts; namely a scarcity of budgetary resources and a weak political infrastructure.

Aside from economic limitations, the government's failure to implement the TRC's recommendations on youth policy related also to the dominance of NGOs and civil society groups in the political sensitisation and empowerment of ex-combatants. The state had effectively outsourced this crucial area of development to NGOs, donors and UN bodies who have funded and managed a vast number of projects aimed at facilitating dialogue between young ex-combatants and Sierra Leonean communities, providing public platforms for consultation and discussion over key issues. Through workshops and surveys, organisations such as the Post-conflict Reintegration Initiative for Development and Empowerment (PRIDE) have played a crucial role in both relaying former RUF fighters' concerns and in informing them of the details of policy and related institutions. In the run-up to elections, such NGOs and donor-funded bodies were instrumental in sensitising ex-combatants to the electoral process, encouraging high voter registration and active participation in the political system. Sierra Leonean-led groups such as PRIDE, which maintain a special focus on the reintegration of former combatants, have further aided political incorporation not only through their work but also through their direct employment of ex-RUF fighters. These initiatives have assisted the political reintegration project by offering former combatants a voice in the environs of peace that they were unable to locate in conflict, providing a real incentive to eschew the way of the gun for peaceful political interaction. The interaction of non-governmental groups with large numbers of young ex-RUF combatants has consequently helped consolidate the official national policy of bringing youth issues to the centre of government.

However, the NGO-led initiatives constitute a double-edged sword. First, it is questionable whether NGOs and civil society groups, formed around immediate conflict-related issues, can provide a long-term forum for political involvement and, indeed, the employment of ex-combatants. As the international presence in Sierra Leone scales down, the capacity of the state, in particular of government bodies such as the Ministry of Youth, Sports and Education, to assume this responsibility and continue this level of political engagement with ex-combatants at a local level will be severely tested. Second, and more ominously, the involvement of ex-RUF fighters in NGO projects and civil-society groups may not ultimately translate into genuine political integration on a national level, particularly as these projects rely so heavily on external actors and donor funds.

The 2003 survey of ex-combatants points towards the high price paid for NGO and UN involvement:

> Ex-combatants have faith more in outsiders than in their own government. The experience with UNAMSIL has been a positive one, but ex-combatants see appeals to the international community and to NGOs as the best ways to hold their government accountable and to achieve positive results.[43]

If former RUF fighters are relying on the presence and work of international organisations to guarantee their political stake in society, their political activity may not have truly assisted their integration into Sierra Leone's political system. This problem is exacerbated by continued widespread cynicism of ex-combatants towards home-grown politicians and institutions, which has strengthened the prevailing belief that Sierra Leone's future depends entirely on international intervention and regulation.[44] In a country severely lacking state capacity even prior to the conflict, the strong presence and footprint of NGOs and international organisations is perhaps to be expected, but nevertheless, the long-term reintegration of former RUF fighters requires that they invest trust in the inherent capacity of Sierra Leone's own political institutions to meet and manage their expectations. The high turnout of former RUF fighters in the 2002 and 2007 elections would seem to indicate some success in this respect. However, the 2003 survey of ex-combatants paints a gloomier picture:

> Ex-combatants believe quite seriously that the most effective means of changing government policy is through pressure from the outside. Internal accountability mechanisms are not seen as credible, when compared to the potential influence of NGOs and the international community more broadly.[45]

Although ex-combatants may have voted in 2002 in order to bring about change and register their commitment to peace, much of their confidence in the ballot was firmly rooted in faith in external actors to act as a guarantor. Progress in building confidence in domestic institutions since the 2002 elections has been limited. A 2007 survey by the BBC World Service Trust and Search for Common Ground, taken in the run-up to the elections, found that most respondents maintained little or no trust in national politicians and felt that political protest against unjust legislation would do little to change government policy.[46] This failure to establish trust among ex-RUF combatants in Sierra Leone's own political institutions is linked to insufficient progress on two key fronts; the fight against corruption, and tackling Sierra Leone's economic underdevelopment.

Building confidence: corruption

Despite voting in large numbers in successive national elections, ex-combatants still feel that corruption and patrimonial politics continue largely unabated.[47] This perception can be traced to post-conflict instances of corruption and abuse in public political institutions. In the run-up to the 2002 elections, the National Electoral Commission (NEC) was dogged by a scandal in which three of its five commissioners were indicted by the Anti-Corruption Commission (ACC), the body established to instil faith in public institutions by rooting out such malpractice.[48] In 2004, the NEC Chairman resigned from office, claiming that the ruling SLPP party had sought to tamper with the results of local elections (NEC also expressed concern over voting irregularities the following year). In 2004, the ICG lamented the lack of commitment by the government in countering corruption, citing the case of Momoh Pujeh, a former Minster of Transport whose conviction for unlawful possession of precious materials was overturned on particularly tenuous grounds.[49] Indeed, in some respects, the government appeared actively to hinder the work of the ACC; delays in processing cases by the Attorney-General's Office consistently slowed prosecutions, and President Kabbah openly condemned the ACC for focussing on the prosecution of government ministers. In 2007, the ICG described the ACC as 'virtually moribund', accusing it of 'sending the wrong message about endemic corruption'.[50]

Alongside these political abuses, ex-combatants were also dismayed by the reappearance, post-conflict, of local and national elites that had dominated Sierra Leone prior to the outbreak of hostilities and represented the inequitable pre-conflict system of patrimony.[51] A pertinent example was the restoration of traditional Paramount Chiefs to positions of authority in the local system of government. Enacted immediately after the war and heavily funded by the UK's Department for International Development (DfID), the move was regarded as an effective means to secure the regional control and stability necessary for post-conflict reconstruction. This 'attempt to restore the past', as President Kabbah described it, was severely criticised for reinforcing the notion of 'same car, different driver'.[52] In a subsequent DfID-sponsored evaluation, it became clear that rural youths in particular resented the restoration of Paramount Chiefs, whom they deemed responsible for imposing unfair and exclusionary private jurisprudence, precisely the grievance that had prompted so many youths to join the RUF.[53] Consequently, although the move initially appeared to hold value for political integration by establishing local political authority, it actually risked undermining this very same objective by restoring socio-political divisions.

Notwithstanding the criticisms aimed at government institutions and public bodies, it is arguable that progress has undeniably been made, particularly given the challenges faced and the long history of endemic corruption in Sierra Leone. An example is the NEC, which in spite of many obstacles has been relatively successful in battling electoral fraud, particularly in its handling of the 2007 elections – for which it took sole responsibility. Nevertheless, such progress may be insufficient to restore ex-combatants' faith in Sierra Leone's political system. In a 2005 report on the battle against corruption, the Campaign for Good Governance (CGG) concluded that 'most Sierra Leoneans are convinced that corruption is on the increase', confirming that many remained 'pessimistic about the Commission's mission to eradicate corruption in the country'.[54] Following the 2007 elections, an internal government investigation found that corruption had indeed been rife under the previous regime of Ahmad Tejan Kabbah. Such corruption, both in its day-to-day effect on Sierra Leoneans and in its impact on perceptions, has deepened ex-combatants' cynicism towards the political establishment, entrenching their political disengagement.

Building confidence: the economy

Sierra Leone's long-term ability to incorporate ex-combatants politically remains intimately linked to its ability to incorporate them economically, a factor that has proven far more critical to an ex-RUF fighter's renunciation of violence than any political incentive. Failure in this area has led to a failure in tackling corruption and meeting the expectations of demobilised RUF combatants.[55] In terms of the number of combatants processed and the apparent consolidation of peace following its eventual completion, the DDR programme is widely regarded as a success.[56] Nevertheless, the reintegration project in Sierra Leone has encountered severe difficulties, not only in securing funding and long-term commitments, but also with the overall desperate condition of Sierra Leone's economy into which demobilised combatants are expected to return. In 2006, the UN estimated that 70 per cent of Sierra Leone's population continued to live below the poverty line, with the concentration of poverty the highest in rural areas away from Freetown, the very areas in which the RUF had previously prospered from economic and political discontent.[57] In 2007, the UN warned of Sierra Leone's 'severe financial crisis', with the ICG also noting that youth unemployment had reached an all time high of 80 per cent.[58] Significantly, according to a report of the Peace Building Commission, the effects of poverty have been felt most acutely by Sierra Leone's youth, a demographic that includes many former RUF combatants:

> Two thirds of the youth population is unemployed and largely marginalized from the political system, and lacks adequate education and training. Significantly, many of the dire conditions that gave rise to the conflict in 1991 remain in 2006, with many youths unemployed, marginalized and lacking hope for the future.[59]

This bleak assessment echoes that of the TRC in its 2004 final report, where it found that ex-combatants' political integration was being undermined by the continued desperation of their social and economic destitution, stating: 'many ex-combatants testified that the conditions that caused them to join the conflict persist in the country, and if given the opportunity, they would fight again'.[60] Accordingly, following DDR, many former RUF combatants have returned to the fringes of Sierra Leone, both geographically and socio-politically, rejoining the growing number of youths seeking profit from alluvial diamond mining in the border regions or taking their place among the swollen ranks of the towns' unemployed.[61] This represents a worrying echo of the pre-war situation, where large groups of unemployed youth and diamond miners were alienated from the Freetown political machinery and came to view conflict as a means of empowerment.

Once again, economic conditions are causing the political marginalisation of former RUF fighters.

Sierra Leone's economic situation also risks engendering a potentially destabilising sense of disillusionment and frustration. Clearly, incentives to eschew violence for peaceful political discourse are quickly diminishing for those former combatants who have failed to realise the economic and social advancement expected from DDR. The majority of demobilised RUF combatants who have remained in Sierra Leone had expectations of extensive economic development, which may very well have outstretched the realistic capacity of the country, at least in the short term. In a 2001 report entitled 'Managing Uncertainty', the ICG warned that failure of the DDR programme and internationally sponsored reintegration schemes to meet the high hopes of former combatants would almost certainly result in their return to violence as a means of securing basic welfare.[62] In some instances, ex-RUF combatants have indeed returned to conflict rather than seek to navigate the complex psychological and economic difficulties encountered in peacetime. For many whose driving motivation has been to seek economic security, integration into regional conflicts such as that in neighbouring Liberia has made far more sense than seeking political reintegration into an impoverished Sierra Leone.[63] The apparently profitable involvement of ex-combatants in regional conflicts – or at least reports suggesting such activity – risks encouraging former RUF fighters still in Sierra Leone to revaluate the benefits of peace.

The 2007 elections

The 2007 presidential and parliamentary elections, widely seen as a crucial test of Sierra Leone's capacity to manage political and security matters independently from external actors, served as a marker-point for the progress of political reintegration and confidence-building efforts. In the absence of a large UN peacekeeping force or international military presence, the task of maintaining a stable security environment for free and fair elections was undertaken by the Sierra Leonean police. Voting arrangements, including the sensitisation of the electorate, monitoring and counting the ballot, fell under the sole responsibility of the NEC. In further contrast to the 2002 election, the incumbent president, Ahmad Tejan Kabbah, was constitutionally required to step down and give way to a newly elected president. In this respect, whatever the result, the conclusion of the election would involve a peaceful relinquishing of power by one leader and regime to another, a major test for any society recently emerged from civil conflict.

The 2007 election saw high voter registration and a subsequent turnout of 75.8 per cent of Sierra Leone's total population. The largely successful political mobilisation of former RUF fighters reflected in part an appreciation by the NEC and civil-society groups of the specific circumstances affecting youth and ex-combatants. Along with workshops and surveys of ex-RUF members, regular radio broadcasts proved particularly effective in mobilising many whose illiteracy, educational background or isolated location rendered election literature or complex political discourse unsuitable or impractical.[64] The promotion of youth issues to the heart of political campaigning may also have played a part in the high turnout, with the major parties presenting themselves as actively seeking to resolve the problems causing discontent among Sierra Leone's youth and ex-combatants. Presidential candidates focused heavily on youth employment, the provision of education and the eradication of corruption, promising at youth rallies that such issues would be the central preoccupation of their presidency.[65] The increasingly youth-centred focus of the parties owed much to the fact that of the 2.6 million Sierra Leoneans registered to vote, almost 40 per cent were under the age of 27.[66]

Despite the political rhetoric aimed at capturing the youth vote, a 2007 survey conducted prior to the polls found that many Sierra Leoneans, particularly the youth, saw the political parties as unrepresentative and as offering little real policy choice.[67] In this sense, the votes of former RUF fighters related more to a desire for change than an investment in one particular party or political strategy deemed to correspond to their interests.[68] Nevertheless, in a country where such dissatisfaction had previously been expressed through violence and a rejection of political authority, the use of the vote by ex-combatants in this manner was deemed a positive sign for the political reintegration project. Optimism also stemmed from the country's ability to survive a number of potentially destabilising factors in the run-up to, and during, the elections, such as the delay of voting by two weeks, the close nature of the contest and, crucially, spates of violence in the lead-up to the second round of voting, which at one point threatened to derail voting altogether.

Yet while encouraging in many respects, the high voter turnout and completion of the elections were not tantamount to successful political reintegration. In fact, the 2007 elections highlighted the maturation of a number of developments, which served to undermine the political reintegration of former RUF combatants. Perhaps most critically, they showed that even where ex-combatants had been politically *incorporated*, some forms of political participation actually proved divisive or detrimental to their long-term political *reintegration*.

The violence in the second round of voting provides a potent illustration of this point and of the need to examine the specific form of political participation achieved among former rebels. Following the failure of any candidate to secure the required 55 per cent of the vote, tensions between supporters of all sides greatly intensified and street rallies often turned violent. Police were forced to use tear gas to disperse battling APC and SLPP supporters across the country, moving President Kabbah to threaten to impose a state of emergency to curb what he described as 'the current state of intimidation, molestation and violent acts'.[69] Tensions on the streets were matched by tensions between the contending candidates and, amid increasing claims and counter-claims of political intimidation, President Kabbah was unable to gain the attendance of both the SLPP's Solomon Berewa and the APC's Ernest Koroma at a public rally to denounce the civil unrest.[70] Despite this setback, the second round of voting was successfully completed and the APC emerged victorious. Having failed to win a court injunction barring the NEC from announcing the results on 17 September, the defeated

SLPP duly conducted a peaceful transition of power. However, looters subsequently ransacked the headquarters of the SLPP and in Mile 91, a base for a large number of ex-RUF combatants, many violent attacks against journalists and SLPP supporters were reported.[71]

Some observers interpreted the tensions of the second round of voting as a positive sign for the health of democratic development in Sierra Leone.[72] It is certainly clear that the closeness of the vote forced the major parties to court the electorate, increasing the likelihood that policies would incorporate ex-combatants' concerns and that ex-combatants would themselves see their votes as having a direct effect on the political landscape. The split of Charles Margai from the SLPP to form the PMDC, which arguably cost Solomon Berewa the election, was widely deemed a positive development for democracy in Sierra Leone in that it limited the chances of a landslide victory for the incumbent regime, and thereby also increased the new government's accountability and reliance on public support.[73] Nevertheless, it is clear that the violence was also far from positive, particularly if the aim of politically integrating former RUF combatants was to consolidate their move away from violence and towards peaceful political intercourse as a means to bring change. An immediate concern was the direct involvement of ex-RUF combatants in the violence, with all sides accused of using former rebel and CDF soldiers to intimidate opposition supporters and candidates. In an interview with Integrated Regional Information Networks (IRIN), the director of PRIDE, Ibrahim Bangura, confirmed the recruitment of ex-RUF combatants by political parties as bodyguards and security, noting that the head of the APC's security operations was ex-RUF fighter Idrissa Kamara.[74] The cynical employment of former rebel combatants in acts of political intimidation and crime in 2007 was a worrying mirror of the abusive practices that had characterised the one-party regime of Siaka Stevens in the 1970s and 1980s. Through their desperate economic situation and experiences of violence, ex-combatants remain particularly vulnerable to such recruitment, a fact underlined by their involvement in regional conflicts. By incorporating former RUF fighters in acts of political intimidation, leaders and political parties in Sierra Leone actually served to reconnect ex-combatants with violence instead of consolidating their rejection of it. Rather than demonstrate politics as an effective substitute for violence, violence was treated as an effective means to influence politics.

The election violence also reflected the wider development of a negative political culture that undermined confidence in the capacity of post-conflict Sierra Leone to transcend the abuses that had fostered conflict in the first place. In the run-up to elections, the UN Peacebuilding Commission observed that 'the discourse from political parties is showing signs of growing intolerance and parties are still striving to become credible vehicles for political expression'.[75] The dangerous promotion of violence as a political method went hand-in-hand with party politics adopting a more confrontational tone, culminating in President Kabbah's injunction that contending parties 'desist from making provocative and inflammatory statements against each other' during the election.[76] The system into which the RUF was being incorporated was increasingly based on zero-sum political competition, with the danger that ex-combatants invest in particular parties over and above the system as a whole.[77] In the long term, the development of such a political atmosphere risks seeing ex-combatants reject the authority of those leaders or parties for whom they did not vote and view any political failure of their party or leader as a defeat of their own aspirations and political stake. Attention to this issue is therefore paramount for political stability. It was precisely such a sense of political marginalisation among many of Sierra Leone's youth that proved instrumental in the onset of civil conflict in 1991.

The resurrection of bitter political rivalries also risked aligning ex-combatants along ethnic and regional divisions, which in the past have informed political allegiances. The PMDC's introduction to the political scene was a potentially positive development in this respect, serving to break regional voting patterns by leading southern Mende voters to back the APC, traditionally reliant on Temne support in the north. However, such divisions were still deemed a pressing concern by the UN Secretary-General in his December 2007 report to the Security Council, in which he spoke of the 'increasing dominance of ethnicity and regionalism in the politics of Sierra Leone', which, he added 'could have a negative impact on peace-consolidation efforts in the country'.[78] The most obvious negative impact on peace-consolidation was precisely the risk that ex-RUF combatants and former CDF fighters become embroiled in such rivalries, undermining their political reintegration and fostering political grievances.[79] The underlying lesson for integration efforts was that not only is the form of political participation achieved by ex-combatants an important consideration, but so, too, is the nature of the political environment into which they are being integrated. The increase in party rivalries and local divisions, leading to violence, illustrated that the environment into which the RUF was being integrated was not conducive to peace or to a view of political discourse as inherently superior to violence as a means of achieving change.

The violence and mutual distrust between parties in the 2007 election further undermined the political reintegration of ex-RUF combatants by failing to build confidence in Sierra Leone's internal political integrity. The 2002 elections had witnessed similarly violent clashes between the short-lived RUFP and SLPP supporters in Freetown, which were eventually quashed by the intervention of international peacekeepers.[80] This did little to reverse perceptions that Sierra Leone was reliant on external actors for its security and political stability. Similarly, despite the ability of the Sierra Leonean police to handle the more widespread outbreaks in 2007, the parties' confrontational and internecine behaviour risked reinforcing the notion that, left to its own devices, Sierra Leone's political system would inevitably default to its previous abusive configuration.[81] Although the NEC performed with relative transparency and competence in 2007, this notion of 'politics as usual', or 'same car, different driver' was not unjustified, with allegations of wider political malpractice remaining well founded.[82] In following the elections, Mats Utas observed the continuing play of patron–client politics in Sierra Leone:

> Hordes of people line up outside the SLPP party leader's mansion in order
> to receive their mandatory money in exchange for promising their votes....
> Although most visible at the SLPP party leader's mansion (simply because
> most money has been given away here) it is clear that all political parties
> and party functionaries on all levels have handed out money in exchange for
> support.[83]

The practice of 'votes for sale' – and its very visibility – represented a further
threat to the building of faith among former RUF fighters in the integrity of the
post-conflict democratic system and its capacity to transcend the exclusionary
politics that previously fostered conflict.[84] The persistence of patrimonial politics
accompanied evidence of a failure to root out endemic corruption in Sierra
Leone's political institutions. Following his inauguration in November, President
Koroma commissioned an audit of government ministries, uncovering the continued and relatively unchecked proliferation of corruption and mismanagement
under the SLPP regime.[85]

The 2007 elections have been viewed by many as a positive development
for the political reintegration of the RUF through their demonstration of ex-
combatants' willingness to channel dissatisfaction politically, through the vote.
However, this underplays the short-term nature of that commitment and the persistence of such dissatisfaction, which poses a continued threat to the longer-
term commitment of former RUF fighters. This long-term political reintegration,
and the ability of Koroma's government to build confidence in Sierra Leone's
political institutions, remained dependent upon Sierra Leone's economic development. The BBC's correspondent in Freetown, Mark Doyle, pointedly observed
that for the presidential inauguration ceremony, boycotted by the SLPP executive, the government was forced to rely on borrowed limousines and UN
helicopters to transport its dignitaries.[86] At the focal point of one of Sierra
Leone's most encouraging signs for the consolidation of peace, the economic
strictures that threaten to undermine it were as apparent as ever.

Conclusion

The case of Sierra Leone demonstrates that the nature of a non-state armed group
and the identity and motivations of its members directly affect the form and relative ease of its political reintegration. In the case of the RUF, the overall absence
of a coherent political project, a limited technical political capacity and the
movement's deep unpopularity with the civilian population rendered it wholly
unsuited for transformation into a political party. The importance of economic
drivers for conflict and the large-scale perpetration of atrocities also undermined
political incentives for peace, particularly when compared to appeals based on
the provision of amnesty, basic welfare and security. In this respect, the political
integration project in Sierra Leone also shows that offers of political power to a
non-state armed actor must be informed by an understanding of the motivations
of both its leadership and rank-and-file combatants, which are likely to differ

widely. In Sierra Leone, the relationship of RUF leaders to their combatants was such that it served to undermine rather than facilitate their political reintegration. Hence, another implication for political integration projects, which may run counter to conventional approaches, is that the dismantling rather than the political formalisation of a non-state armed actor may in fact best serve its political integration. Finally, the Sierra Leone experience shows that decisive military force applied against spoiler elements in a leadership can serve to facilitate combatants' involvement in DDR and wider political re-engagement.

The RUF's unsuitability for conventional political incorporation demonstrated that the success of political integration could not be judged solely by a group's ability to form a party or share power. Instead, a more holistic account is necessary to appreciate the extent to which ex-combatants locate opportunities for expression and resolution of political concerns through a wide variety of formal and informal means, be it through participation in civil society groups, public discussion or interaction with established political institutions. Likewise, the Sierra Leone case shows that the success of this wider process cannot be judged by the narrow terms of electoral participation or the absence of renewed conflict, but must include less tangible indicators such as the faith of ex-combatants in political interaction to deliver results, and the foundations upon which such confidence is based. Directly related to this approach, the experience of the RUF demonstrates that not only does the nature and identity of non-state armed actors impact on the form and potential success of political reintegration, but so, too, does the nature and configuration of the political system into which they are being incorporated. In the case of Sierra Leone, the involvement of international actors in politically incorporating ex-combatants was often positive and needed, but did it result in the RUF investing in external actors and assistance as opposed to Sierra Leone's own institutions? Similarly, the nature of Sierra Leone's political system, as highlighted by the 2007 elections, in many instances served to erode ex-combatants' confidence in political intercourse, or reinforce violence as an acceptable method to achieve change. Finally, underpinning all of these factors, Sierra Leone's continuing experience demonstrates that for a group such as the RUF, political and economic reintegration are two sides of the same coin.[87] For combatants whose primary agenda in conflict was to secure basic economic and welfare security, their long-term commitment to peaceful political interaction over and above violence is predicated upon successful economic incorporation. Given Sierra Leone's severe underdevelopment, and that of many societies emerging from violent conflict, progress in this respect represents one of the greatest challenges for the political reintegration of non-state armed groups.

Notes

1 President Charles Taylor of Liberia resented Sierra Leone's support for ECOMOG (Economic Community of West Africa States Monitoring Group) troops operating against his forces in Liberia. The RUF were actively sponsored by Taylor, who in seeking to destabilise the country, also gained access to its extensive diamond deposits.
2 The reintegration process was officially completed in January 2004.

3 An analyst's comment, cited in Keen, *Conflict and Collusion*, 267.
4 In contrast to this article, Richards and Vincent, 'Sierra Leone: Marginalization of the RUF', 88, argue that the RUF did develop 'a quite coherent political agenda'. However, although political grievances certainly existed, and apparent political instruction of some recruits occurred, the multitude of agendas at all levels, which superseded political aims, resulted in a clear lack of political and organisational coherence.
5 The track record of brutality and the absence of coherent political ideology gave rise to a number of misleading characterisations of the conflict as 'anarchic' or as driven entirely by greed. See, for example, Kaplan, 'The Coming Anarchy'. See Richards, *Fighting for the Rainforest*, for a convincing response to such analysis.
6 Richards, *Fighting for the Rainforest*, 5, puts the initial number of RUF combatants at 100, but Keen, *Conflict and Collusion*, 1, taking into account conflicting estimations, places the number between 100 and 300. This group included a significant proportion of non-Sierra Leoneans, most notably a contingent of Charles Taylor's Liberian combatants.
7 Foday Sankoh regularly invoked pan-Africanist revolutionary ideology and had originally met Charles Taylor in a Libyan training camp. The RUF's 1995 pamphlet, *Footpaths to Democracy*, though often vague, offered some semblance of RUF doctrine. However, though it can be argued that the movement began with overtly political aspirations, the evolution of the RUF and the wider conflict involved a clear subordination of such convictions to a multitude of other disparate driving forces.
8 Although alluvial diamonds are often portrayed as the main resource sought by RUF combatants, access to perceived benefits such as security, food, marriage or women were far more significant aims among the rank and file. See Richards, *Fighting for the Rainforest*, for an examination of the link between the system of patrimonialism and the marginalisation of youth.
9 For discussion of the political economy of war see Berdal and Malone, *Greed and Grievance*, and with particular focus on Sierra Leone, Keen, 'Incentives and Disincentives for Violence'.
10 Keen, *Conflict and Collusion* also highlights psychological functions of conflict, most notably its reversal of power-relationships and hierarchies, which enabled combatants to address complex sensitivities to humiliation and shame, often serving to intensify violence.
11 As pressure for elections had intensified, so too had violence against civilians. Hands or thumbs that could be used to mark the ballot paper were amputated and, in some instances, anti-election slogans were carved into the chests and backs of victims. The perpetrators of such anti-election intimidation included not only RUF fighters but also, apparently, significant numbers of the SLA; Keen, *Conflict and Collusion*, 154.
12 Humphreys and Weinstein, *What the Fighters Say*, 27–29.
13 Keen, *Conflict and Collusion*, 194.
14 Ibid., 194–195.
15 Fears of army–RUF collaboration were epitomised by the notion of the 'sobel' (soldier-rebel) and highlight that the RUF cannot adequately be described as a purely political venture, diametrically opposed to the state. AFRC leader, Major Johnny Paul Koroma, called on Sankoh to take the position of Deputy Chairman but Nigeria did not relinquish the RUF leader. Rather, Nigerian-led ECOMOG forces were deployed to reinstall the civilian government in Freetown.
16 Seven other ministerial posts were allotted to RUF leaders.
17 Keen, *Conflict and Collusion*, 254.
18 UNAMSIL was effectively barred by the RUF from whole regions of north and north-eastern Sierra Leone, where it became a target for attacks and looting. In May 2000, the RUF abducted up to 500 UNAMSIL peacekeepers. See United Nations, *Third Report of the Secretary-General on the United Nations Mission in Sierra Leone*, and

United Nations, *Fourth Report of the Secretary-General on the United Nations Mission in Sierra Leone*, for the UN's assessment at the time of RUF spoiler tactics and the recalcitrance of Sankoh in particular.

19 The abducted soldiers had operated under the original British mandate, restricted to securing Freetown and the international airport.

20 Keen, *Conflict and Collusion*, 272–273.

21 Targeting rebel positions in Sierra Leone and Liberia, Guinean forces overwhelmed the RUF with a combination of airpower and the backing of local militias. So complete was the military reversal that the RUF requested UNAMSIL to deploy in Kono, the region affected by fighting and to which the RUF had previously denied access. As local CDF militias, backed by Guinea, made major inroads into this area, UNAMSIL represented a protection force not only for the local population but also for the RUF.

22 Between May 2001 and January 2002, 19,267 RUF combatants were disarmed. See UN DDR Resource Center, www.unddr.org/countryprogrammes.php?c = 60. However, it is important to note that a significant portion of RUF combatants travelled to neighbouring Liberia to support the increasingly beleaguered Charles Taylor.

23 Humphreys and Weinstein, *What the Fighters Say*, 29.

24 Ibid., 19.

25 Ibid., 20.

26 Richards and Vincent, 'Sierra Leone: Marginalization of the RUF', 82, see the detention of 400 RUFP members in 2000 as severely weakening the party's political capacity. At the time of the 2002 elections, Sankoh was incarcerated. His deputy, Issa Sesay, also failed to meet the minimum age requirement to stand as presidential candidate, paving the way for RUF secretary, Pallo Bangura. However, Bangura faced opposition from many within the RUFP who pledged support solely to Sankoh. This had a debilitating effect on the leadership of the party, as it failed to gain support of Sankoh loyalists.

27 This was also one of the findings of a 2003 survey of RUF combatants. See Humphreys and Weinstein, *What the Fighters Say*, 3. The survey also notes (29) in relation to Lomé: 'Combatants did not consider the substantial political gains of the RUF to be important aspects of the accords.'

28 Ibid., 25.

29 PRIDE, *Ex-Combatant Views*, 15.

30 UNAMSIL, *The DDR Process in Sierra Leone*, 7.

31 See ICG, *Sierra Leone: Managing Uncertainty*, which notes a shift in the RUF in 2001 towards hardliners, away from the more moderate Issa Sesay. Although regarded as a more moderate figure, Sesay was also indicted for war crimes in 2003 and was resented by many in the RUF for the personal wealth he had accrued from the conflict – yet another war-association unlikely to endear the rebel movement to the public.

32 See ICG, *Sierra Leone After Elections: Politics As Usual*, 8.

33 In recognising that the RUF was ill suited for transformation into a political party, this article does not intend to suggest that the *move* to create the RUFP was in itself a mistake. Indeed, it may well have served to ease the transition to peace. Rather, the point here is that whereas in other post-conflict situations the transformation of non-state actors into political entities may constitute to some degree their political integration, this would not be the case for the RUF.

34 See Malan *et al.*, *Peacekeeping in Sierra Leone*, particularly chapter 9, 'Electoral Issues and the Transformation of the RUF'. Richards and Vincent, 'Sierra Leone: Marginalization of the RUF', argue that UN partiality towards the government was also detrimental to the RUF's political capacity.

35 The Special Court also had an important and immediate role to play in addressing the key issues of amnesty and justice, reassuring demobilising combatants that peace would not be an exercise in one-sided recrimination. However, both the Special Court and the TRC failed to sensitise ex-combatants to their work; former RUF remained

confused over the amnesty and concerned that testimonies given to the TRC, aimed at assisting reconciliation, might be passed to the Special Court to facilitate criminal proceedings. A 2002 investigation into this issue found that ex-RUF combatants were poorly informed as to the role and mandate of both the TRC and Special Court. See PRIDE, *Ex-Combatant Views*. The Special Court also at times risked jeopardising the political reintegration of the RUF through its impact on the rebel leadership, particularly when it indicted Issa Sesay, a moderate seen as instrumental in moving the RUF towards peace; see Keen, *Conflict and Collusion*, 273–274.

36 TRC, *Final Report*, Vol. 2, Ch.1.
37 Ibid., Vol. 2, Ch. 3, item 306. It defines youths as those aged between 18 and 35. However, in this article 'youth' also refers to the significant number of young teenagers and child-recruits of the RUF.
38 Ibid., Vol. 3 B, Ch. 5; Vol. 2, Ch. 3.
39 Ibid., Vol. 2, Ch. 3. The Commission recommended that parties be required to ensure that at least 10 per cent of all their candidates in public elections were youths.
40 Republic of Sierra Leone, *Sierra Leone National Youth Policy*.
41 For the limited reach of youth-targeted development policy see IMF and IDA, *Sierra Leone: Annual Progress Report*, and the 'Sierra Leone: Election campaign focuses on youth', Integrated Regional Information Networks (IRIN), 8 August 2007, www.irin-news.org/Report.aspx?ReportId = 73638.
42 The means, in this instance, being funds and an adequate civil service; TRC, *Final Report*, Vol. 2, Ch. 3, item 308. In 2008 the Ministry of Youth, Sports and Education confirmed its aim to establish a National Youth Commission in 2009 (Interview, Civil Servant, Freetown 11 November 2008), a recognition that the 'youth question' remains in dire need of real political commitment in its own right.
43 Humphreys and Weinstein, *What the Fighters Say*, 4.
44 See Clapham, 'Sierra Leone: The Political Economy of Internal Conflict', 10, for the historical roots of such attitudes.
45 Humphreys and Weinstein, *What the Fighters Say*, 44.
46 BBC World Service Trust and Search for Common Ground, *Sierra Leone Elections 2007*, 39–42.
47 See for instance Humphreys and Weinstein, *What the Fighters Say*, 42. The survey found that more than half of respondents believed that levels of corruption had not changed, and possibly gotten worse, since prior the conflict. Clearly, the problem of corruption is strongly linked with economic underdevelopment, a factor covered in the following section.
48 Despite the indictments, no prosecutions were made and the commissioners returned to supervise elections. CGG, *Report on the Government's Fight against Corruption*, 14, notes that of a total of 43 cases investigated by the ACC in 2002, only one conviction was made, suggesting such corruption may still have been relatively safeguarded.
49 ICG, *Liberia and Sierra Leone: Rebuilding Failed States*, 8.
50 ICG, *Sierra Leone: The Election Opportunity*, 9.
51 At both local and national level, this return reflected the scarcity of skilled and experienced leaders among Sierra Leone's particularly young population. The eight presidential candidates in the 2002 elections were mostly veteran politicians, with the notable exception of Johnny Paul Koroma, former leader of the AFRC military junta.
52 Thomson, *Sierra Leone: Reform or Relapse?*, 20–23; and ICG, *Sierra Leone: The Election Opportunity*, 11–12.
53 See Fanthorpe *et al.*, *Chiefdom Governance Reform Programme*.
54 CGG, *Report on the Government's Fight against Corruption*, 24.
55 On the link between economic underdevelopment and corruption, the CGG's *Report on the Government's Fight against Corruption* notes that low wages for civil servants and lack of financial independence for the ACC created fertile grounds for the acceptance of

bribes, misappropriations of public funds and political interference in corruption investigations.

56 Between September 1998 and January 2002, a total of 24,352 RUF combatants were disarmed. Source, UN DDR Resource Centre, www.unddr.org/countryprogrammes. php?c = 60. Humphreys and Weinstein, 'Demobilization and Reintegration', find little evidence of a link between the combatants' completion of DDR and their successful reintegration.

57 United Nations Peacebuilding Commission, *Conference Room Paper for the Country Specific Meeting on Sierra Leone.*

58 United Nations, *Fifth Report of the Secretary-General on the United Nations Integrated Office in Sierra Leone*; ICG, *Sierra Leone: The Election Opportunity.*

59 United Nations, *Report of the Peacebuilding Commission*, 5. See also United Nations, *Fifth Report of the Secretary-General on the United Nations Integrated Office in Sierra Leone*, 4, and 'Sierra Leone: Not a lot of guns but a lot of frustration', IRIN, 6 September 2007, www.irinnews.org/Report.aspx?ReportId = 74151. One ex-combatant interviewed in this report expresses a common disillusionment over DDR: 'We were made promises about what would happen to us after we disarmed but the promises were empty.'

60 TRC, *Final Report*, Vol. 2, Ch. 1, 5, item 20.

61 ICG, *Liberia and Sierra Leone: Rebuilding Failed States.*

62 ICG, *Sierra Leone: Managing Uncertainty*, 15. The report further recognised that economic progress and integration efforts were mutually dependent, calling on those managing DDR to 'reduce combatant's expectations' to realistic levels. Precisely how such a task could be achieved without stirring up disillusionment, however, is far from clear.

63 See HRW, *Youth, Poverty and Blood*; and Ginifer, *Evaluation of the Conflict Prevention Pools*, 16.

64 BBC World Service Trust and Search for Common Ground, *Sierra Leone Elections 2007*, 12, found that those listening to radio were more likely than non-listeners to know the date of elections.

65 'Sierra Leone: Election campaign focuses on youth', IRIN, 8 August 2007, www. irinnews.org/Report.aspx?ReportId = 73638.

66 Ibid.

67 BBC World Service Trust and Search for Common Ground, *Sierra Leone Elections 2007*, 19–20.

68 One unemployed voter told IRIN: 'I voted for the SLPP twice but now I will try another party'. 'Sierra Leone: Election campaign focuses on youth', IRIN.

69 'Emergency Threat in Sierra Leone', *BBC News Online*, 28 August 2007, http://news. bbc.co.uk/2/hi/africa/6966339.stm; 'Sierra Leone: Election tensions could help or hinder democratic process', IRIN, 29 August 2007, www.irinnews.org/Report. aspx?ReportId = 73994. The violence, although significant, must be kept in perspective: casualties were generally restricted to injury from rock throwing, knives and slingshots and, at its peak, never escalated beyond rioting. However, the roots of violence, its potential to destabilise and its impact on perceptions, has great significance for political reintegration.

70 'S Leone poll peace rally snubbed', *BBC News Online*, 6 September 2007, http:// news.bbc.co.uk/2/hi/africa/6981394.stm. Koroma instead announced his commitment to peace in a speech at APC headquarters, also stating: 'Let Berewa allow our people free access all over the country. He has armed people all over the country'. The APC consistently accused the SLPP of rearming the CDF militias.

71 'Violence spreads in Sierra Leone', *BBC News Online*, 20 September 2007, http:// news.bbc.co.uk/2/hi/africa/7004686.stm.

72 See, for instance, 'Sierra Leone: Election tensions could help or hinder democratic process', IRIN.

73 Solomon Berewa of the SLPP was vice-president of Kabbah's government and widely expected to win the contest. However, when Charles Margai split from the SLPP to form the PMDC, the SLPP's support was weakened and, in the second round of voting, Margai's support for Koroma of the APC may have proved decisive.

74 'Sierra Leone: Not a lot of guns but a lot of frustration', IRIN. Bangura also pointed to the absence of firearms in Sierra Leone as significant in minimising fatalities and preventing violence from escalating. As a reflection on the disarmament component of DDR, this would suggest a degree of success, yet the fact that violence has persisted also demonstrates that the removal of arms alone may only alter the form of conflict without tackling its roots, an objective that can only be addressed through the reintegration component. In this respect, Bangura saw little progress, stating that 'under the right conditions all the peace-building efforts we have seen so far may yet collapse'. For the use of ex-RUF as bodyguards, see also Utas, 'Watermelon Politics in Sierra Leone', 64.

75 UN Peacebuilding Commission, *Conference Room Paper for the Country Specific Meeting on Sierra Leone*, 8.

76 'Sierra Leone's leader urges calm', *BBC News Online*, 14 August 2007, http://news.bbc.co.uk/2/hi/africa/6945894.stm.

77 If the system as a whole was deemed corrupt or failing, this might seem logical. Yet, while it was important for parties to hold real political appeal to ex-combatants, building confidence in the wider democratic process also required promoting tolerance of electoral defeat and plurality of opinion.

78 UN, *Fifth Report of the Secretary-General on the United Nations Integrated Office in Sierra Leone*, 8.

79 The ethnic divide in Sierra Leone is often overstated, yet instances of political violence by youths do sometimes reflect this factor. See for example: 'Violence spreads in Sierra Leone', *BBC News*, which reports the targeting of shops of Kabbah's Mandingo ethnicity.

80 Mark Doyle, 'S Leone election turns sour', *BBC News Online*, 12 May 2002, http://news.bbc.co.uk/2/hi/africa/1982817.stm.

81 There was no need for international intervention in 2007, but calls from the UN and international donors for presidential candidates to respect the peace served to reinforce the pattern of external actors as guarantors and political regulators.

82 Despite NEC's encouraging performance, the electoral outcome was actually contested by the SLPP, and two of NEC's own commissioners publicly disassociated themselves from the result: UN, *Fifth Report of the Secretary-General on the United Nations Integrated Office in Sierra Leone*, 9.

83 Utas, 'Watermelon Politics in Sierra Leone'.

84 Utas makes the important point that many Sierra Leoneans accepted money but still voted for their party or candidate of choice, suggesting that this may undermine politicians' attempts to 'shop for votes' and limit its future practice.

85 The BBC obtained a full copy of the report by the Presidential Transition Team, see Mark Doyle, 'S Leone riddled with corruption', *BBC News Online*, 14 November 2007, http://news.bbc.co.uk/2/hi/africa/7092861.stm. The APC's willingness to investigate and expose this problem was a positive step in building confidence in transparent government among ex-combatants and the wider Sierra Leonean community. However, reporting alone is insufficient. Failure to deliver visible results in tackling corruption and abusive practises may irrevocably cement ex-combatants' views of political institutions as inherently exclusionary and self-serving, seriously damaging their long-term political reintegration.

86 'SL Leader pledges graft crackdown', *BBC News Online*, 15 November 2007, http://news.bbc.co.uk/2/hi/africa/7096013.stm. It is also worth noting that despite the 2007 success, the UN expected to assist in organising 2008 local elections due to the logistical and financial limitations continuing to plague NEC.

87 A point also made in 2001 in ICG, *Sierra Leone: Managing Uncertainty*, 10.

References

BBC World Service Trust and Search for Common Ground, 2007. *Sierra Leone Elections 2007: A Comprehensive Baseline Study of Knowledge, Priorities and Trust*, BBC, London.

Berdal, Mats and Malone, David (eds), 2000. *Greed and Grievance: Economic Agendas in Civil Wars*, Lynne Rienner Publishers, Boulder, CO.

Campaign for Good Governance (CGG), 2005. *Report on the Government's Fight against Corruption in Sierra Leone*, CGG, Freetown.

Clapham, Christopher, 2003. 'Sierra Leone: The Political Economy of Internal Conflict', Working Paper no. 20. Clingendael, Netherlands Institute of International Relations, Clingendael Conflict Research Unit, The Hague.

Fanthorpe, Richard, Jay, Alice and Kamara, Victor Kalie, 2002. *Chiefdom Governance Reform Programme (formerly Paramount Chiefs Restoration Programme), Sierra Leone: Project Evaluation and Recommendations*, Department for International Development, London.

Ginifer, Jeremy, 2004. *Evaluation of the Conflict Prevention Pools: Sierra Leone*, Department for International Development, London.

Human Rights Watch (HRW), 2005. *Youth, Poverty and Blood: The Lethal Legacy of West Africa's Regional Warriors*, HRW, New York, p. 17.

Humphreys, Macartan and Weinstein, Jeremy M., 2004. *What the Fighters Say: A Survey of Ex-Combatants in Sierra Leone June–August 2003, Interim Report July 2004.* Produced in partnership with PRIDE, Columbia University Press, New York.

——, 2007. 'Demobilization and Reintegration', *Journal of Conflict Resolution* 51(4), pp. 531–576.

International Crisis Group (ICG), 2001. *Sierra Leone: Managing Uncertainty*, ICG, Brussels.

——, 2002. *Sierra Leone After Elections: Politics As Usual?*, ICG, Brussels.

, 2004. *Liberia and Sierra Leone: Rebuilding Failed States*, Africa Report, No. 87, ICG, Brussels.

——, 2007. *Sierra Leone: The Election Opportunity*, Africa Report, No. 129. ICG, Brussels.

International Monetary Fund (IMF) and International Development Association (IDA), 2006. *Sierra Leone: Annual Progress Report on the Poverty Reduction Strategy Paper*, Joint Staff Advisory Note, IMF, Washington DC.

Kaplan, Robert, 1994. 'The Coming Anarchy', *The Atlantic Monthly* 273:2, pp. 44–76.

Keen, David, 2000. 'Incentives and Disincentives for Violence', in Berdal, Mats and Malone, David (eds), *Greed and Grievance: Economic Agendas in Civil Wars*, Lynne Rienner Publishers, Boulder, CO.

——, 2005. *Conflict and Collusion in Sierra Leone*, James Currey, Oxford.

Malan, Mark, Rakate, Phenyo and McIntyre, Angela, 2002. *Peacekeeping in Sierra Leone: UNAMSIL Hits the Home Straight*, Monograph No. 68, Institute for Security Studies, Pretoria.

Post-conflict Reintegration Initiative for Development and Empowerment (PRIDE), 2002. *Ex-Combatant Views of the Truth and Reconciliation Commission and the Special Court in Sierra Leone*, In partnership with the International Center for Transitional Justice, PRIDE, Freetown.

Republic of Sierra Leone, 2003. *Sierra Leone National Youth Policy*, The Government of Sierra Leone, Freetown.

Richards, Paul, 1996. *Fighting for the Rainforest: War, Youth and Resources in Sierra Leone*, James Currey, Oxford.

Richards, Paul and Vincent, James, 2008. 'Sierra Leone: Marginalization of the RUF', in de Zeeuw, Jeroen (ed.), *From Soldiers to Politicians: Transforming Rebel Movements After Civil Wars*, Lynne Rienner Publishers, Boulder CO.

Thomson, Brian, 2007. *Sierra Leone: Reform or Relapse? Conflict and Governance Reform*, Chatham House, London.

Truth and Reconciliation Commission (TRC), 2004. *Final Report of the Truth and Reconciliation Commission*, 3 Vols, TRC, Freetown.

United Nations, 2000. *Third Report of the Secretary-General on the United Nations Mission in Sierra Leone*, S/2000/186, UN, New York.

——, 2000. *Fourth Report of the Secretary-General on the United Nations Mission in Sierra Leone*, S/2000/455, UN, New York.

——, 2007. *Fifth Report of the Secretary-General on the United Nations Integrated Office in Sierra Leone*, S/2007/704. UN, New York.

——, 2007. *Report of the Peacebuilding Commission*. General Assembly, Sixty-first session, Agenda item 26, A/61/901-S/2007/269, UN, New York.

United Nations Assistance Mission in Sierra Leone (UNAMSIL), 2003. *The DDR Process in Sierra Leone: Lessons Learned*, DDR Coordination Section, UNAMSIL.

United Nations Peacebuilding Commission, 2006. *Conference Room Paper for the Country Specific Meeting on Sierra Leone*, PBC/2/SIL/CRP.1, UN, New York.

Utas, Mats, 2007. 'Watermelon Politics in Sierra Leone: Hope Amidst Vote Buying and Remobilized Militias', *African Renaissance* 4:3–4, pp. 62–66.

8 Beyond bullets and ballots

The reintegration of UNITA in Angola

Alex Vines and Bereni Oruitemeka

Introduction

Angola has enjoyed mostly peace since April 2002 and in September 2008 held legislative elections for the first since 1992. From being one of the most protracted conflicts in Africa, Angola became, within five years, one of the most successful economies in sub-Saharan Africa. This chapter charts the fortunes of the Union for the Total Independence of Angola (UNITA), assesses how successfully it has transformed itself from a rebel movement into the leading party of the democratic opposition, and what its future prospects are following its poor results in the September 2008 legislative elections.

War raged in Angola for four decades, except for the period between May 1991, when a ceasefire was signed, and September 1992 when the first national election was held. The nationalist struggle started in February 1961 with an uprising in Luanda. The next month, strikes, uprisings and massacres of white settlers shook the cotton and coffee-growing areas of northern Angola. In 1964, following splits in the nationalist movement, Jonas Savimbi left the 'government in exile' in which he had served as foreign minister. After visiting a number of mainly communist countries, Savimbi founded UNITA in 1966. UNITA guerrillas began operating in eastern Angola in 1966 and by the early 1970s were responsible for some attacks along the Benguela railway corridor. By exploiting the feelings of exclusion in Angola's largest ethnic group, the Ovimbundu, Savimbi built up his own constituency in the centre and south of the country.

Alvor Accord

Following a military coup in Portugal in April 1974, the colonial government precipitously announced its withdrawal from Angola. In January 1975 UNITA, along with the other Angolan nationalist movements, the Movement for the Popular Liberation of Angola (MPLA) and the National Front for the Liberation of Angola (FNLA), signed the Alvor Accord, an agreement that provided for a joint interim government between the three groups and the creation of an integrated national army. However, as the date for military integration neared, the agreement broke down. By mid-1975, the fronts were at war. During this 'Second War' that involved the Soviets, the US, South Africa and Zaire, the MPLA was able to subdue its opponents and form a single-party socialist government that gained widespread diplomatic recognition, though not from the United States or South Africa who were, during the Cold War, supporters of the FNLA and UNITA.[1] By the end of the 1970s, UNITA took over from the FNLA as the main civil war opponent of the MPLA government. This war reached its peak in the mid-1980s.

Bicesse Accords

Decades of conflict ended with the signing of the Bicesse Peace Accords in May 1991, which ratified a ceasefire and called for UNITA forces to be integrated along with equal numbers of the government's armed forces, the FAPLA,[2] into a new 50,000-strong military to be known as the Angolan Armed Forces (FAA).[3] Remaining troops were to be demobilised. A so-called 'triple zero' clause that prohibited acquisition of new weapons by either party and likewise committed international actors to refrain from supplying such materials complemented demobilisation. However, there were omissions. Although Bicesse effectively forced the reluctant MPLA to adopt a multi-party system with provision for the holding of elections, these were politically dependent on the creation of the FAA, and there was no formal requirement that disarmament and demobilisation be completed.[4] Even the initial quartering and registering of troops was never completed.[5] Despite increasing signs of Savimbi's declining commitment to the peace process, the push towards the elections continued as demobilisation and integration of troops into the FAA fell badly behind schedule.[6] UNITA maintained control over territory and apparently had no intention of losing its advantage by disarming.[7]

Under the terms of Bicesse the UN did not have the same observer status as the 'Troika' of Portugal, the US and Russia; rather it was an 'invited' guest in the process.[8] The United Nations Angola Verification Mission (UNAVEM II),[9] established on 30 May 1991 with a limited monitoring mandate and no powers of enforcement as insisted upon by both parties, was, after a two-and-a-half month delay, backed up with inadequate funding by the Security Council. Inappropriate facilities meant arms could not be locked away securely and troops who self-demobilised were able to take their weapons with them on departure.[10] Conversely, many demobilised troops stayed in the camps because of a lack of transport. Donors – fixated on the coming elections – did not respond to calls to consider seriously the longer-term integration of the former combatants.[11]

Political process

Significantly, no unity government was envisaged at Bicesse for the post election period. As parties and their candidates campaigned furiously across the country in a winner-takes-all contest largely fought along ethnic lines,[12] Savimbi addressed a rally of 50,000 and presented UNITA as a genuinely rural-based African party set against a corrupt, urban Afro-Portuguese MPLA (a strategy that would alienate some of Savimbi's potential non-Ovimbundu support base).[13]

Because the new FAA was a precondition to the 29–30 September election taking place, a symbolic creation thereof occurred on 27 September and elections went ahead as planned.[14] Angola's only nation-wide democratic elections provided the first opportunity for Angolans to express their will. There was a turnout of more than 91 per cent (4.4 million) of registered voters. UNITA was the favourite and Savimbi had expected to win. Early indications of MPLA gains were met with allegations of electoral fraud and Savimbi requested postponement of the announcement of results until the conclusion of a full investigation. UNITA, seeking to unify parties in opposition to the MPLA, formed the cross-party Angolan Democratic Opposition on 7 October, which came to include representatives from sixteen other parties.[15]

The UN declined to meet demands for a pre-announcement investigation. President dos Santos, the government's candidate, received 49.6 per cent and Savimbi 40.07 per cent of the vote. In the election for the legislature, the MPLA won 54 per cent of the vote, 129 seats, and UNITA took 34 per cent with 70 seats.

Savimbi had presented an organised party capable of fielding candidates and able to garner support across the country sufficient to win by a significant margin in some core provinces. UNITA's involvement in the democratic political process and likewise the peace process was however short-lived, as UNITA withdrew its troops from the FAA and the 70 UNITA National Assembly delegates boycotted the seating of the first session of Parliament.[16] The prospect of an opposition role was an unattractive one for Savimbi, and accordingly UNITA declined to participate in a presidential run-off, opting instead for a military response.[17]

Renewed violence

Fighting returned to Angola within one month of the elections. Both sides were maintaining secret armies in violation of the Bicesse Accords. UNITA had used the breathing space offered by the Bicesse peace to rebuild its military. Although between May 1991 and the elections in September 1992 the Angolan government largely neglected its regular armed forces, which were supposed to be demobilising and integrating into the new FAA, the MPLA was able to rely on 'Ninjas' trained in non-standard policing practices backed up by a civil defence initiative, which resulted in tens of thousands of small arms being distributed to civilians.[18] Fierce fighting led to a resumption of civil war.

Lusaka Protocol[19]

Both the government and UNITA had agreed to halt new arms acquisitions as part of the accords. Yet while a Security Council embargo on arms and oil transfers to UNITA had been in place since 1993, the embargo was not enforced and both sides openly continued major arms purchases.

Following early military gains in late 1994 in which UNITA lost ground, the government was reluctant to seek a settlement but nonetheless unable to consolidate its power due to the country-wide devastation.[20] Both sides finally signed a ceasefire protocol on 20 November 1994 in Lusaka, marking the end of Angola's brutal and costly 'Third War'. UNITA leader Jonas Savimbi refused to sign the agreement in person, which ensured that President dos Santos could neither and left it to subordinates to endorse the accord.

The Lusaka Protocol provided for a ceasefire, the integration of UNITA generals into the government's armed forces (which were to become non-partisan and civilian controlled), demobilisation (later amended to demilitarisation) under UN supervision, the repatriation of mercenaries, the incorporation of UNITA troops into the Angolan National Police under the Interior Ministry, and the prohibition of any other police or surveillance organisation.

The major political issues covered in the Lusaka Protocol were the UN's mandate (verification and monitoring of the Lusaka Protocol), the role of peacekeepers (supervision), the completion of the electoral process, and national reconciliation. Under the provisions for reconciliation between the parties, UNITA's leadership would receive private residences, political offices in each province and one central headquarters. UNITA would also hold a series of posts as ministers, deputy ministers, ambassadors, provincial governors and deputy governors, municipal administrators and deputy administrators and commune administrators. The MPLA would retain all other positions of patronage.[21] These provisions formed the basis of a Government of National Unity.

National Unity Government

Parliamentary elections, due to be held in 1996, were postponed for two to four years under the terms of the Lusaka Protocol, and presidential elections would not be held until the UN determined that appropriate conditions existed.[22] In March 1997, UN Secretary-General Kofi Annan visited Angola, hoping to be present for the inauguration of the new government of national unity. While the inauguration was again delayed, the visit stimulated renewed attention to contentious issues.

On 9 April, the Angolan National Assembly took a major step forward with the swearing in of 63 UNITA deputies. Five UNITA deputies who had been participating in the National Assembly since the 1992 elections had earlier been denounced by Savimbi. The National Assembly saw heated debate, the first time since 1992, although votes were clearly along party lines. Perhaps because of international pressure and the change of government in Zaire (now the Democratic Republic of Congo), elements of UNITA finally joined the national unity government, which was inaugurated on 11 April and included representatives from MPLA, UNITA and the Democratic Party of Angola (PDA). Savimbi was not present at the ceremony.

State administration

The handover of control of local municipalities to the government was slow. It began on 30 April, but, citing 'technical reasons', UNITA in May delayed the handover of IS municipalities in Benguela province. Following UN and Troika pressure on UNITA, the UN announced that the expansion of state administration would recommence on 26 May and Vila Nova, just east of Huambo, was handed over on 28 May to a high-level delegation. A few days later in Quibala district of Cuanza Sul, UNITA supporters protesting the handing over of territory to the government managed to assault and injure Isaías Samakuva, head of the UNITA delegation to the UN-chaired Joint Commission, and N'zau Puna, a UNITA defector who had become a vice-minister for the Interior Ministry.[23]

Following a rare telephone conversation between Santos and Savimbi on 9 January 1998, there was an agreement to complete implementation of the key outstanding elements of the Lusaka Protocol.[24] As with so many events in the Angolan peace process, the agreement fell behind schedule. However, by the end of January 1998 it was agreed that the force level of Savimbi's bodyguard corps would start at 400, but would be reduced gradually to 150.

When UNITA declared on 6 March that it had demilitarised all its forces, the government responded by legalising UNITA as a political party and appointing three UNITA-nominated governors and seven vice-governors. Both sides also agreed on the list of six ambassadors nominated by UNITA. On 31 March, a law granting special status to Savimbi as the leader of the largest opposition party was promulgated. On 1 April, Radio Vorgan, the UNITA radio station, ceased broadcasting.

The 1 April deadline for the return of state administration was missed, with only 80 per cent of the localities having been brought under government control. By 1 May 1998, some 60 localities remained in which central authority had not been established, including the UNITA strongholds of Andulo, Bailundo, Nharea and Mongo. The death of UN Special Representative Blondin Beye in an air crash in Côte d'Ivoire on 27 June undermined UN mediation efforts – insecurity increased and UNITA reasserted itself in several areas. Despite repeated calls by the UN for control of UNITA's four strongholds to be handed over to the government, UNITA kept dragging its heels with new excuses. On 1 July, when UNITA again requested at least two further weeks to withdraw from its stronghold, the UN lost its patience and imposed a new package of sanctions freezing their foreign bank accounts, banning their diamond exports, and preventing all air and water transport into and out of UNITA-held territories to try to force compliance. UNITA, however, remained firmly entrenched.

Tensions rise

In anticipation of the enhanced sanctions, UNITA pulled out of the Joint Commission for two months in protest. Upon its return in August, UNITA said it would permit the extension of state administration to 15 October. The government counter-proposed a 31 August 1998 deadline and on that date, it suspended UNITA from the National Unity Government on the grounds of non-compliance by UNITA with its commitments under the Lusaka Protocol.

In a related action, Jorge Valentim and other UNITA members who had served in the government announced a split with Savimbi, launching a party called the Renovation Committee of UNITA. The government stated that it would only negotiate with this 'new' UNITA and urged others to do the same. Although the Southern African Development Community (SADC) branded Jonas Savimbi a war criminal, the 'new' UNITA did not attract strong support inside Angola or outside SADC. Many of UNITA's 70 members of parliament disassociated themselves from the group and many other senior UNITA officials refused to support the breakaway group, despite threats and bribes by the government pressing them to do so.

On 1 September, the government suspended the four ministers and seven vice-ministers who UNITA had designated to serve in the Government of Unity and National Reconciliation. The suspension was lifted on 23 September, when the president also dismissed one UNITA minister and one vice-minister the same day. On 26 September, 53 UNITA deputies signed a declaration seeking clarification of the decision to suspend the ministers and reaffirmed that all 70 constituted the UNITA parliamentary group under the leadership of Abel Chivukuvuku, a former advisor to the UNITA leader. In a statement to the press, Chivukuvuku declared that he had severed all contacts with Jonas Savimbi but did not intend to join the Renovation Committee.

On 27 October, the National Assembly abrogated the law granting a special status to Jonas Savimbi as the leader of the largest opposition party. The decision was attributed to Savimbi's failure to fulfil his party's obligations under the protocol.

Final war

The MPLA held its IV Congress in Luanda from 5 to 10 December. At its opening, President dos Santos stated that the only path to lasting peace was the total isolation of Jonas Savimbi and his movement. The president called for the termination of the mandate of the United Nation's Observer Mission in Angola (MONUA) and an end to the Lusaka peace process.[25] MONUA withdrew from all UNITA-held areas for safety on 6 December.[26]

Savimbi's soldiers advanced across the country once more, denying the government access to more than two-thirds of national territory and again isolating provincial capitals and other urban centres. During the period of peace, government forces had grown complacent. Once more, the military crisis led to political and economic centralisation: the president abolished the post of prime minister in 1999 and assumed the post of head of government. There was only a very small space for political parties – the UNITA deputies were split roughly between those who had openly rejected Savimbi by signing up for Renovation Committee and those (many still in parliament) who adopted an uncomfortable, more ambiguous stance. The government policy now was to pursue Savimbi to the death.

Despite initial battlefield setbacks for the government's forces, by late 2000 the military tide had changed against UNITA. The government embarked upon a brutal scorched earth policy and forcibly removed people to provincial capitals. Commercial technological military assistance, the deployment of agile units and the import of highly trained person-seeking dogs and equipment such as unmanned aerial vehicles (UAVs) from Israel added to UNITA's trouble. Finally, on 22 February 2002, Government forces cornered Jonas Savimbi and killed him.

Luena memorandum of understanding

Following the killing of UNITA's founding leader, which was crowned a military victory by the governing MPLA, and the subsequent death of his immediate successor Antonio Dembo, both sides quickly resumed talks. The process was conducted by Angolans themselves without a mediator present.[27] During talks, the government dealt with military issues with UNITA commanders in the bush and political issues with the Renovation Committee who, in reality, had little legitimacy among UNITA members.[28] After initial suspicions of the process, UNITA's external wing, led by Isaías Samakuva, who had been representative in Paris from September 1998,[29] confirmed support for Paulo Lukamba (General Gato) – the party's Secretary General and, therefore, the next in line for leadership. Fifty-five out of 70 Luanda-based MPs backed General Gato in a declaration, overruling a previous declaration where 46 of the 70 had identified the external wing as the only body with sufficient legitimacy to represent the movement. The remaining 15 continued in their support of Eugenio Manuvakola of the UNITA Renovation Committee.[30]

The absence of a coherent and unified UNITA allowed the government to limit the agreement to essentially military terms, which failed to address adequately the need for a broader process of democratisation, as called for by the Angolan Civic Association. An amnesty for all war crimes committed during the war by both UNITA and the FAA was passed unanimously by the Assembly and in spite of UN resistance, as vocalised by special representative Ibrahim Gambari.[31]

On 4 April 2002 – only six weeks after the assassination of Savimbi, UNITA chief of staff General Geraldo Abreu Kamorteiro and the head of Angola's armed forces, General Armando da Cruz Neto, signed the Luena Memorandum of Understanding in the Angolan parliament building and in the presence of President dos Santos. The agreement largely reaffirmed commitments made at Lusaka in 1994.

Political opposition and the Government of National Unity

In October, following the abolition of its armed wing in August,[32] UNITA declared itself disarmed and became a democratic political party.[33] The UNITA factions agreed to join together under a single authority – the Political Commission – comprised of 250 members, which included Samakuva and was formally sworn in on 8 October. The Renovation Committee was to dissolve and Jorge Valentim, former leader of the breakaway faction, was given a position within the leadership of the unified body.[34] In late October, the government paid an agreed subsidy to UNITA, which UNITA member Horacio Jumjuvili said would 'go towards improving UNITA's political activity throughout the country. It will help rebuild the party's infrastructure that was destroyed during the war so that we can grow as a political party.'[35] The party was in receipt of $13–14 million per year from state funds and UNITA simultaneously became both a member of the Government of Unity and National Reconciliation (with 70 parliamentarians) and the largest opposition party.[36] In mid-November, President dos Santos gave posts to six ambassadors, and the jobs of three provincial governors and four deputy governors to UNITA.[37]

Shortly after it was announced that the UN-brokered Joint Commission for the Angolan Peace Process would be dissolved on 21 November 2002, as according to the spokesman, 'most of the commission's work [was] done'.[38] Marcial Dachala, UNITA's Secretary for Information, complained that the Joint Commission provided 'a forum to discuss the country's many problems', adding that it would now be 'difficult to sustain … dialogue with the government'.[39] The Joint Commission would be replaced by the Bilateral Mechanism of Political Concert.[40] A joint statement declared that the 'government and UNITA commit to no longer resorting to the use of arms'.[41]

In December, the MPLA Political Bureau and the UNITA standing committee signed a Memorandum of Understanding that settled outstanding items of the Lusaka Protocol.[42] On 9 December 2002, the Security Council unanimously adopted resolution 1448 lifting the remaining sanctions on UNITA; Dachala said there would be 'more space which [UNITA] will turn to the advantage of [the] party and for the Angolan people, in order to enhance democracy in Angola'.[43]

On 28 January 2003, parliament's Constitutional Commission agreed on the future role of the president.[44] Observers noted that UNITA's return to war would be unlikely, if only because of its inability to wage war.[45] The United Nations Mission in Angola (UNMA) ended on 15 February 2003 with UN Resident Coordinator Eric de Mul becoming the senior official in Angola.[46] The US followed the UN's lead and lifted sanctions on UNITA in May.[47]

In an interview in early 2003, Samakuva identified the challenges facing UNITA, which included choosing a leader and reorganising the newly reunified party. The party would have to 'formulate policies that appeal to ordinary Angolans' and 'reunite' supporters. Demobilisation and reintegration of ex-combatants was also a priority. Samakuva went on to describe incidents involving MPLA supporters preventing UNITA officials from setting up party offices as 'isolated acts' of those who were 'not willing to embrace the momentum of national reconciliation'.[48]

At UNITA's ninth congress in June 2003, Isaías Samakuva[49] was elected UNITA's new leader, defeating interim leader General Gato, who had led UNITA after Savimbi's death.[50] Gato said 'it is democracy that has won, UNITA and Angola'.[51] Samakuva, who officially took over as UNITA president on 12 July, left Gato out of the 25-member Executive Committee, prompting fears of a split within the party.[52]

Demobilisation, disarmament and reintegration

When the Memorandum of Understanding was signed in April 2002, two structures were created to coordinate disarmament, demobilisation and reintegration (DDR): the Joint Military Commission (JMC) and a Technical Committee (TC). With the assistance of several donors and the World Bank, the Angolan government launched a Programme for Demobilisation and Reintegration (PGDR). The Institute for the Socio-Professional Reintegration of Ex-Combatants (IRSEM) was to coordinate the process.[53] Funded by the Angolan government, the total cost of PGDR was budgeted at $246.3 million, of which $123.5 million was for demobilisation and disarmament. This sum included contingency subsidies and five months salaries to the soldiers quartered, kits and transport to destination areas.[54] By August 2008, $89.33 million was donated for the reintegration process: the World Bank International Development Association (IDA) provided $38.8 million; Multi-Donor Trust Fund $30.23 million, and the European Commission $20.3 million. The Angolan government had provided $157 million as its contribution.[55]

Jointly with IRSEM, an Angola Demobilisation and Reintegration Programme (ADRP) was launched in March 2004 by the World Bank's Multi-Country Demobilization and Reintegration Programme (MDRP). This programme ends in December 2008 and the Angolan government has decided to finance a follow-up project in early 2009 to support ex-combatants from other processes.

Demobilisation

Demobilisation of UNITA occurred quickly but it was dogged with logistical problems. Initial plans were for 50,000 combatants but this proved to be less than half the number of those who eventually reported to the Quartering and Family Areas. The plan was then to demobilise 85,000 former UNITA combatants by the end of 2002 and 20,000 more by the end of 2003.[56]

In April 2002, 5,000 members of UNITA were integrated into the FAA.[57] In a hurry to complete the process, the government announced on 21 June that demobilisation had been concluded, even as more combatants continued to arrive at the concentration areas.[58] Demobilisation formally took place on 2 August 2002,[59] by first integrating all former UNITA soldiers into the FAA, and then demobilising them. Subsequently, though international involvement was kept to a minimum, the UN Security Council (UNSC) authorised the United Nations Mission in Angola (UNMA) to 'contribute to the consolidation of peace'.[60] The JMC announcement that the demobilisation and disarmament process had been completed was premature because there were still many combatants who had not received their demobilisation papers and former combatants and their families were continuing to arrive in the reception areas. Initially there were 27 Quartering Areas allocated, but these were increased to 35, with an extra seven satellite areas around 16 of the country's provinces. These were renamed Gathering Areas in August 2002 to reflect the completion of the demobilisation process and the transition to civilian status.

By the end of July 2002, 85,585 former combatants and 288,756 family members were in the Quartering Areas. A further 14,854 combatants came later, held back probably by UNITA until it was more confident about the peace process. Numbers coming to the areas grew quickly in 2003, putting additional strain on logistical and supply capacities and prolonging the registration and demobilisation from 80 days to approximately four months.

The Office for the Coordination of Humanitarian Affairs reported on 23 October 2003 that the Gathering Areas had been closed and emptied.[61] According to the World Bank, approximately 105,000 UNITA ex-combatants demobilised and 18 UNITA generals were integrated into the Armed Forces of Angola (FAA), with a further 40 joining the national police force.[62]

Disarmament

UNITA and other political parties made repeated calls for the disarmament of civilians. UNITA spokesman Alcides Sakala described this as UNITA's 'number one priority'.[63] UNITA reacted angrily to claims that it had kept arms caches despite mounting calls for a major disarmament campaign ahead of elections.[64] This became an emotive issue in 2008 with UNITA denying any purposeful strategy to hide weapons.

The number of arms handed in by UNITA ex-combatants was surprisingly low – some 33,000 small arms and 300,000 rounds of ammunition were collected – reflective of how depleted these forces had become but also that much heavier weaponry had been cached. Some estimates talk about 90 per cent of UNITA weapons handed in, with a remaining 10 per cent in the hands of the civilian population. Between two and two and a half million small arms and light weapons are thought to remain in civilian possession in Angola although this is very much an estimate.[65] Virgilio Faria, head of the international organisations desk in the Angolan Ministry of External Relations reported that about 158,000 weapons of different calibre had been collected from civilians between 1999 and February 2007. The Government's Programme of Disarmament of the Civilian Population, from April 2002 to April 2005 reported that the National Police collected 75,323 firearms of various calibres. From April 2005 to April 2006, the government's efforts resulted in the recovery of 4,712 firearms. In 2006, FAA collected 28,327 weapons, which had been in the possession of the now abolished Civilian Defence Units.[66]

The government re-launched its disarmament campaign ahead of the elections in 2008, amid calls for a major effort at disarmament. This has had some success and on 10 October the Commander General for Public Order of the National Police, Paulo Gaspar Almeida announced that some 42,000 firearms of different calibres and other lethal weapons, illegally in the possession of civilians, had been seized in police operations in 2008. This campaign is scheduled to continue till 2010.[67]

Hard data on small arms possession is rare. A household survey published in 2006 on weapons possession in the provinces of Huambo, Bié and Huila revealed that 70.4 per cent of respondents believed carrying a firearm was important for security and 46.4 per cent admitted it was easy to access weapons.[68] In Luanda, armed robbery and carjacking has increased significantly in recent years, reflecting the social difficulties of survival in the capital. There has also been increased road robberies, in some provinces, but these crimes cannot be linked specifically to ex-UNITA combatants.[69]

Reintegration

Demobilisation and disarmament since the Luena Memorandum can be judged as largely successful,[70] but while many former combatants would now consider themselves demobilised, reintegration levels have been more disappointing.[71] Both military signatories to the Memorandum took up public posts – Armando da Cruz Neto became ambassador to Spain and General Geraldo Abreu Kamorteiro became the deputy chief of FAA staff for administration.[72] The government also hired 4,100 ex-UNITA combatants for its Ministry of Health and 2,360 for its Ministry of Education.[73] For the majority, finding work is much harder. The profile of the average ex-UNITA combatant was that 57 per cent were single, with an average age of 32 and average military service of 14 years. Of these, 80 per cent did not receive education above fourth grade.[74] Two-thirds of these wanted to return to the agricultural provinces of Bié, Huambo, Huila or Kwanza Sul, but only 20 per cent wanted to return to the land; many wanted new skills and eventually aspired to find work in a town; and many have found employment among Angola's growing number of private security firms.[75]

Government plans for reintegration were not revealed until late 2002 and envisaged support for economic activities, assistance for social reintegration, and support for those with special needs. Each ex-combatant was also eligible for reintegration opportunities such as training and access to micro-credit schemes. The reintegration programme aimed to support 105,000 UNITA ex-combatants and 33,000 government troops (but excluded ex-combatants from Bicesse and Lusaka). A World Bank-funded Angola Demobilisation and Reintegration Programme (ADRP) should quickly have become operational, but negotiations stalled over its financial management (see Figure 8.1).[76] It was finally launched in March 2004 but dispersal of funds was slow and, by April 2005, only 24 projects worth $9 million had reached 23,500 ex-combatants in six provinces.[77]

The IRSEM was responsible for: implementing the ADRP programme (with offices in each of Angola's 18 provinces used as bases to prepare inventories of the different projects on offer); providing assistance for development programmes; and monitoring and coordinating reintegration activities such as economic and social reintegration. Delay in the start-up of the reintegration

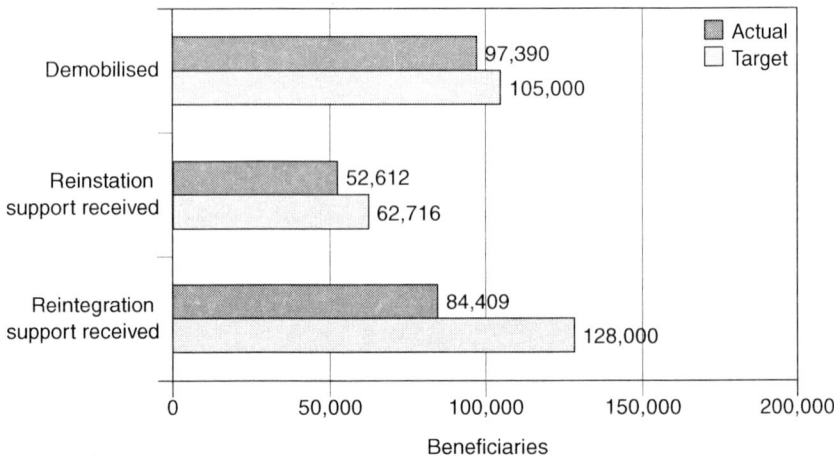

Figure 8.1 Demobilised and reintegrated ex-combatants receiving ADRP support (source: MDRP fact sheet: Angola, August 2008).

programme was not just due to a power struggle over control of money but also due to weak institutional capacity within IRSEM.

By April 2004, the government calculated that around 53,300 former combatants had received help with reinsertion and that 52,200 received payments of $85 and food for one year. Some 3,600 ex-UNITA combatants had received professional training by the Ministry of Employment. Announcements of projects by the government and IRSM had created expectation, and ex-combatants complained at the slowness of the process – some became restive. In September 2005, Isaías Chitombe, overseeing social rehabilitation for UNITA, said 'only 28,000' former soldiers were 'benefiting from rehabilitation projects'.[78] President dos Santos pledged in November 2005 to speed up the reintegration of former UNITA rebels the following year and 'increase assistance to former combatants' as part of the government's commitment to 'consolidating peace'.[79]

President dos Santos' intervention appears to have helped. Gradually more projects have started, mostly implemented by NGOs as contractors. For example, in March 2006, IRSEM announced that the social reintegration of UNITA demobilised combatants cost $3.7 million in Bié province and in September 2006, 4,234 ex-soldiers of UNITA had been involved in five cattle-breeding projects in central Kwanza-Sul province, assisted by the Christian Youth Association, World Vision, Oikos and other NGOs. In 2006 and 2007, the government announced the completion of professional training for 1,200 ex-UNITA and government combatants in Lunda Sul, and the reintegration of 663 former combatants in the labour market in Uije province.[80] In Bailundo, Development Workshop had funded socio-economic projects for the reintegration of 1,200 ex-soldiers and their families. At the same time, the government's continued reliance on NGOs, such as Development Workshop, when implementing its reintegration efforts for ex-UNITA combatants remained dramatic: in June 2007, for example, IRSEM national director, António Francisco de Andrade, admitted that his organisation had failed to assist 4,140 ex-UNITA combatants in the far southern Angolan province of Cuando Cubango because it lacked competent partners and called upon Caritas and World Vision to assist.[81] De Andrade in a March 2008 interview further stated that 'the participation of civil society and private sector in the identification and services rendered towards reintegration is another fact that improves the quality attained'.[82]

By August 2008, 97,390 UNITA ex-combatants were regarded as demobilised and 84,409 individuals benefited from reintegration support while 250 sub-projects had been contracted to offer support for 128,000 ex-combatants and other community members. As of 30 June 2008, some 10,500 ex-combatants were interviewed three to six weeks after receiving reintegration supports. According to the World Bank, 61 per cent of these ex-combatants were self-employed and 4 per cent worked in the formal sector, while up to 35 per cent were unemployed. All but 5 per cent had access to agricultural land, 98 per cent had established families and 93 per cent considered themselves reintegrated into their communities of destination.[83] Fieldwork in 2003 and 2004 by Parsons and Porto showed that a sample of 46,940 UNITA fighters who returned to civilian life after the war was overwhelmingly supported by their communities. This social integration was hugely assisted by their church and political affiliations in the short term and the ex-combatants remained tight with each other, though they are often suspicious of local authorities, who tend to be drawn from the ruling MPLA.[84] These close bonds are less visible in urban areas, and the ties between former UNITA foot soldiers and their leadership are also loosening, as its leadership increasingly looks weak and is corrupted in Luanda.

After five years of laying down their arms, UNITA considers itself a political party but it is the NGOs and faith groups that are mainly assisting the social and economic reintegration of its ex-combatants. Angola retains low human-development indicators five years after the conflict's end and according to the 2006 economic survey by the Catholic University of Angola, unemployment remains high at 27.1–31 per cent.[85] For most, the major challenge has been poverty. Then Vice-Minister of Planning, Carlos Lopes, admitted in 2006 that ex-combatants had serious challenges ahead of them, but that a booming Angolan economy was the best guarantee for their future.[86]

Elections and beyond

Following Savimbi's death, when UNITA was temporarily led by General Gato, politics turned into a bilateral negotiation between the Government and UNITA, with the heavy involvement of figures from the Angolan presidency. The agreement that was reached in December 2002 recognised the president as a head of government who enjoyed discretionary powers to appoint and dismiss a prime minister. It also gave the political party with most votes in a province the right to put forward a list of possible provincial governors from which the president makes the final choice. The president also retained the power to dissolve the national assembly. This shift towards the MPLA model reflected above all the Government's military victory, as well as specific pressures applied on a weakened UNITA during the negotiations.

The incoming UNITA leader, Isaías Samakuva, was unhappy with the agreement and tried to postpone approval to the next legislative assembly. To achieve this outcome, he sought to ally UNITA with a coalition of smaller opposition parties and, in May 2004, all opposition parties withdrew from the constitutional commission responsible for drafting laws, accusing the MPLA of manipulating the commission and holding elections hostage to constitutional approval. The opposition hoped that the MPLA would lose many parliamentary seats at the next election and that the next parliament would be more favourable.[87] The parties retained their unity, in spite of delays to payments due to them from the budget and attacks from the state media, which tried to cast them as 'spoilers'. They demanded a date from the president for legislative and presidential elections and the withdrawal of the MPLA's insistence on a new constitution as a prerequisite for elections. Shortly afterwards, President dos Santos visited the United States where President George W. Bush raised the issue of elections. On returning home, the MPLA's Political Bureau issued a statement saying that elections should take place by September 2006. An MPLA spokesman explained that the government had 'consulted as many key political players as possible' and that they had not wanted to 'rush into any announcement without analysing what needed to happen' before the holding of elections.[88] They also dropped the linkage of the election date to the approval of a new constitution.

UNITA further succeeded in pushing a reluctant dos Santos to undertake a reshuffle, which removed various people from the offices provided for UNITA in the Lusaka Protocol; exiting parliamentarians included Jorge Valentim, formerly UNITA Renovation Committee, from his ministerial position held since 1997.[89] On 22 October 2004, President dos Santos announced that UNITA's original nominee for the position of Minister of Trade, Victorino Domingos Hossi, would be replaced by Joaquim Ekuma Muafumua, also from UNITA but nominated by Samakuva. In addition, Diamantino Sauanbo Kungulo was replaced as Deputy Minister of the Interior by Junior Kuamutali Uambique Kanavanaqui, and Graciano Tulumo, Deputy Minister of Social Communication was replaced by Fonseca Manuel Chindondo. Dos Santos initially refused to remove the Minister of Health, Albertina Hamukwaya, because none of the people put forward by UNITA to replace her were women.[90]

Despite these gains, the MPLA remained far more advanced in its preparations for elections than the opposition parties. The party had commissioned detailed research to assist its task and had been on a recruitment campaign. There was a widespread complaint among opposition parties, and especially UNITA, about a blurring between state and party structures, and that the MPLA was taking advantage of this confusion to promote itself.[91] State media also gave wide coverage to MPLA activities. Some ministers were MPLA Central Committee members and several provincial governors were MPLA first provincial secretaries; there was a similar situation at municipal and communal levels. In many rural areas the MPLA flag remained more common than the national flag (the two also look similar).

In rural areas, most people have only heard of the MPLA and UNITA, and possibly the FNLA, and penetration by smaller parties is minimal. UNITA's provincial governors, who gained their positions through the terms of the Lusaka Accords of 1994, were deprived of effective power, which was instead held by vice-governors who work directly with central government directives. The same problem was replicated at municipal level. The role of UNITA ministers was generally restricted to rubber-stamping pre-prepared projects.[92]

For an opposition party like UNITA, competing against the MPLA with its huge state backing was a daunting task. UNITA received around $14 million per year and the MPLA around $23 million. The MPLA not only had the money from budget but also generated revenue from several large companies it owns and had the choice buildings in many provincial capitals. For UNITA, the issue of funding had risen in importance since the war, because it no longer controlled the diamonds that sustained it until 2002. Although parties generally receive their allocations, the MPLA, on occasions, has used the money as a lever. The MPLA also used other tools, including infiltration, intimidation and bribery, to prevent opposition officials from starting their own business operations. UNITA has failed to get into the construction boom as possible business partners were, according to their officials, frightened off.

A Human Rights Watch report in 2004 acknowledged that although Angolan authorities had become more tolerant of opposition political activity in Luanda, in the county's interior, there were regular violent incidents involving government agents.[93] Numerous reports detail the burning of delegations, beatings and threats, especially of UNITA officials – such as a wave of violence in Luvemba in eastern Angola in July 2004.[94] In March 2005, UNITA complained its members were attacked by a pro-MPLA militia and on 5 April 2005 the ransacking of political offices in Lumbala N'Guimbo was reported. On 2 March 2007, an alleged assassination attempt was made on UNITA leader Samakuva in Cambatela, although this may have been the result of poor firearms management by local police.

In some cases, the violence and hostility was caused by the perception of some communities of ex-UNITA combatants receiving support despite their involvement in serious war crimes. A number of these flare-ups were calmed down after visits to the locations by provincial governors and such incidents are also getting rarer – a testimony to reconciliation.

In advance of elections, the government – through the Interministerial Commission for the Electoral Process (CIPE) and in partnership with the National Electoral Commission (CNE), political parties, NGOs, churches and other entities of the civil society – began a Civic Education Campaign of the Electoral Process to take the message of the importance of elections to the citizens.[95] At the end of 2006, President dos Santos confirmed that the long-awaited legislative elections would take place in 2008 with the presidential elections to follow in 2009.[96]

Virgílio Pereira of CIPE reassured the public of the government's commitment to holding legislative and presidential elections in 2008 and 2009, after the registration period was extended by 90 days to 15 September 2007. The National Platform of Angolan Civil Society for the Elections confirmed good cooperation between the Platform and CIPE.[97]

Following the end of the registration process, the CIPE announced on 12 October 2007 that 8.4 million Angolans had registered throughout the country, against the 7.5 million predicted before the process. UNITA has challenged this process, claiming that it knows of unregistered citizens in areas formerly under its control, though this may have as much to do with the rural location of many of the supporters claimed by UNITA as with any bad faith by the government. In any event, by mid-2008, CIPE had taken onboard UNITA's concerns and voters that had not been registered inside Angola were given a fresh opportunity to have their names added to the electoral lists.

Adding to concerns over the credibility and transparency of the process was the Angolan government's efforts to extend the voting period from one to two days. Under pressure from civil society groups and the opposition led by UNITA, parliament rejected this amendment to the electoral law. It did, however, approve a measure to extend the deadline for announcing election results from ten to fifteen days.[98]

Legislative elections

On 16 September Angola's electoral commission (CNE) released the official results of the 5 and 6 September elections. Turnout was high at over 87 per cent, indicating popular enthusiasm for the first multiparty election in 16 years. This is not very different from the 1992 elections, when turnout was an impressive 90 per cent of registered voters.

Whereas 18 political organisations put forward candidates in the 1992 legislative elections, this time there were fourteen – ten political parties and four coalitions with 5,198 candidates competing.

Out of a total of 6.4 million valid ballots, the MPLA secured 81.6 per cent. UNITA only won 10.39 per cent and other parties secured just 7.97 per cent. UNITA leader Isaías Samakuva on 9 September accepted the outcome of the poll and praised the MPLA, hoping it 'governs in the interest of all Angolans', and added 'after about 80 per cent of valid votes have been counted, despite all that has happened, the leadership of UNITA accepts the results of the elections.'[99]

UNITA, during its election campaign, emphasised change. It highlighted exclusion, poverty, unemployment, the under-funded education system and corruption as the main obstacles to progressive development of the country. UNITA promised a break with the past, by governing in an open and transparent manner. Although these messages resonated with the electorate, the party was disadvantaged by never having been tested in government and also by the behaviour of some of its parliamentarians, including 16 defections in the National Assembly and having former prominent members such as Jorge Valentim calling on voters to turn against the party and vote MPLA.

There were also allegations of official intimidation, corruption and presence of security forces at polling stations. There was some intimidation and damage of UNITA property in the run-up to the elections.[100] For example, on 13 August, some UNITA officials in Londuimbali municipality of Huambo province were attacked by MPLA supporters and the violence was only stopped when police dispersed the crowd by firing shots in the air. But the most serious episode was that, despite a very expensive and high-tech voter registration process only 320 polling stations out of 2,584 polling stations opened in Luanda on election day as voter papers and voter register lists had not been delivered, forcing a second day of voting. According to individuals involved, this was more due to incompetence and inexperience than conspiracy.

UNITA's performance in its traditional heartland, the central highlands of Huambo and Bié provinces, was poor. This outcome was far from unexpected, as the parties parliamentarians had become distant and the MPLA had pumped resources into these areas and vigorously pursued a co-option effort with the traditional authorities since the end of the war.

Other parties did even worse; only three managed to secure more than 1 per cent of the national vote. The opposition now have only 29 seats in total. The MPLA dominated the vote in the provinces except in Bié and Cabinda, where UNITA did better, and the Lunda provinces, where the Partido de Renovação Social (PRS) enjoys strong support from the Lunda/Chokwe people.

UNITA's strongest showing was in Cabinda, due to a protest vote and an official boycott of the election by the armed FLEC separatist group. The FNLA did well in its Zaire province heartland but failed to make an impact nationally.

The five parties that had polled less than 0.5 per cent of the national vote (four of which had held seats in the outgoing parliament) have been dissolved. Angola now has only six officially registered parties compared with 14 parties and coalitions during the election and 108 during the pre-election period. The MPLA, with its 191 seats, now completely dominates the political landscape.

Table 8.1 Legislative election results

	Total votes	*% of total valid votes*	*No. of seats*
MPLA	5,266,112	81.64	191
UNITA	670,197	10.39	16
PRS	204,478	3.17	8
ND	77,405	1.20	2
FNLA	71,600	1.11	3
Other parties	160,615	2.49	0
Total	6,450,407	100.00	220

Source: Comissão Nacional Eleitoral (CNE).

Table 8.2 2008 legislative election: results by province (% of total vote)

Province	MPLA	UNITA	PRS	FNLA	ND	Other
Bengo	90.2	4.0	0.9	2.8	0.8	1.3
Benguela	82.5	12.7	1.3	0.3	1.4	1.8
Bié	74.9	18.3	1.9	0.5	1.7	2.8
Cabinda	62.8	31.4	1.7	0.7	0.4	3.0
Cuando Cubango	79.6	15.0	1.6	0.4	1.3	2.1
Cuanza Norte	94.7	1.4	0.8	0.6	1.2	1.3
Cuanza Sul	87.5	6.1	1.7	0.4	2.7	1.6
Cunene	93.4	2.9	1.0	0.2	1.4	1.1
Huambo	82.1	13.5	1.4	0.3	1.2	1.5
Huila	90.0	4.6	1.2	0.3	2.1	1.8
Luanda	78.8	14.1	1.3	1.5	4.3	0.0
Lunda Norte	65.3	6.8	23.9	0.4	0.9	2.6
Lunda Sul	50.5	3.9	41.7	0.4	0.8	2.7
Malange	93.1	2.2	1.5	0.2	1.3	1.6
Moxico	85.3	5.5	5.6	0.4	1.5	1.8
Namibe	94.4	2.9	0.6	0.2	0.9	1.0
Uige	89.2	4.2	1.2	1.8	1.4	2.4
Zaire	67.5	10.2	1.6	16.5	0.8	3.3

Source: CNE.

International response

The EU, the Pan-African Parliament, the Community of Portuguese Speaking Countries (CPLP), Southern African Development Community (SADC), the US embassy, and the African Union deployed observers. One or two groups from Angolan civil society were authorised to be observers by the government but the CNE failed to accredit nearly half of the 2,640 civil society observers, with 28 out of 370 receiving accreditation in Luanda. This included Chatham House's then Angola researcher who was signed up to be a member of the Angolan civil society monitoring effort in Luanda.

The international observers gave a broadly positive assessment of the poll, but also cited irregularities. The EU mission in particular was critical, especially of the state-controlled radio, television and newspaper, *Jornal de Angola*. On 24 September 2008 the Presidency of EU declared that:

> The Angolan general elections are the fruit of a considerable effort to which the European Union must pay tribute, despite the logistical difficulties noted, and have been considered by all observers as being successful overall. They show the distance Angola has travelled to achieve national reconciliation, six years after the end of the civil war, and are a strong symbol for the whole of Africa.[101]

The US Embassy congratulated Angolans 'on their participation in this important step in strengthening their democracy' but noted that there had been procedural problems encountered with the ballot and hoped lessons would be learnt for future polls.[102]

Just prior to the elections, Chatham House published a report – *Angola's Elections: A Democratic Oil Giant?* – which highlighted the MPLA's enormous financial advantages and how it started its election campaign before the official campaigning start of 8 August 2008.[103] The report also warned that the 'playing field for the political contest is particularly unequal in access to the media' in favour of the MPLA and that the body tasked with the electoral process, the CNE, had problems. The Economist Intelligence Unit believes the MPLA spent some $300 million on its campaign compared with the $17 million shared by the other parties.[104]

Looking ahead

At UNITA's tenth congress in July 2007 Isaías Samakuva was re-elected by a significant majority over Abel Chivukuvuku as party leader and presidential candidate.[105]

When UNITA leader Isaías Samakuva in 2004 met President dos Santos to discuss consolidation of peace and national reconciliation and a reshuffle of UNITA officials in the GURN,[106] Samakuva stated that even if it won the elections 'UNITA does not plan to, nor could it aspire to run the country alone'.[107] One commentator pointed to the danger of 'UNITA growing comfortable as a sort of permanent opposition, leaving Angola as a kind of two-party dictatorship under a veneer of democracy'.[108]

UNITA's options are limited. Following its military defeat, it has made a successful transition from armed guerrilla movement to opposition party in Luanda. A growing obstacle to UNITA is its difficult transition in the rural areas from guerrilla movement into political party. Whereas in Luanda, its parliamentarians have survived through state-support, its ex-combatants in the rural areas have had to survive under difficult circumstances and this is gradually dividing the leadership from its rural constituency. The success of demobilisation and reintegration is mostly due to acute conflict fatigue. Most UNITA ex-combatants had no choice but to integrate and face a daily struggle against poverty. Their efforts have been supported mostly by NGOs and faith groups after initial demobilisation in 2002–03 and this appears to have assisted national reconciliation and reintegration.

Many of the problems that UNITA face today are similar to those of other political opposition parties in Africa and there are few signs that UNITA is no longer disadvantaged by its violent past. Having just lost the majority of its seats in the National Assembly, UNITA no longer enjoys its $13–14 million allowance for its 70 deputies elected in 1992. The September 2008 legislative elections also marked the end of the Lusaka peace process and a government of national unity. The newly appointed government by President dos Santos unsurprisingly includes no UNITA or opposition supporters. UNITA's 54 seat loss was predictable given its disadvantage of competing against a well-organised and funded opponent, the MPLA, and the desire for stability following decades of conflict. The surprise is that other parties did equally badly and that the MPLA gained 81 per cent of the vote and, therefore, a massive majority in parliament. Even the MPLA did not expect to win such a large majority and were caught by surprise. Isaías Samakuva should not expect to win the scheduled 2009 presidential elections and the MPLA will dominate Angola's political landscape for the foreseeable future.

The biggest danger for Angola is that UNITA is now irrelevant to the majority of Angolans. Returning to war is not an option, but social peace is still fragile and many people are frustrated at seeing no tangible peace dividend. Angola benefits from debate and discussion and UNITA could offer important political competition in debating over policies for Angola's post-conflict development. UNITA will now have to work hard to remain relevant by showing its worth in parliament and working with the grass roots. Municipal elections are scheduled for some time after 2009 and these offer UNITA the best chance to regain its standing. This will not be easy, but it is possible, especially as many Angolans increasingly yearn for greater accountability from their politicians and officials.

Notes

1 Vines, 'Angola: Forty Years of War', 76–77.
2 The FAPLA or *Forças Armadas Populares de Libertação de Angola* (People's Armed Forces for the Liberation of Angola) was the armed wing of MPLA, which became the government armed forces when the MPLA came to power.
3 Vines, 'Angola: Forty Years of War,' 75.
4 Porto and Parsons, *Sustaining the Peace in Angola*, 19.
5 Anstee, *Orphan of the Cold War*, 48.
6 Hartzell and Hoddie, *Crafting Peace*, 118. By June 1992 from approximately 192,000 troops only 20,000 soldiers from both sides had been demobilised. Only 37 per cent of government troops and 85 per cent of UNITA troops had been put into the 48 established cantonment areas in spite of the 1 August deadline. By this date, only 8,800 had been integrated into the FAA – Vines 'Angola: Forty Years of War', 78.
7 Messiant, 'Why did Bicesse and Lusaka fail?', 19.
8 Bicesse Peace Accords, 31 May 1991.
9 UNAVEM II was the successor to UNAVEM I, which was established to oversee withdrawal of the Cubans from Angola established by Security Council Resolution 698.
10 Porto and Parsons, *Sustaining the Peace in Angola*, 21.
11 For an insider account of the Bicesse Peace Process see Anstee, *Orphan of the Cold War*, 48–56.
12 Heywood, *Contested Power in Angola*, 217.
13 Ibid., 218.
14 Anstee, *Orphan of the Cold War*, 67.
15 Heywood, *Contested Power in Angola*, 219.
16 Ibid., 219, 224.
17 Required to determine the presidency as neither candidate had secured more than 50 per cent of the vote.
18 Vines, 'Angola: Forty Years of War', 75–79.
19 Vines, *Angola Unravels*, 17–29.
20 Heywood, *Contested Power in Angola*, 230.
21 Angola, *Protocolo de Lusaka*, 31 October 1994.

22 MacQueen, 'Peacekeeping by Attrition'.
23 Vines, *Angola Unravels*, 23.
24 HRW, *Human Rights Watch World Report 1999*.
25 MONUA was established under Security Council Resolution 1118 (1997) 30 June 1997 to assist the parties in consolidating peace and national reconciliation.
26 United Nations, UN Document S/1999/49, 17 January 1999.
27 Springer, *Deactivating War*, 146.
28 Griffiths, 'The end of the war', 25.
29 Angola Peace Monitor (APM), Vol. IX, Issue No. 2.
30 Griffiths, 'The End of the War', 26. Eugenio Manuvakola was the UNITA signatory to the Lusaka Protocol.
31 Ibid., 25–27.
32 Conciliation Resources, chronology of events in Angola available from www.c-r.org/ our-work/accord/angola/chronology.php; ex-combatants were formally demobilised in August 2002.
33 Meijer, 'Introduction: Lessons from the Angolan "Peace Process"', 15.
34 APM, Vol. IX, Issue No. 2.
35 IRIN, 'UNITA welcomes government plan to assist former soldiers', 31 October 2002 www.reliefweb.int/rw/rwb.nsf/db900sid/ACOS-64DB8G?OpenDocumentx&rc = 1&cc = ago.
36 APM, Issue No. 6, Vol. X.
37 Agence-France-Presse (AFP), 'Angola's joint peace commission is dissolved', 21 November 2002 www.reliefweb.int/rw/rwb.nsf/db900sid/ACOS-64BNW8?Open Document&rc = 1&cc = ago.
38 IRIN, 'UNITA disappointed at Joint Commission closure', November 2002 www. reliefweb.int/rw/rwb.nsf/db900sid/ACOS-64CQS9?OpenDocument&rc = 1&cc = ago.
39 Ibid.
40 Government of Angola, 'Lusaka Protocol: Bilateral Commission to handle outstand- ing matters', 21 November 2002 www.reliefweb.int/rw/rwb.nsf/db900sid/OCHA-64- BNCJ?OpenDocument&rc = 1&cc = ago.
41 AFP, 'Angola's joint peace commission is dissolved', 21 November 2002 www. reliefweb.int/rw/rwb.nsf/db900sid/ACOS-64BNW8?OpenDocument&rc = 1&cc = ago.
42 Government of Angola, 'Ruling party and opposition to sign memorandum', 6 December 2002 www.reliefweb.int/rw/rwb.nsf/db900sid/OCHA-64CSDE?Open Document&rc = 1&cc = ago.
43 Government of Angola, 'UNITA pleased with sanctions' lifting', 10 December 2002, www.reliefweb.int/rw/rwb.nsf/db900sid/OCHA-64CEXD?OpenDocument&rc = 1&cc = ago.
44 APM, Vol. IX, Issue No. 5.
45 IRIN, 'Reconciliation crucial to lasting peace', 30 January 2003 www.reliefweb.int/ rw/rwb.nsf/db900sid/OCHA-64CGAY?OpenDocument&rc = 1&cc = ago.
46 APM, Vol. IX, Issue No. 6.
47 AFP, 'US lifts economic sanctions against Angola's UNITA', 7 May 2003, www. reliefweb.int/rw/rwb.nsf/db900sid/ACOS-64C9CS?OpenDocument&rc = 1&cc = ago.
48 IRIN, 'Angola: Interview with senior UNITA leader Isaías Samakuva', 6 March 2003 www.reliefweb.int/rw/rwb.nsf/db900sid/KHII-5ZCB7D?OpenDocument.
49 APM, Vol. IX, Issue No. 2. Samakuva returned to Angola on 1 November 2002.
50 APM, Vol. IX, Issue No. 1.
51 APM, Vol. IX, Issue No. 11.
52 Ibid.
53 IRSEM was created by resolution no. 7/95 of 14 April 1995 after the Lusaka Protocol but it really only became functional after the Luena Memorandum. IRSEM was a suc- cessor to the Gabinete Interministerial de Apoio aos Desmobilizados das Forças Armadas – GIAMDA which was created by presidential decree on 15 November 1991.

54 Ex-combatants were to receive five months back payments of salaries according to military rank, a $100 reintegration allowance and a 'kit' of basic household items and tools and an identity document.

55 'MDRP-Supported Activities in Angola', August 2008, www.mdrp.org.

56 In addition, 33,000 former members of the government's armed forces should have been demobilised by the end of 2005.

57 IRIN, 'Angola: Year-ender 2002 – Political Challenges for the future', 22 January 2003 www.reliefweb.int/rw/rwb.nsf/db900sid/ACOS-64BQ4P?OpenDocument&query = political%20challenges&cc = ago.

58 Springer, *Deactivating War*, 148.

59 Parsons, 'Beyond the Silencing of Guns,' 41.

60 Security Council resolution 7486 (2002).

61 APM, Vol. X, Issue No. 2.

62 De Barros and Njele. *Demobilisation and Reintegration*.

63 IRIN, 'Easy access to guns concern as election nears', 13 March 2006 www.reliefweb.int/rw/rwb.nsf/db900sid/KHII-6MV87Y?OpenDocument&query = number%20one%20 priority&cc = ago.

64 AFP, 'Angola's UNITA denies claims of weapons cache', 9 September 2005 www.reliefweb.int/rw/rwb.nsf/db900sid/ACIO-6G3QJ9?OpenDocument&query   = disarmament &cc = ago.

65 Capapelo and Netswera, *Small Arms and Social Development*, 3.

66 Aragão, Manuel. 'Statement by H.E Manuel Da Costa Aragão, Minister of Justice of the Republic of Angola at the General Exchange of Views of the United Nations Conference to Review Progress Made in the Implementation of the Programme of Action to Prevent, Combat and Eradicate the Illicit Traffic of Small Arms and Light Weapons in all its Aspects', New York, 27 June 2006, 2.

67 'Civis entregam 40 mil armas', *Jornal de Angola*, 10 October 2008.

68 Capapelo and Netswera, *Small Arms and Social Development*, 29–30.

69 For example the murder of an 80-year-old Portuguese Catholic priest Father José Afonso Moreira in Bailundo on 9 February 2006 at his mission home.

70 Parsons, 'Beyond the Silencing of Guns', 40.

71 Porto, Parsons and Alden, *From Soldiers to Citizens*, 60–61.

72 Government of Angola, 'Effective peace is four years old', 4 April 2006, www.reliefweb.int/rw/rwb.nsf/db900sid/YAOI-6NK3T4?OpenDocument&rc = 1&cc = ago.

73 IRIN, 'More needs to be done for reintegration of former soldiers', 29 October 2004.

74 World Bank, Report No. T7580-ANG. Technical Annex for a Proposed Grant of SDR 24 million (US$ million equivalent) to the Republic of Angola for an Angola Emergency Demobilisation and Reintegration Project, March 2003, at www.mdrp.org/PFs/Country_PDFs/AngolaDoc_TechAnnex.pdf, p. 21.

75 IRIN, 'Demobilised soldiers find work in the security industry', 14 June 2004, www.reliefweb.int/rw/rwb.nsf/db900sid/KHII-5ZY42U?OpenDocument&rc = 1&cc = ago.

76 There had been donor discussions headed by the World Bank in May and July 2002 but agreement was only reached in January 2004. It appears that the World Bank wanted to head this process but the government opposed and the creation of a Management Unit was the eventual compromise.

77 Due to this delay, UNDP created a $4.3 million Special Project to Support the Re-integration of Ex-Combatants in the Framework of the Peace Process in Angola. The project provided agricultural reintegration for 44,816 ex-combatants and training for 4,891 ex-combatants through 48 projects in six provinces; technical assistance and training for IRSEM between 20 August 2003 and 30 June 2005. See project appraisal document, dated 13 January 2006, at www.mdrp.org/PDFs/Implem_comple_Ang_UNDP.pdf.

78 AFP, 'Former Angolan rebels criticise delay in rehabilitation of ex-fighters', 1 September 2005, www.reliefweb.int/rw/rwb.nsf/db900sid/ACIO-6FTRGW?OpenDocument&query = Chitombe&cc = ago.

79 AFP, 'Angola pledges model post-war elections as it fetes key anniversary', 11 November 2005, www.reliefweb.int/rw/rwb.nsf/db900sid/EVOD-6J2KKN?Open Document&query = consolidating%20peace&cc = ago.

80 The Association for Cooperation, Exchange and Culture financed $323,000 of projects for the re-integration of 802 ex-UNITA combatants in Huambo province between December 2005 and June 2006. It calculated that its funds for reintegration projects in Bié, Huila and Luanda, targeted some 82,000 linked to UNITA. 2,919 resettlement kits were also delivered to demobilised combatants.

81 Lourenço, 'Irsem precisa de parceiros para implementer programas'.

82 'The Angolan Reintegration Strategy: an interview with General Antonio Francisco de Andrade, Director General, IRSEM, Angola', News and Noteworthy, 4, 7 March 2008, www.mdrp.org.

83 'MDRP-Supported Activities in Angola: August 2008', www.mdrp.org.

84 Porto, Parsons and Alden, From Soldiers to Citizens.

85 Universidade Católica de Angola, Relatório Económico de Angola 2006. Luanda: Centro de Estudos E Investigação Científica, July 2007, 9–10.

86 'Governo aposta na criacao de emprego para demobilizados', Jornal de Angola, 25 June 2006.

87 Interview with opposition party leaders, Luanda, September 2004.

88 IRIN, 'Electoral table announced', 25 August 2004. www.reliefweb.int/rw/rwb.nsf/db900sid/SZIE-647PE9?OpenDocument&rc = 1&cc = ago.

89 APM, Vol. XI, Issue No. 3.

90 APM, Vol. XI, Issue No. 2.

91 Interview with MPLA officials, Luanda, September 2004 and February 2007.

92 Pearce, 'L'Unita a la Recherche de "son peuple"'.

93 Marques and Pearce, Unfinished Democracy.

94 Author visited one such location that had just been attacked in central Angola in August 2004.

95 Government of Angola, 'Government calls for Politics-Free Election Civic Campaign', 3 October 2006 www.reliefweb.int/rw/rwb.nsf/db900sid/HMYT-6U8RM7?Open Document&rc = 1&cc = ago.

96 AFP, 'Angolan president confirms election dates', 28 December 2006.

97 Swiss Peace Foundation, FAST Update Angola No. 3: Trends in conflict and coop-eration, May–June 2007 www.reliefweb.int/rw/rwb.nsf/db900sid/AMMF-75FDCS? OpenDocument&rc = 1&cc = ago.

98 Amundsen and Weimer, Opposition Parties and the Upcoming Parliamentary Elections in Angola.

99 'Angola: Elections free and fair, sort of', IRIN, 9 September 2008.

100 Human Rights Watch. 'Angola: Doubts Over Free and Fair Elections: Intimidation of Opposition, Media Before First Poll Since 1992'. *Human Rights News*, 13 August 2008.

101 'General Elections in Angola: Declaration of the Presidency on behalf of the European Union', 24 September 2008, www.diplomatie.gouv.fr/en/country-files_156/angola_256/the-eu-and-angola_6561/general-elections-in-angola-24.09.08_11923.htm.

102 'Angola: Elections free and fair, sort of', IRIN, 9 September 2008.

103 Campos, *Angola's Elections: A Democratic Oil Giant?*

104 Economist Intelligence Unit, *Angola Country Report, October 2008*, 11.

105 Swiss Peace Foundation, *FAST Update Angola No. 2: Trends in conflict and cooper-ation*, March–April 2007 www.reliefweb.int/rw/rwb.nsf/db900sid/YZHG-733MKA? OpenDocument&rc = 1&cc = ago.

106 Government of Angola, 'Opposition UNITA's Political Commission to Review Situation', 28 January 2004 www.reliefweb.int/rw/rwb.nsf/db900sid/ACOS-64BFWB?OpenDocument&query = samakuva&cc = ago.

107   AFP, 'Angola needs national unity government for at least another decade: UNITA', 13 February 2004 www.reliefweb.int/rw/rwb.nsf/db900sid/ACOS-64D4VU?Open Document&rc = 1&cc = ago.
108   IRIN, 'Savimbi's ghost still haunts UNITA', 23 February 2004, see Nicholas Shaxon's comments at www.reliefweb.int/rw/rwb.nsf/db900sid/ACOS-64CFG4? Open Document&rc = 1&cc = ago.

References

Amundsen, I. and Weimer, M., 2008. *Opposition Parties and the Upcoming Parliamentary Elections in Angola*, Chr Michelsen Institute, Bergen, August.

Anstee, M., 1996. *Orphan of the Cold War: The Inside Story of the Collapse of the Angolan Peace Process, 1992–93*, Macmillan, London.

Campos, I., 2008. *Angola's Elections: A Democratic Oil Giant?*, Chatham House Africa Programme Paper, 9:1, September.

Capapelo, M. and Netswera, F., 2006. *Small Arms and Social Development: A Survey in Angola*, Angola2000, Luanda.

De Barros, M. and Njele, F., 2005. *Demobilisation and Reintegration: The Case of Angola*, Angola Center for Strategic Studies, Luanda.

Griffiths, A., 2004. 'The End of the War: The Luena Memorandum of Understanding', in Meijer, G. (ed.), *Accord: From Military Peace to Social Justice? The Angolan Peace Process*, Conciliation Resources, London.

Hartzell, C. and Hoddie, M., 2007. *Crafting Peace, Power-Sharing Institutions and the Negotiated Settlement of Civil Wars*, Pennsylvania State University Press, University Park.

Heywood, L., 2000. *Contested Power in Angola: 1840s to Present*, University of Rochester Press, New York.

Human Rights Watch (HRW), 1998. *Human Rights Watch World Report 1999*, HRW, New York.

Lourenço, M., 2007. 'Irsem precisa de parceiros para implementer programas', *Jornal de Angola*, 7 June.

MacQueen, N., 1998. 'Peacekeeping by Attrition: The United Nations in Angola', *Journal of Modern African Studies* 36:3.

Marques, N. and Pearce, J., 2004. *Unfinished Democracy: Media and Political Freedoms in Angola*, HRW, New York.

Meijer, G., 2004. 'Introduction: Lessons from the Angolan "Peace Process"', in Meijer, G., (ed.), *Accord: From Military Peace to Social Justice? The Angolan Peace Process*, Conciliation Resources, London.

Messiant, C., 2004. 'Why did Bicesse and Lusaka Fail? A Critical Analysis', in Meijer, G., (ed.), *Accord: From Military Peace to Social Justice? The Angolan Peace Process*, Conciliation Resources, London.

Parsons, I., 2004. 'Beyond the Silencing of Guns: Demobilisation, Disarmament and Reintegration' in Meijer, G. (ed.), *Accord: From Military Peace to Social Justice? The Angolan Peace Process*, Conciliation Resources, London.

Pearce, J., 2008. 'L'Unita a la Recherche de "son peuple". Carnets d'une non-campagne sur le Planalto', *Politique Africaine* 110, June.

Porto, J.G. and Parsons, I., 2003. *Sustaining the Peace in Angola: An Overview of Current Demobilisation, Disarmament and Reintegration*, BICC, Bonn.

Porto, J.G., Parsons, I. and Alden, C., 2007. *From Soldiers to Citizens: The Social, Economic and Political Reintegration of UNITA Ex-Combatants*, ISS, Pretoria.

Springer, N., 2006. *Deactivating War: How Societies Demobilise after Armed Conflict*, NDC, Rome.

Vines, A., 1999. *Angola Unravels: The Rise and Fall of the Lusaka Peace Process*, HRW, New York.

——, 2004. 'Angola: Forty Years of War', in Batchelor, P. and Kingma, K. (eds), *Demilitarisation and Peace-Building in Southern Africa*, Vol. II, Ashgate, Aldershot.

Index